Egypt
faith after
the pharaohs

Egypt
faith after
the pharaohs

Edited by
Cäcilia Fluck
Gisela Helmecke
Elisabeth R. O'Connell

With the assistance of Elisabeth Ehler

DAS ÄGYPTISCHE MUSEUM UND PAPYRUSSAMMLUNG, DIE SKULPTURENSAMMLUNG
UND MUSEUM FÜR BYZANTINISCHE KUNST AND DAS MUSEUM FÜR ISLAMISCHE KUNST DER
STAATLICHEN MUSEEN ZU BERLIN AND THE BRITISH MUSEUM, LONDON

The British Museum

This publication accompanies the exhibitions *One God: Abraham's Legacy on the Nile*, Bode-Museum, Berlin (2 April–13 September 2015) and *Egypt: faith after the pharaohs*, the British Museum, London (29 October 2015–7 February 2016).

Egypt: faith after the pharaohs is generously supported by the

BLAVATNIK
FAMILY FOUNDATION

The exhibition at the British Museum has been made possible by the provision of insurance through the Government Indemnity Scheme. The British Museum would like to thank the Department for Culture, Media and Sport, and Arts Council England for providing and arranging this indemnity.

First published in the United Kingdom in 2015
by The British Museum Press
A division of The British Museum Company Ltd
38 Russell Square, London WC1B 3QQ
britishmuseum.org

A catalogue record for this book is available from the British Library

ISBN 978 0 7141 5114 4

Designed by Raymonde Watkins
Printed in Italy by Printer Trento SRL

Frontispiece: A half-conserved early 14th-century wall painting depicting Mary Theotokos. From the church of the Monastery of Shenoute (White Monastery). See fig. 135.

Many of the images illustrated in this book are from the collections of the British Museum and the Ägyptisches Museum und Papyrussammlung, the Skulpturensammlung und Museum für Byzantinische Kunst and the Museum für Islamische Kunst, Staatliche Museen zu Berlin. Further information about the museums and their collections can be found at britishmuseum.org and smb.museum/home.html.

Conventions

A note on conventions used in this book is necessary because it covers a number of academic disciplines. For the spelling of words in Egyptian, Hebrew, Greek, Latin, Coptic and Arabic, we have aimed to use the most readily recognizable transliteration or transcription in English, even if it is inconsistent with the transliteration system employed elsewhere in the book, thus Cleopatra, not Kleopatra, and Mecca, not Makkah. Dates are given in BC/AD throughout, and the Hijra date (AH) given when it is written on the object, for example, a document, inscription or coin. Ancient authors and sources are cited in accordance with the *Oxford Classical Dictionary* (Hornblower and Spawforth 2012), the *Dictionary of Byzantium* (Kazhdan et al. 1991), and the *Oxford Dictionary of the Christian Church* (Cross and Livingstone 1997). Papyri are abbreviated according to Oates et al., *Checklist of Greek, Latin, Demotic and Coptic Papyri, Ostraca and Tablets* http://library.duke.edu/rubenstein/scriptorium/papyrus/texts/clist_papyri.html (last accessed September 2015).

Contributors

Roger Bagnall [RB] Institute for the Study of the Ancient World, New York University

Martin Bauschke [MB] Stiftung Weltethos, Berlin

Dominique Bénazeth [DB] Musée du Louvre, département des Antiquités égyptiennes, Paris

Elizabeth S. Bolman [ESB] Temple University, Philadelphia

Florence Calament [FC] Musée du Louvre, département des Antiquités égyptiennes, Paris

Karsten Dahmen [KD] Münzkabinett, Staatliche Museen zu Berlin

Marie Delassus [MD] Musée du Louvre, département des Antiquités égyptiennes, Paris

Alain Delattre [AD] Université Libre de Bruxelles

Jitse Dijkstra [JD] Department of Classics and Religious Studies, University of Ottawa

Arne Effenberger [AE] Director Emeritus, Skulpturensammlung und Museum für Byzantinische Kunst, Staatliche Museen zu Berlin

Elisabeth Ehler [EE] Skulpturensammlung und Museum für Byzantinische Kunst, Staatliche Museen zu Berlin

Sebastian Elsässer [SE] Seminar für Orientalistik, Christian-Albrechts-Universität zu Kiel

Cäcilia Fluck [CF] Skulpturensammlung und Museum für Byzantinische Kunst, Staatliche Museen zu Berlin

David Frankfurter [DF] Department of Religion, Boston University

Dorota Giovannoni [DG] Musée du Louvre, département des Objets d'art, Paris

Wlodimierz Godlewski [WG] Instytut Archeologii UW, Warsaw

Florence Gombert-Meurice [FGM] Musée du Louvre, département des Antiquités égyptiennes, Paris

Peter Grossmann [PG] Deutsches Archäologisches Institut, Kairo

Clara ten Hacken [CTH] Institute for Area Studies, Leiden University

Mahmoud Hawari [MH] Department of the Middle East, The British Museum, London

Marina Heilmeyer [MHe] Botanischer Garten und Botanisches Museum, Berlin

Jana Helmbold-Doyé [JHD] Ägyptisches Museum und Papyrussamlung, Staatliche Museen zu Berlin

Gisela Helmecke [GH] Museum für Islamische Kunst, Staatliche Museen zu Berlin

Karel C. Innemée [KI] Faculteit der Archeologie, Universiteit Leiden

Cécile Jail [CJ] Musée du Louvre, département des Antiquités égyptiennes, Paris

Carine Juvin [CJu] École Pratique des Hautes Études, Sciences Historiques et Philiologiques, Paris

Mary Kupelian [MK] Faculty of Tourism and Hotel Management, Helwan University, Cairo

Verena Lepper [VL] Ägyptisches Museum und Papyrussammlung, Staatliche Museen zu Berlin

Michael Marx [MM] Berlin-Brandenburgische Akademie der Wissenschaften

Amandine Mérat [AM] Department of Ancient Egypt and Sudan, The British Museum, London

Cédric Meurice [CM] Musée du Louvre, département des Antiquités égyptiennes, Paris

Elisabeth R. O'Connell [ERO] Department of Ancient Egypt and Sudan, The British Museum, London

Arietta Papaconstantinou [AP] Department of Classics, University of Reading

Peter Parsons [PP] Ioannou Centre for Classical and Byzantine Studies, University of Oxford

Mladen Popović [MP] Faculteit Godgeleerdheid en Godsdienstwetenschap, Rijksuniversiteit Groningen

Venetia Porter [VP] Department of the Middle East, The British Museum, London

Siegfried G. Richter [SGR] Institut für Ägyptologie und Koptologie, Münster

Tonio Sebastian Richter [TSR] Ägyptologisches Seminar, Freie Universität, Berlin

Vincent Rondot [VR] Musée du Louvre, département des Antiquités égyptiennes, Paris

Renate Rosenthal-Heginbottom [RRH] Independant scholar, Berlin and Großsolt

Agnes Schwarzmaier [ASch] Antikensammlung, Staatliche Museen zu Berlin

Peter Sheehan [PSh] Abu Dhabi Tourism and Culture Authority

Petra Sijpesteijn [PS] Institute for Area Studies, Leiden University

Jürgen Tubach [JT] Martin-Luther-Universität, Halle-Wittenberg

Gertrud J.M. van Loon [GVL] KU Leuven and Leiden University

Esther-Miriam Wagner [EMW] Woolf Institute, University of Cambridge

Helen Whitehouse [HW] Emerita curator of Ancient Egypt and Sudan, Ashmolean Museum, Oxford

Gregor Wurst [GW] Katholisch-Theologische Fakultät, Universität Augsburg

Contents

Forewords

The exhibition *Egypt: faith after the pharaohs* is the result of a collaboration between the Staatliche Museen zu Berlin and the British Museum. Following display at the Bode Museum on the Museum Island of Berlin, where it was titled *Ein Gott – Abrahams Erben am Nil* (2 April –13 September 2015), the exhibition opened at the British Museum on 29 October 2015, generously supported by the Blavatnik Family Foundation.

The cooperation between three Berlin museums and the British Museum offers a unique opportunity to present the incomparably long, joint history of the three Abrahamic religions in Egypt. The exhibition's central theme is the on-going development over twelve centuries of a cultural and artistic identity, from a mainly polytheistic society to one of monotheistic religions, though developing in dialogue with Graeco-Roman traditions. Until now this part of Egyptian history, from the time of the Roman Empire to the end of Fatimid rule in the twelfth century AD, has been in many ways under-represented, in favour of the better-known Egypt of the Pharaohs. Objects from the collections in Berlin and London, combined with selected manuscripts from the Ben Ezra Synagogue in Old Cairo and other loans, vividly reflect the shared lives of Jewish, Christian and Muslim communities in Egypt in this period. Egypt is unique in allowing such perspectives, given the preservation of architecture, documentary texts and objects of daily life, particularly richly decorated textiles.

The present book was conceived to accompany the exhibition at both venues, gathering together essays written by world-renowned specialists across a number of disciplines, including archaeology, history, art history, epigraphy and papyrology. Presenting 1,200 years of religious history, using Egypt's unique wealth of preserved material culture, it is hoped that the exhibition and book will introduce to audiences a fascinating chapter of cultural and religious complexity, which substantially shapes the modern world.

Michael Eissenhauer
General Director
Staatliche Museen zu Berlin

Neil MacGregor
Director
British Museum

The original idea for the exhibition project goes back to 2010, when a temporary exhibition *Coptic Art Revealed* was staged on the 100th anniversary of the Coptic Museum in Cairo. Egyptian colleagues suggested that a second version of this exhibition was displayed in Berlin. It soon became clear that, in Berlin, the exhibition needed to also explore Islam and Judaism.

At the suggestion of colleagues in Berlin, the exhibition was then developed in partnership with the British Museum, with curators working together to select objects – and edit this accompanying book – that convey the transformation of an ancient land into one in which Jews, Christians and Muslims co-existed, but also lived through times of conflict. This remains of great relevance to contemporary Egypt, and beyond.

The exhibition comprises material from the three participating collections from the Staatliche Museen zu Berlin and the British Museum, supplemented by generous international loans. Our thanks go to the scholars and colleagues who, with their contributions to this book, have made possible fascinating and extensive insights into the history of the three faiths in Egypt. We are delighted that, through this cooperation between colleagues in Berlin and London, along with many other scholars and partners, a project has been able to take shape which can represent, in a unique way and for the first time, the early history of Jews, Christians and Muslims in Egypt.

It is particularly pleasing to see that this project has inspired a temporary display in the Egyptian Museum, Cairo. At the request of the Minister of Antiquities, Dr Mamdouh Eldamaty, curators selected objects from across museums in Cairo to reflect the three faith communities and their interaction across the centuries. The exhibition, entitled *One God – Three religions: Religious tolerance on the Nile* opened 15 May 2015, was the first display of its kind in Egypt.

Neal Spencer
Friederike Seyfried
Julien Chapuis
Stefan Weber

Acknowledgements

Without the help of colleagues at the British Museum, the Staatliche Museen zu Berlin, the Stiftung Preußischer Kulturbesitz, and numerous institutions and individuals, it would not have been possible to realize the exhibition and its accompanying publication. From the outset we were warmly supported in our plans by the Ministry of Antiquities of the Arab Republic of Egypt. His Excellency Nasser Kamel, Egyptian Ambassador to the UK, also provided invaluable advice, and the Egyptian State Tourist Office assisted with a press trip to see relevant sites in Egypt. Particular thanks are due to Friederike Seyfried, who initiated this project.

The editors warmly thank the authors for their essays and object descriptions for the book accompanying the exhibition. Valuable advice and/or illustrative material with permission for publication were gratefully received from Daniele Colomo, John Cooper, Nicholas De Lange, Antoine De Moor, Andreas Effland, Jas Elsner, Nikolaos Gonis, Neil Hewison, Henry Hohmann, Hugh Kennedy, Maja Kominko, Carolyn Ludwig, Sonja Marzinzik, Roberta Mazza, Judith McKenzie, Liam McNamara, Wolfgang Müller, Chris Naunton, Ben Outhwaite, Peter Parsons, Yossef Rapoport, Dominic Rathbone, Christoph Rauch, Dietrich Raue, Emilie Savage-Smith, Stephan Seidlmayer, Keith E. Small, Philipp Speiser, Maia Wachtel, Susan Walker, Bryan Ward-Perkins, Alasdair Watson and Helen Whitehouse.

Cäcilia Fluck
Gisela Helmecke
Elisabeth R. O'Connell

The British Museum

The London exhibition is generously supported by the Blavatnik Family Foundation. The generosity of Ahmed and Ann El-Mokadem in supporting research on the Coptic collections of the British Museum is gratefully acknowledged. We thank the lenders to the British Museum exhibition for their generosity: Ägyptisches Museum und Papyrussammlung, Staatliche Museen zu Berlin; Antikensammlung, Staatliche Museen zu Berlin; Ashmolean Museum of Art and Archaeology, University of Oxford; Biblioteca Medicea Laurenziana, Florence; Bodleian Library, University of Oxford; British Library, London; Cambridge University Library; Egypt Exploration Society, London; Sackler Library, University of Oxford; Fitzwilliam Museum, Cambridge; Institut für Altertumskunde, Universität zu Köln; John Rylands Library, University of Manchester; Musée du Louvre, Paris; Museum für Islamische Kunst, Staatliche Museen zu Berlin; Skulpturensammlung und Museum für Byzantinische Kunst, Staatliche Museen zu Berlin; Taylor-Schechter Genizah Research Unit, Cambridge University Library; Victoria and Albert Museum, London; Whitworth Art Gallery, University of Manchester.

At the British Museum we thank the Directors, Neil MacGregor, Jonathan Williams and Joanna Mackle. For exhibition and research assistance, we thank especially Amandine Mérat and Sabrina Ben Aouicha. In the Department of Ancient Egypt and Sudan, Neal Spencer, Caroline Barton, Daniel Bowmar, Mark Haswell, Sylwia Janik, Marcel Marée, Claire Messenger, Simon Prentice, Emily Taylor, Marie Vandenbeusch, Evan York and volunteer Ruiha Smalley; in the Department of Britain, Europe and Prehistory, Roger Bland, Chris Entwistle, Richard Hobbs, Ralph Jackson and Angela Rowbottom; in the Department of Coins and Medals, Philip Attwood, Richard Abdy, Vesta Curtis, Amelia Dowler, Amanda Gregory, Janet Larkin and Ian Leins; in the Department of Greece and Rome, Lesley Fitton, Trevor Coughlan, Peter Higgs, Thorsten Opper, Paul Roberts and Ross I. Thomas; in the Department of Middle East, Jonathan Tubb, Dean Baylis, Rupert Chapman, Mahmoud Hawari, Venetia Porter and St John Simpson; in Conservation and Science, David Saunders, Karen Birkhoelzer, Hayley Bullock, Duygu Camurcuoglu, Alexa Clifford, Adrian Doyle, Hazel Gardiner, Anna Harrison, Michelle Hercules, Philip Kevin, Capucine Korenberg, Nicola Newman, Susan La Niece, Bridget Leach, Nic Lee, Tomasina Munden, Saray Naidorf, Julianne Phippard, Fleur Shearman, Kathleen Swales, Tracey Sweek, Clare Ward, Carol Weiss; and in Photographic and Imaging, Ivor Kerslake, John Williams, Stephen Dodd, and especially Kevin Lovelock; in Exhibitions, Carolyn Marsden-Smith, Matthew Weaver, Olivia Bone, Elizabeth Bray; in Loans, Jill Maggs, Julia Evans and Christopher Stewart; the designers Caroline Ingham, Rebecca Hayward, Peter Macdermid, James Alexander, Elbow Productions and Benchworks; in Learning and National Partnerships, Harvinder Bahra, Daniel Ferguson, Freddie Matthews and David Shelton; together with colleagues in Marketing, Merchandising and Operations.

At the British Museum Press, we thank Rosemary Bradley, Laura Fox, Coralie Hepburn, Axelle Russo-Heath and Kate Oliver, with Ray Watkins (design), Miranda Harrison (editing of the English texts) and Vicki Robinson (index).

The Staatliche Museen, Stiftung Preußischer Kulturbesitz

We are grateful for the generous support of the sponsors who made the exhibition in Berlin and the German-language edition of the publication, namely the Bundesministerium für Kultur und Medien, the Sawiris Foundation for Social Development, the Ernst von Siemens Kunststiftung, Museum & Location Veranstaltungsgesellschaft der Staatlichen Museen zu Berlin mbH, the Verein zur Förderung des Ägyptischen Museums Berlin e.V., Mercedes-Benz, the Kulturstiftung des Bundes, the Kulturstiftung der Länder, the Brigitte und Martin Krause-Stiftung and the Kaiser Friedrich-Museums-Verein. We thank the lenders to the exhibition in Berlin: Botanisches Museum and Botanischer Garten Berlin-Dahlem; the British Museum, London; the British Library, London; Musée du Louvre, Paris; Musée Historique des Tissus, Lyon; Staatsbibliothek der Stiftung Preußischer Kulturbesitz; Staatliche Museen zu Berlin, Stiftung Preußischer Kulturbesitz: Antikensammlung and Münzkabinett; Taylor-Schechter Genizah Research Unit, Cambridge University Library; Victoria and Albert Museum, London.

We thank especially Elisabeth Ehler, Christina Hanus, Michael Klühs and Mary Kupelian for exhibition management and research assistance; exhibition design and production management, Marion Stenzel; Exhibition graphics, Bettina Gojowcyzk, Anna Netzel, Marion Stenzel; exhibition construction, exhibit arrangement and lighting: Firma EMArt (Ruben Erber) with Jürgen Burkhard, Thomas Schreiber and Ingo Valls; facilities and operations staff of the Staatlichen Museen zu Berlin; transport: Hasenkamp Internationale Transporte GmbH; Conservation care (in collaboration with the participating establishments), Hiltrud Jehle; Gisela Engelhardt, Stephanie Fischer, Rhoda Fromme, Iris Hertel, Myriam Krutzsch, Nina Loschwitz, Kathrin Mälck, Frank Marohn, Boris Meyer, Nora Pfeiffer, Anne Schorneck, Jutta Maria Schwed, Irina Seekamp, with the collaboration of the Conservation departments of the participating institutions; temperature control, ArtGuardian GmbH; film production, Sammler und Jäger Filmproduktion GmbH; translation of the film and exhibition texts, Anna Hodgkinson and Mary Kupelian; for the media stations, Uwe Büttner, Stefan Gross, Achim Schlüter; Publicity and communications, Fabian Fröhlich, Mechthild Kronenberg; design of communications media, Ingo Morgenroth; and others, including Stefan Bentzien, Bodo Buczynski, Karsten Dahmen, Wolfgang Davis, Sabine Dettmann, Maren Eichhorn, Klaus Finneiser, Julia Gonnella, Hans-Jürgen Harras, Michaela Humborg, Yelka Kant, Johannes Laurentius, Tanja Lipowski, Cédric Magniez, Wolfgang Maßmann, Andrea Müller, Andreas Paasch, Armin Peupelmann, Claudia Pörschmann, Bettina Probst, Perihane Radwan, Joachim Rau, Kathleen Reinert, Marna Schneider, Andreas Scholl, Agnes Schwarzmaier, Doreen Siegert, Sandra Steiß, Daniela Vandersee-Geier, Antje Voigt, Ute Wolf and Olivia Zorn.

The German edition was produced by the Verlag Michael Imhof, and we thank Karin Kreuzpaintner in particular, together with the Publication Department of the Staatlichen Museen zu Berlin, namely Sigrid Wollmeiner, assisted by Andrea Schindelmeier.

THE THREE RELIGIONS IN EGYPT

30 BC – AD 1171

1

1 INTRODUCTION

EGYPT's arid climate has preserved an abundance of material culture that is unparalleled for the ancient and medieval worlds. Egypt therefore presents a privileged point of access to examine the material context of lived religion in the first 1,200 years AD.[1] During this time the majority population of Europe, North Africa and the Middle East converted to monotheism. The adherents of Judaism, Christianity and Islam, and their formative relationships in this period, shape today's world. Using Egypt as a lens through which to examine the development and interaction of these three faiths, the long history of not only tension and conflict but also peaceful co-existence comes into sharper focus.

Part I offers introductions to the three religions as they developed in Egypt. Jewish, Christian and Muslim scriptures demonstrate ambivalent attitudes towards Egypt itself. For Jews it is portrayed as a haven for escaping famine and finding opportunity, but also slavery and false refuge. Inheriting this ambivalence to a lesser or greater degree were Christians, for whom Egypt was a place of escape from Herod for the holy family, and Muslims, for whom 'Pharaoh' was a villain par excellence.[2]

Whereas literary sources, passed down through generations, are susceptible to reinterpretation and redaction over time, ancient and medieval texts that have been discovered through excavation or have otherwise survived untouched for millennia in Egypt provide more immediate access to the people who produced and used them (ch. 2, ch. 3, ch. 4). Thus texts bearing the earliest copies of the Jewish and Christian bibles and the Muslim Qur'an found in Egypt show us where and how individuals and communities read, copied and used scripture. The rich remains of other kinds of literary texts – and especially documentary texts such as legal texts, letters and receipts – provide named and often titled people operating in both inter- and intra-communal networks. We meet a community of Jews at a military installation on Elephantine Island at Egypt's southern border who served on behalf of the Persian king and maintained regular contact with the Temple in Jerusalem (focus 1). Only in Egypt do otherwise 'lost' Christian gospels survive in abundance, along with other texts that were eventually excluded from church canon (focus 2). So, too, the earliest documentary evidence for the administration of the Islamic caliphate as well as for Hajj survives in Egypt (ch. 4).

But Egypt offers much more than Jewish, Christian and Muslim texts. Its archaeology provides a richness and variety of sources that enable both complementary and contradictory readings of religious identities in the past. In addition to the stone monuments, ceramics, glasswork and metalwork that is abundant in the contemporary milieux, Egypt preserves organic material such as the garments and accessories people wore; the curtains, hangings and cushion covers with which they furnished their synagogues, churches, mosques, other public buildings and their homes; children's writing exercises and toys; and funerary assemblages.

Egypt provides an intimacy with the ancient past like nowhere else in the ancient and medieval worlds. [ERO]

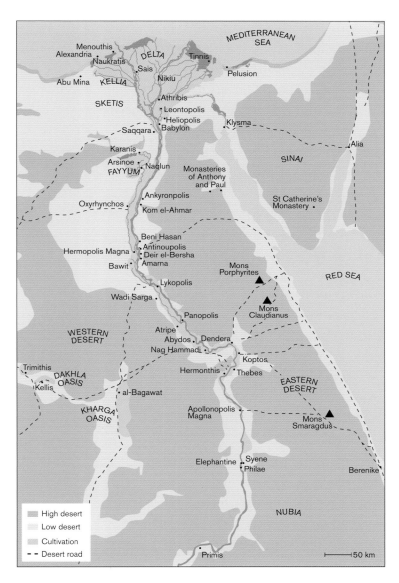

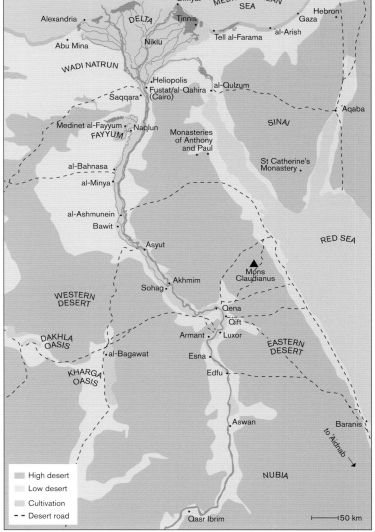

1 **Map of Egypt in the Roman and Late Antique period, showing selected sites mentioned in this volume**

2 **Map of Egypt in the medieval period, showing selected sites mentioned in this volume**

Chronology

Major chronological periods for historic Egypt are given here, including selected rulers and events. All dates before 690 BC are approximate. Note that the reigns of rival rulers or co-rulers sometimes overlap.

	BC
Predynastic period	5500–3100
Early Dynastic period	3100–2686
Old Kingdom	2686–2181
First Intermediate period	2181–2055
Middle Kingdom	2055–1650
Second Intermediate period	1650–1550
New Kingdom	1550–1069
Third Intermediate period	1069–747

Late period: 747–332	
Dynasty 25 (Kushite)	747–656
Dynasty 26 (Saite)	664–525
Dynasty 27 (1st Persian period)	525–404
Cambyses	525–522
Darius I	522–486
Jewish community at Elephantine	494–399
Xerxes I	486–465
Dynasty 28	404–399
Dynasty 29	399–380
Dynasty 30	380–343
Nectanebo II	380–362
Dynasty 31 (2nd Persian period)	343–332

Macedonian dynasty: 332–306	
Alexander the Great	332–323
Foundation of Alexandria	331
Ptolemy son of Lagos satrap of Egypt	323–306

Ptolemaic dynasty: 306–31	
Ptolemy I Soter (with Berenike I)	306–282
Ptolemy II Philadelphos (with Arsinoe II)	282–246
Ptolemy VI and Cleopatra II	163–45
Cleopatra VII Philopator and Ptolemy XIII	51–47
Julius Caesar in Egypt	48–47
Cleopatra VII and Ptolemy XIV	47–44
Cleopatra VII and Ptolemy XV	44–30
Mark Antony sometimes in Egypt	41–30
Battle of Actium	31

Deaths of Cleopatra VII and Mark Antony, after which Egypt becomes a part of the Roman empire

Roman empire: 27 BC–AD 330	
Augustus (previously Octavian)	27 BC–AD 14
Tiberius	14–37
Gaius (Caligula)	37–41
Alexandrian Greeks attack the Jews	38
Claudius	41–54
Titus	79–81
Trajan	98–117
Jewish Diaspora Revolt in Egypt	116–17
Hadrian	117–38
Hadrian visits Egypt	129–30
Marcus Aurelius	161–80
Antonine plague in Egypt	167–c.79
Septimius Severus	193–211
Septimius Severus visits Egypt	200–01
Caracalla	211–17
Constitutio Antoniniana (grant of Roman citizenship)	212
Decius	249–51
Decian 'persecution' of Christians	250

Roman empire: 27 BC–AD 330 continued

Valerian and Gallienus	253–60
Palmyrenes control Egypt	270–72
Diocletian	284–305
Diocletian in Egypt	298
The Great Persecution	303–13

Byzantine empire: 330–619

Constantine I	306–37
Athanasius Bishop of Alexandria	328–73
Inauguration of Constantinople at Byzantium	330
Constantine II	337–40
Constans II	337–50
Constantius II	337–61
Julian ('the Apostate')	361–63
Theodosius I	379–95
Roman Empire divided into east and west	395
Theodosius II	408–50
Council of Chalcedon	451
Leo	457–74
Zeno	474–91
Justin I	518–27
Justinian	527–65
Justin II	565–78
Heraclius	610–19; 629–39

Sasanian Persians occupy Egypt: 619–29

Arab conquest of Egypt under General 'Amr ibn al-'As: 639–42

Rashidun caliphs: 640–58

Abu Bakr	632–34
'Umar ibn al-Khattab	634–44
Foundation of Fustat	642
'Uthman ibn 'Affan	644–56
'Ali ibn Abi Talib	656–61
'Amr ibn al-'As, governor of Egypt	658–64

Umayyad caliphate: 659–750

Marwan I	684–685
'Abd al-Malik	685–705
Coin reform	696
'Umar ibn 'Abd al-'Aziz	717–20
Marwan II	744–50

Abbasid caliphate: 750–969

Tulunid Emirs in Egypt	868–905
Ahmad ibn Tulun	868–84
Ikhshidid Emirs in Egypt	935–69

Fatimid caliphate: 909–1171

al-Mu'izz	953–75
Fatimids establish their capital at al-Qahira in Egypt	969
al-'Aziz	975–96
al-Hakim	996–1021
al-Mustansir	1036–94
al-Amir	1101–30
Regent al-Afdal ibn Badr al-Jamali	1101–30

Ayyubid sultanate: 1171–1258

Salah al-Din (Saladin)	1171–93

Mamluk sultanate: 1250–1517

Ottoman rule: 1517–1867

French occupation	1798–1801
Muhammad Ali	1805–49

Khedivial Egypt: 1867–1914

British Protectorate:	1882–1922

Kingdom of Egypt: 1922–53

Arab Republic of Egypt: 1953–present

1 The Role of Abraham in Judaism, Christianity and Islam

Martin Bauschke

3 Fragment of illustrated Cotton Genesis manuscript

Egypt, Alexandria (?) 5th or 6th century
Parchment. 27.3 × 22.2 cm (original size of each leaf)
British Library, London. Cotton MS Otho B VI, 26v

This miniature from a luxury illustrated copy of Genesis, once belonging to the collection of Sir Robert Cotton (d. 1631), depicts Abraham standing before 3 angels (2 preserved) who appear to him as men by the oak of Mamre and are waited on by him (Genesis 18:2). The illustrations are in the tradition of Hellenistic and Roman painting. The sumptuous quality of the volume, despite its near-destruction by fire in 1731, provides valuable evidence for the high quality of Late Antique book production. [CF/ERO]
Bib: Weitzmann and Kessler 1986

ABRAHAM has enjoyed a recent surge of interest.[1] A semi-nomad, who is said to have lived about 4,000 years ago in the Near East, he is more current than ever. Anyone who studies the patriarch in greater detail discovers that 'the' Abraham does not exist – whether Jewish, Christian or Islamic. Instead we find very different images of the patriarch, not only by comparing between the religions but also *within* the three religions. Who Abraham really was is not known. His existence cannot even be proved historically. On the other hand, what he has meant to individual groups at particular times can certainly be grasped. Abraham is always an ideal projection and identification figure. In him the most varied religious concepts are mirrored. For rabbis learned in the Torah he was a Hebrew-speaking rabbi; for seekers after God he became the first monotheist; for Cosmopolitans the epitome of the citizen of the world; for the doubter he was an example of faith; and for those willing to make sacrifices he was one who was ready to give up everything. As a model individual Abraham has given answers and set an example of behaviour which matched the challenges to his heirs in later times. Thus he served as a figure of legitimization, whose authority was to secure the key issues for the respective group. 'Father Abraham', as all three religions call him, is the archetype for the belief in the one God. He bears the honoured name 'Friend of God'. He is so called unanimously in the Hebrew Bible (Isaiah 41:8), the New Testament (James 2:23) and the Qur'an (Sura 4:125). The other side of Abraham's friendship with God is his hospitality. Entertaining humans and divine messengers was a matter of honour for him, as all three religions report. Thus Abraham was not only a friend of God, but of men too.

The three religions have each put their own emphasis on their conceptions of Abraham. In Judaism, Abraham – *Awraham* in Hebrew – is considered the forefather and progenitor of the Jewish people through his son Isaac, born of Sarah. However, this has never meant that Abraham has been there only for the Jews; he was always considered as a blessing for the whole world (Genesis 12:1–3). The heathen from Ur in Mesopotamia becomes a migrant at God's behest. He moves into a land that is promised to him and later becomes the home of the Jews. In his intercession for the inhabitants of the cities of Sodom and Gomorrah, when they are threatened with destruction, the potential for the blessing emanating from Abraham is revealed – he becomes the advocate for the others, the heathens, the aliens. God concludes a covenant with Abraham and his descendants through circumcision (Genesis 17).

4 Funerary stela of the Christian monk Abraham

Egypt. 7th century
Sandstone. 60 × 37 cm
British Museum, London. EA 1257

Before the 4th century the name Abraham was a good indication that a person's parents were Jewish. The use of the name in Egypt increased exponentially in the 4th and 5th centuries as it also became popular among Christians. In addition to attesting the Christian inheritance of a Jewish name, this funerary stela of 'Abraham, the perfected monk' captures the intersection of Classical, Christian and Egyptian cultural markers. The rectangular stela is carved with a Classical architectural motif comprising a foliate pediment supported by columns, together with a *tabula ansata* (handled tablet) bearing the inscription. Below, the *staurogram* (cross-monogram) – comprising the Greek letters tau and rho – together with the alpha and omega inscribed in the upper left and right quadrants respectively, symbolize Christ's death and resurrection. The *cruces ansatae* (handled crosses) occupying the lower 2 quadrants derive from the ancient Egyptian ankh hieroglyph meaning 'life' and, together with the use of Coptic to write the inscription, establish an unequivocal Egyptian context. [ERO]
Bib: Hall 1905, p. 134, pl. 95

Down to the present day proselytes to Judaism are considered sons and daughters of Abraham. A cardinal virtue of Abraham is his faithfulness, as demonstrated in the story of the Sacrifice of Isaac on Mount Moriah. In the Talmud, the Midrash and other non-biblical Jewish texts, new motifs appear. Abraham is depicted for instance as a fighter (and not just preacher) against the astral religion of his forebears, understood as the cult of idols. Through the observation of the heavens and the stars, hitherto revered as gods, he comes to the realization of the true God. In the conflict with Nimrod, the haughty ruler, Abraham is portrayed as an iconoclast and martyr, whom God protects from being burnt at the stake.

If Abraham is considered in Judaism as the first circumcized Jew, he is advanced in Christianity as the exemplary Christian. According to Paul, membership of the people of Israel is not the determining criterion for participation in Abraham's blessing. Rather, this is said to be based on the faith which comes before circumci-

**5 Tapestry depicting the Sacrifice
of Isaac**

Egypt. 7th – 8th century
Wool and linen. 13.5 × 27 cm
Musée Historique des Tissus, Lyon. Inv. 24400/55

The central field of this tapestry border
depicts an often-represented scene from
the story of Abraham in Genesis (22:1–
19), in which Abraham is on the point of
sacrificing his son Isaac at God's command.
Abraham grasps Isaac by the hair and
is about to thrust his sword. However,
an angel of God – here symbolized by a
hand reaching down from the firmament
– orders him to stop. Prepared to give up
his son for God, Abraham is rewarded for
his obedience. Instead of Isaac, Abraham
sacrifices a ram. This image has its origins
in the iconography of subduing a captive
enemy found in Classical antiquity – see
fig. 12. [CF]
Bib: Cat. Paris 2000, p. 192, no. 213

sion. All who believe belong to Abraham and, like him, are blessed. But all who live according to the law are cursed (Epistle to the Galatians 3). With the emergence of Gentile Christianity a religious argument began about who is the true heir and beneficiary of Abraham's blessing. The Christian tendency to disinherit the Jews is already intimated in Paul. In the later Gospel of John, Abraham becomes the weapon of argument, the instrument of burgeoning Christian anti-Semitism. If in the genealogies of the New Testament in Matthew and Luke Jesus is naturally considered to be a son of Abraham, in John this genealogy is theologically inverted. Jesus is declared to be the father of Abraham: 'Before Abraham was, I am' (John 8:58). Unfortunately this is linked with the accusation that, as the sons of Abraham, the Jews are in fact the children of Satan (John 8:44). In Abraham the Protestant tradition has seen, above all, the embodiment of the man justified through faith rather than through legality or his good deeds. Common to all confessions is the christologically new interpretation of the sacrifice story, which makes a cosmic-divine drama out of the account of Abraham and Isaac. Since God only nearly demanded the sacrifice of Isaac, and yet in the sacrifice of his Son on the hill of Golgotha this actually happened, it is the risen Christ and not Abraham who is the foundation of Christian identity.

In Islam, Abraham – *Ibrahim* in Arabic – has become precisely that founding figure. If Moses is at the centre of Judaism and Christ at the centre of Christianity, Abraham is at the heart of Islam. It was not Muhammad but Abraham who was the first model Muslim. He is the archetype of belief in the one God and at the same time the *imam* (leader) of believers (Sura 2:124). He has been a *hanif* (a true seeker after

6 Funerary stela of Ishaq ibn Ibrahim

Egypt, probably from Cairo. 30 November 859
(1 Ramadan 245 HJ)
Marble or limestone. 59 × 44 cm
Museum für Islamische Kunst, Staatliche Museen
zu Berlin. Inv. I. 579

While the name of the deceased, 'Isaac
son of Abraham', is Jewish in origin, the
content of the stela expressly confirms his
Muslim faith. The last 2 lines give the date
of death, written out in words according to
the custom. The 11-line inscription is incised
in elegant, decorated Kufic script and
framed on 3 sides by arabesque tendrils.
The script of the last 5 lines lacks the
decorative elements on the stems; they
are a little smaller and closer together
than the first 6 lines. [GH]
Bib: RCEA 2 1932, no. 437

7 The tomb of Abraham, Hebron

View of the tomb of Abraham and its
surroundings in Hebron, today located in
the West Bank, south of Jerusalem.
Engraving by W. Finden, drawn by
D. Roberts from a sketch made on the
spot by Mrs Bracebridge, c.1850.

God). The Islam founded by Muhammad shows itself to be the restored *milla* (religious community) of Abraham. Thus Muslims can say that Islam is the oldest and at the same time the newest monotheistic religion. As the original Muslim, Abraham has already exemplified almost all the pillars of Islam – the declaration of faith, ritual prayer, obligatory almsgiving and the pilgrimage to Mecca. Muhammad sees his own fate prefigured in that of Abraham. The latter's departure from Ur is the model for his Hijra (emigration) from the heathen Mecca. The cleansing of the Ka'ba by Muhammad is the imitation of the renovation of the Ka'aba by Abraham and his son Ishmael, who in Islam takes the place of Isaac (Sura 2). The Festival of Sacrifice is unthinkable without the sacrifice story also told in the Qur'an (Sura 37). All in all, the Qur'an paints an idealized picture of the patriarch as a 'beautiful example' (Sura 60:4), a perfect believer without a blemish and beyond reproach. The stories familiar from the Bible, in which Abraham's weaknesses are shown, are withheld. Other tales in the Qur'an, for example about the destruction of the idols and the contemplation of the stars, do not appear in the Bible. In the post-Qur'anic tradition an important role is played by the legends of Abraham and Nimrod, as in the Jewish tradition, as well as the legend of Hagar and Ishmael in Mecca.

That Abraham died and is buried in Hebron (al-Khalil in Arabic) is self-evident for Muslims as well as Jews and Christians. His last resting place is considered a place of prayer in all three religions. At the same time there is constant unrest and violence there. Abraham both unites and divides the three religions. At the present time there is trialogue but also terrorism 'in the name of Abraham' (for example, the Salafist organization 'Millatu Ibrahim'). The patriarch remains an ambivalent figure to this day.

2 Judaism

Mladen Popović

8 The First Gaster Bible

Egypt. 9–10th century
Parchment codex. 33 × 24.2 cm
British Library, London. Or. 9879

The First Gaster Bible is named after its
owner, Dr Moses Gaster (1856–1939), the
head of the Sephardic community in London.
It represents one of the earliest surviving
examples of Jewish manuscript illumination
from the Middle East. The style of the
Hebrew script decoration parallels that of
contemporary Qur'ans. [ERO]
Bib: Cat. New York 2012, no. 113, pp. 112–13

EGYPT figures prominently in the Hebrew Bible, or what Christians call the Old Testament. Egypt is the land where Abraham and Sarah go because of famine in the land of Canaan, and where the famous story unfolds of Abraham telling Sarah to say to the Egyptians that she is not his wife but his sister (Genesis 12:10–20). Connecting the stories of the patriarchs with that of Moses, Egypt is the land where Joseph rises to prominence having been sold by his brothers to traders (Genesis 37–50) (see ch. 20). Most importantly, Egypt is the land of the Exodus, the land from which Hebrew slaves escape under the leadership of Moses from an oppressive pharaoh – a focal memory for the formation of Jewish identity throughout the ages. For example, the prophet Hosea from the eighth century BC says: 'When Israel was a child, I loved

him, and out of Egypt I called my son' (Hosea 11:1). Not surprisingly, in light of the Exodus tradition, Egypt is not looked upon favourably in many biblical texts. At the same time, it is clear from a historical perspective that people in ancient Israel and Judah looked for support from Egypt, rightly or wrongly, in light of the lethal threats posed by the Neo-Assyrian and Neo-Babylonian empires in the eighth and late seventh/early sixth centuries BC. For example, the prophet Isaiah at the end of the eighth century says: 'See, you are relying on Egypt, that broken reed of a staff, which will pierce the hand of anyone who leans on it. Such is Pharaoh king of Egypt to all who rely on him' (Isaiah 36:6). Facing the Babylonian threat in the early sixth century, Judeans fled to Egypt, taking the prophet Jeremiah with them, probably against his will (Jeremiah 43:6).

Notwithstanding the Exodus tradition and negative perceptions of Egypt in biblical memory, Jews lived in Egypt (at least from the First Persian period, 525–404 BC, onward) when a Jewish garrison was stationed at Elephantine Island, southern Egypt. Letters, ostraca (pottery or stone sherds), documentary and literary texts belonging to the people of this garrison illustrate Jewish life in Egypt in the fifth century and connections with Persian-controlled Samaria and Jerusalem (see focus 1).

After the conquests of Alexander the Great (332–323) many Jews settled in Egypt, primarily in the new city of Alexandria on the Mediterranean coast but also elsewhere. Jews served as mercenaries, police, tax collectors or administrators to Ptolemaic kings, but most of the Jews were either farmers or artisans. According to tradition, king Ptolemy II Philadelphos (282–246) instigated the translation of the Bible into Greek. It was named Septuagint after the number of translators – allegedly six from each of the twelve traditional tribes.[1] Probably starting with the translation of the first five books of Moses, and subsequently the other books over a period of perhaps two centuries, the Greek translation of the Bible illustrates that Jews were at home in Alexandria, and that they were in need of access to their ancestral traditions in a language they could understand (see ch. 5).[2] This cultural need is also borne out by the wisdom book of Jewish author Ben Sira (later known in Latin as Ecclesiasticus). Originally composed in Hebrew early in the second century BC in Jerusalem, it was translated into Greek, purportedly by Ben Sira's grandson, during the latter third of the second century BC in Egypt. While sources such as these suggest Jews were

9 Wall painting depicting the Exodus

The Necropolis of al-Bagawat in the Kharga Oasis contains both 'pagan' and Christian graves from the 5th and 6th centuries. A section of the wall painting in the dome of the so-called Exodus Chapel shows the Israelites' exodus from Egypt. Shown here are Egyptian soldiers driving Moses and the Israelites towards the Red Sea. The Israelites hurry ahead with their goods and chattels. The Promised Land is depicted at the end (not shown here). [CF]

10 Glass pendant with *menorah*

Eastern Mediterranean. 4th century
Glass. 2.1 × 1.81 cm
British Museum, London. BEP 1983,1108.61

Worn as amulets for protection, this type of translucent glass pendant was popular in the 4th century. Most depicted deities and heroes from Classical and Egyptian mythology, or astrological motifs. A small proportion depicted the *menorah* (the Jewish symbol par excellence in Late Antiquity) or the Christian cross, or scenes from the New Testament such as Christ teaching. The same workshops may have produced for clientele of various religious persuasions. [ERO]
Bib: Entwistle and Corby Finney 2013, no. 87, p. 163

11 Petition mentioning the annual celebration of the suppression of the Jewish Diaspora Revolt (*P.Oxy.* IV 705)

Oxyrhynchus. After 202
Papyrus. 21.1 × 46 cm
Cambridge University Library, Cambridge.
Add. Ms. 4416

Over 80 years after the Diaspora Revolt of 116–17, the town of Oxyrhynchus celebrated an annual festival commemorating its suppression. In his petition to Emperor Septimius Severus, the wealthy landowner Aurelius Horion seeks benefactions for his town, reminding the emperor of their 'goodwill, faithfulness and friendship towards Romans, which they showed both by joining in the war against the Jews and by celebrating even now, each year, the day of the victory'. [ERO]

Bib: Parsons 2007, p. 66, p. 77

well integrated into their Hellenistic-Egyptian cultural environment, other sources indicate that cultural tensions existed between Jews and non-Jews and that also outright hostilities occurred.[3]

In the early Roman period, starting after the Battle of Actium in 31 BC between Octavian and the combined forces of Mark Antony and Cleopatra, Jewish individuals could rise to high prominence. Tiberius Alexander became prefect of the Roman province of Egypt (AD 66 – 69), apparently after having renounced his ancestral Jewish traditions. Before that he was procurator of Judea (*c.*46–48), and in 70 he was one of the commanders of Titus' Roman army during the siege of Jerusalem and the destruction of the Temple. Jewish relations with non-Jews in Alexandria seem to have been strained. The Jewish philosopher Philo of Alexandria (*c.*25 BC – AD 50), who was Tiberius Alexander's uncle, headed a diplomatic mission in 40 to Emperor Gaius Caligula on behalf of the Jews of Alexandria after anti-Jewish riots and hostilities in 38.[4] Caligula did not reassert Alexandrian Jews' rights as requested by Philo. After Caligula's death in 41, Jews massacred Greeks in Alexandria. Jewish literary works such as 3 Maccabees and Wisdom of Solomon[5] illustrate the tense relations between Jews and non-Jews in Alexandria during the late Hellenistic and early Roman period.

In the context of the start of the First Jewish Revolt against Rome in Judea (66–70), Flavius Josephus in his *Jewish War* describes Alexandrian relations between Jews and non-Jews in a familiar manner – dire. The prefect Tiberius Alexander sent two legions and 2,000 extra soldiers against the Jews to end the unrest, killing purportedly 50,000 or more than 60,000.[6] Josephus relates that, after the revolt, one of the rebel groups, the Sicarii, fled to Egypt and caused unrest there before they were stopped.[7] Also, in 73 the Romans destroyed a Jewish temple that had been at Leontopolis (now Tell al-Yahudiya), northeast of Memphis since *c*.170 BC.[8] After the revolt Rome established a special Jewish tax, *fiscus Iudaicus*, to be paid annually to the Capitol as Jews formerly contributed to the Jerusalem temple. This *fiscus Iudaicus* had to be paid by Jews everywhere in the Roman empire. Tax receipts written on ostraca from Egypt show that Jews in Egypt paid this tax well into the second century AD.[9]

It is difficult to gauge the exact causes of the Diaspora Revolt in 116–17 under Emperor Trajan. It was possibly a combination of the long-term effects of the First Jewish Revolt, such as the *fiscus Iudaicus*, togetherer with messianic and apocalyptic ideas. It was widespread, and initially successful.[10] Revolts broke out in Cyrenaica, Egypt and Cyprus, and in Mesopotamia in relation to the Roman invasion of Parthia. These simultaneous revolts and the Roman responses caused the destruction of Diaspora communities. The Roman crackdown had a devastating impact on Jewish life in Egypt in particular. It is not until the late third century that significant evidence of Jewish life reappears. In the meantime it seems that Christians had taken over the production and transmission of biblical (Septuagint) and other Jewish texts in Greek, since the social frameworks for text production and transmission by Jews were lacking in Egypt. This coincides broadly with the process of Jews exclusively using the Hebrew text and Aramaic renderings

12 An emperor subduing a captive

Egypt. 2nd century
Terracotta figure. 17 × 10.5 cm (max);
depth 5cm (max)
British Museum, London. G&R 1983,0723.1

Images of Roman emperors subduing enemies were powerful statements of dominance. They appeared on public monuments and coins, or as small everyday statues as here. Wearing a diadem and with an eagle on his shoulder, a Roman emperor wields a sword in one hand and grasps a half-kneeling enemy by the hair with the other. The emperor's curly hair and full beard date the statue to the 2nd century, contemporary with the Jewish Revolt in Egypt. [ERO]
Bib: Bailey 2008, no. 3509, p. 139, pl. 93

13 Description of plots of land formerly in Jewish possession (*SB* XII 10892)

Egypt, Fayyum (?) After 188
Papyrus. Left section: 14 × 76 cm; right section: 13.9 × 45.5 cm
Ägyptisches Museum und Papyrussammlung, Staatliche Museen zu Berlin. ÄMP P 8143 A-C R and P 7397 R

This Greek text, assembled from 2 fairly large fragments of papyrus, contains a list with a description of plots of land that had previously been in the possession of Jewish and Greek occupants and had been confiscated by the State. This is one of the few surviving documents from the time between the Jewish Revolt and the resettlement of the Jews in Egypt in the 3rd century. [CF]
Bib: Pucci Ben Zeev 2005, pp. 56–68, no. 38

14 Ivory pyxis with Daniel in the lions' den

Syria or Egypt? 5th–early 6th century
Elephant ivory. 7.6 × 10.5 cm
British Museum, London. BEP 1877,0706.3 (donated by A.W. Franks)

Christians drew upon both Jewish and Classical
iconographic sources. Here, a series of scenes from the
Old Testament and extra-biblical sources illustrates salvation
through faith on this luxury *pyxis* (lidded box). Daniel with
arms raised in prayer is flanked by 2 lions, with a guard
looking on in surprise to the right (Daniel 6), while to the
left (not shown) the prophet Habakkuk is carried by the
hair by an angel to deliver stew and bread to Daniel, in
accordance with the apocryphal story of Bel and the Dragon
(1.30–1.42). In a separate scene (not shown), an angel
rushes forward behind a ram, with both looking intently
ahead – referring to but not representing the moment before
the latter is substituted for Abraham's son Isaac (Genesis
22:11–13). [ERO]
Bib: Cat. New York 1979, no. 436, p. 485

15 Wooden architectural element with Daniel in the lions' den

Egypt, said to be from Bawit. 6th century
Tamarisk wood. 96 x 41 × 14 cm
Skulpturensammlung und Museum für Byzantinische Kunst, Staatliche
Museen zu Berlin. Inv. 3019

Like the *pyxis* above, this Christian architectural element
depicts the miraculous rescue of Daniel from the lions' den
(Daniel 6). He stands frontally with his hands (now lost)
raised in prayer. He is dressed in a typical Eastern costume
with trousers, gathered gown, a rider's cloak and a Phrygian
cap. The lion on the left sits facing outwards, while the one
on the right stands on his hind legs. The lower, undecorated,
part of the architectural element served as a support for a
beam. [MK]
Bib: Cat. Hamm 1996, p. 134, no. 92, 134; Cat. Berlin 2006,
pp. 80–81

(Targumim), probably because of the Greek text being associated with Christians. When Jewish life becomes visible again in Egypt in the third century, it is probably due to immigration from Roman Palestine and elsewhere. As had happened before, during the fourth and fifth centuries the new Jewish communities became integral elements of their cultural surroundings.

Little is known concerning the conditions of Jewish life in Egypt from the pogrom in Alexandria in 415[11] until the Sasanian (619–29) and Arab (639) conquests, and then until the tenth century. Under the Fatimids, from the tenth century onwards conditions changed for the Jews in Egypt. The treasure trove of the Cairo Genizah in the Ben Ezra Synagogue in Old Cairo (Fustat), comprising more than 200,000 documents, provides a unique window onto historical, social, economic, religious and cultural aspects of medieval Jewish life – of Jews amongst themselves and with others – thriving in Mediterranean Egypt during the Fatimids and later (see ch. 18). The documents attest ties with other Jewish communities across the Mediterranean and Near East, and also show a variety of Jewish groups in Egypt at the time, most notably the Qaraites next to the well-known Rabbinic Jews, who could disagree with each other but also could live together.

16 Book of Exodus in Arabic

Egypt. 1005
Paper codex. 23.5 × 17.5 cm
British Library, London. Or. 2540

The Book of Exodus gives the account of the flight of the ancient Israelites from Egypt. This incomplete Arabic manuscript contains Exodus 1:1–8.5. In the medieval period Jews spoke and often wrote in Arabic. Whereas Rabbanite Jews rendered their Arabic translations of the Bible using Hebrew script (today called Judeo-Arabic), so-called Qaraite Jews sometimes used Arabic script to render Hebrew. This codex features Hebrew and Arabic vocalization signs in red and green ink, giving it the appearance of contemporary Qur'ans. [EE]
Bib: Cat. New York 2012, no. 77, pp. 114–15

FOCUS 1 THE JEWISH COMMUNITY AT ELEPHANTINE

Verena Lepper

OPPOSITE the city of Syene (modern Aswan), on the east bank of the Nile, lies the island of Elephantine (fig. 17). In the fifth century BC, when Egypt was under Persian rule (Dynasty 27), an Aramaeo-Jewish Diaspora community lived on the island. This famous so-called 'Jewish colony' of Elephantine has been the subject of numerous studies, especially in the fields of Jewish studies. The existence of a Jewish Diaspora in Egypt was already attested in biblical sources (Jeremiah 41:16ff; Jeremiah 42 and 43; Jeremiah 44:1ff; cf. 2 Kings 25:22–26).

A sensational discovery of fifth-century documents on papyri and ostraca found on the island confirmed the presence of Jews even at Egypt's southern border. Since the beginning of the nineteenth century several pieces from this papyrus discovery have made their way through various dealers to Europe, including today's papyrus collection of the Ägyptisches Museum und Papyrussammlung, Staatlichen Museen zu Berlin.[1] The texts of this find are all written in Aramaic, the lingua franca of the western Persian empire and therefore also of Egypt. They explain in detail the life of the Aramaic-speaking Jewish community, stationed on the border between Egypt and Nubia as a 'military colony'. A temple

to Yahweh, which must have originated before the start of Persian rule, is attested in this township. The Aramaic papyri from Elephantine were all written over a period of less than one hundred years. Many texts are precisely dated, some in accordance with the Babylonian Jewish calendar, some with the Egyptian calendar, and most of them more specifically providing the regnal year of the current Persian ruler. The uniqueness of these texts in terms of their historical importance can therefore hardly be underestimated. The oldest document to bear its own date is from year 27 of Darius I (494 BC), while the latest dates from the year 5 of Amyrtaeus (399 BC), the first post-Persian ruler of Egypt (Dynasty 28).[2]

The Aramaic texts of the Diaspora community of Elephantine were mainly written by its members. They are contemporary with the events they describe, without there being – as is common in biblical texts – any major time lapse, textual corruption or even later editorial intervention. Today these documents on papyri and ostraca are scattered all over the world, in various museums. They reveal aspects of political, economic and religious life, as well as family and community life. They can be grouped as follows:

- The communal archives of Jedaniah, leader of the community. Letters report on, for example, the destruction of the Jewish temple at Elephantine by Egyptians.
- The private family archives of the temple official Ananiah, who was married to an Egyptian slave woman. The archive consists mainly of legal contracts.
- The private family archives of Mibtahiah, aunt of Jedaniah. These documents cover a period of three generations or about sixty years, and also reflect private law.
- Numerous letters of an administrative and private character.
- Lists and catalogues of persons or goods (often on ostraca, rather than papyrus).
- Literary and historical works: the *Story of Ahiqar* and the so-called Behistun Inscription of Darius I.[3]

These documents are the oldest non-biblical evidence of any Jewish community in Egypt.

17 Elephantine Island

View from the south of the archaeological site where the Aramaic papyri were found.

18 Aramaic document with seal from the Ananjah Archive

Found 1906 on Elephantine Island, Egypt. 13 December 456 BC
Papyrus. 56 × 29 cm
Ägyptisches Museum und Papyrussammlung, Staatliche Museen zu Berlin. P Berlin 13491

The subject of this originally sealed document is a loan agreement concerning silver. The woman Jehohen borrows the sum of 4 shekels from Meshullam, son of Zaccur, with an interest rate of 5% per month. The writer is Nathan, the son of Ananjah. The seal of the document is made of clay and is stamped with Egyptian hieroglyphs. [VL]

3 Christianity

Gregor Wurst

ALTHOUGH Egypt is mentioned many times in the New Testament, the beginnings of Christianity here are largely obscure. The flight of the Holy Family into Egypt (Matthew 2:13–15, 19–21) is a pious legend.[1] The existence of a Christian community is not verified either by the naming of Egypt in the list of peoples in the story of Pentecost (Acts 2:10), or by the single person of the Alexandrian Jew Apollos, who attached himself in Ephesus to St Paul's mission (Acts of the Apostles 18:24). The historical value of the story of the conversion of the Ethiopian (Nubian) eunuch (Acts of the Apostles 8:27) is likewise questionable.[2]

The earliest evidence of Egyptian Christianity is found in biblical texts, written on papyrus, dated as early as the second century AD and definitely used by (Judeo-) Christian communities.[3] Amongst them is a fragment known as P52 (fig. 19) with the text of John 18:31–33, 37–38. Probably the oldest textual material of the New Testament, it is traditionally dated to the second half of the second century, but some experts date it to around the turn of the second and third centuries.[4] From early

19 Papyrus fragment with New Testament text (*P.Ryl.* III 457)

Egypt, probably from Oxyrhynchus. Early 2nd or late 2nd / early 3rd century
Papyrus. 8.9 × 6 cm
John Rylands Library, Manchester. P52

The text preserved on this fragment of papyrus comes from the Gospel according to John (18:31–33). It contains the scene in which Christ appears before Pilate. The fragment is thought to be the oldest written evidence of the New Testament discovered to date. [CF]
Bib: Bagnall 2009, p. 12

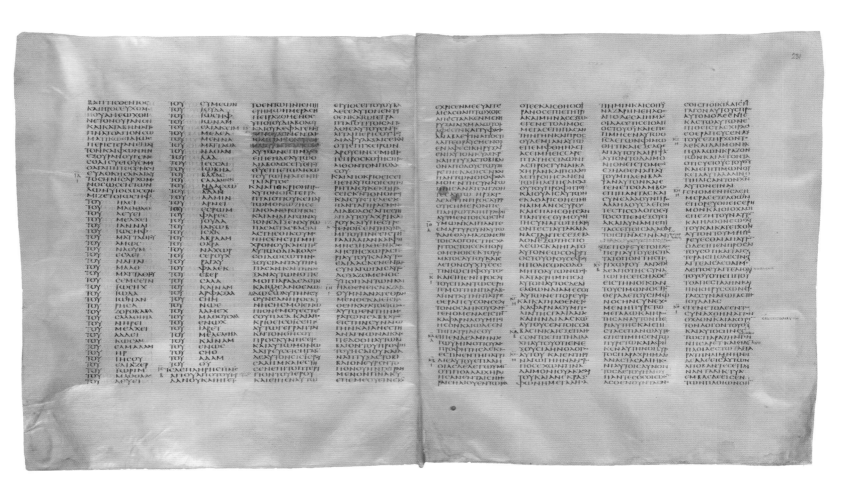

patristic sources the place of composition is assumed to be Alexandria or Egypt, with varying plausibility, for the Epistle of Barnabas, the so-called 2 Clement and the Preaching of Peter. However, in no case can it be proved,[5] and even if it were these texts contain no information about a Christianity that is distinctively Egyptian.

The oldest surviving copies of some gospels that did not receive canonical status – for example the Gospel of the Egyptians, the Gospel of the Hebrews and the Gospel of Thomas – come from Egypt. Whilst the first two texts may also have been composed in Egypt,[6] the Greek fragments of the Gospel of Thomas (*P.Oxy.* I 654, 655; cf. NHC II 2; see fig. 26), and the quotations from the Gospel of the Egyptians used by Alexandrian theologians, show the existence of Gnostic or semi-Gnostic Christian communities in Egypt from an early period (see focus 2).[7] This is likewise supported by the heresiological (and therefore polemical) reports about the Gnostic teachers Basilides and Valentinus from the second century, the historical value of which is however somewhat questionable.[8] The vitality of the so-called Gnostic tradition in Egyptian Christianity is shown in the second half of the fourth century by a group of at least fifty-two manuscripts in Coptic translation, mostly of Gnostic provenance from various schools, found near Nag Hammadi in Upper Egypt.[9]

20 Codex Sinaiticus

Egypt, Sinai, Monastery of St Catherine, until 1859.
Mid-4th century
Parchment, modern binding. 38 × 34.5 cm
British Library, London. Add. MS 43725, ff 230v–231r

Codex Sinaiticus ('The book from Sinai') is a Greek manuscript containing the earliest complete version of the Christian New Testament. It is also the best and most complete witness to many of the books of the Greek translation of Jewish scripture (i.e. the Septuagint or Christian Old Testament), and attests works that did not later receive canonical status. Together with Codex Vaticanus, it is the most important textual witness to the Christian Bible. Now distributed between London, Leipzig, St Petersburg and Sinai, the codex was preserved for centuries in the Monastery of St Catherine near the foot of Mount Sinai. Shown here is the text giving the genealogy of Jesus from Joseph to Adam (Luke 3:23–38). [CF/ERO]
Bib: McKendrick et al 2015; Codex Sinaiticus Project (http://www.codexsinaiticus.org/en/)

21 Relief with preaching apostle (?)

Eastern Mediterranean (Syria or Alexandria?). Middle
or second half of the 6th century
Elephant ivory. 15 × 12 × 0.35 cm
Département des Objets d'art, Musée du Louvre,
Paris. OA 3317

This exceptionally thick ivory block, deeply
carved on its convex face, presents a group of
smaller figures standing around a man with a
halo, who sits on a throne and dominates the
composition. Above is a city surrounded by a
wall flanked by 2 towers, and populated by
spectators who throng the windows and
balconies. The identification of the city and
the scene is uncertain. It could represent
St Mark, the first Bishop of Alexandria, and his
35 successors. The 36th was Anastasius, who
occupied the seat of Alexandria from 607 to
619. This identification leads to a dating for
the ivory of the early 7th century. No element
in the architecture provides us with evidence
to identify positively the city represented, and
none of the characters is wearing clerical dress.
However, the appearance of the central figure
and the strong overall relief reveal an affinity
with the ivories of the second half of the 6th
century attributed to the workshops of the
Eastern Mediterranean or Constantinople, such
as the binding of the St Lupicinus gospels (Paris,
BnF) and the Etchmiadzin gospels in Armenia
(Yerevan, Matenadaran). [DG]
Bib: Gaborit-Chopin 2003, pp. 55–57
(with bibliography)

22 Oil lamp with inscription 'St Mark the Evangelist'

Egypt, acquired in Cairo. 5th–8th century
Terracotta. 4.5 × 6.4 × 11.7 cm
Skulpturensammlung und Museum für Byzantinische Kunst,
Staatliche Museen zu Berlin. Inv. 9617

The inscription on the lamp – 'St Mark the
Evangelist' (MARKOY E[-]ΥΓΓΕΛΙC) – refers to
the legendary founder of the Church at Alexandria.
Originally the inscription would have been partially
obscured by an applied handle (subsequently lost).
The cross, decorated with dots between the discus
and the nozzle, would nevertheless have left its
Christian message in no doubt. [EE]

The Egyptian church traces its own origins back to the Evangelist Mark, the colleague and *hermeneutes* (interpreter) of the apostle Peter. This legend is first attested in the *Church History* of Eusebius of Caesarea (AD 260/64–339/40). Apart from a few isolated and scattered reports, the Egyptian church only enters the historical record with the long episcopate of Demetrius of Alexandria (AD 188/89–231/32).[11] It seems that until this time there was only one Egyptian bishop, in Alexandria, and that the other communities were led by presbyters (ch. 6). Demetrius ordained three other bishops for the Egyptian hinterland, and his successor Heraklas ordained a further twenty. Thus, at the turn of the second to the third century, a primary ecclesiastical organization had come into being.[12]

Papyrus documents discovered in Egypt provide direct contemporary attestation of what has been recorded in the writings of the Church Fathers as Roman persecution of Christians. So-called *libelli* (sacrifice certificates) from the reign of Decius show local administrative commissions giving receipts for the carrying out of a pagan sacrifice. One such sacrifice certificate dated 250 was made out for a pagan priestess from the Fayyum: 'Aurelia Ammonous, [daughter] of Mystus, priestess of the great, mighty and immortal god Petesouchos'.[13] In contrast to the Church Fathers' accounts, such documents show that Decius had enacted a general sacrifice decree directed to the whole population of the country rather than an explicit persecution of Christians.[14] By sacrificing in accordance with the edict, Christians faced exclusion by their community; by not doing so, they faced potential imprisonment and even death – namely, martyrdom. Later edicts by Emperors Valerian and Diocletian targeted Christians specifically. Although absolute numbers of martyrs cannot be ascertained because of the incomplete sources, the conclusion from Eusebius' reports in his *Church History* and in Coptic martyr accounts is that Egyptian Christians suffered severely, especially under Diocletian.[15] The importance of these events for the Egyptian church is shown by the fact that the Egyptian Christians renamed a 'pagan' calendar, the so-called 'Diocletian Era', originally used for the calculation of Easter for all Christian churches/Christians, in the 'Era of the Martyrs' when the Islamization of Egypt started from the eighth century onwards. This calendar is still used today.[16]

At the same time as the episcopate of Demetrius, Alexandria was an important centre of theological learning – Pantaenus (active *c*.180), Clement of Alexandria (died *c*.220) and Origen (died *c*.254) were the formative teachers at the famous Catechetical School of Alexandria. Origen, who left Alexandria in the second decade of the third century because of a dispute with his bishop, is rightly considered as the most influential theologian of his time. It was due to his conception of Christian theology – that the Son (the Logos) must be understood from eternity to be the Son – that the Trinitarian disputes started decades after his death because of the dissent of the Alexandrian presbyter Arius. These controversies arising in Egypt largely

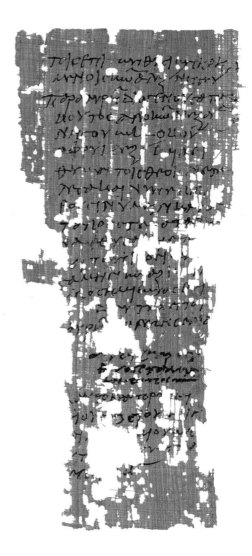

23 Receipt confirming sacrifice (*BGU* I 287)

Egypt, Theadelphia (Batn al-Harit). 26 June 250 (year 1 of Decius, 2 Epep)
Papyrus. 20.5 × 8 cm
Ägyptisches Museum und Papyrussammlung, Staatliche Museen zu Berlin. Inv. P 7297

A man named Aurelius Diogenes asks Aurelius Syros, the person responsible for issuing receipts in the village of Alexandrou Nesos, to confirm that he has sacrificed to the gods in accordance with legislation issued by the emperor Decius. The empire-wide requirement to sacrifice posed a special problem for Christians, since people who refused faced prison or death. All 46 such receipts found in Egypt were written between 12 June and 14 July 250, indicating that the official registration of sacrifice took place within a specific time span and was the result of a coordinated bureaucratic effort. [CF/ERO]
Bib: Luijendijk 2008, pp. 157–74

24 Book of Proverbs in Akhmimic Coptic

Egypt, probably the Monastery of Shenoute (White Monastery) near Sohag. Late 4th century
Papyrus in modern leather binding. 13.5 × 14.5 cm (page size)
Orientabteilung, Staatsbibliothek zu Berlin.
Inv. SBB Ms. or. oct. 987

This codex contains the complete Book of Proverbs, the authorship of which is traditionally ascribed to Solomon, the son of David. In reality this collection of wise sayings was assembled over a longer period. The Proverbs are a part of both the Jewish Bible and the Christian Old Testament, while the New Testament also refers to them in several places. This codex is one of the earliest Christian records, written in the Upper Egyptian Akhmimic dialect of Coptic. Fine lines separate the individual verses from one another. Only 2 pages are decorated. Shown here, page 140 has an ornamental border below the text, as well as a panel with an ornamental frame with an ankh or Christian 'handled cross' (*crux ansata*) to the left and right of it. The original binding of the book has been preserved and is stored separately. [CF]
Bib: Buzi 2014, pp. 214–16, no. 17

determined the theological discussions of the fourth century throughout the empire. The Council of Nicea (convened by the emperors) and, after numerous further meetings, the Council of Constantinople (381), fixed Christian orthodoxy on this point. The Alexandrian Archbishop Athanasius (died 373) played a decisive part in these controversies.[17]

If Alexandria and Rome were in agreement on the question of the Trinitarian doctrine in the fourth century, this alliance failed in the fifth century on the theological problem of the Incarnation of the Son. The archbishops of Alexandria, Cyril (died 444) and especially Dioscorus of Alexandria (died 454), supported a position that is described, albeit controversially, as monophysite or miaphysite by modern scholars in the history of theology. The problem was whether Jesus of Nazareth, born a man, was not only entirely God but also entirely human, and how one can understand such a union of a divine and human nature. The Alexandrian patriarchs committed themselves to a position that taught 'the one nature of the Word Incarnate'. However they were unsuccessful in their bid to have this language adopted at the Council of Chalcedon (AD 451).[18]

The unity of Christendom in Late Antiquity shattered on the acceptance or rejection of the christological definition of Chalcedon (the Son of God become Man), which teaches both a divine and a human nature. In spite of various attempts at unity by the Byzantine emperors, there developed in the Eastern Mediterranean the so-called monophysite national churches that exist to this day, including the Coptic Church. Freed from the grip of the Eastern Roman emperors, this church developed under Arab rule from the Patriarchate of Benjamin I (died 661) onwards. Yet, over the centuries, Egyptian Christianity came into a minority position, which characterizes it to this day.[19]

25 Psalter in Bohairic Coptic

Egypt, Monastery of St Antony (?)
11th–12th century, and 18th century
Parchment and paper codex; leather and wood binding. 28 × 20 × 8 cm (closed)
Ägyptisches Museum und Papyrussammlung, Staatliche Museen zu Berlin. Inv. P 22160

The manuscript contains the Psalms of David written in the Coptic dialect of Bohairic. In the 18th century the book was re-bound, and replacements for missing pages in the middle and a number of pages at the end were added.

The older part of the manuscript, written in the Fatimid period, contains Psalms 1–142.3. The flyleaf is decorated with copious ornamental illuminations, framing the beginning of the book of psalms. The individual psalms that follow are embellished with coloured paragraph markers, sometimes entwined with initials, and the headpieces picked out in red. Psalms play an important part in the liturgy for both Jews and Christians. [CF]
Bib: Kaiser 1967, p. 135, no. 1174

FOCUS 2 GNOSTICISM AND MANICHAEISM

Siegfried G. Richter

THE term Gnosticism – from the Greek *gnosis* meaning 'knowledge' – refers to the religious and philosophical belief systems that emerged at the latest in the second century AD and, in this definition, are limited to Late Antiquity.[1] Understood in a broader sense, the term gnosis refers to epistemological doctrines in general and thus can be applied to many philosophical systems from the Graeco-Roman period onwards.[2]

Manichaeism, as a variety of Gnosticism, is a syncretistic religion that was consciously founded by the Persian Mani in the third century AD, with the intention to unite all existing knowledge and to spread it via missionary endeavour. Characteristics and names from different regions were thus adapted and transferred into Mani's own system. The Manichaeans presented themselves as the true Christians, who alone possessed the genuine tradition about Jesus Christ; Mani referred to himself as an apostle of Jesus Christ. Their most prominent, if temporary, adherent was the Church Father Augustine – who went on to write several anti-Manichaean works after his conversion to Christianity. Manichaeism reached its zenith in the Uighur empire, where it was the state religion in the eighth and ninth centuries.[3] Its cultic afterlife can be detected in China today. There is a Manichean temple in Quanzhou, where Buddhists revere an image that was originally a depiction of Mani in the shape of the Buddha.[4]

In addition to the tradition of the Church Fathers, who were vehement opponents of these religious phenomena, the main sources survive in Coptic and come from finds at Nag Hammadi (with Christian-apocryphal, Gnostic and Hermetic texts), Medinet Madi in the Fayyum and Kellis in Dakhla Oasis (with Manichaean texts) (fig. 27).[5] But additional original sources have been found in Egypt, written in both Coptic and Greek.[6] Among the numerous apocryphal texts written in the New Testament tradition, there are gospels, apocalypses and other texts that have at least some Gnostic features.[7] Subsequent original sources for Manichaeism include various texts in different languages and from different regions (such as Turfan in Central Asia), and also high-quality miniatures and paintings.[8]

The Gnostic belief systems sought to answer the basic questions of human existence in a philosophical and speculative way. In the second century, theological schools had already emerged that represented different views but shared a close kinship with Christianity. The transition from 'Christian' to 'Gnostic' thought is fluid, and modern scholars continue to debate it.[9]

A characteristic feature of such systems (which vary greatly in detail) is the notion of a spark that has fallen from its home of light into the realm of matter, which is substantially evil. This spark is mainly found in human beings and needs to return to its origins. The mythical descriptions of divine spheres serve to answer the question of where human beings come from, and how they can fulfil their destiny – in other words, return to the kingdom of light. In Gnosticism there is a primordially good God who creates other beings. But in the ongoing process of evolution, a mishap occurs through which something imperfect and evil arises. This evil is viewed in some systems as identifiable with the God of the Old Testament, who jealously keeps human beings in a state of ignorance. The world is seen as dualistic in character and fundamentally separated into spirit and matter, light and darkness, good and evil.

Manichaeism, however, represents a dualism that exists from the beginning. The Manichaean system recognizes a good principle (the father of the realm of light) and an evil principle (the prince of darkness). As the creatures of darkness grow envious of the light, the realm of light defends itself by a cunning tactic that causes the light to become mixed into the realm of darkness and thus initiates a development that again leads in the end to a separation, with the darkness being left behind in a clump. The deities of

26 Fragment of the Gospel of Thomas (*P.Oxy.* IV 654)

Egypt, Oxyrhynchus. 3rd century
Papyrus. 24.4 × 7.8 cm
British Library, London. Pap 1531 Vo

This fragment of a Greek papyrus roll contains a text headed 'These are the [secret] words that the Living Jesus spoke [and Judas also called] Thomas [wrote down]'. The text itself, like 2 other fragments from 3rd-century Oxyrhynchus, consists of sayings of Jesus (some not known from other sources), strung together without the biographical narrative found in the canonical gospels. Scholars inferred that all 3 fragments came from the lost Gospel of Thomas, and this was confirmed when a complete text, in Coptic, was published from the Nag Hammadi Library. This Gospel shares some features of contemporary Gnosticism; the Greek version was probably the original, dating back to the 2nd century AD. [PP]

27 A church at Kellis

View over the Large East Church at ancient Kellis. One of the earliest churches discovered in Egypt, it probably dates to the reign of Constantine I. Works of Mani and other Manichaean literature and letters from nearby houses demonstrate the presence of a Manichaean community at the town before its abandonment c.AD 400.

28a–b Cologne Mani-Codex

Egypt. 5th century
Parchment. 3.5 × 4.5 cm (shown at actual size)
Institut für Altertumskunde, Universität zu Köln. Inv. Nr. 4780

This tiny book dates from the 5th century. Shown below at actual size, it is written in Greek and contains a biography of Mani, the founder of Manichaeism. [CF]
Bib: Koenen and Römer 1988

light sent out to take part in this combat of light against darkness are identical in substance with the Father.

Basically Manichaeism is also a Gnostic system. However, it was presented as a highly developed religion with a binding canon of scripture, a church hierarchy, and organized communities whose members were divided, according to their way of life, into Elect and Catechumens. Through targeted proselytizing, Manichaeism became a world religion which left its mark on the three continents of Europe, Africa and Asia. One central aspect, demonstrating its close connection to Gnosticism, was the doctrine of the soul's ascent into the kingdom of light. The soul of a deceased person had, with the support of a Requiem Mass, to follow the same path, with different stations along its route, that the light (in a mythological past, as it were) had descended in the shape of various divine figures.[10]

In principle, Gnosticism and Manichaeism promised to provide human beings with knowledge of their true position in the world and, with revelatory scriptures, a well-established ethical life and cultic rituals to bring about their salvation. The existence of evil is explained by its manifestation as matter and body, so that good and evil represent not only philosophical opposites, but are also active substances.

As the enemies of Gnosticism continued to debate with the proponents of philosophically inclined Gnostic systems, they were impelled to develop a Christian theology – a scientific way of thinking about religious revelations – with which Gnosticism could be combated with arguments.[11] Alongside this intellectual debate they also repeatedly resorted to the burning of books,[12]

but they could not prevent the survival in Egypt of both the smallest and thickest books from antiquity – the Greek Cologne Mani Codex, with a biography of the religion's founder (figs 28a–b), and the Coptic Manichaean Psalm book respectively – as examples of Manichaean book production.[13]

4 Islam

Petra Sijpesteijn

THE entry of the Arab armies into Egypt in 639 followed a long period of cultural, economic and political engagement. Muhammad had already recognized the patriarch of Alexandria, Cyrus (in office 630–41), as one of the political leaders of his day, inviting him to join Islam. The patriarch's polite refusal was accompanied by precious gifts, including two slave-girls, one of whom would bear the Prophet his only (short-lived) son, Ibrahim. Sayings attributed to Muhammad predict the Muslims taking control of Egypt and emphasize the special relationship that existed between Egyptians and Muslims. The great Arab general and first governor of Egypt, 'Amr ibn al-'As (died 664), knew Egypt from his commercial travels – 'the wealthiest of lands and least well defended'[1] – thus convincing the caliph 'Umar (reigned 634–44) in Medina to conquer it. Raiding, and possibly a treaty under which the Egyptians kept the Arabs at bay by paying them a yearly tribute, preceded the invasion, while the presence in 'Amr's army of (Christian) Arabs who had resided on Egypt's eastern border under the Byzantine empire would also have increased familiarity with the country.

Once 'Amr crossed into Egypt at al-'Arish, his limited and ill-equipped troops did not encounter much resistance. The Roman fortress of Babylon, located at the entrance of the Delta, was taken, after which the Arabs advanced on the Fayyum oasis and the Delta, taking Alexandria in 641 and reducing Upper Egypt by stages in the years that followed. For the next fifty years, however, their position remained precarious with continuous Byzantine counterattacks, most famously occupying Alexandria in 645.[2] A numerical minority, afraid of diluting their faith and customs by mingling with the Egyptian population, the Arabs were confined to garrisons, and made only temporary, military related forays into the countryside.[3]

The Arabs did not introduce into Egypt, let alone impose, a fully developed and worked-out religion, nor did they initiate a complete overhaul of Byzantine administration and culture. Only the highest administrative positions were taken over by Arabs, while the daily management remained in the hands of Christian Egyptians (see also ch. 26). The Arabs did, however, implement some significant changes, displaying the authentically different administrative, linguistic and cultural traditions that they brought with them. Babylon was renamed Fustat, and a huge volume of building materials was shipped there from the rest of Egypt to construct the new capital.[4] For the first time since the reforms of Emperor Justinian (reigned 527–65),

29 Bilingual document (*SB* XVIII 13218)

Egypt. 22 November 713 (12th Indiction, 26th Hathur)
Papyrus. 22 × 23.7 cm
Ägyptisches Museum und Papyrussammlung, Staatliche Museen zu Berlin. P 13352

This document contains instructions in Arabic and Greek, with the same content. The Arab governor of the Umayyad Caliphate in Egypt, Qurra ibn Sharik al-Absi, asks the inhabitants of the farmstead Bubaliton (in the Peri Polin district of the city of Antinoopolis) for a contingent of sailors for ships that are to be sent to ʿAbdallah ibn Musa ibn Nusair. They are to agree to pay the costs of 2.5 sailors and their wages and travels expenses as far as Pentapolis (in Cyrenaica in modern-day Libya). Musa ibn Nusayr was the Umayyad governor in Ifriqiya (Libya, Tunisia and eastern Algeria) from 703 to 714. He took part in the conquest of Spain in 712/713 and returned to Ifriqiya in 713. [GH]

Egypt had one political centre.[5] A poll tax was introduced, and other administrative and political–military organizational measures launched. Arabic was instituted as an administrative language next to Greek and Coptic, and the Arabs initiated distinctive documentary practices.[6]

References to Muslim institutions and ideas that appear in fully developed form in later literary works already appear in the documentary record in this early period. The *basmala* ('in the name of God, the Compassionate, the Merciful') heads the earliest Arabic document dated 22 AH / AD 643, and was also used in Greek and Coptic texts.[7] The statement of faith, 'there is no god but God', also appears in the earliest Arabic texts. The Hajj (Muslim pilgrimage to Mecca) is first mentioned in a text dating to 705–9.[8] In a will dated to 721 a *hubs* (pious endowment) – consisting of a house – was set up by a woman for her female slave to live on after her mistress's death.[9] The

30 Abbasid coin (dinar)

Egypt. 790–91 (174 AH).
Gold. Diameter 1.8 cm; weight 4.09 g
Münzkabinett, Staatliche Museen zu Berlin.
18205161

This dinar was minted under
Dawud ibn Yazid al-Muhallabi,
who was briefly governor of Egypt
under caliph Harun al-Rashid. The
inscriptions in upright Kufic script
represent the Muslim confession of
faith, the declaration of the oneness
of God and part of the 33rd verse of
the 9th Sura of the Qur'an. The year
of minting and the forename of the
governor also appear on the reverse.
The caliph and the place where it
was minted are not named. [GH]

dhimma (protection), which non-Muslim subjects possessing a Holy Book were entitled
to in exchange for paying a tax (according to the Qur'an), appears for the first time in
a papyrus dated AD 680 from Nessana.[10] Without a narrative context, however, it is
difficult to determine to what extent these references form a coherent and consciously
distinctive religious practice.[11]

The Mosque of 'Amr ibn al-'As in Fustat (see ch. 14) is said to have been extended several times to house growing numbers of Muslims in the decades following the
conquest. Serving not only religious goals, mosques were also built in Alexandria and
in other administrative centres. Arabic inscriptions, including religious ones with
paraphrases of the Qur'an, were used on these buildings. The architecture, although
drawing upon pre-Islamic traditions, was strikingly new.

Some important changes took place in the first half of the eighth century,
coinciding with empire-wide Islamicizing and Arabicizing measures.[12] Arabs started
to take over administrative posts outside the garrisons, leading to permanent Arab
settlements in the Egyptian countryside. Greater interaction with a more self-
conscious and self-confident Arab population led to an increasing Arabicization and
Islamicization – and even conversion – of the Egyptian population, albeit still on a
small scale at this time.

The first attestation of Muhammad and of 'the people of Islam' also dates from
this period.[13] Islamic legal institutions, including the *qadi* (judge) and other expressions of Islamic law, appear more widely. Dating from the eighth century are the
earliest preserved literary and semi-literary texts, such as amulets and pious writings
containing Qur'anic verses and Hadith (reported teachings, sayings and deeds of the
Prophet Muhammad), as well as historical and literary narratives.[14] As a result of the
administrative reforms under caliph 'Abd al-Malik, exclusively Arabic (as opposed to
bilingual or non-Arabic) texts occur on measurements and coins, the latter containing also selected Qur'anic verses (fig. 30). The earliest fragments of Qur'anic codices
from Egypt – all on parchment – date to the early Abbasid period (750 to the ninth
century) (fig. 31).[15]

Alexandria had always been a centre for study in the Classical world, and it
seems to have continued to be so into the Islamic period. Under Islamic rule Egypt
again developed into an important scholarly centre. Egypt developed its own
Hadith tradition and history schools.[16] Indeed, it was to Egypt that two famous
biographers of Muhammad – Ibn Ishaq (died 768) and Ibn Hisham (died *c.*833)
– came to collect accounts about the Prophet's life.[17] The great Muslim lawyer al-Shafi'i (died 820) moved from Baghdad to Egypt, where his works of legal
reform were written down.[18]

By the ninth century the use of Arabic had also become widespread amongst
Egypt's non-Muslim inhabitants. The close interaction of indigenous and Arab written culture resulted in the introduction of terms and expressions from Greek and

Coptic into Arabic's legal and administrative language. Egypt continued to have a majority non-Muslim population for centuries to come, but some literary expressions point to an increased Muslim presence. The so-called rescript (legal response) of 'Umar – attributed to the Umayyad caliph (reigned 717–20) but more probably a product of the ninth century – prescribes distinctive clothing and behaviour for non-Muslims, while also prohibiting public expressions of non-Muslim religious rituals. These rules express an anxiety about the loss of a distinctive Muslim identity resulting from increasing numbers of converts. At the same time, local Egyptian Muslims cultivated a stronger regional identity, articulated in the literary genre of describing *fada'il misr* (Egypt's wonders) and regional histories.[19]

Local identification was also advanced by Arab Muslims in Egypt, especial-ly those who could trace their descent to the first conquerors. They felt entitled to a special status and a generous share of the land and its income. The relationship between the caliphal court and the province had always been subject to tensions,

31 Leaf from a Qur'an

Middle East. *c*.8th century
Parchment. Leaf: 12 × 20 cm; leather binding: 20 × 28 cm
Stiftung Preußischer Kulturbesitz, Staatsbibliothek zu Berlin. Inv. No. Wetzstein II 1916

Parts of the 4th, 5th and 10th Suras are reproduced on the 50 leaves of this early Qur'an. The beautiful, regular Kufic script is large and spread out, so that only around 14–18 characters appear on each page. Vowel signs are often present in the form of red dots, while the diacritical marks (which make it possible to distinguish between characters with similar forms) appear as small lines. The page shown here contains parts of verses 162 and 163 of the 4th Sura on the revelation of the divine word: '(and believe) in God and the last day, to these We will surely give a great reward./Surely, We have sent revelation to thee, as we sent revelation to Noah and the Prophets after him, and We sent revelation to Abraham and Ishmael and Isaac and Jacob, and his children and to Jesus…' [GH]
Bib: Ahlwardt 1887, no. 316

especially over the division of fiscal revenue and the degree of independence of the (local) ruling Arab elite vis-à-vis the caliph. Egyptians were instrumental in opposing the centralizing policy of the caliph 'Uthman (reigned 644–56), which threatened to infringe upon provincial autonomy, and eventually in murdering him.[20] During the Umayyad period rivalry over the caliphal seat gave rise to interferences in Egypt's governing elite.[21] The threat to their privileged position perceived by the first genera-tion of Arabs in Egypt at the arrival of new elite populations was expressed in the first history of Egypt, written by Ibn 'Abd al-Hakam (died 870).[22]

Turkish rule and Persian administrative practice and culture were introduced into Egypt with the arrival of governors and their officials from the Abbasid court – after the army of the caliph al-Ma'mun (reigned 813–33) had reconquered the province in 825–26 in the aftermath of the great civil war with his brother al-Amin (reigned 809–13). Slave soldiers had long started to fill other functions at the Abbasid court in Samarra, with members of the Turkish elite being appointed governors over Egypt. Ahmad ibn Tulun, of Turkish origin, arrived in 868. He founded Medinat al-Qata'i' – a new capital to house his troops – of which the Mosque of Ibn Tulun is the most conspicuous and only remaining display of Samarran influence (fig. 32; see also ch. 14). Ibn Tulun stopped forwarding Egypt's taxes to Samarra, although he continued to use the Abbasid caliph's name in the Friday prayers and on coins. Making use of the Abbasid court's preoccupation with dynastic quarrels and the African Zanj slave uprising (869–83), the Tulunid dynasty was one of several local dynasties that rose up against the empire. Financially independent, Ibn Tulun used his growing army to extend control over Syria, building on a long-standing relation between the two provinces.[23] Increased spending of the local fiscal income made Egypt prosper under the 135 years of Tulunid rule, but in 905 an Abbasid army re-established central control. The pattern was repeated under another governor appointed in 935, who obtained the right to use the title *ikhshid* (prince) commonly used by Central-Asian rulers and whose family, thus known as the Ikhshidid dynasty, ruled in Egypt until the arrival of the Fatimids in 969.

Abbasid administrators, bearing Persian names, accompanied the armies and governors sent from the East introducing their administrative practices in Egypt.[24] The use of star-shaped signatory signs at the bottom of administrative and legal doc-uments from Egypt resembles similar practices attested earlier in documents from the eastern empire.[25] Eastern influences can also be traced in fiscal and legal technical terms introduced at this time.[26]

From their new capital city of Cairo (al-Qahira, meaning 'the victorious'), the Shi'ite Fatimids established an empire that extended at its height in the eleventh century from North Africa throughout Palestine and the Upper Red Sea coast. The Fatimid caliphs were acknowledged in the prayers in Mecca and Medina. In spite of an ambitious and wide-ranging missionary programme extending throughout

the Muslim empire, and energetic building activity in Egypt, religious rituals and doctrines of the Egyptian population were hardly affected. New openings arose for non-Muslim religious minorities in the expanding Fatimid administration, while economic opportunities were provided by the intensifying and extending of trade networks that reached from the western Mediterranean to South Asia, in which Egypt played a central role. The writings produced by the Jewish communities of Cairo, as preserved in the Genizah in the city's Ben Ezra Synagogue, are witness to such activities (see ch. 18).

32 Mosque of Ibn Tulun, Cairo

Completed in 879 and built in Samarran style, the Mosque of Ibn Tulun formed the focal point of the new Tulunid capital, today part of modern Cairo.

ROMAN EGYPT

2 INTRODUCTION

IN 31 BC Octavian (later, Augustus) defeated the navy of his Roman rival Mark Antony and the Ptolemaic queen Cleopatra VII at the Battle of Actium. After the deaths of Antony and Cleopatra in 30, Egypt became a province of the Roman empire. The Romans inherited a land that had been under foreign rule periodically from the eighth century BC onwards, by Kushites, Persians, Assyrians and Macedonians (i.e. the Ptolemies). In time Egypt became a fully constituent part of the Roman empire, but like other provinces it also remained distinctive. Like their counterparts elsewhere, people in Egypt drank wine (ch. 26), ate and drank from a common tableware, wore tunics and accessories (ch. 25), and participated in the Roman imperial cult. In other spheres, such as funerary practice, Egyptian custom was conservative (ch. 6). The Roman practice of commemorating the dead with naturalistic portraiture was matched to the quintessential Egyptian burial practice of mummification, resulting in Romano-Egyptian portrait mummies and shrouds (ch. 27).

Residents of Roman Egypt had hundreds of gods to choose from for assistance with aspects of this life and the next. People from different cultures usually understood one another's gods in relation to the deities they knew from their own traditions. In this way deities accumulated the qualities and attributes of others. Isis was absorbed or was equated with so many other divinities that she acquired a universal character. Such universalizing tendencies were a product of Hellenistic philosophy as it developed in the late ancient world, and in the capital, Alexandria, in particular. The city had long been the cultural heart of the Eastern Mediterranean – famous for philosophy and rhetoric, science and medicine, literatur[...] (ch. 5). Under the influence of Platonis[...] philosophical schools a system of thoug[...] whereby many deities like Serapis were [...] as manifestations of the One God (heis t[...] this context that Judaism developed and [...] emerged in Egypt. Their God was one a[...] The name of the God of the Jews and C[...] with his angels and figures from the Bib[...] and Solomon, was regularly invoked in [...] alongside the gods of the traditional pa[...]

By the Roman period, Jews had a [...] Egypt (ch. 2, focus 1). Like the Ptolemies[...] the Romans recognized Judaism as an a[...] But this special status was challenged fol[...] Jewish revolts in the first and second cen[...] the Jewish population was significantly c[...] the Diaspora Revolt of AD 116–17 (ch. [...]

The first Christians were Jews. In [...] were the heirs to the Hellenized Judaism[...] such as Philo (remembered, erroneously[...] centuries later, as Philo the Bishop). The[...] Neo-Platonism espoused by Plotinus – [...] Upper Egyptian city of Lykopolis – rea[...] Egypt's borders as the philosopher joine[...] circles, eventually settling in Rome. Dev[...] philosophy influenced early Christianity[...] are recognizable in early Christian work[...] Judaism, Christianity was considered a [...] even criminal sect by the Roman admin[...] third century, when the borders of the [...] were threatened by Germanic tribes to [...] Sassanian Persians to the east, emperor[...] variety of strategies in order to neutraliz[...]

Jews were exempt from edicts calling upon residents to regain the 'peace of the gods' (*pax deorum*) by sacrificing to them, but Christians faced exclusion from the community if they did sacrifice, and imprisonment and even death if they did not. The results of such imperial legislation contributed to the self-definition of the emerging Christian communities and came to define the Church of the Martyrs. The unique body of evidence preserved in Egypt shows how people responded to their individual sets of circumstances, often cleverly circumnavigating the system. [ERO]

(Previous page)
33 Bronze head of Augustus

Sudan, excavated at Meroe in 1911. *c.*27–25 BC
Bronze (head); calcite, glass and plaster (eyes).
46.2 × 26.5 × 29.4 cm
British Museum, London. G&R 1911,0901.1

This head was originally part of an over life-size statue erected near Egypt's southern frontier, probably at Syene. The rival Kingdom of Kush, in what is now Sudan, challenged Roman control of Egypt's southern border, capturing statues such as this one in 24 BC. In near-perfect condition, the head was buried as a trophy in front of the threshold of a small temple at the Kushite capital at Meroe. The defeated enemy, represented by the Roman emperor, would have been trodden on when people entered the temple. [ERO]
Bib: Opper 2014

34 World map of Claudius Ptolemy

Florence. *c.*1455–62 copy; 2nd-century original
Parchment. 59 × 44.5 × 9 cm (closed volume)
Biblioteca Medicea Laurenziana, Florence.
Pluteo 30.2, ff. 68v-69r

The 2nd-century Alexandrian scientist and mathematician Claudius Ptolemy compiled a geography of the *oikumene* (inhabited world), from the Atlantic coast of Africa to China, and the northernmost British Isles to sources of the Nile in East Africa. He provided instructions for calculating latitude and longitude, and for representing a sphere on a two-dimensional surface. Originally in Greek, it was transmitted through the manuscript tradition into Latin and Arabic. Today it survives in several copies, dating no earlier than *c.*1300. [ERO]

5 Alexandria

Roger Bagnall

35 Cameo with the city goddess of Alexandria

Egypt. 1st century BC
Plasma. 1.7 × 1.4 × 0.3 cm
Ägyptisches Museum und Papyrussammlung,
Staatliche Museen zu Berlin. Inv. ÄM 9781

On twisted columns rests a tympanum in the middle of which there is a star or cross. Both the pediment and the capitals are decorated with vegetal motifs, most likely palm branches. The centre is filled by a female bust seen in left-side profile; the figure is wearing a richly pleated gown. The headgear can be interpreted as an elephant hood whose skin is indicated by lozenge shapes. If this interpretation is correct, this is a relatively rare depiction of the goddess of the city of Alexandria whose attributes include two ears of corn. [JHD]

ALEXANDRIA was the greatest city of the Eastern Mediterranean, second in the Roman empire only to Rome itself. With an urban core of about 10 square kilometres and a population at its peak of perhaps a half million, it was by ancient standards huge; only Antioch in Syria came close to rivaling it. Because it is buried so deep under the modern city, we know much less about it from archaeology than we do about its rivals, with even the location of some of its most famous monuments still hotly debated. Some of ancient Alexandria now lies under the waves of its harbour, thanks to the subsidence of the land. Compared to Rome, it has given us only a small number of inscriptions on stone.[1] But energetic and opportunistic archaeological exploration in recent decades has given new life to its study,[2] and the growth of Late Antiquity as a field of study has brought into view much more of its rich literary and theological production.

The city was laid out from its foundation by Alexander the Great in 331 BC on a grid, with the longer dimension running east-west parallel to the sea. Its larger harbour was bounded by the promontory of Cape Lochias on the east and the artificial dyke of the Heptastadion on the west, connecting the mainland with the island of Pharos – on which Ptolemy II built the great lighthouse that was reckoned to be one of the wonders of the world (fig. 38). To the west was a smaller, but still sizable, harbour. Together these gave Alexandria one of the finest harbours in the ancient world, drawing the commerce that was a major contributor to Alexandrian cosmopolitanism. The population was exceptionally diverse for an ancient city. Alexandria was not only the hub of Eastern Mediterranean trade but the capital of Egypt under the Ptolemies and the Romans. The Ptolemies had attracted or simply imported many settlers from all over the Greek world but also the Levant, including a large Jewish population from early in the Ptolemaic period.[3] Roman commerce with East Africa, Arabia and India largely passed through the city on its way up and down the Nile and across the desert. Of Alexandria's five quarters, one and part of a second were occupied by the Jewish population. But we know next to nothing of these quarters and what they were like, thanks to the poverty of the archaeological record. Only a handful of Hellenistic houses have been even partly excavated, and no temples or synagogues of the period have been located; things are hardly better in the Roman period.[4]

Governing a population of this diversity was no simple matter. The Alexandrians were famous for their unruliness and, on occasion, mob violence. Although Ptolemaic

36 Mosaic depicting Alexandria

Mosaic from the Church of St John the
Baptist at Jerash, Jordan, depicting the
city of Alexandria c.531.

Alexandria had laws modelled on those of Athens, it did not import Athenian democratic institutions. The Ptolemies preferred to control their capital more directly. The evolution of civic institutions is poorly known, but the Romans were no fonder than the Ptolemies of giving free rein to a fractious populace, and it was not until the third century AD that Alexandria even got a city council. Alexandrian citizenship was limited to Greeks, and tightly restricted under the empire, but it was highly prized for, among other things, the exemption from the poll tax, paid by Egyptians, that it brought.[5] The question whether Jews were, or could be, full Alexandrian citizens proved a perennial source of conflict under the early emperors.[6]

As the seat of Roman power in Egypt, Alexandria housed the offices of the prefect (an equestrian official), along with the other high officials who supported him in running a highly centralized power structure.[7] It was also the centre for the imperial cult in Egypt, based in the Caesareum temple located near the sea at a spot not yet securely identified (see focus 4).[8] Just outside the city, at Nicopolis, was the most important Roman garrison post in Egypt. It is hardly surprising that the imperial government kept Alexandrian government limited and relatively powerless for more than two centuries. Septimius Severus, at the beginning of the third century, permitted Alexandria to have a council, at the time that he allowed the same privilege to the fifty or so capitals of the Egyptian administrative districts called nomes. But it should not be supposed that he intended this to weaken the power of the central government over this critical city.

38 **Plan of the city of Alexandria**
in Late Antiquity

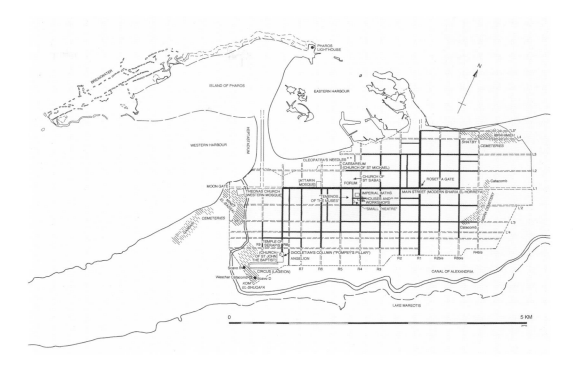

39 Drachma of Hadrian

Egypt, Mint of Alexandria. 130–31
Bronze. Diameter 3.3 cm; weight 30.61 g; die axis 12 h
Münzkabinett, Staatliche Museen zu Berlin. Object. no.
18245941

This drachma of Hadrian dates from the 15th
[Greek IE] year of the emperor's reign. The use
of bronze embossing, still widespread in the 2nd
century, with the nominal value of the drachma,
is equivalent to six *obols* (silver coins), i.e.
small values. A drachma corresponded roughly
to the daily wage of a worker. The image on
the reverse of the coin here alludes to the
demonstrative solidarity between the province
and the emperor. On the left is a personalized
depiction of Alexandria with an elephant hood,
and on the right is Emperor Hadrian in his toga
and bearing his sceptre – he is being greeted by
Alexandria with a kiss to the hand. The historical
background to this numismatic design was a
visit made by the emperor to Egypt between
summer 130 and spring 131. [KD]

40 Drachma of Antoninus Pius

Egypt, Mint of Alexandria. 148–49
Bronze. Diameter 3.5 cm; weight 29.20 g; die axis 12 h
Münzkabinett, Staatliche Museen zu Berlin. Object. no.
18200455

The important Roman province of Alexandria,
under imperial supervision, was supplied
with coins embossed with the name of the
capital; these circulated only in the province.
Inscriptions are in Greek and, on the obverse
of this coin, indicate the portrait of the reigning
emperor. The reverses often include Egyptian
or local references. The coins often bear the
name of the regnal year of the emperor. Here,
the reverse refers to the 12th [Greek IB] year of
the reign of Antoninus Pius. The famous Pharos,
the 3rd-century BC lighthouse of Alexandria,
is shown with the goddess Isis Pharia/Pelagia
in characteristic headdress, sistrum and cloak
blowing in the wind. This also alludes to the
great feast of the goddess, as protector of
seafaring, on 5 March. [KD]

41 Drachma of Hadrian

Egypt, Mint of Alexandria. 127–28
Bronze. Diameter 3.5 cm; weight 26.43 g; die axis 1 h
Münzkabinett, Staatliche Museen zu Berlin. Object no.
18245942

In the lower part of the reverse of this
drachma, the regnal year is written out in full,
as 'dodek[atou]', i.e. the 12th year. Above the
reclining river god of the Nile, another numeral
appears (Iς – i.e. 16). This indicates the optimal
level of the Nile, a height of 16 cubits. If the
waters of the Nile were too low, the fields
were left dry; any higher than 16 cubits and
the river caused great damage to dykes and
flood barriers. So a high tide of 16 cubits was
ideal for agriculture. The person of the emperor,
pictured on the obverse of the coin, was seen
as a guarantor of the population's security. The
importance of the Nile is emphasized here by
the figure of the personified river-god, and the
reference to the optimal high tide. [KD]

42–43 Statues of Emperors Marcus Aurelius and Septimius Severus

Egypt, Alexandria. c.176–80; c.193–200
Imported marble. 182 × c.192 cm
British Museum, London. G&R 1802,0710.1–2

Both imperial statues were reportedly found together in 1801 among ruins
along the coast of the Eastern Harbour of Alexandria, identified by the
Napoleonic expedition as the location of the Caesareum. They were part of the
group of about 20 monumental sculptures – together with the Rosetta Stone
and the Sarcophagus of Nectanebo II (see fig. 105) – conceded by the French
to the British according to the terms of the Treaty of Alexandria on 30 August
1801. King George III gave the group to the British Museum upon their arrival
to London. The two statues represent different aspects of an emperor's public
persona – Marcus Aurelius wears the formal and official civilian garment of a
Roman citizen, while Septimius Severus wears full military costume. Their flat,
minimally carved backs confirm that they were both produced to be displayed
in an architectural setting. [ERO]
Bib: Tkaczow 1993, no. 185, cf. 186; Bierbrier 1999, no. 7, pp. 111–12; pl. 30

44 Painted panel with the family of Emperor Lucius Septimius Severus

Egypt
Late 2nd – early 3rd century
Wooden panel painting. Diameter 30.5 cm
Antikensammlung, Staatliche Museen zu Berlin.
Inv. ANT 31329

In the winter of 199/200, Septimius
Severus travelled to Egypt with his family,
and there implemented a comprehensive set
of administrative reforms. During his reign
conversion to Christianity was made a penal
offence, and there were local persecutions
of Christians in Egypt and other places.
This unique circular painting – believed to
have been painted during the trip to Egypt
– shows the imperial family in official garb.
To the right of the emperor is his wife, Julia
Domna, and in front are their sons, Geta
and Caracalla. The emperor and princes
are holding sceptres and wearing jewelled
gold wreaths. After the death of their father
in 211, both sons of Septimius Severus
succeeded him, according to plan, but
towards the end of the same year Caracalla
had his brother murdered. Images of Geta
were subsequently destroyed, as on this
painted panel. [CF]

If Septimius Severus thought that an Egypt endowed with more substantial
civic institutions would be less turbulent, he would have been disappointed. Hostility
to his son Caracalla triggered a destructive slaughter in 215. The Palmyrene occupation and Aurelian's recovery of Alexandria in 272 led to extensive damage, including
perhaps to whatever remained of the city's famous library.[9] Before the third century
ended, another slaughter followed Emperor Diocletian's capture of Alexandria at the
end of the revolt of Domitius Domitianus in 298. From that point to the Persian invasion in the seventh century, Alexandria played no role on the world stage that would
expose it to such harm.[10] The extensive damage to the city's fabric suffered in the third
century took many decades to make good, and probably Alexandria never quite fully
recovered the physical splendour of earlier times.

The absence of external political shocks should not make one think that Alexandria enjoyed more than three centuries of calm, however. Internal strife remained an endemic part of Alexandrian life as much as it had in previous centuries. In the early fourth century the last and greatest wave of imperial persecutions of Christians helps to give this period a flavour of Christian–pagan struggle. From Constantine onwards, with Christianity the religion of the emperors except for the

45 *Tetradrachm* of Diocletian

Egypt, Mint of Alexandria. 290–91
Billon. Diameter 2.0 cm; weight 7.28 g; die axis 11 h
Münzkabinett, Staatliche Museen zu Berlin. Object no. 18245940

From AD 20–21 *tetradrachms* (coins worth four drachmas) were issued in Egypt, made from an alloy with a small quantity of silver known as 'billon'. The noble metal content decreased further over the next two centuries, falling to less than 1% at the end of the 3rd century. Emperor Diocletian, who set out to reform the State in the areas of management, currency, and military and economic affairs, decentralized the production of coinage. From the 12th year of his reign (295–96), the independent coinage of the province was discontinued. It was replaced by the production, in Alexandria, of money that was valid throughout the empire. The familiar Egyptian coinage would be issued once again in the reign of the soon-ousted usurper Domitius Domitianus, in 297–98.

On the left side of its reverse this *tetradrachm* shows the father of the gods, Zeus, carrying a bowl in his right hand. His left arm is resting on a sceptre. At his feet is an eagle – this was the animal associated with him. Not unconventionally for a coin, this image depicts not only the main deity of the Graeco-Roman pantheon, but also the new imperial order of the Roman empire under Diocletian, with two main and two sub-emperors. The father of the gods was seen to be on a par with Diocletian as senior emperor, who also had himself referred to as 'Iovius'. [KD]

46 Stela of Diocletian offering to the Buchis bull

Egypt, Hermonthis, excavated at the Bucheum. 288
Sandstone. 68 × 39 × 11 cm
British Museum, London. EA 1696

In Egypt, Roman emperors were often depicted in the traditional roles of ancient Egyptian kings. Here, Diocletian offers before the mummified bull-god, Buchis, whose cult was practised in the Upper Egyptian capital of Hermonthis. The hieroglyphic text records the year in which the bull died. However, the last recorded burial of a Buchis bull dates to year 57 of Diocletian (AD 340), long after the emperor's death – during the reign of Christian emperor Constantius II, 337–61. The priests of the Buchis cult seem to have circumnavigated the traditional system of dating, as this would have required an inappropriate representation of a Christian emperor offering to an Egyptian deity. [ERO]
Bib: Mond and Myers 1934, vol. 2:18-19, 34, 52, pl. XLVI; Grenier 1983

47 Engraving of 'Pompey's Pillar', by Luigi Mayer, 1804

By the medieval period this column had already been misidentified as 'Pompey's Pillar', recalling Julius Caesar's rival who died in Egypt in 48 BC. As the dedicatory inscription states, it is in fact a victory column erected after the emperor Diocletian's 8-month siege of Alexandria in 298, when he recovered the city from the usurper L. Domitius Domitianus. The column shaft is carved from a single piece of Aswan granite measuring 20.46 m high with a diameter of 2.71 m. Standing almost 27 m high – with its capital and base atop the already high ground of the promontory occupied by the Temple of Serapis (Serapeum) – the victory column was visible throughout the ancient city. [ERO]
Bib: McKenzie 2007, pp. 203–9

brief interlude of Julian's reign (361–63), the dominant struggles are those within Christianity itself. Our sources for these contests for power are almost exclusively written by Christians and must be used with caution. They show how Christian leaders could use battles with Alexandria's pagans for their own advantage, most dramatically in the destruction of the temple of Serapis in 391 or 392 (see ch. 7).

The central figures in these developments were the bishops. The office of Bishop of Alexandria, although traced in legends recounted by the church historian Eusebius all the way back to St Mark the Evangelist, becomes securely attested only in the Severan period.[11] The supremacy of the Alexandrian bishop over all of Egypt was still hotly contested in the early fourth century, as we can see in the attempt of Meletius, Bishop of Lykopolis (now Asyut), to challenge the sole right of the Alexandrian bishop to name other bishops in the province.[12] The long tenure of Athanasius (bishop 324–73), marked by constant struggles with the successors of Meletius as well as the Arians, and punctuated by confrontations with emperors and several exiles from Alexandria, did little to unify Egyptian Christendom – but it did establish the supremacy of the Bishop of Alexandria. His power over the church is often compared to that of the prefect over the civil administration. This is an exaggeration, certainly, but it is suggestive of his central importance all the same. The bishops were able, with the support of Emperor Constantius II, to take over the old imperial cult temple of the Caesareum and convert it into an episcopal church.[13] In the dying days of Roman rule, in the decade before the Arab conquest of 640–42, the offices were even united in the same individual – Cyrus.

48 Torso of an emperor

Egypt, Alexandria, found in the garden of the former
German Consulate, acquired in 1909. 4th century
Porphyry. 96 × 45 × 36 cm
Skulpturensammlung und Museum für
Byzantinische Kunst, Staatliche Museen zu Berlin.
Inv. 6128

The almost life-size torso of the statue
of an emperor, made from porphyry, is
of the traditional Roman kind. A purple
stone, porphyry was quarried from Mons
Porphyrites near the Red Sea. In Late
Antiquity it was reserved for imperial
representations. Several statues of a related
type, but executed in a more severe style,
date from the time of Diocletian and his
co-rulers in the late 3rd century. Apart from
the material, the costume and the attitude of
the figure indicate that he was a member of
the imperial family. The softer figure style is
typical of the first half of the 4th century, the
time of Constantine the Great and his sons.
The figure is wearing a soldier's clothing,
consisting of a tunic, a short cloak pinned at
the right shoulder by a studded brooch, and
a wide belt. The right hand is reaching for a
sword held by a strap. [CF]
Bib: Cat Hamm 1996; Tkaczow 1993, no.
273, p. 287

The Meletius controversy brought into high relief within the Christian sphere a central element of Alexandria's secular life – its role as capital of Egypt. The often-quoted name of the city, *Alexandria ad Aegyptum* (Alexandria by Egypt) is regularly misunderstood as a mark of separation. It is more nearly an indication of connection. 'Egypt' in this phrase means, as usually, the Nile valley; Alexandria was in fact 'by' and linked to the Nile valley rather than directly in it. It was Egypt's largest port (the port of Pelusium at the opposite side of the Delta was also very important). A complex administrative apparatus throughout Egypt reported to the administration in Alexandria. Even when Egypt was divided into multiple provinces from the time of Diocletian onwards, Alexandria remained the head of the whole. Grain for shipment to Rome or Constantinople was funnelled through Alexandria, money taxes were gathered there, and there was a constant flow of information and orders back and forth within the bureaucracy.

In private life as well, Alexandria was the hub of Egypt's activity. Wealthy Alexandrians owned land throughout the *chora* (the term used for the rest of Egypt's land). The upper classes of the nome *metropoleis* aspired to become Alexandrians, and certainly many of them had property in Alexandria and spent time there on all sorts of business. Particularly for legal business, such as registration of important documents or litigation before imperial officials, Alexandria was the indispensable centre. The culture of Alexandria was what the provincial cities and their elites aimed to take part in, and its styles were widely copied throughout the *chora*.

It is in this context that we must see the energetic attempts of the bishops of Alexandria to control the ecclesiastical life of Egypt. It is often remarked that the church of Egypt, which included the Cyrenaica (the eastern coastal region of today's Libya), had no regional bishops governing groups of cities on behalf of the archbishop, as many other provinces did. Instead, each of the dozens of bishops reported directly to Alexandria. The absence of these metropolitans is not an aberration. The relationship of the other Egyptian cities to Alexandria was not comparable to that of cities in other provinces to their regional heads.

Alexandria's economic role was equally central. The roughly quarter of a million metric tons of wheat exported each year for the public grain distribution of the imperial capital was only part of the vast commerce in grains, which included grain for Alexandria itself and a huge private market in exports. The internal trade to feed the city itself was obviously enormous, with every type of foodstuff along with large amounts of wine drawn into it from its vast extended hinterland. Better quality wine, however, mainly came from imports, along with much of the olive oil required for a large Greek city to feed and light itself. Even after the Arab conquest, when the wheat formerly sent to Constantinople was diverted to Arabia by way of the canal that began at Fustat (see ch. 14), Alexandria's domestic demand remained substantial for many years. We have little evidence to trace its eventual decline in any detail.

49 Comb of Helladia

Egypt, probably Antinoopolis. Late 5th–early
6th century
Elephant ivory. 17.5 × 6.8 × 0.5 cm
Département des Antiquités égyptiennes, Musée
du Louvre, Paris. Inv. E 11874

In the central part of the comb, 3 people
raise their hands in acclamation. They seem
to be performing a mime or pantomime
scene, a performance of the kind that was
frequent in the hippodrome. Wearing a long
tunic, a dancer stands in front of an arcade
and brandishes a wreath, while the other
2 figures stand on either side – a man in
a short tunic holding an object and playing
a *scabellum* (sandal fitted with cymbals),
and a young woman with her mouth open,
perhaps a chorister. The Greek inscription
at the base of the comb's teeth reads
'Long live the Fortune of Helladia and the
Blues. Amen'. This refers to the winner of
the contest organized as part of the circus
games where rival factions competed. [MD]
Bib: Cat. Paris 2009, no.114, pp. 133–34

50 Spherical censer

Egypt. 5th century
Silver. Height 16.2 cm; diameter 10.2 cm
Département des Antiquités égyptiennes, Musée
du Louvre, Paris. Inv. E 11705

Comprising a cup with a tapered foot, the
censer's shape is similar to that of a chalice.
A hemispherical lid rests on the incense
burner to form a complete sphere. At the
top a wreath encircles the end of a chain
with double links, giving the receptacle
the appearance of a pomegranate. Four
incised masks from the tragic theatre
tradition decorate the lid. Their expressive
faces, surmounted by tall headdresses,
have pierced eyes and mouths to allow the
fragrant smoke to escape. This decoration
combines aesthetic effect and apotropaic
value (the power to ward off evil or bad
luck), and is consistent with the function of
the object, which was probably intended for
use at home. [MD]

In production as well, Alexandria was both workshop and way station. The Egyptian countryside and its cities produced textiles in quantity, particularly linen. The cotton for which Egypt is renowned in modern times is largely a nineteenth-century development, although modest amounts were produced, especially in the oases, in the Roman period. Alexandrian glass, despite its fragility, was widely exported and then imitated. Egypt was of course a monopoly provider of that most essential material: papyrus. It, too, largely passed through Alexandria. If we had more of Alexandria's living and producing quarters available for excavation, we would have a better sense of what was undoubtedly a much richer array of goods for export than we can now identify.[14]

But there is one area of Alexandrian trade that we know about entirely from external sources – its role as the transit point for the Indian Ocean trade. Enormous quantities of pepper, ivory, nard (an oil derived from plants), *malabathron* (aromatic plant leaves) and other exotic and valuable substances travelled each year from India to Egypt, passing mostly by way of the Red Sea port of Berenike (today Baranis), by camel caravan across the desert to Koptos (today Qift), and by boat to Alexandria.[15] The imperial treasury banked the taxes on this trade – a quarter of its value – and from there the goods were shipped to Rome and other centres of consumption. No doubt a fair amount stayed in Alexandria to be used there. Papyrus evidence for the value of these cargos makes it possible to realize that the taxes from this trade amounted to a substantial share of the imperial revenues.

Alexandria was thus at once producer, consumer and distributor of a wide variety of goods and services, public and private. Its administrative role in the economy was also central to the eastern part of the empire, not merely to Egypt itself. Although the Roman world was in many ways a market economy, the imperial government devoted substantial resources to creating and maintaining the infrastructure of that economy and to regulating and taxing it. All of this happened to a high degree in Alexandria.

Much of Alexandria's reputation came from its role as a centre of Greek culture. The Museum ('sanctuary of the Muses') turned traditional Macedonian patronage of artists and scholars into an institution for science and literature alike. The great library built as part of the Museum complex was legendary in its own time, with book collections as comprehensive as royal resources could make them.[16] Ptolemaic patronage turned Alexandria into a magnet for scholarly and scientific luminaries from around the Mediterranean world. This patronage disappeared with Roman rule, and indeed had been anaemic in late Ptolemaic times. But its traditions survived the funding, and the wealthier classes of Alexandria and the other cities of Egypt proved a more durable support for research and education over the entire period, down to and beyond the end of Roman rule.

But Alexandria was not only a Greek city; it was an Egyptian one. It is hardly

51 Stela commemorating a Platonic philosopher

Antinoopolis, excavated 1913/14. Late 2nd century
Marble (?) 33 × 44 × 3 cm
British Museum, London. EA 1648

The stela honours Flavius Maecius Severus Dionysodorus, a Platonic philosopher and city council member of Antinoopolis. As 'one of those maintained by the Museum, exempt from taxes', he received fiscal privileges granted to the intellectual elite affiliated with the 'Temple of the Muses'. It is not clear if it is the famous Museum at Alexandria or a similar institution in Antinoopolis that is meant here. The individual may be the same Severus whose work is quoted in Neo-Platonist authors Porphyry (3rd century) and Proclus (5th century), and by Church historian Eusebius of Caesarea (4th century). [ERO]
Bib: O'Connell 2014c, no. 41, pp. 482–83

surprising that its vital economy, needing large numbers of craftsmen, labourers and other service workers, drew many people from the countryside in search of a better livelihood than that of a farm labourer (fig. 52). Roman governors and emperors disliked the large Egyptian presence in the capital, and periodically ordered the natives to return to their homes. These edicts had no lasting effect – Alexandria was the home of these workers, and without them the economy of the metropolis would have collapsed. While Alexandrian art and architecture, as we think of them today, were Greek, or eventually Graeco-Roman in character, the city also had its share of Egyptian-style art. Much of this was brought from old sanctuaries, like that of Heliopolis, by the Hellenistic and Roman rulers and used to decorate the capital. These statues have come to light in large numbers from underwater excavations in recent decades, helping to reshape our mental image of what Alexandria looked like.[17]

Alexandria also had the largest Jewish community outside Palestine in the entire Eastern Mediterranean.[18] Profoundly Hellenized, it produced both high-ranking officials and philosophers, sometimes in the same family. The famous philosopher Philo produced both Platonic treatises and works on the Hebrew scriptures. His Platonizing, allegorical readings of these scriptures (which he read in the Septuagint,

the Greek version of the Hebrew Bible produced in Ptolemaic Alexandria) had a vast influence on later Christian writers. Philo was the uncle of Tiberius Julius Alexander, who became prefect of Egypt and served with Titus in the Jewish War that ended with the capture of Jerusalem in AD 70. The family included successful business-men as well. The Ptolemaic origins of this community and its large scale have already been mentioned, along with the periodic conflicts over rights and privileges in the first century AD between the Jews and at least some segments of the local Greek citizenry. The Roman emperors seem on the whole to have been sympathetic to the Jewish community and unwilling to give free rein to the hostility expressed by representatives of the Alexandrian elite. But when a revolt of the Jewish population in the Cyrenaica under Emperor Trajan spread to Egypt, the era of even hostile coexistence was over. Much of Egypt was swept up in the war that followed. As was usual with revolts against Rome the outcome, early in the reign of Hadrian (117–38), was a disaster – both for the Jews of Egypt, whose numbers were dev-astated to the point that the abundant papyrus documentation of the Jewish population in the period down to Trajan simply vanishes for a century and a half after Hadrian, and for the entire cosmopolitan Jewish culture that their Alexandrian presence created and sustained.

Given the small numbers and indeed invisibility of Christians in Alexandria until the late second century,[19] the city was dominated by the cults of the Greek and Egyptian gods – and of the more Hellenized versions of Egyptian cults – for more than a century after the destruc-tion of Alexandrian Judaism. There are traces of the beginning of the rebuilding of a Jewish population in Egypt in the middle to late third century, around the time the numbers of Christians also become sig-nificant. Alexandria probably continued to manifest the many parallels that mark the efforts of Late Antique Judaism to recast itself in a mode more competitive with Christianity, but there is no evidence that the Jewish community ever recovered a numerical strength comparable to that in earlier centuries.

The picture is complicated by the tendency of Christian rhetoric to use 'Jew' as a term with which to attack enemies, including enemies within the church.[20] This tendency is only part of a long history of such anti-Judaic rhetoric, but it offers a pro-found challenge to the historian in attempting to know when an ancient writer talking about Jews is actually referring to a real Jewish community and when it is a stick with which to beat a fellow Christian. It can at any rate hardly be doubted that by the end of the fourth century the dominance that Christianity had achieved in political terms in the early to middle parts of that century was essentially complete, and that

52 Charioteer papyrus
Egypt, Antinoopolis, excavated 1914. c.500
Papyrus. 12 × 7.5 cm
Egypt Exploration Society, London

This fragmentary page from a codex shows a group of charioteers in their distinctive helmets and protective strapping, one holding a whip. A yellow arc behind them perhaps evokes the arched starting-gates or entrance of a hippodrome. Their clothing displays 3 of the 4 colours – red, green and blue – associated with the Roman circus factions (white is the missing colour). Rivalry between supporters, divided on both social and political lines, was intense. The writing surviving on both sides of the page suggests that the context of the illustration was a literary text, but too little remains to identify it. The papyrus was retrieved from one of the rubbish dumps at Antinoopolis, where a monumental hippodrome was situated just outside the city wall. [HW]
Bib: Cat. New York 1978 no. 93, pp. 102–3; Humphrey 1986, pp. 515–16

53 Terracotta Horus as rider

Egypt. 1st–3rd century
Fired Nile clay with traces of paint (red-pink, black, formerly white). 26.2 × 18 × 6.8 cm
Ägyptisches Museum und Papyrussammlung, Staatliche Museen zu Berlin. Inv. ÄM 9685

This unique terracotta shows the falcon-headed god, riding on a caparisoned horse. Horus, almost frontally turned to the viewer, is wearing the Egyptian royal kilt, with a tunic and a cloak. On his head he wears the double crown, and his hair frames his face in thick strands. With a broad, sweeping gesture he pierces an enemy, not shown here. The enemy of Horus was the god Seth, who is usually depicted in one of his forms, either animal or human. Comparable representations of Horus are mainly familiar from the temple of the god in Edfu, but also from other regions of Egypt. The crown shows him as ruler of the two parts of the country – as for any reigning Egyptian king. Images of this type also form part of the royal succession. [JHD]

Bib: Cat. Berlin 1899, p. 369; Wilhelm 1914, p. 89, no. 82, pl. 7; Philipp 1972, p. 9, p. 13, p. 32, no. 46, fig. 42; Trioche 2012, pp. 96–97, fig. 3

54 Horus as rider in stone relief

Nubia (modern Sudan), Faras. 1st–3rd century
Sandstone. 46.1 × 32 × 7.5 cm
Département des Antiquités égyptiennes, Musée du Louvre, Paris. Inv. E 4850

This relief seems to be the exact illustration of the text in which Plutarch (*De Iside* 39, 19, 358C) describes how Horus claimed to have chosen the horse as a fighting animal 'to avenge his father and mother for the evil that had been done to them'. The figure of Horus as rider is a theme increasingly attested in late paganism, just as Horus-avenger-of-his-father is a god as old as Egyptian religion itself. Here, pharaonic and Classical styles can be seen mingled, at a time when Hellenism was spreading across the provinces of the empire. The figure of the god – dressed as a senior military Roman officer, his weapon a mixture of lance and harpoon – is seated as vertically as a hieroglyph in the centre of the composition, while the crocodile embodies the enemy. All these elements help to convey the victory of divine power and give it a visible form for the supplicant. [VR]

55 **The so-called Small Theatre at Kom el-Dikka, Alexandria**

Built in the middle of the 4th century, this open-air building was equipped with a scene structure, suggesting it was used for entertainment. Significantly remodelled in c.500, when it was domed, the theatre may have had multiple purposes such as poetry performance, pantomime and lectures. In this latter phase of use, architectural elements were decorated with crosses, and graffiti dating up to the early 7th century praises the Greens circus faction. [ERO] Bib: McKenzie 2007, pp. 209–12, figs 357–65

struggles of religion were largely between factions in the Christian community. The supposed expulsion of the Jewish population of Alexandria in 414–15 by Bishop Cyril should be viewed with some scepticism.[21]

In the midst of all of these struggles, however, Alexandrian high culture experienced a late flourishing, in the form of the 'university' of which two dozen or so classrooms are now visible in the central archaeological zone of Kom el-Dikka (fig. 55), excavated by the Polish mission over more than a half century.[22] Although most of the learning imparted in these halls was Classical and even what might be called 'pagan', the professors and students were in large part Christian. Classical culture was not only the common inheritance of the educated elites of Late Antiquity, it was systematically used in the development of Christian theology and philosophy. Alexandria was the most important home of that fusing of traditions.

6 Religion in Roman Egypt

Jana Helmbold-Doyé

DURING the rule in Egypt of Alexander the Great and his successors – the Ptolemies (332–30 BC) and, later, the Roman emperors (30 BC–AD 330) – two main lines of development in relation to the world of the gods can be discerned. On the one hand was the continuity of pharaonic traditions, and on the other was change.[1] Whereas funerary practice largely continued, other aspects of traditional Egyptian practice, such as animal cults, ceased in the Roman period. The cults of several ancient Egyptian deities including that of Isis flourished, while new cults, such as that of Serapis and Mithras, were further developed or introduced.

Traditional ancient Egyptian conceptions of the afterlife demonstrate remarkable continuity (ch. 35). In adopting these traditions, immigrants to Egypt from throughout the Mediterranean world evidently also found comfort and hope. The conservativeness of Egyptian funerary practice was no doubt due to the inherent appeal of a religion that respected ancient traditions. Grave finds and the design of the tombs evidence a pronounced affinity for pharaonic culture. In contrast to practice elsewhere in the ancient world at this time, cremation was generally avoided in Egypt. The preservation of the body of the deceased was a prerequisite for the effectiveness of Egyptian afterlife, as it was placed under the protection of the god of the dead, Osiris (figs 56, 57). Since the dead were seen as part of the world of Osiris, distinctions between the deceased and Osiris were rarely made in representations. He usually appeared in the form of a mummy, enveloped in skilfully wrapped linen bandages and wearing a lozenge-patterned robe, like a net, which acted as a full body amulet and symbolized the transformation that he underwent during the transition from this world to the next. Dating from the Ptolemaic period onwards, a new feature appeared – a cape to protect its wearer.[2]

56 Mummy label of Tekysis

Egypt, probably originally from Akhmim or Sohag.
1st–2nd century
Wood inscribed and painted with black ink.
6.5 × 14 × 1.3 cm
Ägyptisches Museum und Papyrussammlung, Staatliche
Museen zu Berlin. Inv. ÄM 10585

Egyptian mummy labels are little wooden tablets, usually inscribed with the names of the deceased. They can be seen as a substitute for a grave stela, and were hung on the mummy as a label. The inscription is a formulaic invocation to the ba-soul of the deceased, which is often found on tablets of this kind. Unusual, however, are the figurative pictures on both sides with the mummiform god of the dead, Osiris, and the deceased himself as a mummy, wound in the way that was typical during the Roman period. Noteworthy is the lying in state on a Greek *kline* (couch) with lathe-turned legs. Forming part of the supplies for the afterlife provided for the dead, there are two vessels on a table and a wine amphora next to them, with a long ladle. [JHD]
Bib: Erman 1899, p. 361; Möller 1913, p. 60; Lüddeckens, Thissen and Brunsch 1979–2000, p. 1052; Vleeming 2011, p. 505, p. 170, p. 801

57 Deceased as Osiris on a lion console

Egypt, cemetery of Tuna el-Gebel. 1st–2nd century (?)
Stucco, painted in polychrome and almost completely gilded.
Length 47 cm; width 16.5 cm; height 3.1 cm (Osiris); length 7.8 cm; width 3.4 cm; height 0.5 cm (fragment of cloak)
Ägyptisches Museum und Papyrussammlung, Staatliche Museen zu Berlin. Inv. ÄM 24151

The god wears the plumed Atef crown on his head, with a shoulder-length headscarf, and on his chin is a divine beard. On his breast there is a broad collar, while in his fists he holds two flails. He wears an ankle-length net robe, which imitates the artful winding of mummy wrappings. His bare feet stand on a raised platform, under which is a lion's face. Originally he was wrapped in a cloak, of which only a fragment is preserved. This is the representation of the deceased, in his manifestation as one who has become Osiris. His majestic status is reflected in the frontal presentation and the depiction of the lion console. This covering was part of the foot-end decoration of a wooden coffin, which was originally supplemented with an *aedicula* and a floating, winged sun disc with two uraeus figures. [JHD]
Bib: Helmbold-Doyé 2015. Cat. S. 16, p. 71

58 Terracotta of the god Harpocrates on a ram

Egypt. 2nd–3rd century
Nile clay, formerly primed and painted. 12.6 × 8.2 × 3.7 cm
Ägyptisches Museum und Papyrussammlung, Staatliche Museen zu Berlin. Inv. ÄM 8794

A plump Harpocrates rides on the sacred ram. The child is naked except for a cloak, and his head is bare except for his side-lock. The right index finger is placed on the mouth, and with his left hand the boy clings to the ram's fleece. Around the neck of the animal a bulla hangs from a long chain. This small figure can be seen as an example of a widespread mode of terracotta production, even if no identical piece is available for comparison. Since Harpocrates was a child-god, he was regarded as a protector and patron of children. However, as he is here shown with a ram the emphasis may be on his role in fertility, as this function was also closely associated with him. [JHD]

Bib: Erman 1899, p. 368; Weber 1914, no. 94; Bonnet 1952, p. 274, fig. 69; Kaiser 1967, p. 104, no. 1006 (with fig.); Philipp 1972, p. 8, p. 11, pp. 13-14, p. 30, no. 38, fig. 34a

59 a–b Cameo with Isis

Egypt. 1st century
a) Jasper, red, set in a modern silver ring: 1.6 × 1.2 × 0.2 cm
b) Jasper, red: 1 × 0.8 × 0.2 cm
Ägyptisches Museum und Papyrussammlung, Staatliche Museen zu Berlin.
(a) Inv. ÄM 9819 (b) Inv. ÄM 9823

Both these cameos depict Isis, with a cow's horns and the solar disc on her head indicating important divine aspects. The right-hand cameo, enclosed in a ring, presents the enthroned goddess turned three-quarters towards the viewer. On her lap she holds the little Harpocrates in her right arm; he is playfully raising his arms. He is naked and on his head, above the sketchily indicated locks of hair, is the solar disc. Isis has moved her tunic down on the left to offer her breast to the child.

In the second cameo Isis' body faces us, in a somewhat squat posture, with the head turned to the right. Her sleeveless tunic is characterized in a few brief lines, and her heavy cloak is wrapped in thick folds around the lower body. In her left hand she holds a *sistrum* (musical rattle), while her right hand bears both a *situla* (urn) and, on a *patera* (dish for pouring libations), a crouching goat. The Greeks equated the ram of Mendes with a goat. The sacred animal of Mendes was a symbol of fertility and is the incarnation of Osiris who, in the divine triad, is the male equivalent of Isis. [JHD]

Bib: a) and b) Langener 1996, p. 123, cat. KN 208; Philipp 1986, p. 59, pp. 62–63 no. 62, p. 71, pl. 16–17; Toelken 1835, pp. 16–17, no. 36, p. 41; Tran Tam Tinh 1973, pp. 156–57, cat. A-157

60 Finger-ring

Egypt. 1st century
Gold. 2.3 × 2.7 × 2.3 cm
British Museum, London. EA 2965

The divine triad Serapis, Harpocrates and Isis are depicted as *agathoi daimones* (good spirits) in serpent form, their entwined tails forming the ring. [ERO]

While Osiris ruled only in the afterlife his sister and wife, the goddess Isis, exercised power in this world (figs 59, 60, 64, 65, 66, 82, 84). As the mother and protector of their divine child Horus (or Harpocrates, meaning 'Horus-the-Child') (Figs 58, 59b, 60, 63, 64b), Isis guaranteed the legitimacy of rule from one generation to the next. In addition to her role as mother and guardian goddess, she had the power to avert cosmic catastrophes and cure diseases. This family triad was familiar to the Greeks, Romans and others who sought to understand such deities in relation to their own, as evidenced in the assimilation of Osiris–Isis–Horus to, for example, Dionysus–Demeter–Apollo.

62 Seated Horus

Egypt. 1st–3rd century
Painted limestone. 54.5 × 31.8 × 25.6 cm
British Museum, London. EA 51100

While standing and equestrian figures of falcon-headed Horus are common, seated figures are rare. Here the god is represented in the pose of senior Olympian deities and Roman emperors, sitting with one sandal-clad foot forward, his knees apart and draped in a garment. He wears a cloak pushed back over the shoulders and a shirt of feathered mail armour that ends just above his elbows, but double as the falcon's feathers above the collar. A crown, now missing, once fitted into a hole in the top of the head. Traces of original black, red, yellow, green and blue pigment show that the sculpture was once brightly painted. [ERO]
Bib: Dyer, O'Connell and Simpson 2014

61 Standing Horus

Egypt. 1st–3rd century
Bronze. 48.5 × 30.5 × 14 cm
British Museum, London. EA 36062

In ancient Egypt the god Horus was the divine representation of the living king, commonly shown as a man with the head of a falcon. Images of Horus in Roman military costume expressed the ancient Egyptian god's power by using distinctively Roman symbols of authority. They also served to validate Roman political dominance by clothing the divine manifestation of the ancient Egyptian king in Roman costume. Here Horus wears an ancient Egyptian headdress and military dress worn by the Roman emperor. [ERO]
Bib: Cat. Marseille 1997, no. 251, p. 229

63 Necklace with Horus and Serapis

Egypt. 2nd century
Gold, chased and hallmarked. Length 86 cm; height of the figures 2.5 cm
Antikensammlung, Staatliche Museen zu Berlin. Inv. Misc. 11863, 6

The braided strand of the foxtail chain is decorated with a
heart-shaped pendant and two small movable figures in the
form of the gods Serapis and Horus. In the body of the heart is
engraved the inscription ΕΥΨΥΧΙ (be happy); it is finished on
the upper edge with a waveband. Serapis is depicted with
a wild mane and bearded, in the costume of a philosopher, while
Horus is shown in military costume, holding a shield in his left
hand. [CF]
Bib: Greifenhagen 1975, Gr.II 28, 3 and 6; Cat. Berlin 1988,
p. 363, no. 12

64 a–c Gods in gold: Isis, Harpocrates and Bes

Egypt. 1st–3rd century
a) Gold. 2.9 × 1.4 × 0.6 cm
b) Gold. 3.7 × 2.8 × 1.3 cm
c) Clay, fired with gold plating. 2.6 × 2.6 × 0.8 cm
Ägyptisches Museum und Papyrussammlung, Staatliche Museen zu Berlin.
(a) Inv. ÄM 12700 (b) Inv. ÄM 10752 (c) Inv. ÄM 11158

Far right is a pendant depicting the goddess Isis, wearing a crown
consisting of two plumes, the solar disc and a pair of horns. She
also wears earrings and a wide pearl collar, under which a breast
board or clumsily tied Isis knot is visible. The second piece (centre)
shows Harpocrates sitting on a goose. Both the curled strands of
hair on the right and the gesture of the right index finger to the
lower lip symbolize childhood. On his head he wears the double
crown, and in his left arm he holds a cornucopia. He appears
here in Hellenized form with reduced Egyptian iconographic
features such as double crown, finger and side-lock, which are
typical of terracottas of the Roman empire. With a cornucopia
as an attribute, Harpocrates appears as bringer of fertility. His
connection with the goose has not yet been satisfactorily resolved;
perhaps the animal, with its Egyptian reading of the hieroglyph for
'son', indicates the family status of Harpocrates, the child of Isis
and Serapis. The bearded god with a high crown of plumes (below)
represents the god Bes, who was invoked against night demons,
especially for women during pregnancy and childbirth, and for
newborn infants. All three pieces were amulets that could be fixed
to eyelets, and served to protect the living or the dead. [JHD]
Bib: a) Erman 1899, p. 362; Schäfer 1910, pp. 84–85, no. 142,
fig. 81 (eyelet) pl. 19
b) Schäfer 1910, p. 84, no. 140, pl. 19; Lauer and Picard 1955,
p. 195 note 1; Cat. Hamm 1996, pp. 202–3, no. 204
c) Erman 1899, p. 362; Schäfer 1910, p. 84, no. 141, pl. 19

65 Terracotta of a standing Isis Lactans

Egypt, the Thebaid. c.200 to mid-3rd century
Fired Nile clay, white primed and painted (dark
green, dark red, maroon, black). 19.1 × 9 × 5.2 cm
Ägyptisches Museum und Papyrussammlung,
Staatliche Museen zu Berlin. Inv. ÄM 16150

In her left arm the standing goddess holds
the small Harpocrates, who reaches for her
breast. She wears a tight garment that falls
to the ground and a fringed cloak, knotted
on her chest. On her head there are two
lotus buds, supporting her typical crown. In
her right hand Isis holds a *sistrum*. In cult
ceremonies to worship the goddess, this
musical instrument played a significant role.
The shape of the framing is reminiscent
of cloth decorated with stars. The various
attributes represent different aspects of the
goddess – Isis as sky goddess and as divine
mother. [JHD]
Bib: Weber 1914, p. 49, no. 26, pl. 2; Philipp
1972, pp. 8-9, pp. 13-14, p. 28, no. 32, pl. 6b;
Tran Tam Tinh 1973, pp. 193–94, cat. D-2,
pl. LXXV fig. 197

66 Standing figure of Isis-Demeter

Egypt. 1st–3rd century
Marble. 83 × 31 cm; diameter 17 cm
Ägyptisches Museum und Papyrussammlung, Staatliche
Museen zu Berlin. Inv. ÄM 12440

The cult statue stands in the Greek posture, with
one leg standing and the other free – known as
contrapposto. The goddess is dressed in a *chiton*
(simple garment) and *himation* (mantel or cloak),
with sandals on her feet. She holds a vessel with a
handle in her left hand, and a writhing snake in her
right. While the vessel is not recognizable as a woven
basket, it probably alludes to the old *cista mystica* of
Demeter. Her hair is let down in ringlets, and on her
head sits a crown of ears of corn, a solar disc and
a snake. All of the above attributes can be linked
with those of the goddesses Demeter and Isis, and
stand as guarantors for the fertility of the earth and
for a bountiful harvest. They also indicate general
regeneration and the protective aspects of the
goddess. [JHD]
Bib: Scharff 1923, pp. 32–33, pl. 8; Priese 1991,
p. 208, no. 127; Cat. Berlin 1999, no. 423, pl. 79;
Albersmeier 2002, p. 74, note 443

67 Stela with the god Tutu

Egypt. 1st–3rd century
Sandstone. 53 × 54 × 9 cm
Ägyptisches Museum und Papyrussammlung, Staatliche
Museen zu Berlin. Inv. ÄM 20914

The name of this god can be translated as 'he who
keeps enemies at bay'. His apotropaic power over
demons is particularly evident in the manner of his
presentation. Thus, on this stela, Tutu has taken on
the shape of a lion with the Atef crown, around which
rises a whole series of animal heads. In addition, a
crocodile's head is projecting out of his chest. Under
it we see a cobra, which he holds with his front
left paw, while his tail also ends in a cobra. Above
him is a lunar disc, and in the upper left corner is
a winged solar disc with another cobra. One of the
few exceptions is the representation of the moon,
probably indicating the aspect of a sky-god, whose
eyes were the sun and moon. It is likely that this stela
was erected as a votive offering in a temple. [JHD]
Bib: Schulman 1972/73, pp. 73–74, fig. 32;
Castiglione 1975, p. 471, pl. 73; Kaper 2003, pp.
329–31, no. S-33 (fig. p. 330); parallels: Kaper
2003, pp. 67–75, pp. 331–32, no. S-34; on the
name: Kaper 2003, pp. 19–25

Acquiring the attributes of other deities and accumulating their spheres of influence, Isis became popular far beyond the borders of Egypt. Due to her great capacity for transformation, combined with her stability, she had already become a universal goddess between the second and first century BC. It has been suggested by modern scholars that representations of Isis nursing Horus-the-Child influenced Christian iconography of the Virgin Mary nursing the Christ child (focus 3).[3] But it was not only these deities who were worshipped into Roman imperial times. Other gods were revered too, such as Bes, the patron deity of pregnant women (fig. 64c), or the zoomorphic god Tutu, who appears both in tombs and temples from the mid-sixth century BC to the beginning of the third century AD (fig. 67).[4]

A significant, Egypt-wide tradition was the worship of animals. Animal cemeteries contain thousands of mummies, from bulls and crocodiles to dogs, cats and snakes, among others. The expansion of animal cults under Ptolemy I (367/66–283/82 BC) was economically motivated. There were government-mandated burials associated with the institution of a temple and its related organization. It has not been established when this practice was abandoned at each archaeological site. However, numerous indications suggest that such burials ended in the early Roman period, no later than the middle of the first century AD.

The god Serapis can be described as a new development, as he is first attested in the Ptolemaic period (figs 60, 63, 68). He represents the Hellenization of Egypt that took place from this time. Initially he appears with a beard, long curly hair, a Greek robe and a high *kalathos* (grain-basket) on his head. Serapis was revered not only in his famous sanctuary in Alexandria, but in all forty-two regions of Egypt (the so-called nomes). He is linked to the Egyptian god (Osiris-)Apis, who had the form of a bull (figs 46, 72).[5] In the Roman empire Serapis first appears in this shape, but at the end of his development, like the goddess Isis, he had become a universal deity.

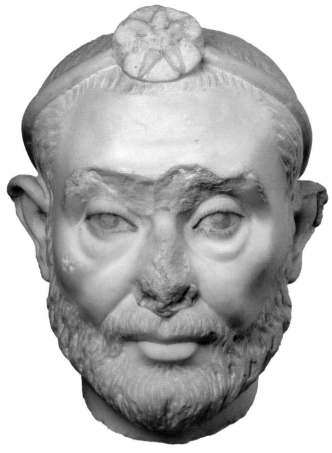

68 Bust of Serapis

Italy. Last quarter of the 2nd century
Marble. 61.5 × 27 × 29 cm
Antikensammlung, Staatliche Museen zu Berlin. Inv. SK 252

Serapis is depicted in the so-called 'fringe type', customary in the Roman empire. His face is looking towards us and surrounded by long, thick, curly hair and a shaggy beard. In the left section of hair, reddish-brown traces remain. The *kalathos* (lily-shaped container) on his head is mostly reconstructed. Under Emperor Hadrian, Egyptian cults in Italy were particularly encouraged, explaining the large number of portraits of him that have been found in Italy. [CF]
Bib: See database http://arachne.uni-koeln.de for Berliner Skulpturennetzwerk, Nr. 105718

69 Head of a priest of Serapis

Egypt. 230–40
Marble. 31 × 21.5 × 21 cm
Antikensammlung, Staatliche Museen zu Berlin. Inv. SK 1810

The figure depicts the head of a bearded older man with short hair. The almond-shaped eyes make the face appear vibrant, due to the remaining pigment. The most conspicuous attribute is, above his forehead, a diadem with an attached circular medallion in the centre, showing a star with seven rays. Here too traces of colour can be seen. Moreover, reddish colour has been preserved in the gap between the lips. The diadem with the medallion of rays could be connected with the cult of the Egyptian god Serapis, who was equated with the sun god. Similar images from Egypt with this symbol suggest that men depicted in this way fulfilled a role as priests in the cult of Serapis. [AS]
Bib: see database http://arachne.uni-koeln.de for Berliner Skulpturennetzwerk, Nr. 2112

70 Gold ornament

Egypt. c.1st–3rd century
Gold. 3.4 cm
British Museum, London. EA 26328

This ornament, with eight rays radiating from
a central circular bose, has a ring soldered
on the back that enabled it to be suspended.
[ERO]
Bib: Cat. New York 2000, no. 109, p. 153

**71 Mummy-portrait of a priest of
Serapis**

Egypt, excavated at Hawara. 140–60
Limewood panel painted in encaustic technique.
42.50 × 22.2 × 0.4 cm
British Museum, London. EA 74714

Roman and ancient Egyptian funerary
practice combined in innovative ways in the
first centuries AD. The Roman custom of
commemorating the dead with naturalistic
portraiture – as survives elsewhere in the
Mediterranean in stone sculpture – was
combined with the quintessential ancient
Egyptian practice of mummification. The
deceased wears a white tunic with red *clavi*
(vertical strips), and has long curly hair and
a full beard characteristic of the Antonine
period. The three locks that fall on the brow
are typical of men associated with the cult
of Serapis at this time, as is the seven-
pointed gold diadem ornament. [ERO]
Bib: Cat. New York 2000, no. 21,
pp. 59–60

72–73 Anubis (right) and Apis (left) as emperors
Egypt. 1st–2nd century (?)
a) Bronze. 7.8 × 4.8 × 1.9 cm
b) Bronze. 7 × 4.5 × 1.7 cm
a) Ägyptisches Museum und Papyrussammlung, Staatliche Museen zu Berlin. Inv. VÄGM 2002/120
b) Ägyptisches Museum und Papyrussammlung, Staatliche Museen zu Berlin. Inv. ÄM 22396

Both of these figures of ancient Egyptian gods stand in *contropposto*. Rather than wearing Egyptian costume, each wears the armour and cloak of a Roman officer, with a military belt – the *cingulum militare*. Originally the feet (now broken) would have been wearing sandals. The animal heads in combination with a crown in Anubis (a) and the solar disc in Apis (b), between the ears, can be understood as genuine Egyptian characteristics. In their right hands they originally held lances. They appear in the pose of a victorious Roman emperor. In an allusion to the Egyptian king, whose job it was to maintain *maat* (truth, balance, order, law, morality and justice) in the country and ward off evil, the gods are here both warriors and protectors. The jackal-headed Anubis and the bull-headed Apis can be seen defending the body of the god Osiris and protecting the dead deity. It is highly probable that these figures were votive offerings from a temple or grave. [JHD]
Bib: Roeder 1956, p. 62, § 95d (without fig); Riederer 1978, p. 41, Analysis – no. 503 (on the material composition)

The god Mithras and his worship was an innovation of the Roman period and was practised throughout the empire.[6] He was depicted as a youth with special head-gear (the Phrygian cap), a tunic and a cloak that is often decorated with a starry sky. Many portraits show him killing a bull with a dagger, while he averts his face from the animal. These scenes are surrounded by other animal representations and torch-bearers, as well as the god of the sun and moon. How this image, with all its layers of meaning, is to be read is largely unknown to us today. It includes astronomical features, as well as the presence of a mighty god clearly depicted as victorious. Since the (exclusively masculine) cult was one of the mystery religions, its followers were not permitted to record or spread their knowledge of the beliefs and rituals involved, either orally or in writing. For this reason, many questions about this god and his role remain unanswered.

LATE ANTIQUE
EGYPT

3

3 INTRODUCTION

LATE Antiquity spans the period between about 250 and 800. In 330 the capital of the Roman empire shifted from Rome to Constantinople, and by the sixth century the population had become a Christian majority. Later, from the second quarter of the seventh century, much of the Eastern Roman empire (and, farther east, the Sasanian Persian empire) fell to the Arabs, who introduced Islam.

In Late Antiquity Christianity became legal, first with the Edict of Toleration issued by Galerius in 311 and, later, with the Edict of Milan issued by Constantine in 313. Within a few short years of being recognized by the state Christianity became the favoured religion of the imperial dynasty, and elites throughout the empire converted. By the end of the fourth century imperial legislation began to

75 Cross pendant from Asyut hoard
Egypt, near Asyut. 5th century
Gold and emerald. 6 × 4.1 cm
Antikensammlung, Staatliche Museen zu Berlin.
Inv. 30219,508d
Bib: Greifenhagen 1970, p. 70, pl. 51.4; Cat. Hamm 1996, 207, no. 209b; Cat. Munich 2004, 294, no. 489

76 Necklace and earrings from the Asyut hoard
Egypt, near Asyut. c.600
Gold and precious stones. Chain 99.6 cm (length); medallion 7.5 cm (diameter); earrings 12.1 cm (length)
British Museum, London. BEP 1916,0704.2-4

At the beginning of the 20th century a large hoard of gold was recovered in the Asyut region. The jewels are of excellent quality and were certainly made for the imperial court. Some are decorated with precious stones, like the chain with medallion and the earrings. Others bear Christian motifs, such as the large piece of jewellery designed to hang on a person's chest with an Annunciation scene (fig. 186), or the comparatively simple cross with sockets for beads or stones. On official artwork this was possible only after Christianity was declared the state religion, and thus not before the end of the 4th century. Presumably the treasure came to Egypt as a gift from the imperial capital Constantinople. As a representative testimony it combines political power with Christian ideas. [CF]
Bib: Cat. Munich 2004, pp. 300–1, nos 495–96

74 World map of Cosmas Indicopleustes
Greece, Mount Athos? 11th-century copy; 6th-century original
Parchment. 27.5 × 20.5 × 10.5 cm (closed volume)
Biblioteca Medicea Laurenziana, Florence.
Pluteo, 9.28, fol. 92v

Known today as Cosmas Indicopleustes ('he who has sailed to India'), the anonymous author was a 6th-century Alexandrian merchant and Christian whose treatise was written explicitly to refute the theory that the universe is a sphere with the globe of the earth in the centre. In his world view, argued in text as well as depicted in illustrations, the earth is flat with the heavens arching over it like the curved lid of a box. The author presents time and space collapsed in the service of God's plan for salvation, while at the same time providing a first-hand account of parts of the Red Sea and Indian Ocean coasts. [ERO]
Bib: Kominko 2013

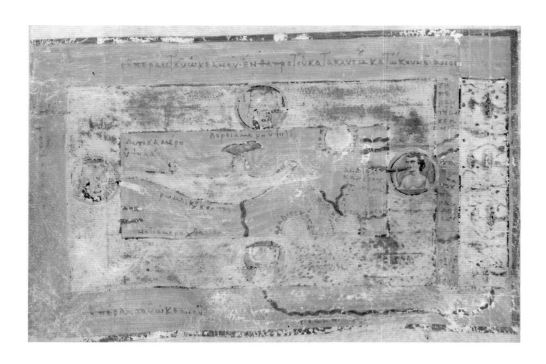

penalize adherents of traditional religion, just as Jews and Christians had been penalized in earlier times (ch. 2, ch. 3). In the Greek-speaking Eastern Roman empire Christian authors used the word *Hellene* ('Greek') to identify non-Christians, and in the Latin-speaking west the word *paganus* (of uncertain origin but implying 'rustic') was used, from which the English 'pagan' derives. As it was used pejoratively to identify practitioners of traditional religion, and mainly in the Latin west, 'pagan' is avoided or placed in quotes in this book. Christian sources depict both 'pagans' (ch. 7) and Jews (focus 3) as villains.

Legislation in 391/92 is traditionally used by scholars to mark the close of temples in the empire. At Philae the last temple in Egypt, long exempted for political reasons, was reportedly closed in the reign of Emperor Justinian (r. 527–65).

The rate of conversion across the empire is debated by modern scholars. The best data for calculating the rate of conversion is to be found in the unparalleled survival of evidence from Egypt. By analysing the personal names of people in the tens of thousands of documents surviving on papyrus, we can trace trends in onomastic practices whereby parents chose to name their children after, for example, figures from the Bible. However, the method is imperfect since both Jews and Christians used names from the Greek translation of the Jewish Bible (the Septuagint), and many originally 'pagan' names such as Ammon and Serapion were also used by Christians who named their children after martyrs or other prominent Christians.[1] Nevertheless, using the broad brush of statistical analysis, a trend becomes discernible whereby most people in Egypt had Christian names or names that were compatible with a Christian identity by the sixth century AD.

Despite the impression gained from ancient Christian historians, the evidence on the ground demonstrates a relatively gradual transformation in the course of the fourth and fifth centuries. Already in the

reign of Emperor Constantine coins were minted with Christian symbols. Nevertheless, in most media a distinctively Christian material culture was slow to develop, at first mainly adopting and adapting earlier models – such as civic basilica for churches (ch. 8), and iconography, as is possibly the case with Isis imagery for Mary (ch. 6, focus 3; cf. focus 4). Even in the fifth and sixth centuries, staunch Christian leaders like Shenoute, abbot of the so-called White Monastery, were trained in Classical Greek rhetoric. The same poet might draw upon both Biblical and Classical literature,[2] and textiles and other media were decorated with scenes from Classical mythology (ch. 10, ch. 25).

Gradually, churches, saints' shrines and monasteries came to define the sacred landscape

of Egypt. Monasticism, as it developed throughout Christendom, had its origins in Egypt (ch. 11). Due to the typical locations of monasteries outside the cultivated land along the Nile, they tend to be well preserved and are over-represented in the archaeological record by comparison to cities and towns. Thus monasteries are a plentiful source for the study of material culture in this period (ch. 12, focus 5, focus 6). Local and international travellers connected Christian sacred places through a web of processional and pilgrimage routes (ch. 13). Visitors from throughout the empire came to Abu Mina, outside of Alexandria, for example, and took away with them the blessings of St Menas in the form of earth, oil or water in flasks that have been found from Britain to Uzbekistan. [ERO]

77 Clavus fragment with a rider

Egypt. 7th – 9th century
Wool and linen. 16.5 × 12 cm
Skulpturensammlung und Museum für
Byzantinische Kunst, Staatliche Museen zu Berlin.
Inv. 6943

The fragment is from the *clavus* of a tunic. Bordered by two narrow panels with a stem of palmettes and lotus blossoms, the middle panel depicts a rider on a horse bridled with strings of pearls. He wears a belted robe, a cloak fluttering backwards, and a jewelled turban-like headpiece. In his right hand he holds a dagger; with his left hand he lifts up a garland. The horse and rider motif that recurs in many depictions of saints, and to this day enjoys special popularity in Egypt, has its origin in the image of the victorious emperor returning to the capital after a campaign. [CF]
Bib: Wulff and Volbach 1926, p. 90, pls 27 and 103

78 Relief with mounted Christ between angels

Egypt, probably from the Monastery of Shenoute (White Monastery) at Sohag. 6th – 7th century
Limestone. 43 × 61 × 9 cm
Skulpturensammlung und Museum für
Byzantinische Kunst, Staatliche Museen zu Berlin.
Inv. 4131

Christ is depicted in the middle as a triumphant ruler riding side-saddle on a donkey. A nimbus with a cross surrounds his head, and his face is turned to the viewer. He is represented with wide-open eyes, no beard and long hair. He wears a long-sleeved tunic and raises his right arm in a gesture of blessing. An angel with head turned back is walking ahead of him, while another follows. The scene is based on the iconography of the Adventus Augusti, the triumphant arrival of the emperor accompanied by winged Victory figures after defeating enemies, which also inspired depictions of rider saints that were so popular in Egypt. [MK]
Bib: Cat. Hamm 1996, p. 110, no. 55; Cat. Berlin 2006, p. 76

7 Religious Violence in Late Antique Egypt

Jitse Dijkstra

RELIGIOUS violence – if we are to believe our newspapers and other media – seems to be omnipresent in today's world. This is not dissimilar to the Late Antique world, for which our sources are full of dramatic stories of zealous Christians attacking temples, statues and even 'pagans'. Not surprisingly, the idea that religious violence was endemic in this period has remained influential among scholars.[1]

All the attention to violence, however, has obscured the fact that most of the time religions coexist peacefully. Moreover, students of religious violence in its modern context have demonstrated that we are dealing with a highly complex phenomenon that is of all places and times, and almost always involves other factors (psychological, political, social and economic). Thus religious violence needs to be analysed on a case-by-case basis, in the particular local and regional circumstances in which it arises.[2] This theoretical premise has now also been applied to Late Antiquity.[3] At the same time, scholars are becoming increasingly sceptical of the (mostly Christian) literary sources that describe violent exchanges between Christians and 'pagans'. They are often highly ideological and need to be compared, where possible, with the other sources available. For example, the archaeological evidence indicates that the destruction of temples and their reuse as churches were exceptional events rather than routine (see focus 4).[4]

It is from this perspective that we intend to approach religious violence in Late Antique Egypt. We shall do this by focusing on three iconic events that are well documented in ancient literature, and that at first sight may seem good illustrations of the supposedly pervasive nature of religious violence in the Late Antique world, and in Egypt in particular.[5] These are the destruction of the Serapeum at Alexandria, the anti-'pagan' crusade of Abbot Shenoute in the region of Panopolis, and the closure of the Isis temple at Philae. As we shall see, when we take away the emphasis on a stark Christian versus 'pagan' conflict that is so characteristic of the literary works, and place the events in their regional contexts, a more nuanced picture arises.

The case of the Serapeum needs to be seen in the urban setting of Alexandria. The city, with its huge, multi-ethnic population, was rife with deep-seated social tensions and had a long history of violence (see ch. 5). Among these incidents, the so-called 'destruction' of the Serapeum in 391/92 is by far the best-documented.[6] We have no fewer than five accounts, which were all written within slightly over a half-century of the incident – four by the Church historians Rufinus, Socrates, Sozomen and Theodoret, and one non-Christian account by the sophist Eunapius.[7]

Yet these authors contradict each other on several important points, which makes it hard to reconstruct what exactly happened. From what little information we have it seems that, partly through the involvement of Bishop Theophilus, riots broke out over the Christian reuse of a former temple, which soon became centered on the Serapeum and resulted in its plundering and the end of its cults.

The archaeological research that has been carried out at the site enables us to evaluate the statements on the fate of the Serapeum in the literary sources. There is no evidence for new structures on the temple terrain in the fourth century, which argues against the account by Sozomen who says that the temple was turned into a

79 The Serapeum at Alexandria

This fragment of a 6th-century copy of an illustrated 'Alexandrian World Chronicle' now in Moscow depicts the Archbishop of Alexandria, Theophilus, in the left margin, standing upon the Temple of Serapis. An image of Serapis, wearing his distinctive headdress, is just visible. In the right bottom margin, the same temple is also depicted. [JD]

80 Monastery of Shenoute (White Monastery) near Akhmim

Interior view of the nave of the church.

church. Moreover, the monumental temple would not have been suitable architecturally to be turned into a church. Christian buildings, including a church, were constructed to the west of the complex, which seems in line with Rufinus' remark that churches were built on either side of the Serapeum.[8] The extent to which the Serapeum was destroyed will probably remain unknown. In the post-conquest period the colonnade surrounding the complex was still intact, and it seems most likely that, as is the prevailing picture elsewhere in Egypt, initial damage to the building was limited and that it was only gradually reused for building material after the riots.[9] Nevertheless, the impact of the incident, which was soon perceived as a triumph of the Alexandrian Church, cannot be ignored, as is illustrated by the famous picture of Theophilus on top of the Serapeum in the margin of a fragmentary sixth-century papyrus codex (fig. 79).[10]

The second much-quoted act of religous violence to look at here involves Shenoute, the charismatic abbot of the so-called White Monastery (Monastery of Shenoute) near Sohag in Upper Egypt (fig. 80) and prolific author of Coptic literature.[11] He is often seen as a fervent anti-'pagan' crusader roaming the region around Panopolis (Akhmim) c.400, on the lookout to destroy temples and idols. Under close scrutiny, however, only one secure case of a temple destruction can be found in his works, that of the temple of Atripe, in which statues were destroyed and the temple set on fire. Shenoute also came to the defence of some Christians in the nearby village of Pneuit, who were accused by the local priests of destroying their temple. The abbot is most well-known, however, for his actions against the local aristocrat Gessios, whom he singled out as a 'pagan' and robbed of his house statues on a nightly raid.[12] As with the 'destruction' of the Serapeum, here also we have to be careful before assuming wholesale destruction of temples and idols on the basis of literary sources. An archaeological study of the temple of Triphis at Atripe, almost certainly the one that Shenoute targeted, shows no signs of systematic dismantling and the 'destruction' could at most have amounted to a fire in an abandoned building.[13] Moreover, Shenoute's anti-'pagan' actions need to be seen in the context of his power struggle with the local elite at Panopolis, as embodied especially in the person of Gessios, in which the anti-'pagan' discourse played a prominent role.[14] While the literary evidence no doubt goes back to actual events, the image of Shenoute as an anti-'pagan' crusader is thus incorrect and clearly more rhetoric than reality.

The last case that we will discuss here is that of the Isis temple at Philae. Owing to its position on the southern Egyptian frontier, the famous temple island retained its attraction to the peoples south of the frontier and stayed open for much longer than any other major Egyptian temple complex. According to the sixth-century historian Procopius, the sanctuaries on Philae continued to function until his time, when Emperor Justinian decided to end this situation and sent his general Narses to 'destroy' them in 535–37.[15] The incident has often been connected to the Greek inscriptions that commemorate the dedication of a church of St Stephen inside the temple of Isis (see ch. 8 and focus 4), especially the one stating 'The cross has conquered, it always conquers!' (fig. 81).[16] Thus having forcefully suppressed the still active 'pagan' cults, Christianity finally triumphed on the island.[17]

This picture does not hold, however, when we include the other sources from the region. First of all, the temple of Isis is among the best preserved temples in Egypt and cannot therefore have been destroyed. Procopius also completely ignores the impact that Christianity must have had on the local community. Philae had an episcopal see from *c*.330 onwards, and Christians and Isis worshippers lived peacefully side-by-side on the island for well over a century. Moreover, the inscriptions left by the last priests of Isis point to an unmistakable dwindling of the cults from the early fourth century onwards, so that the conclusion is unavoidable that when the last of these was incised, in 456/57, the cults also came to an end. As a result, the event that Procopius describes, about eighty years later, cannot have been more than a symbolic closure. There is also no reason directly to connect the closure of the temple and the dedication of the church, as the inscriptions are undated and mention Theodoros, who was Bishop of Philae until after 577. The reuse of the temple as a church, then, is best seen as the decision of a local bishop to find a new purpose for an empty building.[18]

This brief discussion of the three most commonly cited cases of religious violence in Late Antique Egypt shows that, when we take into account other sources, it becomes clear that where the literary works mention a 'destruction', in reality the violence was something less extreme. Moreover, placing each incident against a local or regional background demonstrates that factors other than religious ones (social and political) were equally at stake. A much less dramatic picture emerges, in which religious violence only occasionally broke out in specific local or regional circumstances. Indeed, despite the fact that the discourse of violence is so much more abundantly attested in this period, compared for instance with the first centuries of Arab rule (see ch. 4), Late Antique Egypt does not seem to have been a particularly violent society.[19]

81 Christian inscription from the Temple of Isis at Philae

View of the Greek inscription to the right of the entrance to the *naos* (main sanctuary) of the former Temple of Isis. The inscription reads: '+ The cross has conquered, it always conquers! +++' [JD]

FOCUS 3 **AN ICON OF MARY IN ALEXANDRIA?**

Arne Effenberger

THROUGHOUT the Roman world Isis was worshipped as the Mother of God, the giver of life and the goddess of healing (see ch. 7).[1] The most common images of Isis are sculptures and paintings that depict her with the child Horus, where she is often breastfeeding him (fig. 82). Many of these characteristics were transferred to Mary, on whom the reverential term of Theotokos (Mother of God, literally 'bearer of God') was bestowed.[2] Like Isis, Mary in Egypt was from early times shown as a breastfeeding mother – known in Greek as Theotokos Galaktotrophousa and in Latin as Maria Lactans (both meaning 'giver of milk'). Whether or not the iconographic models for the Theotokos Galaktotrophousa are actually to be sought in the figure of the breastfeeding Isis is still controversial.[3]

From the third century onwards representations of Mary with the Christ Child on her lap are found in Roman grave art (catacombs, sarcophagi), where the Three Magi present him with gifts.[4] It is not Mary but her child who is here being adored – in him, according to the Christian view, the magi could already see the future Messiah. It was only after a prolonged dispute that Mary was officially recognized, at the Council of Ephesus (431), as Theotokos, because the mystery of the incarnation of the god-man Saviour had been accomplished in her.[5] Only from that time onwards was Mary worshipped in the church.

In Roman Egypt wooden panels with images of 'pagan' deities were used in both the public and private sectors for the purpose of worship (figs 83, 84). The Christians adopted this practice, replacing the deities with Christ, the Virgin, saints and angels. Examples of this practice are the several panel paintings in the possession of the Monastery of St Catherine on Mount Sinai (fig. 86).[6]

Given these indisputable historical facts, it would be quite amazing if a miracle-working icon of Mary were to have been in existence in Alexandria soon after 400. This, at least, was the

claim made in a sermon preached by the Bishop of Alexandria, Theophilus (385–412), on the Feast of the Assumption of Mary into heaven (fig. 85).[7]

The preacher tells of a wooden board with the image of the Virgin owned by a Christian, who lived with his family in a store on the outskirts of the city. When the owner of the store, a Jew, raised the rent, the poor Christian could no longer pay and was thrown out onto the streets with his young children. In his haste he forgot to take the painting with him. Workers who came to clean the store greeted the image with great respect, embracing it and kissing the hands and feet of the Virgin. On learning from them that it was an image of Mary the Jewish owner became angry, broke the wooden board and put the pieces into a basket with ashes. One of the workers was told to throw the remains

82 **Terracotta with enthroned Isis Lactans**

Egypt. Early 2nd century
Fired Nile clay, red-slipped. 9.4 × 5.1 × 3.5 cm
Ägyptisches Museum und Papyrussammlung, Staatliche Museen zu Berlin. Inv. ÄM 8704

The goddess Isis sits on a throne with a high back. She is dressed in a tunic and a knotted cloak decorated with fringes. Her hair falls in long ringlets on her shoulders. On her head, next to two lotus buds, she wears her characteristic crown, consisting of cow horns, solar disc and plumes. With her left hand she supports the head of her son Harpocrates, offering him her breast, for which he reaches with his right hand. The back of the throne is decorated with small square panels and carefully carved armrests. This image is a frequently repeated type, which also appears on coins after Trajan. The fractured surface on the back indicates that this would have been a lamp attachment. [JHD]
Bib: Cat. Berlin 1899, p. 367; Weber 1914, p. 47, no. 17, pl. 2; Bonnet 1952, p. 329, fig. 84; Kaiser 1967, p. 102, no. 998 (without fig.); Philipp 1972, p. 8, p. 13, p. 26, no. 27 fig. 24; Tran Tam Tinh 1973, p. 31, pp. 86–87, cat. A-45, pl. XLIII fig. 71; Langener 1996, p. 72, p. 111, cat. KN 188, fig. 4

83 **Painted wooden panel with one of the Dioscuri**

Egypt. 2nd–3rd century
Wood. 38 × 6.5 × 5 cm
Département des Antiquités égyptiennes, Musée du Louvre, Paris. Inv. E 10815

In Greek mythology the divine twins Castor and Pollux (the Dioscuri) were sons of Zeus and Leda, brothers of Helen of Troy. On this fragmentary panel, the extant figure stands *contrapposto*, with a *nimbus* (halo) and a cloak thrown over his shoulder to reveal scale armour over a short, white tunic. [ERO]
Bib: Rondot 2012, pp. 176–77, pp. 267–73

84 **Panel painting with a female goddess (Isis?)**

Egypt. 2nd–3rd century
Wood, painted in tempera. 25 × 9 × 1 cm
Ägyptisches Museum und Papyrussammlung, Staatliche Museen zu Berlin. Inv. ÄM 14443

On the wooden panel is the image of a voluptuous female figure wearing a necklace. A veil (or a *nimbus*?) surrounds her long hair. She wears a purple tunic with gold *clavi*, under which is a bright tunic with a delicate pattern decorating the neckline. Her head is crowned with a crescent-shaped object. It could be a crescent or cow horns, so an interpretation as Isis is possible. [CF]
Bib: Rondot 2012, pp. 119–21

85 Oration on Mary Theotokos by Theophilus of Alexandria (P.Lond.Copt. II 162)

Egypt, copied in Esna for the Church of the Holy Archangel in Esna. 974
Parchment codex. 32 × 26.5 cm
British Library, London. 6780 fol. 7V

One of a group of up to 22 10th- and 11th-century manuscripts from, or said to be from, the monastic site of Hagr Edfu, Egypt. This Coptic codex contains an oration on the Archangel Gabriel by the Archbishop of Rome, Celestine I, and is 'An oration which our holy and in all ways glorious father Theophilus archbishop of the great city of Alexandria delivered on the lady of us all, the holy Theotokos (Mary …)'. In addition to his role in closing the Serapeum, Theophilus is also said to have cleared out the Mithreum and confiscated images of gods to be melted down and recast into Christian church equipment. [ERO]

86 Panel painting of the enthroned Virgin and Child

A unique collection of Christian icons, painted on wooden panels, is held in the Monastery of St Catherine in Sinai. Here they survived the iconoclastic controversy of the 8th century unscathed. This large 6th-century painted panel (68.5 × 49.7 cm) shows a representation of the enthroned Virgin with Child accompanied by angels, and flanked by St Theodoros Stratelates and St George. [CF]

into the river, but he was stopped on his way and accused of murder because there was blood dripping from the basket. The man was brought to the Bishop's Palace, where Theophilus and the clergy recognized the portrait, with its melancholy gaze, as the Virgin Mary. They carried the fragments into the church, washed them with water and fragrant oil, put the image back together and attached it to the wall above the altar, from where it now performed miracles of healing. The Jewish store owner was thereafter converted and baptized, and shortly afterwards died a blessed death.

In this text, the preacher also refers to the way the imperial image could be used for asylum – although the emperor was only a mortal man, he would protect anyone who sought refuge by fleeing to his portrait in the market. All the more, then, should one honour the image of the Virgin Mary. The preacher's story concludes with the

store being torn down at the Bishop's command and, in the Caesareum district, he builds a hospital where the sick could now be healed by the image of the Virgin.

However, we know that the hospital was built under Patriarch John the Merciful (609–19), a later date than the time of the story. Scholars agree that the text of the sermon dates from well into the seventh century and is, to put it mildly, a fake.[8] Nevertheless, it is a good story and presupposes a certain amount of historical knowledge. The preacher calls himself a bishop and mentions 'his nephew' Cyril as a member of the clergy. Cyril, in fact, was the nephew of Theophilus and began his ecclesiastical career in 403 as a lector.[9] Later he became Archbishop of Alexandria (412–44) and was the driving force at the Council of Ephesus.

In the story it appears the sermon was preached after 403 and before 412, and that

the discovery of the icon of Mary and the conversion of the Jew occurred in this period. Yet the question must be raised as to whether there may not be a kernel of historical truth in the account of this image of the Virgin. Its credibility ultimately depends on whether one especially ancient image of Mary was present in Alexandria. What iconographic features might have predestined the painting being seen as a representation of Mary, we do not know. If we are to believe the words of the author, who claims that the workers kissed the Virgin's feet, it must have been a full-length representation. There is nothing to counter the suspicion that an older painting on a wooden panel showing a woman or a goddess – perhaps even an Isis with the Horus child – was interpreted as an icon of Mary, and provided with a corresponding legend in which it shed blood and was able to perform miracles of healing.

8 Sacred Architecture

Peter Grossmann

THE cult buildings of the three so-called Religions of the Book have always observed the respective requirements of their divine liturgies. Synagogues, churches and mosques are all buildings in which people can gather and move freely. The creation of such assembly rooms relied on pre-existing types of architecture. The civic basilicas of the Roman empire that were used for the transaction of legal matters provided one such suitable model.[1] They were in use from the first half of the second century BC and later spread throughout the empire.

SYNAGOGUES

Despite Roman reservations about Jews – a prejudice that peaked in AD 70 with the destruction of the Temple in Jerusalem under the future emperor Titus (79–81) – in the early centuries of the empire the Roman authorities practised tolerance towards even the most alien of religious practices, and in this context Judaism was a fully recognized and respected religion (see ch. 5). The Romans accepted individual Jewish rites and rules of conduct, but steps were taken against cults that were seen to undermine morality or endanger the safety of the state – for example, Christianity.

In the early fourth century, the situation changed with the recognition of Christianity under Emperor Constantine. Judaism became a religion that was still just about tolerated, while Christianity was not only fully recognized but was promoted by the state. Except for a few dedications from the Hellenistic period,[2] in Egypt no architectural remains from ancient synagogues have survived. We do have a brief description of a large, richly decorated synagogue – the so-called *diplostoon* (double porticos) in Alexandria[3] – that was destroyed when the Jewish Diaspora Revolt of AD 116–17 was suppressed by Emperor Trajan (AD 98–117). According to the description, the building consisted of an elongated central space surrounded on all sides by two aisles, and so it largely corresponded to the large civic basilicas of the high imperial period.

How synagogues must have looked in smaller towns can be conjectured from examples in the neighbouring Roman province of Arabia, later Palestine. This area was the Jewish heartland and contains several early synagogues, which the Egyptian buildings must have resembled. The earliest examples were surrounded on all four sides by aisles, like the civic basilicas (fig. 87),[4] with rows of seats for those taking part in services. Later, the aisles were constructed on just three sides. On the middle fourth

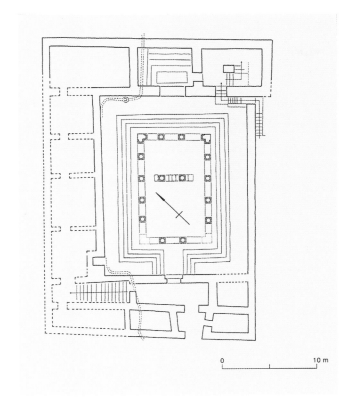

0   10 m

87 a – b **Plan and view of a basilica-like synagogue at Gamla**

side was the large niche in which the Ark of the Covenant was kept with the Torah scrolls. The *hazzan* (prayer leader) took his place on a *bima* (podium) in the middle of the room.[5] Basically this arrangement corresponded to the order of the service in the synagogue.

People met not only to pray together, and to attend a sacred rite, but to follow the teachings of the *hazzan*. To some extent, the internal space of the synagogue was adapted to the needs of a university auditorium of a type known from Alexandria.[6] Not by chance was this shape adopted for Christian churches in the period before Constantine, especially as in the early days preaching to the faithful and giving them instruction was one of the main activities of the service. The external appearance of the rectangular synagogue, with its longitudinal axis pointing towards Jerusalem, was modest. The entrances mostly lay on the side opposite the Torah niche. The decor consisted of items modelled on the usual Classical orders of the day (see also ch. 9).

88   View of the Temple of Isis on the island of Philae

Vue des temples de l'isle de Philae, Baron Dominique Vivant Denon.
c.1802
Ink on paper. 28.7 × 10 cm
British Museum, London. P&D 1836,0109.110

Built under the Ptolemies on the island of Philae at the
First Cataract, the Temple of Isis remained in use for
traditional worship until at least the 5th century. It is the
location of both the latest dated hieroglyphic (436) and
demotic (452) inscriptions in Egypt. From the 6th century
it was the location of the church of St Stephen. The
entire temple complex was dismantled and removed to
another nearby island as part of a major UNESCO salvage
campaign during the construction of the Aswan High Dam
in the 1960s before the region was flooded in 1970. This
drawing by a member of the Napoleonic expedition to
Egypt records its position before it was moved. [ERO]
Bib: Dijkstra 2011, p. 398

CHURCHES

Egypt seems to be the only province where the origin of the internal structural layout of the church can be clearly recognized from the civic basilica; this is especially
the case in Upper Egypt. Until the end of the Umayyad period (mid-eighth century)
the nave was, as with the basilica, surrounded on all four sides by narrower aisles.
In contrast, throughout the empire outside Egypt, the front and rear side aisles to
east and west were soon abandoned,[7] and no examples survive. However, there is no
doubt that churches with several aisles existed, especially in the third century.

Even today Christian churches are predominantly oriented to the east, the
rising sun being the direction from which the return of the Lord is expected. The
entrances of Egyptian churches were, with few exceptions, on one of the long sides,
even if the churches were equipped with a vestibule (narthex) on the narrow western side (such as the Temple of Dendera, in Upper Egypt).[8] Although the Sunday
meetings in the churches served mainly for the instruction of the faithful, they were
always connected with the memory of Christ's sacrificial death on the cross as
well as the preparation and distribution of the Eucharist, and for this an altar was
required. Usually this was in an eastern apse-like extension of the nave. Later, in
parish churches, the altar – now surrounded by *cancelli* (barriers) – was moved into
the lay area, while the old rules continued to be observed in the monastery churches.

From the fifth century onwards churches were also built in some 'pagan' temple
complexes in the Roman empire. The most famous example from Egypt is the reported
destruction of the Temple of Serapis in Alexandria, under the Archbishop Theophilus

89   Foliate capital

Egypt, Philae. 7th–8th century
Sandstone. 35 × 47 cm; diameter 27 cm (bottom)
Skulpturensammlung und Museum für Byzantinische Kunst,
Staatliche Museen zu Berlin. Inv. 4737

In its basic form the capital goes back to the Corinthian
type. The garland sits on a ring of fluted strips. The leaves
on the corners are ribbed, the outer lobes above are
rolled up in volutes. On two opposite sides of the capital
a rounded leaf lies in between, and the design is filled
out with a stylized flower motif. The other two sides have
a deep cut in the middle recess. This suggests that the
capital was once integrated into a sanctuary screen. The
abacus (the upper covering plate) is decorated with a vine
in two strips. Presumably, the capital comes from the East
Church of Philae. [CF]
Bib: Wulff 1909, p. 68, no. 199

90   Capital with ornamental interlaced band

Egypt, Philae. 8th–9th century
Sandstone. 30 × 33.5 cm; diameter 20 cm (below)
Skulpturensammlung und Museum für Byzantinische Kunst,
Staatliche Museen zu Berlin. Inv. 4763

With its ornamental interlaced band, the capital clearly
stands apart from other models of Classical capitals and is
instead similar to architectural decoration from Nubia. Only
the ribbed leaves emerging from the lower interlaced band
still recall the highly typical acanthus leaves. This capital
also has cuts on two sides. It could come from the East
Church of Philae, but it belongs to a later phase. [CF]
Bib: Wulff 1909, p. 69, no. 204; Cat. Hamm 1996,
pp. 100–1, no. 4

91   Niche head with shell and cross

Egypt, Philae. 6th–7th century
Sandstone. 54 × 53.5 cm; diameter 20 cm (below)
Skulpturensammlung und Museum für Byzantinische Kunst,
Staatliche Museen zu Berlin. Inv. 4766

Shaped like shells (conches), niche heads formed part
of the church interior. The design originates from Syro-
Palestinian representations of *loca sancta* (sacred place),
recalling the place where Jesus was baptized in the
Jordan River. This conch, as well as the adjacent one and
(probably) the two capitals, was part of the architectural
decoration of the East Church of Philae. [CF]
Bib: Wulff 1909, pp. 75–76, no. 233; Cat. Hamm 1996,
pp. 101–2, no. 43

92   Niche head

Egypt, Philae. 6th–7th century
Sandstone. 63 × 60 cm
Skulpturensammlung und Museum für Byzantinische Kunst,
Staatliche Museen zu Berlin. Inv. 4741

This niche head is designed as a shell, the grooves of
which emerge from a finely ribbed palm leaf in the centre.
A nearly identical example is now in the Coptic Museum
in Cairo. The conches and capitals illustrated on this page,
along with other architectural elements, came to the Berlin
Museums as a result of the work in the churches of Philae
conducted by H.G. Lyons and L. Borchardt at the end of
the 19th century. [CF]
Bib: Wulff 1909, p. 76, no. 234

93 a–b Plan and view of the bishop's church at Hermopolis Magna

The 5th-century transept basilica was the city's episcopal church, and one of the largest churches in Egypt. It was built on the foundation of an earlier Ptolemaic building, and reused elements of Roman-period public buildings. [ERO]

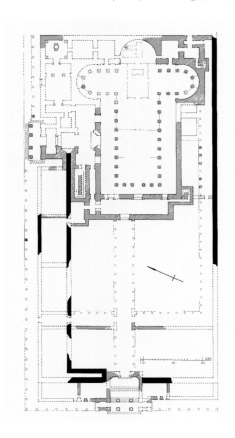

(386–412), and its conversion into the Church of Arcadius[9] – named after Emperor Arcadius (383–408) (see ch. 5, ch. 7 and focus 4, cf. ch. 7). Archaeological remains attest that the Great Church of the Kastrum Memnonion was installed within the second courtyard of the so-called mortuary temple ('house of a million years') of Ramses III at Medinet Habu,[10] and that St Stephen's Church was built in the *pronaos* (vestibule) of the Temple of Isis at Philae.[11]

In its later development Egyptian church architecture – at least in the northern part of the Nile Valley – followed the general trend in the Roman empire. To increase the area for the laity, churches in some major cities and towns were enlarged with a transept, for example at Abu Mina, Hermopolis Magna (fig. 93), and Marea. At Abu Mina, the great pilgrimage centre outside Alexandria (ch. 13), what had been originally planned as a one-nave transept in the Great Basilica was converted into a three-aisled transept (while the building was still under construction in the first half of the fifth century). From the sixth century onwards several centralized buildings were erected in Egypt, of which a rotunda[12] and a large cruciform church,[13] both in Pelusium, as well as churches with four apses on either side of a square central chamber (so-called *tetraconchoi*),[14] two in Abu Mina, are worth special mention.

In the second half of the ninth century two new types of central building were developed in the Byzantine empire under Emperor Basil (AD 867–86). One type was the 'cross in square' churches, whose spatial structure in the *naos* area (central area where the congregation gather) arose from the interpenetration of two perpendicular barrel vaults, the resulting dome of which was supported by four columns, while the other was the 'octagon-domed churches', the square central *naos* area of which was free of intermediate supports and covered by a single large dome. The latter type is due to influences from the East and is represented in the Fatimid era in several churches in the area of Aswan,[15] but also occurs in Tura,[16] in the so-called Monastery of St Arsenios (south of Cairo), and in Nubia (at Qulb).[17] In the late sixth and early seventh century in Egypt isolated examples of the four-pillar churches shaped with aisles on all four sides were already to be found, for example, at Elephantine[18] and the North Church at Bawit.[19] Due to favourable conditions for preservation, in Nubia several churches of this type have survived.[20] In these the barrel vaults that formed a cross in the *naos* area as well as the vaults of the other bays were replaced, probably under Islamic influence, by suspended domes, which resulted in a tensionless uniformity of the whole building.

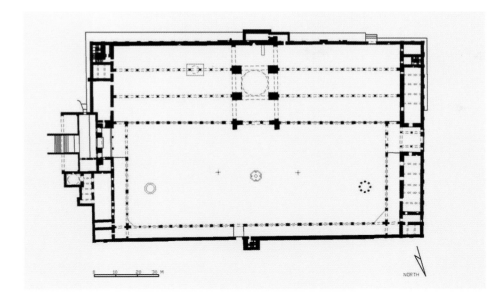

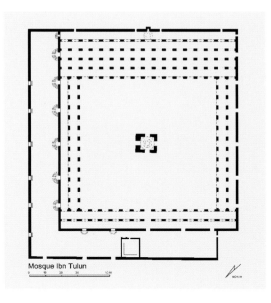

MOSQUES

Because no buildings from the early Islamic period survive, the original model of the Roman basilica is unrecognizable in Islamic places of worship in Egypt. But the fact that Islam was following the same path is shown by the Great Mosque of Damascus (fig. 94),[21] built in AD 706 to replace the demolished Church of St John. It used to be regarded as a reused Christian church because of its central floor plan, resembling a basilica, but the mosque was in fact commissioned anew on the site of the earlier church.[22] The shape of the original Mosque of 'Amr ibn al-'As in Fustat in Babylon (Old Cairo) is no longer traceable, due to the building's numerous alterations and renovations. It must initially have been a simple, uncovered place of prayer with a *qibla* wall standing transversely to the direction for prayer, namely Mecca.

Churches confiscated from Christians in Egypt were frequently converted into mosques, and they must have retained their multi-aisled basilican appearance. One change was first effected under Ahmad ibn Tulun (868–83), who declared himself an independent ruler of Egypt (figs 32, 95). According to the tradition of his native city of Samarra, the mosque named after him was built between 876 and 879. The ceiling of the *liwan al-jamia* (covered prayer hall) was supported by many oblong fired-brick pillars, and extended full width to open at the front onto a large *sahn al-jamia* (courtyard). The *qibla* wall was decorated in the middle by a *mihrab* (niche with a pointed arch). The main bay located immediately in front of the *mihrab* was covered with a small dome rising high above it. Although this type of mosque was not native to Egypt, it remained unchanged for several centuries, even after the Fatimid era (969–1171). In more recent mosques of this type, the pillars were mostly replaced by columns reused from demolished Christian buildings. In the middle of the courtyard there was usually a fountain where the faithful washed.

94 Plan of Umayyad mosque in Damascus

95 Plan of the Mosque of Ibn Tulun in Cairo

FOCUS 4 LIVING WITH THE MONUMENTAL PAST

Elisabeth R. O'Connell

IN Late Antiquity, people recycled, adapted and reused and reimagined their monumental past. In Egypt, they had an exceptionally rich range to choose from. For example, by around AD 400, the Great Pyramids at Giza were viewed by some visitors through a biblical lens to be the granaries of Joseph.[1]

Despite the claims of Christian literature, there is little archaeological evidence to support the conversion of still-active traditional temples in the Mediterranean, and Egypt is no exception.[2] Instead, as the Roman state removed the patronage of temples lavished by the Ptolemies, temples declined and were thus available for other uses.[3] In the fourth century AD Alexandria was said to be the site of dramatic temple (and also synagogue) 'conversions', most famously the imperial donation of the Caesareum (the temple to the imperial cult), probably by Emperor Constantius II.[4] Thus, at a time when other episcopal churches were built on the edges of the empire's great capitals (for example at Rome), the archbishops of Alexandria occupied a prominent position at the heart of the monumental city. Nevertheless, the precise mechanics of this process cannot be verified in the archaeological record. Beyond Alexandria the textual evidence is less plentiful, but archaeological evidence for churches within or around temples is widely demonstrable.[5] For example, in about AD 300 the largely pharaonic Luxor temple was converted into a Roman fort that was enclosed by a massive wall with typical U-shaped towers. A chapel to the imperial cult was installed within a pharaonic courtyard, the walls of which were plastered over and decorated with a high-quality, if now fragmentary, programme of imperial wall paintings (fig. 96). Several centuries later, from around AD 600, at least four churches were installed within the ancient complex.[6]

The Egyptian landscape was arguably more radically reworked when Christians transformed the ancient cities of the dead into cities of the living. Throughout Egypt, where

ancient monumental stone funerary temples and tombs were accessible, Christians moved in. Most of these men were monks, identifiable by inscriptions and excavated documents on papyrus and ostraca. While the literary tradition describes both of the fourth-century traditional founding fathers of Egyptian monasticism – Antony and Pachomius – as occupying tombs, the archaeological evidence of Late Antique habitation of earlier necropoleis dates no

96 Wall painting from the imperial cult chapel at Luxor Temple

The New Kingdom Luxor temple complex was extended and modified over successive millennia. When the complex was converted into a Roman fortress in *c*.300, a chapel to the imperial cult was installed within one of its courtyards and richly decorated with wall paintings. This scene depicts a group of Roman senators gathering below the imperial throne. [ERO]

97 a–b Ancient Egyptian temple to Christian monastery

Before it was 'cleared' by Egyptologists at the end of the 19th century, the remains of a c.600-800 monastery dedicated to the holy martyr Phoibammon still stood upon the earlier, pharaonic Temple of Hatshepsut. The 2006 photograph at left shows the temple as it stands today, reconstructed in the 20th century; the c.1892 photograph at right shows the monastery's mud-brick tower and other remains in situ. [ERO]

earlier than the sixth century.[7] This is the case in the Theban Necropolis, located on the West Bank of the Nile just opposite Luxor Temple.[8] Surrounded by hermitages, saints' shrines and other monasteries installed among pharaonic funerary monuments, the Monastery of Phoibammon at Deir al-Bahri was built in and around the mortuary temple of Hatshepsut of c.1500 BC (fig. 97). The monastery was owned, and probably founded, by Bishop Abraham of Hermonthis, c.AD 590–620. Among the thousands of papyri and ostraca from the site (fig. 98), about 200 letters to, from or concerning this bishop survive from the site today.[9] His name appears on pieces of a silver treasure, on an ivory diptych (fig. 100) and, remarkably, he is also depicted on a painted wooden panel that was probably produced on his appointment as bishop (fig. 99).[10] The c.AD 610 Greek legal document by which Bishop Abraham's heir Victor eventually inherited the property – namely Abraham's last will and testament – details the monastery's contents, 'from the cheap to the costly, down to a cinder' (fig. 101). While the archaeological evidence for the reuse of this complex suggests that practical considerations motivated the adaptation and reuse of the complex, literary sources suggest ideological motivations for, or explanations of, the practice.[11]

Earlier structures were also dismantled for *spolia* (building materials) or put to other purposes in Egypt, just as other cultures with a long history of monumental building have done for millennia. While the fifth-century tri-conch churches of the so-called White and Red monasteries near Sohag are remarkable for their in situ contemporary, purpose-carved niche heads and other sculpture, these and many other new building projects also depended on reused blocks and building sculpture. Such material was

brought from ancient Egyptian and also more recent structures.

Reuse of near-contemporary, Late Antique sculpture depicting Classical themes has sometimes confused excavators and art historians, who have failed to recognize that it had been covered in plaster or was otherwise invisible – for example at the Monastery of Apa Jeremias at Saqqara.[12] In other cases at this same site, reused earlier sculpture was clearly put to decorative effect, as when fragments of Old Kingdom relief sculpture depicting fish were reused to frame the threshold of a doorway. The doorway itself reused two doorjambs, probably originating from a recent (fifth or sixth century)

98 Ostracon depicting Jonas praying (*O.Deir el-Bahari* dessin 1)

Egypt, Western Thebes, Temple of Hatshepsut/Monastery of Phoibammon, excavated 1900. c.600–800
Limestone ostracon. 15 × 13.5 × 4cm
British Museum, London. EA 33254

Thousands of papyri and ostraca, mainly in Coptic and some in Greek, were excavated from the c.600–800 Monastery of St Phoibammon, built in and around the ruined Temple of Hatshepsut. While papyrus was used for official documents, ostraca provided abundant writing surfaces for more ephemeral writings such as letters and receipts as well as drawings. This figural *ostracon* depicts a schematic figure with his arms raised in prayer. His name is given in the label: Jonas. [ERO]

99 Portrait of Bishop Apa Abraham of Hermonthis

Upper Egypt, probably Luxor. 590 –600
Tempera on Acacia wood. 36.5 × 26.5 × 3.2 cm
Skulpturensammlung und Museum für
Byzantinische Kunst, Staatliche Museen zu Berlin.
Inv. 6114

This portrait depicts Apa Abraham, the 14th Bishop of Hermonthis, and abbot of the Monastery of St Phoibammon at Deir al-Bahri. It is the only surviving official portrait of an historically identified bishop in Egypt from Late Antiquity. Apa Abraham is depicted with eyes wide open in an expressive gaze, while his firmly closed mouth gives a severe impression. His long beard reaches to his chest, and he wears a purple *dalmatic* (tunic) and an *omophorion* (a long, bright scarf identifying the wearer as a bishop). He holds a decorated Gospel in one hand and supports it with the other. On either side of his golden nimbus is an inscription giving his name and title: 'Apa (father) Abraham the bishop'. At the side 4 drill holes show that this portrait was intended to be hung for display. [MK]
Bib: Wulff 1909, p. 301, no. 1607; Cat. Hamm 1996, p. 259, no. 287; Fluck 2010, pp. 213–25

100 Diptych naming the Bishop Abraham

Egypt, purchased in Luxor in 1903. Palimpsest: hand 1 undated; hand 2 written after 623; hand 3 written after 662
Elephant ivory with copper alloy fastenings. 25.5 × 12 × 4.5 cm (with leaves open)
British Museum, London. BEP 1920,1214.1

Read aloud in the liturgy, church diptychs ('twofold') bore the names of persons whom the local church wished to commemorate in its services. They typically name a combination of foundational figures and historical bishops, effectively defining the apostolic heritage of a given see. While the contents of diptychs are known from other sources, this is a unique ancient object. On the left are listed the archbishops of Alexandria beginning with St Mark's legendary successor, Ananias. On the right are the bishops of Hermonthis, including Abraham. [ERO]
Bib: Cat. Hamm 1996, no. 287, p. 259

101 The Will of the Bishop Abraham (*P.Lond.* I 77)

Egypt, Theban region. c.600 – 25
Papyrus. 111.8 × 35.5 cm
British Library, London. P. 77

In his last will and testament Bishop Abraham bequeathed the Monastery of St Phoibammon to his heir, the priest Victor. The will is written in Greek on behalf of Abraham, who is explicitly said not to have known Greek letters. Although he could read and write Coptic and could almost certainly speak and understand Greek, he was not Greek-literate. The will also states explicitly that Abraham wishes to be buried 'according to the customs of the country', and indeed burials from the monastery itself confirm its residents were buried in mummiform (cf. figs 144 and 285). Three additional wills, all in Coptic, transmit the property over the course of four more generations until the death of the last known abbot, also named Victor (last attested 711/712). [ERO]
Bib: O'Connell 2007

102 Portrait of Germanicus

Egypt. c.14–20
Basalt. 47 × 30 × 24 cm
British Museum, London. G&R 1872,0605.1

Germanicus visited Egypt shortly before he died in Antioch in AD 19, around which time this bust was probably commissioned and carved. Centuries later a cross was incised upon the forehead and the bust was intentionally mutilated, with hacking scars marring the bust's nose, right ear and neck. Whether or not these two episodes were part of the same event is unknown, as are their precise motivations. [ERO]
Bib: Kristensen 2012, pp. 39–40, p. 55

103 Stela of a nursing woman

Egypt, Medinat al-Fayyum (?) 4th–5th century
Limestone. 56 × 32 cm; diameter 7 cm
Skulpturensammlung und Museum für Byzantinische Kunst, Staatliche Museen zu Berlin. Inv. 4726

The mother sits on a folding bench and bares her left breast for her child. On either side of her head are two large crosses. The relief was long considered one of the earliest examples of 'Maria Lactans' – the Mother of God nursing her child. In fact, the remains of a painted inscription contain a funerary formula that proves the relief was a grave stela, and thus the interpretation as a Maria Lactans is invalid. The relief can be seen to demonstrate a transition from the familiar image of the nursing goddess to a Christian context. [CF]

Late Antique tomb superstructure.[13] In addition to practical and aesthetic motivations for reusing architectural elements, it is sometimes difficult to avoid recognizing ideological interpretations as well. The threshold of the same doorway was a fine quartzite stela, measuring over a metre and a half in height and originally belonging to the Dynasty 30 king, Nectanebo II (reigned 360–43 BC). The figures of both the king and Apis, the bull-god to whom he offers, were pecked out – according to the excavator they were 'willfully destroyed'. Everyone in the monastery who crossed the threshold would have trodden on the image of these royal and divine figures.[14]

Sculpture where the findspot is unknown can display modifications that require consideration of ideological motivations. Like other sculpture from throughout the empire, the forehead of the basalt bust sculpture

of Germanicus (c.AD 19), great-nephew and grandson-in-law of Augustus, was later inscribed with a cross (fig. 102).[15] Although the act was performed with intention, modern observers can only speculate as to why – to neutralize spirits thought to dwell in images, or perhaps retroactively to 'Christianize' a popular member of the imperial family? Given the ancient practice of marking slaves with tattoos, was it to mark Germanicus as a 'slave of God,' just as we are told some Christians voluntarily did this to themselves?[16]

A relief sculpture once thought to bridge the chronological gap between representations of Isis Lactans and Maria Lactans is now identified by its Greek inscription as the funerary stela of a young woman aged twenty-one (fig. 103). If, as has been argued, the crosses that flank her seated figure were added later, it is possible that the image also had the double meaning of evoking

the woman and the Virgin to ancient viewers.[17] So too, Muslims reused and re-imagined the material past.[18] Located not far from the location of the Caesareum at Alexandria, the al-'Attarin Mosque reused over a hundred Late Antique capitals and columns presumed to come from churches, perhaps including the Great Church of Alexandria (fig. 104). Within the courtyard of the mosque, an octagonal structure used for washing by Muslims ahead of prayer, stood the massive stone sarcophagus of Nectanebo II – modified by twelve drains drilled along the bottom (fig. 105). Local tradition identified it as the tomb of Alexander the Great.[19] Just as elite Christians collected ancient statues for display, as had their earlier, 'pagan' counter-parts,[20] the status incurred of owning and displaying already ancient monumental sculpture may be identified among the range of possible motivations for reuse.

104 Al-ʿAttarin Mosque, Alexandria

The octagonal structure in the courtyard of al-ʿAttarin Mosque c.1800 contained a basin for washing which was originally carved as a sarcophagus for the last king of pharaonic Egypt, Nectanebo II.

105 Sarcophagus of Nectanebo II

Egypt. c.345 BC
Agglomerate granite. 118.5 × 162 × 313.5 cm
British Museum, London. EA 10

Taken by the Napoleonic expedition from its location in al-ʿAttarin Mosque, this ancient Egyptian sarcophagus was one of about 20 objects conceded by the French to the British according to the terms of the Treaty of Alexandria in 1801 (cf. figs 42–43). At that time the sarcophagus was known as the tomb of Alexander the Great. This association possibly recalls the legendary connection between Alexander and Nectanebo II, as presented in the Alexander Romance – a collection of legends, several versions of which were transmitted from as early as the 3rd century and into the medieval Arabic tradition. Members of the Napoleonic expedition understood al-ʿAttarin Mosque as the location of the earlier episcopal church of Alexandria. This church is known to have been installed within the temple complex of the Caesareum after the land was granted to the church by the emperor in the middle of the 4th century. [ERO]
Bib: McKenzie 2007, pp. 258–59

9 Synagogues

Renate Rosenthal-Heginbottom

106 Inscription with renewal of a decree of asylum for a synagogue

Egypt, Tell al-Yahudiya. 146–116 BC and 47–31 BC
Marble. 42 × 25 × 6 cm
Ägyptisches Museum und Papyrussammlung, Staatliche
Museen zu Berlin. Inv. ÄM 7733

The marble stela bears an original Greek and a secondary Latin inscription. This is the renewed dedicatory inscription of a synagogue, allowing it to be granted asylum status. The original dedication dates back to Ptolemy VIII Euergetes II, while the secondary inscription, with the Latin text, was added under Cleopatra VII and Caesarion. It is probable that this was the synagogue of Leontopolis, today's Tell al-Yahudiya, northeast of Cairo. An unusual feature is the stone material – marble – which was imported to Egypt. [JHD]
Bib: Erman 1899, p. 331; Rigsby 1996, pp. 571–73, no. 228; Rigsby 2003, pp. 127–42

THE splendour of the Great Synagogue of Alexandria, probably the building referred to by Philo of Alexandria as 'the largest and most magnificent in the city' – although destroyed under Trajan in the Diaspora Revolt of AD 116–17 – was still lingering in the Jewish cultural memory centuries later. In Jewish sources, the Tosefta of the early third century and in the Jerusalem and Babylonian Talmud, the synagogue is highly praised.[1]

Written sources document the construction of the first synagogues in Ptolemaic Egypt; however, there is no physical evidence from that period. Thus, conclusions about structure, furnishing and decoration of Egyptian synagogues can only be drawn from comparison with excavated buildings in Roman and Byzantine Palestine and in the Diaspora.[2] In view of the existing diversity in basic and essential furnishings resulting from geographical and chronological differences and developments, the suggested analogies are conjectured. Unsubstantiated through archaeological evidence, for instance, are the suggestions that the synagogue at Gamla in the Golan Heights was built under Alexandrian influence in the reign of Herod the Great (37–36 BC), and that the Great Synagogue of Alexandria, following the plan of the Gamla synagogue,[3] had a double ambulatory colonnade on the interior and aisles filled by tiers of benches.

In fact, while it appears that the Great Synagogue in Alexandria was a basilica structure (ch. 11), the arrangement of the *dyplastoon* (double colonnade) is equivocal: the term allows colonnades above or beside each other, either a hall with two rows of columns on each side or a second-storey gallery, as well as colonnades on two, three or four sides.[4] Talmudic sources mention a wooden platform (*bima*) in the centre of the hall, indicating that the principal forms of the synagogue ceremony were the reading of the Torah, sermons and interpretations, and that the platform or podium was a vital component in the synagogue hall. Yet its location can vary and, depending on the size of the hall, the lectern could have been a portable wooden table.[5] In the same texts, seating arrangements are disclosed twice. Firstly, we read of seventy-one golden thrones – a number not based on reality, but on a custom of describing ruling bodies. These probably refer to seats reserved for distinguished private and official personages, mentioned in some literary sources as Cathedra or Seat of Moses, for instance in Matthew 23:1-6. However, the number of seats found in excavations is insignificant, and does not speak for their widespread use as synagogue furnishings.[6]

Secondly, separate seating according to professional groups of craftsmen – goldsmiths and silversmiths, weavers and forgers – is mentioned, apparently as an Alexandrian peculiarity. A plausible explanation is the acceptance of the Roman custom of group seating according to social and political affiliations in public places of assembly such as theatres. Analogous to synagogue architecture and literary sources, fixed stone benches as well as wooden benches and floor mats can be assumed.[7]

Home to the largest and most influential Jewish community, Alexandria had several synagogues. In Egypt the earliest evidence for the construction of synagogues by the local Jewish communities comprises inscriptions, papyrus documents and literary sources, using the frequent term *proseuchê* (prayer, place or house of) and the rare term *synagôgê* (place of assembly), dating from the third century BC to the first century AD. *Proseuchae* are documented in inscriptions at Arsinoe/Krokodilopolis, Schedia, Nitria, Xenephyris and Athribis, and mostly dedicated to the Ptolemaic king and his queen (fig. 106).[8]

Philo records that, in Alexandria, synagogues were adorned with inscriptions on stone stelae set up in honour of the Roman emperor, and with golden crowns and shields placed within the building. Inscribed statue bases have been found in Alexandria and reportedly found in Naukratis.[9] However, such practices were never common, and were generally rejected on religious grounds in the late Hellenistic and early Roman periods.

From the beginning of synagogue architecture to this day, the main feature and the focal point of interior furnishings is the Torah shrine, complete with the *aron-hakodesch* (Torah ark), the repository for the Torah scrolls. The shrine was permanently installed in several ways on a *bima* in the Jerusalem-oriented wall.[10] Essential furnishings included objects like the seven-branched *menoroth* (candlesticks), either of bronze, marble or limestone.[11] They were placed at either side of the Torah shrine, as depicted on mosaic floors, stone reliefs, gold glasses and clay plaques (fig. 107).[12] After the destruction of the Temple in AD 70 and the Temple *menorah* being transferred to Rome to be displayed in the emperor's triumph (as shown on the Arch of Titus),[13] the *menorah* became the most distinguished visual symbol of Judaism. Ritual objects were the *ner tamid* (meaning eternal light, this was a lamp suspended either from the gable of the Torah shrine or hanging from standing *menoroth*), the *mahta* (incense shovel), and the *shofar* (ram's horn), which was blown from the first day of the Hebrew month Elul until the *rosh hashanah* (New Year) and on *yom kippur* (Day of Atonement). There was also the four plants of the *sukkot* (Feast of Tabernacles) – in the right hand is held the closed frond of the *lulav* (date palm tree), together with boughs of *hadassim* (myrtle) and *arawot* (willow), while in the left hand is held the *ethrog* (citron).[14]

Mosaic pavements were particularly favoured in the Byzantine period. Patterns and subjects range from geometric and floral carpets to representations of human

107 Clay plaque with depiction of menoroth

Unknown origin
Collection of the Archaeological Institute of the
Hebrew University of Jerusalem (HUJI 2473)

108 Interior view of Ben Ezra Synagogue in Old Cairo

and mythological figures, biblical scenes and ritual implements, and attest a new approach to figural art despite the prohibition of the second commandment. Furthermore, they reflect a Late Antique Jewish tradition in visual arts that was in close contact and interchange with 'pagan' and Christian communities, in Palestine in particular as well as in the Diaspora.[15] Whether or not the Jewish communities in Egypt were part of this world cannot be answered, due to the lack of physical and literary evidence.

In AD 412 Cyril of Alexandria became archbishop. His intolerance towards alternative Christian beliefs and Judaism resulted in the expulsion of Jews from the city in AD 415. Their synagogues were reportedly taken over for use as churches (see ch. 5).[16]

The ancient synagogue was a multi-functional hall where a wide range of religious, educational, social and juridical activities took place, such as Torah reading, sermons, instructions, and possibly prayer as well as study and fasting. In addition it served as school, court, hostel and as a place for charitable engagement and financial donations. The buildings discovered from the time before the destruction of Jerusalem in AD 70 confirm that synagogues existed parallel to the Temple and did not replace it. The Temple was singular, while synagogues could be built anywhere. Leadership was open to everybody, including women to a certain extent. By the third century AD the architectural and liturgical components of all synagogues were the orientation of the direction of prayer and the placing of the Torah shrine in the wall towards Jerusalem.[17]

Under Fatimid rule two synagogues existed within the former Roman fortress of Babylon (Old Cairo or Fustat) – the Synagogue of the Palestinians (the Ben Ezra Synagogue) and the Synagogue of the Babylonians.[18] The probable foundation of the medieval Ben Ezra Synagogue took place around the middle of the tenth century, and is first mentioned in a Genizah document of the year AD 1006. (The Cairo Genizah, a treasure trove of discarded documents and manuscripts, was discovered at the synagogue in the nineteenth century; see ch. 18.) Demolished by order of al-Hakim in 1013, the building was rebuilt in 1039–41 by wealthy Jews from Fustat and, though suffering from periods of neglect and damage, existed until 1888

109 Lamp with several light holders (*polycandelon*)

Egypt, 4th–6th century
Copper alloy. 18 × 48.5 cm (open)
Département des Antiquités égyptiennes,
Musée du Louvre, Paris. Inv. E 11916.3

In Late Antiquity lamps with multiple
openings gradually disappeared, to be
replaced by metal *polycandelon* with
glass inserts. They take the shape of
punched discs or crowns with articulated
arms. This chandelier, with 3 chains
for hanging, is decorated with 12
dolphins which extend from the main
cylindrical piece. Their jaws are hinged
for mobility, while their round tails
support the candle-ring filled in with
oil. This chandelier reminds us of the
golden and silver chandeliers decorated
with numerous dolphins which used to
ornament the great Roman basilicas in
the 4th century. The openwork Greek
inscription, which translates as 'Mary,
daughter of Levy', is in memory of the
donor who gave this chandelier, possibly
to a synagogue. [MD]

when the roof collapsed. In 1892 the synagogue was rebuilt on the eleventh-century foundations.[19] In the 1980s the synagogue was restored. No excavations were undertaken, with the exception of restricted soundings in the course of which the existence of at least one or probably two earlier synagogues were revealed.[20]

It is assumed that the first structure of the Ben Ezra Synagogue and the rebuilding after the destruction followed the same ground-plan – a basilica with nave and aisles, divided by six columns on each side, an entrance from the west and a tripartite division on the eastern wall. The second story served as a women's gallery. The plan resembles a church, though in the middle of the eastern wall there is no apse but an exedra, framed by the two easternmost columns. Since the builders and craftsmen were most likely Christians, the similarity should not come as a surprise.[21] The furnishings of the medieval synagogue can only be conjectured. The Torah ark was housed in the exedra of the eastern wall, flanked on either side by rooms with cupboards for the Torah scrolls; in the centre of the synagogue the *bima* was placed.[22]

Among the Genizah documents there are inventories of movable furnishings,[23] such as mats for the synagogue floor, precious fabrics for walls, the *bima* and important books, hanging candelabra and lamps, chests for the storage of ritual objects, lists, books and documents. This and other information is evidence for an affluent Jewish community under Fatimid rule, with leaders willing to invest in the synagogue and thereby manifest their religious and cultural identity. The most important remains of the medieval synagogue are wooden carvings, which decorated the Torah shrine and ark as well as the *bima*. There are five inscriptions on wooden panels, in which personalities of the thirteenth century are mentioned.[24] A precious walnut carving is considered to be part of the hinged door of the Ben Ezra's Torah ark from the time of the synagogue's reconstruction in AD 1039–41; later re-decoration and modern pigments were also revealed on the surface (fig. 111).[25]

Four points key points provide a conclusion here. First, the greatest achievement of the Jewish community in Ptolemaic Egypt – presumably under the leadership of Jews from Alexandria – was the creation of the synagogue as a multi-functional communal institution, parallel to the existing Temple in Jerusalem. The establishment of

110 Fragment of an arch with a Hebrew inscription

Egypt, Old Cairo, Ben Ezra Synagogue. 13th century
Carved cypress wood. 147.5 × 33 × 2.7 cm
Département des Arts de l'Islam, Musée du Louvre, Paris.
Inv. OA 6348

This fragment of the lower part of an arch belonged to a doorframe. It contains a Hebrew inscription: '...His altar [and the] edification of His sanctuary and His portico soon and in a near future', alluding to the end of the world, when the Temple of Jerusalem will be rebuilt. Nevertheless, this inscription cannot be identified with any biblical or liturgical text to date. The components of the vegetal decoration

are part of the shared repertoire of Fatimid period wooden panels also appearing in Muslim and Christian contexts, and thus demonstrating that different communities used an identical stylistic vocabulary with the same craftsmen working for all three. The Ben Ezra Synagogue of Old Cairo was rebuilt in the 11th century, then demolished and subsequently rebuilt in the 1880s. On this occasion fragments of the decoration may well have circulated, as they are found today in museum collections such as the Museum of Islamic Art in Cairo and the Israel Museum in Jerusalem. [CJu]

111 Panel decorated on both sides, with Hebrew inscriptions

Egypt, Old Cairo, Ben Ezra Synagogue.
Mid-12th century
Walnut wood, remains of painting and gilding.
87.3 × 36.7 × 2.5 cm
Walters Art Museum, Baltimore. Inv. 64.181

Part of the door of a Torah shrine. Shrines for the Torah scrolls are opened only during the liturgy, something to which one of the inscriptions alludes: 'Open to me the gates of righteousness: I will go into them, and I will praise the LORD' (Psalm 118:19). The arabesque medallions and the other designs are consistent with the general Fatimid repertoire of decoration, as also used by Muslim and Christian clients. [GH]
Bib: Cat. Chicago 2015, p. 114, no. 1

synagogues was not the result of the Temple's destruction in AD 70, but preceded it. Second, no physical remains of synagogues have so far been discovered in Ptolemaic and Roman Egypt. No records survive of synagogues under Byzantine rule, though the first structure on the site of the medieval Ben Ezra Synagogue might date already to the seventh century; the ground-plan of the latter does not differ from that of contemporary churches. Third, a major difference between the Great Synagogue in Alexandria and the Ben Ezra Synagogue is the introduction of the women's gallery.[26] Fourth, in both of them the focal point was the Torah shrine; for the former the reading of the Torah from the *bima* in the centre of the hall is assured, for the latter it is assumed. Created as an institution in ancient times, the synagogue and its essential furnishings preserved its central and prominent role in the Jewish community up to the present.

10 Churches

Dominique Bénazeth

112 Panel with cross

Egypt. 12th century
Lemon wood. 29 × 28.7 × 3.9 cm
Département des Antiquités égyptiennes, Musée
du Louvre, Paris. Inv. E 13882

Adorned with a cross, this panel may have
belonged to a Christian religious building
such as a church. Wood was very common
and used for many entrances, including
those of the rail or screen separating the
sanctuary from the nave where the faithful
stand. On these church screens, as in
synagogues or mosques, we sometimes see
radiating compositions composed of multiple
elements of various geometric shapes
combined with each other by a tongue-and-
groove system – a protruding edge fits into
the recessed groove of the neighbouring
element. These places of worship share
the same decorative repertoire based on
long leaves and florets, forming very flexible
interlacing. [CJ]

I N Egyptian churches the separation between the sacred space of the sanctuary and the part where the faithful gather is marked by barriers, wooden
partitions, doors and curtains. Archaeology has shown the existence of
wooden partitions in the oldest known churches.[1] But it is not until the
beginning of the Islamic era that we find, in one of the churches at the
Monastery of Apa Apollo at Bawit, pieces of sculpted and painted panelling actually belonging to partitions. Developed in the medieval period, this system of dividing
spaces was interdependent with the architecture – partitions were used as supports
for decoration and, later, for icons. The sculpted panels in al-Mu'allaqa church in
Old Cairo (fig. 113) are particularly successful examples of such decoration. Others
are produced using a collection of small geometric segments, some in the form of a
cross (fig. 112). The panels are recessed in the structure, which is made of uprights
and crosspieces. This method and the style of decoration are entirely similar to the
processes used in mosques for the construction of the *minbars* (prayer pulpits) (see ch.
16). In the Bawit church, moreover, there is a large piece of furniture with steps that
greatly resembles these Muslim pulpits.[2]

113 Two panels from the Church of
the Virgin, Old Cairo

Egypt, Old Cairo. *c*.1300
Boxwood. 31 × 13.1 × 2.5 cm (maximum
dimensions for each of the 10 panels)
British Museum, London. BEP 1878,1203.1 and 8

From the Church of the Virgin – also known
as al-Mu'allaqa (the Hanging Church) – are
10 panels that probably once decorated the
doors to the baptismal chapel of St George.
While 4 of the panels are carved with ornate
crosses, 6 represent a series of 8 feast
scenes. Traces of gesso on 3 of the panels
suggest that they were once at least partially
painted or gilded. Shown here is one panel
with a cross (right) and a 2nd panel (left)
pairing the Nativity and the Adoration. The
Annunciation to the shepherds (Luke 2:8-
20) appears along the left. Two of the Magi
approach the Virgin and Child (Matthew
2:1-22) along the left, the 3rd having been
squeezed up to a higher register where he
joins the shepherds and beasts gazing upon
a bank of angels above. Below the Virgin and
Joseph, midwives wash the Christ child in
accordance with apocryphal tradition. [ERO]
Bib: Hunt 1989

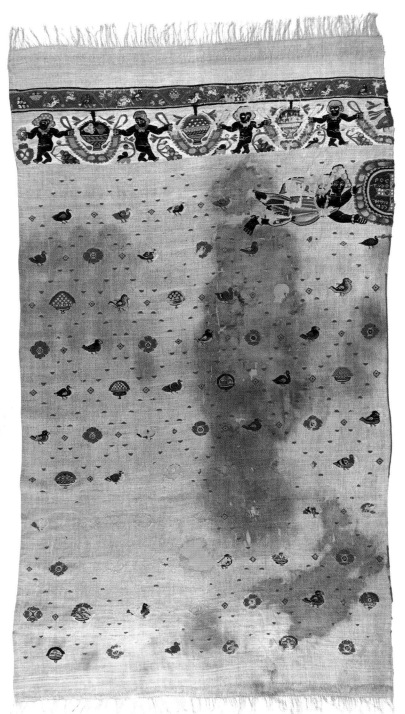
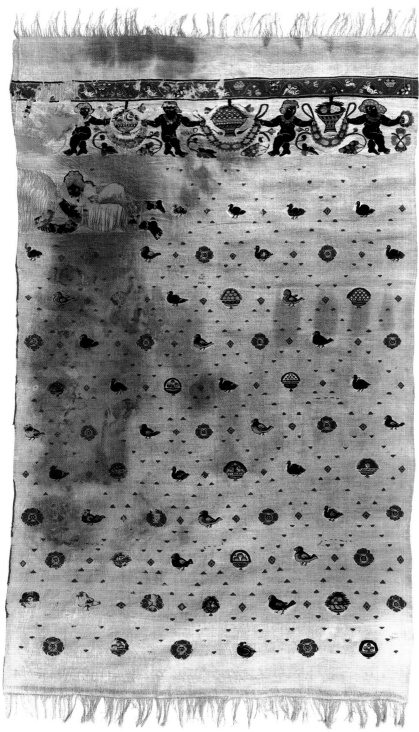

114 Curtains

Egypt, Akhmim. 6th –7th century
Linen; wool. 274 × 213.5 cm
British Museum, London. EA 29771

This pair of curtains was probably hung from the top of a door. The body of each curtain is simply ornamented with birds and vegetal motifs in floral lozenges to facilitate gathering, while the top parts, on view whether or not the curtains were gathered, are more elaborate. Under a decorative band containing an inhabited vine scroll are *erotes* holding floral garlands that stand between baskets of produce. Below them, two winged *nikai* (Victory figures) hold a wreath containing a jewelled cross with the remains of a Greek inscription in the surviving quadrants formed by the cross. Both *erotes* and *nikai* figures come from the Classical repertoire of representation, the latter often depicted holding busts of mythological figures or victorious emperors. Later such figures were 're-employed' to present the bust of Christ or other Christian symbols. This pair of curtains, through its decoration, represents a good example of continuity and reuse of Classical themes throughout Late Antiquity – here in a demonstrably Christian context. The curtains themselves were reused when they were put to a new purpose, serving as a burial shroud, which is why they have survived nearly intact. [AM]

Bib: Cat. London 1994, no. 112, pp. 102–3

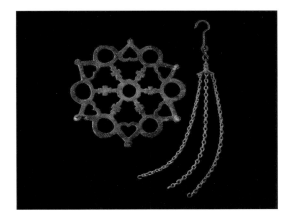

115 *Polycandelon*

Egypt. 6th – 7th century
Bronze. Diameter 24 cm
Skulpturensammlung und Museum für Byzantinische Kunst, Staatliche
Museen zu Berlin. Inv. 19/62

Polycandeloi were used to illuminate both private spaces and
places of worship. This *polycandelon* consists of an openwork
bronze disc. From a central ring radiate out 6 cross-shaped
supports that lead to rings. These served as holders for round
glass lamps. Between the outer rings a total of 6 heart shapes
are fitted. On 3 of these, chains can be hooked into small loops
to hang the lamp holder. The chains used today were added later.
The *polycandelon* will probably have hung in a church given the
cross-shaped supports. Similarly crafted lamp holders were also
part of the equipment of synagogues and mosques. [EE]
Bib: Cat. New York 1978, pp. 622–23, no. 558, fig. p. 622

116 Lamp stand

Egypt. 5th – 7th century, with modern additions
Bronze. 118 × 34 × 34 cm
Skulpturensammlung und Museum für
Byzantinische Kunst, Staatliche Museen zu Berlin.
Inv. 4906

The rather unusual candelabra shape is
explained by the fact that the foot and shaft
were originally worked separately and then
combined into one object. The foot is made
up of round-pointed leaves formed with
button ends resting on panther-like animals
and leading up to the short hexagonal shaft.
Here sits the 2nd piece, a shaft formed from
a multi-profiled base, pillar and Corinthian
capital, that in the middle swells out and
then curves back in. The attachment for
fastening a lamp is missing. On the shaft
and pointed leaves of the foot, as well as in
several other parts, hieroglyphic signs such
as wavy water lines and quail chicks were
engraved after casting, but the characters
together do not make sense and were
added in modern times. Such candelabras
were not limited to use in churches, but also
found in other buildings and private homes.
[EE]
Bib: Wulff 1909, p. 208, no. 991

The presence of curtains hanging in front of the doors or between the columns
is shown in numerous depictions, not only in the churches of the Middle East but also
in synagogues.[3] A rare pair of Late Antique curtains has survived because they were
reused in a burial (fig. 114). It is not known for sure that they were originally used
in a church, but they give a good idea of what these furnishing textiles looked like.
They are woven in linen, with polychrome tapestry decoration. At the centre of the
closed curtains is a triumphal cross, but *erotes* holding garlands are straight out of the
Classical, 'pagan' repertoire. Other fragments, with biblical subjects, are more certain
evidence of church hangings (fig. 265).

Metal or oil lamps provide the lighting for religious buildings.[4] To increase their
limited light, the lamps were placed on candelabra (fig. 116) or in suspended stands
with openwork designs. The proliferation of light sources on a *polykandelon* (light fit-
ting with chains and cone-shaped lamps)[5] is another way of lighting important
spaces (figs 109, 115). Late Antique chandeliers have been discovered that were used
to illuminate mosques, and there are examples still present in the Great Mosque of
Kairouan, in Tunisia.

For services the priest wore a special costume adorned with Christian subjects. As
seen depicted on lustreware ceramics in Fatimid style (figs 117, 118), he wears a tunic

117 Bowl fragment with a monk

Egypt. 10th–11th century
Quartz fritware, lustre painting. 17 × 16 cm
Museum für Islamische Kunst, Staatliche Museen zu Berlin.
Inv. I. 43/64138

Fragment of a bowl with an angled edge. The
exterior is lightly painted with rings and line
sequences. Inside is the figure of a monk or hermit
in a tower-like dwelling, the dome of which bears an
equilateral cross. Swinging a censer (this has not
survived), he looks at a person of which only a hand
raised in benediction can be seen. He wears a dark
robe with long wide sleeves and dark tall headgear.
The wrinkles on his face identify him as an older
man, but he is depicted beardless. This is one of
the few purely Christian scenes on the figural lustre
ceramics of Fatimid Egypt. [GH]
Bib: Museum für Islamische Kunst 1971 and 1979,
no. 275

118 Lustre bowl with a priest

Egypt, probably Cairo. 11th century
Quartz fritware, lustre painting. 10.4 cm; diameter 23.5 cm
Victoria and Albert Museum, London. Inv. C.49-1952

This is the only known complete representation of
a Christian priest on a Fatimid lustre ceramic. He
waves a censer in the shape of a hanging basket.
The tree-like motif on his right could be interpreted
as a Christian ankh cross (cf. fig. 308). The long,
belted robe with its wide, tapered sleeves and the
tiraz bands on the upper arms correspond to the
secular clothing of the period. But the sock-shaped
footwear and the bonnet-shaped headgear mean
that the figure is to be identified as a priest. The
bowl may have been produced in a well-known
workshop in Fustat/Old Cairo, if the word Sa'd on
the outside is read as a signature. [GH]
Bib: Contadini 1998, p. 86, pls 34a and 34b

with long sleeves and a pointed cowl, and swings a censer in a gesture symbolic of his
function. Preserved at the Louvre, such a costume has the name of a priest from the
Monastery of the Archangel Gabriel, Naqlun, embroidered on one sleeve. The cowl
goes with the loose-fitting woollen tunic (see ch. 11). Monks, when they are also priests,
still wear the *schamla* (a very long band of material which goes over the head and falls
down to the feet). Another kind of stole, richly embroidered with crosses and biblical
figures, distinguishes the bishops and the patriarch at the top of the ecclesiastical hierarchy. In Greek it is called the *omophorion* (fig. 119). More recent, from the Mamluk period,
are cotton tunics embroidered with Coptic and Arabic script, and motifs dear to the
Egyptian Christians – the cross, the Virgin and Child, angels, the holy horsemen killing
the demon. This tradition has survived down to the present day.[6]

Apart from the curtains and liturgical vestments, fabric also has its place in the
sanctuary. Cloths, veils and napkins are arranged on the altar, on the liturgical objects
and the hands of the officiant. The fragments of a beautiful piece of material decorated with symbols of Christ are regarded as having been part of this altar linen (figs
120, 121). The principal object used during Mass is the chalice (fig. 124), the place of
the mystery of the Eucharist. Together with the paten and the spoon with which the
priest distributes communion, it is consecrated.[7] Other articles used in the liturgy are
not consecrated, such as the censer (fig. 122), the benedictory cross (fig. 123), the fans
and the casket containing the Gospels.

119 Omophorion

Egypt, Akhmim. Canvas fabric: 890–1016;
Ikat fabric: 894–1015 (carbon-14 dating)
Linen and silk. Overall length 217 cm;
width 10 cm (per strip)
Skulpturensammlung und Museum für
Byzantinische Kunst, Staatliche Museen zu
Berlin. Inv. 9182, 9185, 9187 and 9188

Placed together, the fragments form
about half the original length of the
omophorion (the scarf-like band
belonging to a bishop's garb, worn
around the shoulders). On a strip of
linen fabric, oval, cross-shaped and
diamond-shaped applications of
recycled silk fabrics are attached on
top of one another, alternating with
rectangular embroideries. The latter
present scenes and individual figures
from the life of Christ – including Christ
as teacher and judge of the world, the
denial of Peter, the raising of Lazarus,
the healing of the blind man, Christ on
the Cross, Mary and angels before the
grave and archangels. A striped silk
fabric probably formed one of the two
original ends. [CF]
Bib: Cat. Munich 2004, pp. 134–35,
no. 171

120–121 Textile fragments with handled crosses

Egypt, Akhmim (?) 6th–7th century
Linen and wool. 30.4 × 35.5 cm
Victoria and Albert Museum, London. Inv. 258-1890

Egypt, Akhmim (?) 6th–7th century
Linen and wool. 30 × 46 cm
Département des Antiquités égyptiennes, Musée du
Louvre, Paris. AF 5556

Both fragments come from a textile that probabl
served as an altar cloth. The ankh, an ancient
Egyptian hieroglyph meaning 'life', represented
for Egyptian Christians the glorious cross of
Christ and the Resurrection. In the loops of 2
of them there is a chrism, consisting of the first
2 letters of the name of Christ, chi and rho.
This fabric also has the Greek letters alpha and
omega, from the text of the Apocalypse of St
John: 'I am alpha and omega, the beginning
and the ending, says the Lord, who is, and who
was, and who is to come, the Almighty.' The
monumentality of the crosses, their disposition
in registers, the luminous colours – violet and
madder red, indigo blue and green of weld –
contribute to the majesty of the scenery. The
edges give the width of the piece; the height,
incomplete, can be added to that of the London
fragment if the join is established. [CF/ CJ]
Bib: Kendrick 1921, pp. 12–13, no. 309, pl. IV

124 Chalice

Egypt. Late 6th – early 7th century; inscription: after the Arab conquest of Egypt
Silver and silver gilt. Height 20 cm; diameter of the cup 15.5 cm
Département des Objets d'art, Musée du Louvre, Paris. OA 11311

The chalice consists of a deep hemispheric cup of hammered silver soldered to a tapered foot, also hammered and provided with a flattened spherical node. A Greek cross and 3 gold points adorn the body. Its material, shape, dimensions and manufacturing techniques are common to a type of Byzantine cup from the 6th–7th centuries. The chalice is provided, as often occurs with Byzantine liturgical objects of that time, with a dedicatory inscription – engraved here on a narrow gold band that runs around the lip. Written in Fayyumic Coptic, the inscription reads 'In the name of God, this is a precious belonging of the Virgin of Pelcisok-burs. In peace. Amen'. The chalice was probably a dedication to a shrine of the Virgin in the village of Pelcisok-burs in the Fayyum region, and was engraved later by a local artist, as evidenced by the rather clumsy extended gilding on the lip, used to adapt the chalice for the liturgical use of an Egyptian Christian community. The double toponym is the name, in Coptic and Arabic, of a medieval village mentioned in a papyrus from 947. This fact, and the Islamic phraseology of the first words of the inscription, mean the latter can be dated to after the Arab conquest of Egypt. [DG]

122 Censer

Egypt. Period unknown
Bronze. 24.5 × 12.2 cm
Département des Antiquités égyptiennes, Musée du Louvre, Paris. E 11704

The censer could be used in religious and private spheres. Simple in shape, this one is nevertheless rare. It consists of a deep bowl and a conical lid. Both parts are simply decorated with incised lines, and are interconnected by a hinge. The lid can be closed for safety. The cone has holes for combustion and fumigation with incense or aromatic substances according to use. The object ends in a flat button and a ring serving to attach a chain. Thus the censer could be swung, but, as shown by the bottom of the bowl, it could also be placed on a surface. [CM]

123 Processional cross

Egypt. 6th–8th century
Bronze. 10.8 × 6.8 cm
Département des Antiquités égyptiennes, Musée du Louvre, Paris. E 11715 (7)

The arms of this cross are of equal length (the so-called 'Greek' cross), decorated at their ends on the front and back by punctiform pierced balls. On each side of the intersection of the arms an X is engraved. The reverse bears markings that are difficult to interpret, while the obverse shows the main decoration: on each arm a Greek letter is shown (the initials of Jesus – iota and eta – as well as alpha and omega, symbols of Christ as the beginning and end of all things), plus a small rectangle that probably imitates a gem. The cross was easily attached by the pin at its lower end to a metal or wooden stick, and used to bless worshippers. [CM]

11 Hermits and Monks

Siegfried G. Richter

INSPIRED by the varied forms of ascetic life described in early Christian writings,[1] in the second half of the third century a movement developed in which Christians renounced worldly goods, broke away from normal secular life, and often moved into the solitude of the desert. Various monastic ways of life developed. These flourished and declined depending on political circumstances, but played an important role in Egypt, and some continue to do so.[2]

The word 'anchorite' comes from the Greek *anachoretes*, meaning someone who lives in a retreat. In this context it describes a hermit who leaves the world behind. In his fourth-century biography of St Antony (*c*.251–356),[3] Athanasius, the Archbishop of Alexandria, writes that the saint is said to have followed Matthew 19:21 and sold all his possessions, giving them to the poor, in order to be perfect. He apparently withdrew deeper and deeper into the wilderness, until he died at the site of the present Monastery of St Antony near the Red Sea. In his *Vita* (Life), he is depicted not only as an ascetic – i.e. as a follower of Christ fighting against the demands of the flesh – but also as struggling against the demons who, for both Christians and non-Christians of the time, were real beings (see ch. 22). The biography depicted an ascetic ideal to which monks throughout Christendom should aspire, and cast Antony in the role of father of all monks. Through a Latin translation, the *Vita* became widespread in the West. The surviving letters (though their authenticity is not entirely beyond doubt)[4] and the collected sayings of the saint fill out our picture of Antony, who is characterized in the *Vita* as a relatively uneducated man. In the monasteries and hermitages of the ascetic movement lived individuals who covered the spectrum from healers to scholars.[5]

Travellers in Egypt, and Church Fathers who themselves sometimes followed the monastic lifestyle for a period, left reports of the lives of hermits and monks.[6] Another source is the *Apophthegmata Patrum*. This contains the relatively short 'Sayings of the Fathers' (and three 'Mothers'), collected from the fifth century onwards and covering topics such as anger, humility, the right way to pray, fasting and observance of the rule of sexual abstinence.[7] Furthermore, there are biographies of famous anchorites and collections of stories about monks written in Coptic. For example, a certain Apa Paphnutius[8] tells of how he went into the wilderness, met various ascetics and asked them questions about their lives. One of the most famous among them was Apa Onnophrius.

In contrast to the ideological motivation given in literary texts for withdrawing from the world, documents and other archaeological sources demonstrate that

125 View of the Monastery of Shenoute (White Monastery)

Dara el Abead, the Coptic Monastery, 1868, by Shallcross Fitzherbert Jacson Widdrington

the majority of ascetics were not actually very far removed from nearby cities and towns, and nor did they cease to interact with their neighbours.[9] The first mention of a *monachos* (monk) in a documentary text is on a papyrus from Karanis dated AD 324 in which the monk, together with a deacon, saves a man from a beating on the outskirts of a village.[10] Women with the title *monache* (female monk) were also involved in worldly activities in a wide range of urban, village and other contexts.[11]

After this first phase of monasticism, which we are obliged to imagine on the basis of almost purely literary sources, a new period began that was led by the desire for intellectual exchange, the way the young could learn from the old – starting with the development of monastic colonies that arose in the early decades of the fourth century in Kellia, Nitria and Sketis (see fig. 1). An impression of the extent of this movement is given by the archaeological excavations in Kellia, an area located on the western edge of the Delta, about 3 × 12 km wide, where there were more than 1,500 hermitages located within earshot of each other. Two or more monks lived in each hermitage (see ch. 12).[12] The dwellings, partly decorated with high-quality wall murals, corresponded to a standard of living significantly higher than that of a simple farmer or farm worker. In addition, these settlements offered the opportunity to socialize and gather in community meetings.

However, the Egyptian invention that proved groundbreaking for the whole development of Christianity was the foundation of the first *cenobitic* monasteries (from the Greek *koinos*, meaning 'communal'), with monastic rules incumbant upon all to follow. Pachomius, the founder of communal monasticism, was born in 292 in Upper Egypt, had been a soldier, became a Christian and joined a hermit named Palamon. Before his death in 346 he is said to have founded (according to his *Vita*)

126 Relief with a depiction of Apa Shenoute

Egypt, probably from Sohag. 5th century
Limestone. 53 × 31 × 8 cm
Skulpturensammlung und Museum für
Byzantinische Kunst, Staatliche Museen zu Berlin.
Inv. 4475

This initially inconspicuous relief depicts a male figure under an arcade, identified by an inscription as Apa Shenoute. Both the title 'Apa' and his costume show him to be a monk. Most probably this is meant to be the famous founder of the monastery, Shenoute of Atripe, who, *inter alia*, was known for his outspoken attacks on 'pagan' practices. He wears the monk's costume as he describes it in his own monastic rules: a long tunic, a belt, an undergarment, a large cowl lying on the shoulders, a goat skin on the right side of the body and a long strap over the left shoulder. With his right hand he grasps a walking stick. Some examples of original monks' costumes from Late Roman Egypt can be seen in figs 127, 128, 130. [CF]
Bib: Cat. New York 2012, p. 78, no. 46

nine monasteries with over 5,000 monks.[13] Binding rules arranged everyday life down to its smallest details, including on the powers of superiors, on the communal liturgy, on the times for meals and prayers, as well as instructions for treating diseases, who could cut your hair and how much distance you should keep when sitting with your fellow monks. From the start, a high value was placed on literary studies – newly accepted monks had to know parts of the Scriptures by heart. In many monasteries and even hermitages, such as in Deir el Naqlun in Fayyum (see focus 6), writing exercises on ostraca have been preserved, attesting the existence of school lessons. The early Pachomian monasteries reportedly had their own fields and boats, and became economically very significant. The monks could rely on support in sickness and old

127 Monk's hood

Egypt, Esna. 8th–9th century
Wool. 27 × 22 cm (lying flat)
Skulpturensammlung und Museum für Byzantinische Kunst,
Staatliche Museen zu Berlin. Inv. 9927

According to the excavator Carl Schmidt, this hood was
found – together with a cowl and a tunic – in a grave in
Esna. No further details are known. Since the Second
World War the tunic has been labelled as missing, but an
archival photo shows its similarity to the one shown in fig.
130. Hoods and cowls have been components of monastic
costume since Late Antiquity. [CF]
Bib: Fluck, Linscheid and Merz 2000, pp. 194–95, no. 127

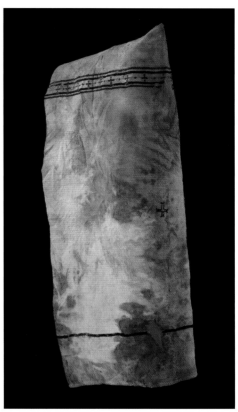

128 Monk's cowl

Egypt, Naqlun (Fayyum). 8th–10th century
Wool and linen. 79 × 35 cm (folded)
Département des Antiquités égyptiennes, Musée du Louvre, Paris.
Inv. E 26798

Made of natural, brushed wool, this cowl is decorated
with red and blue lines, cross motifs and lozenges of
linen and wool yarn. Although seen as an independent
clothing accessory, it belongs to a well-preserved tunic
from the Louvre (inv. E 26798). Unusually, the tunic's
sleeves feature a Coptic inscription, giving us the name
of the owner. It was a certain Papa Kolthi (a variant of the
name Kolluthos), a monk and priest from the Monastery
of the Archangel Gabriel, Naqlun (see pp. 130–33). The
inscription places him under the protection of God, whose
name stands 'in first place in all things'. [FC]

age. Thus, even in their early phase, Egyptian monasteries were already cultural and
economic centres. An alternative way of life was founded, whose importance for
global missionary activity and the spread of Christianity cannot be overestimated.
On the edge of the fertile countryside and in the desert mountains of Egypt, a dense
network of hermitages and monasteries arose, which was involved in lively social and
economic exchange with the surrounding settlements.[14]

Monasticism enjoyed another flowering in the fifth century with the Monastery
of Shenoute (the White Monastery) at Sohag in Upper Egypt. It was founded with its
own rules by Pigol, whose nephew Shenoute succeeded him (figs 125, 126) in the post
of abbot. Shenoute founded further monastic institutions, so that eventually a reported

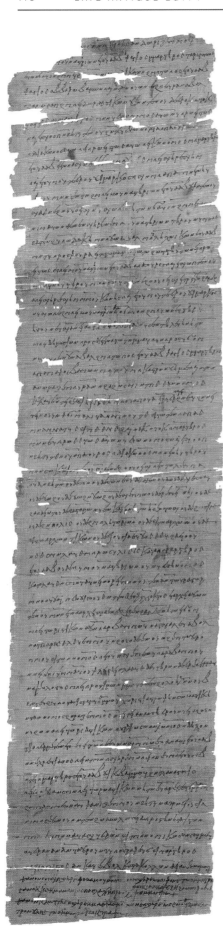

129　Coptic deed gifting a child

Egypt, Western Thebes, Monastery of Phoibammon
(Deir al-Bahri). 770 – 80
Papyrus. 107 × 24.5 cm
Ägyptisches Museum und Papyrussammlung, Staatliche
Museen zu Berlin. Inv. P 3209

This long sheet of papyrus is one of some 20 surviving
8th-century Coptic documents, in which a parent or
parents give their child – a boy – to the Monastery of

St Phoibammon at Deir el-Bahri (see pp. 93 – 95). The
texts usually start with a formulaic report: the little boy is
seriously ill, his parents ask St Phoibammon to cure him
and promise, in the case of a cure, to present him to the
monastery as a servant, following the biblical model of
Hannah and her son Samuel. The donation includes the
usual legal formulas, which are commonly used for the sale
of land. In this document a man named Papas and his wife
Anna present their son Mark to the monastery. [TSR]

2,200 monks and 1,800 female monks lived in them; on one occasion, 20,000 refugees are said to have been taken in from the southern border of Egypt.[15] Shenoute has remained the most significant author writing exclusively in Coptic. It is recorded that he was a pragmatic man who led his monasteries with great severity, and did not shrink from violence when it came to conflict with 'pagans' in his region (see ch. 7).[16]

Monastic life is often depicted in literary sources as strictly ascetic and deprived of possessions, but as we have seen this is not entirely accurate in historical terms.[17] Documents and archaeological finds provide evidence that possessions were partly allowed, and the community not only ensured regular care for its members but also guaranteed a quality of life that was far above the average level of the majority of the population at that time. In the monastery, individuals had not only a cell at their disposal, but also communal facilities such as refectories, workshops, clinics and, last but not least, churches. Above all, it must have been very attractive to learn or practise a craft trade. The communal ownership of books written and produced in scriptoria can already be seen from the Pachomian rules.

After the Arab conquest of Egypt many monasteries flourished in the twelfth to fourteenth centuries, but the monastic movement then declined. Poll taxes were collected, which was probably a major reason for more and more monasteries being deserted and private property being increasingly preferred. Thus, for example, in the ninth century, monks in the Monastery of Apa Apollo at Bawit could buy cells and, in a St Menas monastery in Middle Egypt[18] they could purchase the title of abbot.[19] These phenomena can be seen as survival strategies.

Travel writings of the nineteenth and early twentieth century show that even major monasteries such as the one in Wadi Natrun harboured only a few monks. It was not until the mid-twentieth century that, under the Coptic patriarch Cyril VI, a revival began, in the course of which monasteries again became centres of Coptic life.[20] The new form of Christian life invented in the Egypt of Late Antiquity led in the following centuries to the founding of religious communities and orders throughout the world. In the West, the reputation of the Thebaid (Upper Egypt) as the primeval landscape of Egyptian monasticism survived up to modern times. Its reception history extended even into the landscape gardens of the eighteenth and nineteenth centuries, where men employed as hermits or mechanical monkish figures could be seen by the guests.[21]

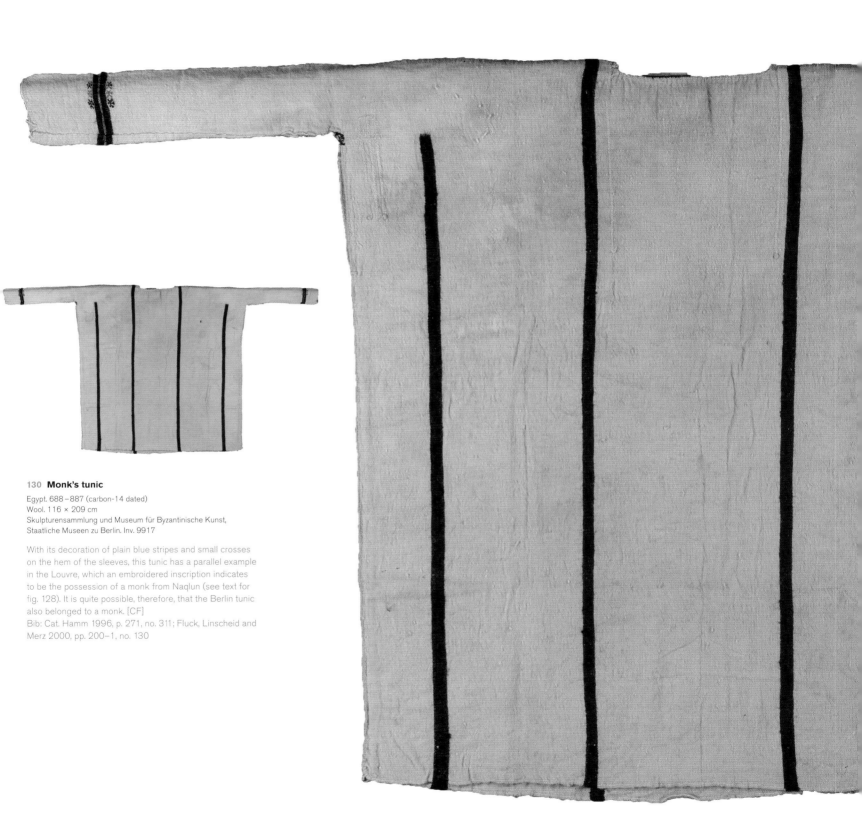

130 Monk's tunic

Egypt. 688–887 (carbon-14 dated)
Wool. 116 × 209 cm
Skulpturensammlung und Museum für Byzantinische Kunst,
Staatliche Museen zu Berlin. Inv. 9917

With its decoration of plain blue stripes and small crosses
on the hem of the sleeves, this tunic has a parallel example
in the Louvre, which an embroidered inscription indicates
to be the possession of a monk from Naqlun (see text for
fig. 128). It is quite possible, therefore, that the Berlin tunic
also belonged to a monk. [CF]
Bib: Cat. Hamm 1996, p. 271, no. 311; Fluck, Linscheid and
Merz 2000, pp. 200–1, no. 130

12 Monastic Architecture

Karel C. Innemée

IN antiquity the monk detached himself from society and its splendour. Neither his dress nor his residence were meant to impress, but rather to serve practical purposes. From the very beginning of the monastic movement there were varying degrees of isolation and social contacts between society and anchorites, or coenobitic or semi-coenobitic communities. A number of literary sources – such as the *Apophthegmata Patrum, Historia monachorum in Aegypto* and *Historia Lausiaca* – provide us with idealized depictions of the way early desert fathers lived, but archaeological evidence is also an indispensable source. Different lifestyles are reflected in the variety of monastic architectural remains. These buildings can be 'read'. From their layout and shape we can learn what purposes they served and how the residents lived.

The most basic kind of monastic dwelling hardly deserves the designation of 'architecture'. Hundreds if not thousands of hermits have lived in caves (man-made or natural), or in reused tombs from earlier periods. In many cases only crosses, graffiti and modest painted decorations show that such tombs were inhabited by hermits.[1] In a number of other cases we see that enlargements and adaptation have led to the shaping of what we can call a monastery. At the so-called Monastery of Epiphanius on the West Bank of Thebes, additions were made to six pharaonic tombs so that a small settlement developed over time.[2] A remarkable number of communities and individuals once lived in or around ancient necropoleis (see focus 4).

At the western edge of the Nile Delta lies the site of Kellia (or rather what is left of it, since most of the area was turned into cultivated land from the end of the 1960s). Here we find purpose-built architecture for smaller groups. Hundreds of complexes were built for groups of two to five semi-anchoretic monks each.[3] Living conditions must have been reasonably comfortable for the inhabitants, usually comprising two rooms per person with shared facilities such as a kitchen, latrine and food storage, all located within a perimeter wall that enclosed the buildings and a central court. Each unit was inhabited by an older spiritual father with one or more hermits under his guidance. The complexes had *oratoria*, which were rooms for prayer with a niche, often decorated with paintings, directed towards the East. There was no chapel or church, which indicates that few hermits were priests. A number of communal centres with churches have been found, while in some complexes chapels were added only later.

About 50 kilometres south from Kellia, and more isolated from civilization, is the region of Wadi Natrun (known as Sketis in Late Antiquity). According to

tradition it was St Macarius who settled here as one of the first hermits. He was in search of more solitude than he had experienced in Nitria, a region now within the Nile Delta, where numerous hermits have lived. The earliest dwelling places (*manshubiyya* in Arabic, from the Coptic *mansjoope*) must have consisted of little more than (half-)underground constructions, with additional rooms and vaults above ground. Only a few of these hermitages have been investigated. They show a more austere character than the monastic villas of Kellia. Remains of mud-brick constructions, intended for small numbers of inhabitants and resembling the housings in Kellia, have also been found.

Monastic life in Kellia went into decline after the seventh century, but in Sketis a gradual development towards the formation of full-grown monasteries took place. The first stage in the development in Sketis was the *laura*, a settlement with a church and a defence tower in the centre and *manshubiyyas* in a radius of about 3 kilometres. This indicates that communal life consisted of a weekly liturgy, which would have been celebrated in the night of Saturday to Sunday, possibly followed by a meal, after which the members of the community would return to their cells. The exact building dates of the towers are difficult to establish. In the case of Deir al-Baramus there are reasons to believe that such a tower existed already by the end of the fourth century.[4]

132 The Church of the Monastery of Apa Jeremias at Saqqara

View of the church from the southeast. The Monastery of Apa Jeremias is located in the Old Kingdom pyramid field of Saqqara, to the south of the causeway of the pyramid of the Old Kingdom pharaoh, Unas. The church and other buildings in the monastery were constructed using a range of reused pharaonic and Late Antique funerary sculpture alongside purpose-carved pieces. [ERO]
Bib: Severin 1982

Repeated raids of Berber nomads necessitated more elaborate defence works at Sketis. Textual and archaeological evidence shows that defensive perimeter walls were built (not earlier than the ninth century).[5] From that period onwards, walled complexes of approximately 50 × 50 metres developed in Sketis. They contained common facilities such as a kitchen, store rooms and a church (fig. 131). Some were located close together, as in the case of the twin monasteries whose origin goes back to the early sixth century.[6] At St Macarius' monastery, numerous walled complexes were in use, surrounding the central complex of the settlement that contained the main church. Many hermits must have decided to give up their life of solitude in exchange for the safety of a walled monastery but, even so, many cells outside the defensive walls will have remained inhabited. Thus we see a diversity in the social structure of monastic communities reflected in the form and structure of the architecture. Developments in Sketis demonstrate a shift over time from anchoretic to (semi-)coenobitic life (see focus 6).

If we define coenobitic monasticism as a way of life where monks share a common rule regulating the daily activities and hours of rest and prayer, there are reasons to believe that between the *ideorhythmic* (purely anchoretic) lifestyle and a strict coenobitic lifestyle a number of varieties in a semi-coenobitic existence have existed.

The Monastery of Apa Jeremias near Saqqara was possibly founded around AD 470, although the oldest architectural remains date back to the sixth century.[7] Here we have a different type of settlement, where monks live in small, usually two-room houses, arranged in irregular blocks and separated by narrow alleys. Thus the settlement resembles a village, with common facilities in the centre such as a church (fig. 132) and a refectory, plus a number of buildings whose function is difficult to establish. Enlarged in the middle of the seventh century, the church was constructed of ashlar blocks and contained some reused architectural sculpture (see focus 4). While the monasteries in Sketis gradually developed from diffuse settlements into fortresses, at Apa Jeremias we have a settlement where the architectural structure seems to reflect a more coenobitical character from an early stage. One important characteristic that illustrates an aspect of individuality for the inhabitants is the presence of prayer-niches in the cells. Their decoration resembles the apse-compositions of churches, and it seems to indicate that not all devotional or liturgical activities took place in the main church.

The monastery at Bawit in Upper Egypt was dedicated to its founder, a certain Apa Apollo, possibly at the end of the fourth century.[8] Buildings belonging to the monastery are to be found over a wide area, giving it the character of a village. It may also have been built on the location of an earlier necropolis, from which building material was reused.[9] As in the case of Saqqara, it is likely that the daily life of the monks was regulated according to certain rules. According to the *Historia monachorum in Aegypto*, the monks would celebrate the liturgy daily, apparently in one of the churches,[10] but as in Saqqara, numerous cells have been found that were equipped with *oratoria* (see focus 5).

Unfortunately we know very little about the total layout of the coenobitic monasteries that were founded by Pachomius (*c.*291–348) and Shenoute (died 465). The Pachomian monasteries of Pbow and Tabennesi have not survived, apart from a few remains of the foundation of the church in Pbow (Faw Qibli).[11] From descriptions of the Pachomian monasteries, however, we can deduce that the accommodation for both male and female monks was rather uniform, with 'houses' in which each had a cell.[12] Apart from prayer, the daily schedule included manual labour in order to gain income for the community. In the Monastery of Shenoute near Sohag, traces of industrial activity (large basins, possibly for dyeing textiles) and a large storeroom were found.[13] The churches of these coenobitic monasteries were of impressive proportions, showing not only the large numbers of monks that lived here, but also their wealth, and therefore the economical role that these buildings played in regional society.

FOCUS 5 MONASTIC WALL PAINTINGS

Elizabeth S. Bolman

DESPITE their fragile nature, a surprisingly large number of wall paintings has survived from Egyptian desert monasteries dating to the Late Antique and medieval periods, best exemplified by painted programmes at the so-called Red Monastery (Monastery of Bishay), near Atripe (figs 133, 134) and the Monastery of St Antony near the Red Sea coast (fig. 137).[1] While the oldest were probably executed in the fourth century, densely coloured and elaborate programmes were more common beginning in the fifth century. They continued to be widely produced until the fourteenth century (fig. 135), when there was an abrupt decline in the tradition. Often incorrectly described as frescoes, these paintings were applied directly to dry plaster using pigments mixed with a binding agent, either of tempera (animal protein) or encaustic (molten beeswax). The range of painted subjects that have survived in hermitages, oratories, assembly rooms and churches displays the extraordinary richness of Egyptian monastic culture. Although some paintings were purely ornamental, such as the geometric dado panels from the Monastery of Apa Apollo at Bawit, many were figural and functioned actively in the lives of the monks in multiple ways (fig. 136). Iconographic images could chart an ascetic ancestry, provide holy models for imitation, and make visible the spiritual world that the monks believed was all around them.[2]

There were once thousands of decorated churches and monastic buildings, in both urban and desert settings, but only a handful, most outside cities and towns, have survived. Nevertheless, a strong connection can be hypothesized between images in these two environments.[3] Thus monastic paintings outside of towns and cities are especially precious, and probably represent the visual richness of many types of Late Antique and medieval buildings. As far as we know, the extant monastic paintings were created by and for men. Although textual sources indicate that large numbers of women also joined monasteries, very few material

remains of female communities have survived. While a small number of images of female ascetics has been found, the vast majority of images come from men's establishments and the only holy woman is Mary, the Mother of God.[4]

Virtually no monastic paintings from the fifth and the sixth centuries have survived, except in Egypt. The Egyptian material shows ties to paintings elsewhere in the empire, in other contexts. While even Upper Egypt was part of the strong cultural dynamic of the Mediterranean region until the Arab conquest in the seventh century, in the following centuries monastic centres were increasingly – although not immediately – cut off from these trends. New centres of culture, for example Baghdad, informed visual production in Egypt, although some monasteries seem to have maintained older traditions.[5]

The character and quality of monastic paintings, like the monasteries themselves, varied widely, but figural representations, ornamental motifs and *dipinti* (painted texts) were popular additions to the interiors and probably also the exteriors of many buildings. The most intensely decorated seem to have been monumental churches and small oratories for prayer (sometimes for both prayer

and habitation, such as at Saqqara). At the Monastery of Shenoute (White Monastery), the abbot's tomb (d. 465) is designed and painted following a type common elsewhere in the Mediterranean. The barrel-vaulted burial chamber includes popular subjects in funerary contexts, with a typical emphasis not on death but on rebirth. These include gemmed crosses, peacocks, gazelles and rosettes, among others (figs 138, 139).[6] The small chapels at Kellia, near the Delta, included many paintings. Some are immediately recognizable as devotional subjects, such as crosses and figures of saints (for example, St Menas, see below). Others might at first sight appear to be only ornamental in nature, but were actually also charged with religious meaning. For example, many of the chapels at Kellia had running motifs of triangles topped with pomegranates.[7] These represented the hill of Golgotha, where Christ was crucified, along with one of the types of fruit associated with rebirth. Thus this abbreviated design was a reminder of Christ's sacrifice and also signified resurrection.

The paintings of St Menas from Kellia and the Three Hebrews from Wadi Sarga near Asyut exemplify the character of many monastic representations. These holy figures

133 **Detail from a wall painting at the church of the Red Monastery near Atripe**

This detail is from a preliminary sketch in the east semi-dome, depicting the face of an angel (c.late 5th century).

134 **The church of the Red Monastery near Atripe**

The east semi-dome of the church has 4 phases of painting, in various states of preservation. The 1st painting depicts the Ascension of Christ (late 5th century), while the others show Christ in Majesty (c.6th–7th century).

135 Wall painting from the church of the Monastery of Shenoute (White Monastery)

This half-conserved early 14th-century wall painting depicts Mary Theotokos.

136 Wall painting from the Monastery of Apa Apollo at Bawit

Work taking place on the wall paintings at the monastery during the 2009 fieldwork season, Room 7, north wall.

137 Wall painting from the Old Church of the Monastery of St Antony, near the Red Sea

In the nave of the Old Church of St Antony this wall painting, dated 1232–33, depicts SS Bishoy, John Little, Sisoes and Arsenius.

138 Detail from a wall painting in a tomb at the Monastery of Shenoute (White Monastery)

This detail from the south wall of a burial chamber depicts a gemmed cross, flanked by birds and gazelles or unicorns.

139 Wall painting from a tomb at the Monastery of Shenoute (White Monastery)

View of the barrel-vaulted burial chamber of the painted tomb, looking west to the vestibule.

140 Wall painting from dwelling at the Monastery of John the Little at Sketis

Fragments of a late 9th–10th-century wall painting depict an equestrian saint, possibly St Claudius, from Residence B, Monastery of John the Little, modern Wadi Natrun

were popular *foci* for devotion. They stand frontally, inviting eye contact from the viewer. Paintings enabled people to communicate with the subjects represented. Images were believed to provide a point of access to holy figures. Therefore, viewers could have directed prayers to them. An image of St Menas shows him standing with his arms raised in prayer (fig. 148). A soldier in the Roman army, he converted to Christianity and died for his beliefs (see ch. 13). His pose intentionally imitated Christ's position on the cross. The monks looking at the painting could have chosen to model themselves on the martyr Menas, unwaveringly faithful to his beliefs, embracing

physical mortification and death. They would thus have created a chain linking themselves first to the saint, and then beyond him to Christ, through the imitation of suffering. One might also imagine military saints such as Menas serving a protective function.

The Three Hebrews, from the Book of Daniel (part of both the Hebrew and Christian bibles), could also have functioned as models, because they exemplify steadfastness in the face of a very painful death by fire (fig. 184). They also represent salvation, because the Bible tells us that an angel delivered them from the inferno into which they had been put to perish. In this way figures from the Jewish tradition,

claimed by Christians as Old Testament ancestors – as well as more recent saints such as Menas – could be models for spiritual transformation.

New discoveries indicate that painted hermitages, previously known only from Late Antiquity, continued to be created. A lavishly decorated space in a multi-roomed compound was recently found in the Wadi Natrun (the ancient Sketis; see ch. 12). It was once filled with large figural paintings that are now in fragments (fig. 140). These include equestrian saints, hermits and texts. They date to the tenth century, and already show the bold outlines and saturated colours of medieval painting.[8]

FOCUS 6 MONASTERY OF THE ARCHANGEL GABRIEL, NAQLUN

Włodzimierz Godlewski

141 Naqlun

View of Naqlun from
the desert hermitages
over the medieval and
modern monasteries

142 Map of Naqlun

THE Monastery of the Archangel Gabriel in Naqlun was one of the largest in the Fayyum, and yet it escaped the notice of historians of ancient monasticism in Egypt until recently. The first mention of the Naqlun monastery appears in the *Life of Samuel of Qalamun* and probably represents a summary description of the monastery in the 630s, the years just before the Arab conquest of Egypt. Medieval texts referring to Naqlun cite two different foundation traditions, one of which is closer to the character of the anchorite complex at Naqlun and suggests St Antony's formative influence as the author of the monastic rule.[1] A later tradition – accepted by the medieval Coptic community and still current today – attributes the foundation to celestial forces and the legendary Aur, said to have been Fayyum's first bishop.[2] By contrast archaeological remains, being excavated by a Polish team from the University of Warsaw since 1986, provide vivid testimony for the development of the monastery and its successive generations of inhabitants.[3]

The oldest hermitages were established *c.*AD 450–500 and functioned for about fifty years (figs 141, 142).[4] The modest textual evidence suggests that the residents had their origin in wealthy Fayyum society. Technically and functionally, three complexes under investigation represent the same tradition. The inhabitants of two of the hermitages (nos 85 and 87), at the southwest of the site, presumably came from affluent Greek-speaking families – judging by the size of the interiors, as well as the Greek texts and imported ceramics and glassware found therein. The incorporation of a small church in hermitage no. 85, next to a separate oratory, suggests that the resident was a priest (fig. 143). Surviving texts indicate that the monk Phibamo, of a near-contemporary hermitage (no. 44) located on the hillside (Gebel Naqlun), operated in a Coptic-language milieu. He wrote magical texts in Coptic for

143 Naqlun dwelling

Hermitage no. 85, viewed north with the apse
of a small church at the left and an oratory to
the right.

his patrons and he may have been a physician.[5]
His hermitage did not have an oratory but, like
numbers 85 and 87, it was furnished with its
own grain containers, bread-baking ovens and
a kitchen. All three had special reception areas
to welcome visitors seeking the spiritual wisdom
or healing skills of the resident monks. Were
these early hermits responsible for establishing
the Naqlun complex? We cannot know for sure,
but they seem to have been pioneers setting
down spiritual and social beacons for others,
and 'testing' the most appropriate form and
furnishing of a hermitage.

The hermitages of the sixth century
differed from the earlier complexes, benefiting
from a central supply system and centrally
organized religious services. They were cut
into the rocky hills by professional stonecutters.
Although they were better executed and more
permanent in character, these hermitages
are much more poorly furnished. One large
hermitage (A), of a different architectural
formula, was built of mud-brick on the plateau
and comprised a massive keep and another
building, perhaps including a church or
sanctuary, as suggested by traces of an apse.
Numerous Greek and Coptic texts found in
the sixth- and seventh-century rubbish dump

associated with this hermitage, as well as in
the storage bins of the hermitages in the hills,
provide tantalizing insights into Naqlunian
monastic history in this period. More than sixty
hermitages have been recorded (five have been
fully excavated), testifying to the size of the
monastic community of around AD 600–50
– namely, about a hundred and twenty monks
and two hundred *pistoi* (layperson believers).
At this time, a non-monastic cemetery (C)
extended to the west of the plateau. Of the
approximately two hundred graves that have
been identified here, sixteen have been explored
to date. They are rock-cut burial chambers,
containing typical Late Antique mummiform
burials wrapped in shrouds and bound by so-
called mummy bands (fig. 144).[6]

Probably at the end of the seventh
century the monastery in Naqlun was seriously
damaged – by all appearances, intentionally.
The destruction and subsequent rebuilding are
particularly evident in the large hermitage on
the plateau (A). The non-monastic cemetery (C)
was cleared away when the superstructures were
dismantled; limestone blocks and architectural
decoration elements were salvaged for use in
the construction of the apse and walls of the
Church of the Archangel Gabriel in the early

years of the eighth century. Most of the central
part of the monastery complex burned down
about a century later, probably before 945. The
catastrophe has been dated on the grounds
of archaeological evidence – pottery sealed
in the debris, and coins found in a small jar.[7]
The architecture in this part of the plateau was
never rebuilt and is thus well-preserved in the
archaeological record. The extensive economic
potential of the monastery, evidenced by gold
coins and numerous financial texts, coupled with
the presumed generosity of the local community,
led to substantial development of the complex to
the north and south of the deserted ruins in the
central part. A new complex (D) comprised
two tower keeps, multi-story dwellings and
probably a library and codex-binding workshop.
It appears to have been the most important part
of the new foundation in the monastery, which
now incorporated all the open hermitages in
the hills to the east as well as the extensive and
mainly domestic architecture on the plateau.

The turn of the tenth and eleventh centuries appears to be the most dynamic period in the economic growth of the monastery, best evidenced by the splendour of the Church of Archangel Gabriel. An entirely new set of wall paintings, dating from before 1034, represents a high level of artistic quality (fig. 145).[8] A foundation inscription preserved in the church apse records that the work was supported by the bishop and the monastic community, as well as by people from outside the monastery. The decorative programme demonstrates the emergence of a strongly so-called monophysite orthodoxy in the Fayyum community,[9] expressed by including the main founders of the Alexandrian Church – the Apostle Mark, Peter the Martyr and Bishop Athanasius – in the apse. The decoration in the *naos* represents martyrs on horseback and monastic figures, as well as the Virgin Mary enthroned between archangels and an enthroned Christ on a shining rainbow inside a *mandorla* (body halo) supported by angels. Only for this period in the monastery's history is the name of an archimandrite of the monastery known to modern scholars – Papnoute.

In the second half of the eleventh century,

probably as a result of the dwindling Christian community in Fayyum Oasis, the number of monks in the complex diminished and the hermitages were gradually deserted. At that time the Christians buried there were dressed like contemporary Muslims; their clothes were ornamented with Arabic inscriptions and typical so-called *tiraz* bands (focus 7). Only a probable deacon was found buried in a traditional-style dress with a Coptic inscription.[10] An example of an older monks' habit, a hood now in the Louvre (fig. 128) also originates from Naqlun. In time, the economic activity of the monastery came to a standstill and the monastic site shrank to a limited area concentrated around the Church of the Archangel Gabriel.

Little is known of the monastery in later medieval times.[11] By 1985 just the holy Mesicha, an old monk venerated by the local people, lived there in the company of a few laypersons staying temporarily in the monastery. In the course of the past twenty years, however, the monastery has enjoyed a complete social and economic renaissance. Over forty monks and novices have joined the community, and many pilgrims visit it throughout the year.

144 Naqlun mummiform burial

This Late Antique mummiform burial, wrapped in shrouds and bound woven mummy bands, is seen with a modern monastery in the background.

145 Church of the Archangel Gabriel, Naqlun

On the western wall of the *naos* at the Church of the Archangel Gabriel, Naqlun, this 11th-century wall painting depicts the equestrian saint Pichoshe.

13 Jewish and Christian Pilgrimage

David Frankfurter

146 Small jug with *menorah*

Jerusalem. 6th–7th century
Dark brown glass. 13 × 6.5 cm
Antikensammlung, Staatliche Museen zu Berlin.
Inv. 30219, 168

On the hexagonal body of this little jug is a *menorah*, a
palm tree, lozenges, a niche and a four-leafed rosette.
Such vessels with Jewish or Christian symbols
served as pilgrims' bottles for oil, water or the earth
of sacred sites, and are found throughout the Eastern
Mediterranean. This is a typical product of a glass-
blowing factory in Jerusalem, which produced work
to this model for several decades. [CF]
Bib: Cat. Halle 2005, pp. 301–2, A.14
(G. Platz-Horster)

To understand pilgrimage in pre-modern cultures like Late Antique Egypt, we must first understand how local societies distinguish places and perceive powers in their own intimate landscapes. A pond is associated with a harmful demon, while a fallen statue has brought pregnancies to women who rub it; a tomb is a place to pray for favour in business, while the monks in those hills can give you a charm to use against your enemy.[1] It is this sense of the landscape as a geography of potentially helpful, ambiguous or harmful spirits, or simply of appealing loci, that anthropologists have described across contemporary local cultures,[2] and that also emerges in complaints that Christians 'practice abominations in city and village … that some of them ablute their children in polluted water and water from the arena [and] from the theater'.[3]

Pulling back from the specificity of such complaints to recognize people's engagement with local landscapes by means of ritual gestures and appeals for the resolution of crises, we can understand more clearly their sense of the variety of powers present in their immediate environments. People will travel from their homes to sites near and far that might provide resolution. All pilgrimage sites, from the cell of a holy man to the grandeur of the Abu Mina complex, represent accentuations and developments of this more basic regard towards the landscape. The difference, anthropologists have observed, lies in the shrine's relationship to the village world – as an intimate centre in a familiar landscape or as a distant site of appeal, on the periphery of society and the familiar, requiring travel and effort to reach. This kind of 'regional shrine' might offer people a kind of outside perspective on local conflicts and crises. Such regional shrines are well-known from Graeco-Roman Egypt – for example, the oracles of Deir el-Bahri, Abydos and Siwa Oasis – and characterize the growth of a Christian sacred landscape in Late Antiquity.

How did Jews fit into this general model of familiar landscapes with familiar spirits? Unfortunately, there is little evidence for Jews at all after AD 117 – when most of the Egyptian Jewish community was annihilated in the messianic uprising of the Diaspora Revolt that spread from Cyrene – until the medieval period (see ch. 5, ch. 14, ch. 18). Before AD 117 Egyptian Jews, at least those outside Alexandria, probably shared their neighbours' relationship with holy places in their environments. Jerusalem and its mythical environs were probably imagined in song and legend, but there is little evidence for religious travel there. Like other Egyptians (and Jews in Palestine), they would have visited their ancestors' tombs for intercession in family crises, an inevita-

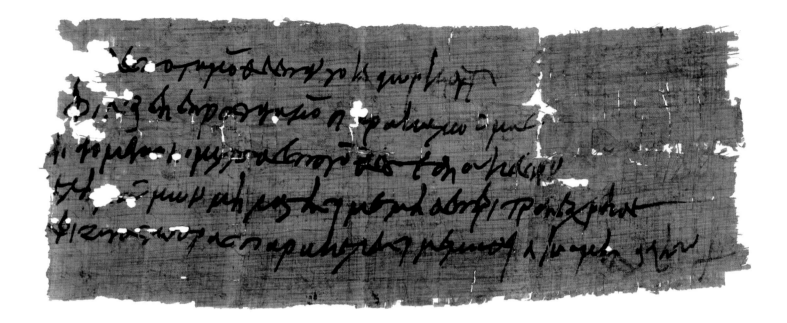

ble form of local pilgrimage.[4] It seems likely from graffiti and inscriptions that Jews in Egypt shared a sense of the potency of other religions' spirits and shrines, even to the point of visiting Egyptian temples and participating in local and regional festivals, much as Muslims and Orthodox Christians or Hindus sharing the same landscapes have developed devotional traditions toward each others' shrines.[5]

Other possible Jewish pilgrimage sites before AD 117 are dubious – a supposed tomb of the prophet Jeremiah or places associated with the Patriarch Joseph,[6] the mountain of God in Sinai or Onias' Jewish temple in Heliopolis (2 Maccabees 4; Josephus, *Jewish Antiquities*, Book 13, I: 65-68), or even Jerusalem itself. However Jewish identities were constructed in early Roman Egypt, they do not seem to have depended on travel to distinctively Jewish religious centres.[7] And although there is evidence for a reconstruction of Jewish communities in later centuries, there is no evidence for their pilgrimages in Late Antiquity.

Christians would have shared this enmeshment in local landscapes. However, a distinctively *Christian* sacred geography emerges in Egypt in the third century as a development of tomb visitation, remythologized through legends of martyrs. The *Elijah Apocalypse*, datable to this period, envisions an Egypt full of holy places and as the site of eschatological martyrdoms – one in particular being 'the virgin Tabitha' whose 'blood will be a healing for the people'. It is because of such saints, the text says, that 'the earth gives fruit ... the sun shines upon the earth, [and] ... the dew falls upon the earth!'[8] These literary images of a landscape brimming not just with local spirits but now with heroic martyrs' relics do not necessarily prove specific pilgrimage places. They show a more general ideology – that of the spatialization of the martyrs' powers. However, reports from the fourth century, when the cult of

147 Oracle ticket (*P.Oxy*. XVI 1926)

Oracle ticket of the 6th century, from the cult of St Philoxenos at Oxyrhynchus. The petitioner would submit 2 questions about the same problem – a positive version ('Should I?') and a negative ('Should I not?'), – on different tickets. The saint and his God would decide by returning one or the other ticket. Here we have the negative question, 'Is it your will that I should *not* speak about the bank business?'. The positive question, written by the same hand on the same papyrus and then cut off, survives in another collection. [DF]

martyrs was gaining importance, suggest some incipient pilgrimage practices. It is 'to the tombs of martyrs' that people travel, according to Bishop Athanasius (296/98–373), to be healed of afflicting spirits and to hear oracular messages from the demons.[9] Within a few decades Abbot Shenoute (died *c.*465) of Atripe (cf. ch. 7, ch. 11) complains of local folk discovering bones they claim to be martyrs' and bringing them into the church, claiming miraculous prodigies as a result.[10] These documents show a popular Christian interest in locating the new legends of martyrs, establishing them as shrines in the landscape to which a journey would be fruitful, even amazing.[11]

A different geography of holy powers develops in the fourth century with the phenomenon of the Christian holy man. Both an ascetic figure and a charismatic prophet, the holy man typically set himself up on the periphery of village culture as a dispenser of blessings, an interpreter of Christian scripture and ideology, and a master of spirits. Indeed, for many holy men, their interpretations of Christianity lay specifically in the area of demons, angels and the perception of supernatural worlds.[12] But holy men like Antony (*c.*251–356), John of Lykopolis (died 394), and Shenoute of Atripe also functioned regionally as seers, healers and arbitrators of civic disputes. It is for these powers that they attracted throngs of lay visitors, both local and distant, as well as teams of monastic acolytes.[13] Fourth- and fifth-century hagiographies – like Athanasius' *Life of Antony*, the anonymous *History of the Monks of Egypt*, Palladius' *Lausiac History* and Paphnutius' *History of the Monks of Upper Egypt* – celebrate not only their superhuman austerities and remote habitats but their visions, their charismatic powers and the benefits gained from their words and blessings.[14]

By the late fourth century Christianity in Egypt was a religion of saints both living and entombed, with a new geography of local, regional and peripheral holy places that called villagers to regular or crisis-inspired travel to gain blessings. The saints' acolytes themselves formed monastic complexes to administer the saints' availability, so that pilgrimage to a saint amounted to visiting a monastery, its church, its liturgical cycles and its scribal services.[15] Such monastic complexes became instrumental in the commemoration and ritualization of the holy man after death. Shenoute of Atripe, for example, earned a stunning tomb (see focus 5), a stational procession through the vicinity of the monastery and a lively legend tradition, detailing his miraculous powers and heavenly mediation (eventually compiled as his *Vita*).[16] These were the types of commemorative activities that monasteries offered pilgrims. Over the course of the fifth and later centuries, monasteries compounded their attraction as pilgrims' goals by incorporating the relics of martyrs as well as those of their own holy men.[17]

150–152 Menas *ampullae*

Egypt, probably from Abu Mina. 6th–7th century
a) Terracotta. 15.3 × 2.9 cm; diameter 10 cm
b) Terracotta. 9.7 × 3.2 cm; diameter 9.1 cm
c) Terracotta. 15.6 × 3.4 cm; diameter: 10.7 cm
Skulpturensammlung und Museum für
Byzantinische Kunst, Staatliche Museen zu Berlin.
(a) Inv. 3396 (b) Inv. 3394 (c) Inv. 3397

According to tradition, St Menas was a
soldier in the Roman army who suffered
martyrdom in the reign of Diocletian *c.*300
for professing his Christian faith. His tomb
near to Alexandria thereafter developed
into a popular pilgrimage shrine. From the
5th through to the mid-7th century, lentil-
shaped flasks were mass-produced for
pilgrims as devotional objects and souvenirs.
The body of each *ampulla* was moulded in
two halves and joined with separately made
handles, and a short cylindrical neck with a
moulded mouth applied. They were probably
filled with consecrated water, oil or earth, to
heal or otherwise convey spiritual power to
the owner.

The *ampullae* typically depict the saint
standing within a victory wreath with arms
raised in prayer, wearing a soldier's costume
– a short, belted tunic, cloak and boots. To
either side a camel kneels at his feet, head
lowered to fit the available space, and his
name is given in a Greek label above. The
decoration on the reverse is more varied,
sometimes repeating the same image of
Menas, or depicting another saint, a ship
or an inscription, or some combination
thereof. On the reverse of flask b is a rare
representation of a saint called Apa Konon,
standing with a large *amphora*. [MK]
Bib: a) Wulff 1909, pp. 268–69, no. 1378,
pl. LXVIII; Witt 2000, p. 113, no. 3
b) Wulff 1909, p. 265, no. 1359, pls LXVIII
and LXIX; Cat. Munich 2004, p. 203,
no. 288
c) Witt 2000, p. 115, no. 5; Cat. Berlin 2012 ,
pp. 58–59, no. 33b

Most shrines in Late Antique Egypt, however, were devoted to martyrs. While a great many dotted the land, some gained international renown. A small building for the 'doctor' saints John and Cyrus in Menouthis, outside Alexandria, claimed in its miracle accounts pilgrims from as far as Rome, but documentary evidence suggests it was a mostly regional clientele, like the shrines of St Philoxenos in Oxyrhynchos, St Colluthos in Antinoopolis and SS Apollo and Phib in the Monastery of Apa Apollo at Bawit.[18] Each of these shrines offered visitors specific ways of experiencing the saints' intervention – divination by ticket-oracle at St Philoxenos (fig. 147), dream-visions and healing at SS John and Cyrus, healing by contact with the tomb of SS Apollo and Phib (perhaps by means of figurines bought at the site), and the full range of incubation, ticket-oracle and *Sortes*-book (collection of oracles) mediation at the shrine of St Colluthos.[19]

The most famous pilgrimage complex to develop around martyrs' relics was undoubtedly Abu Mina (ch. 8), 60 kilometres southwest of Alexandria. The ruins of the basilica, courtyard and pilgrims' city of workshops and hostels still stand. The miracle legends of St Menas celebrate his dream-appearances, and it may be that a building just outside the basilica was curved so as to provide the sleeping pilgrims equal proximity to the crypt.[20] But the shrine is best known for its workshops' abundant production of *ampullae* (two-handled ceramic flasks) used for holding sacred sand or oil from St Menas (figs 150, 151, 152), impressed on both sides with the image of St Menas between two camels. These *ampullae* have been found throughout the Roman and Byzantine world, testifying to the diversity of pilgrims who made it out to the Abu Mina complex. The workshops also produced a good number of female figurines – some pregnant, some holding tambourines – perhaps to leave hopefully as votive images or to take home as another form of blessing from the saint.[21] The Abu Mina complex flourished from the fifth to the eighth century. Dwindling with the spread of Islam, it has become active once more since the second half of the twentieth century as a modern monastery.

153 Votive figure of a woman

Egypt, Abu Mina. 6th–7th century
Terracotta. 17 × 8 × 4 cm
Skulpturensammlung und Museum für Byzantinische
Kunst, Staatliche Museen zu Berlin. Inv. 6032

In addition to the pilgrim bottles, a number
of female figurines have been excavated
at Abu Mina. These objects may have been
related to fertility, or used to ensure protection
from harm to its owner, or both. Such figures
could have been used as votive offerings for
persons seeking to be blessed with children.
Since they have also been found outside
the sanctuary, they may also have served
as pilgrim souvenirs. The majority of extant
figures are plain and take a variety of forms.
In general they are everyday objects made in
large numbers and in inexpensive material.
This one wears a long wide-bottomed robe.
A circle frames her face imitating a halo.
The curved belly is usually understood as an
indication of pregnancy. [MK]
Bib: Wulff 1909, p. 282, no. 1475, 282, pl.
LXXI; Cat. Hamm 1996, p. 158, no. 126

MEDIEVAL EGYPT

4

4 INTRODUCTION

WITH the Arab conquest starting from the end of 639 to 642, Egypt became part of a new and growing empire that would reach from Spain to India a hundred years later. The old administrative structures were retained for the time being. However, the proceeds from taxes now went to the East – under the Umayyads to Damascus and its hinterland, and under the Abbasids to Iraq, especially Baghdad (founded 762). The grain surplus from the country, which had previously supplied Constantinople, now flowed to the holy cities of Islam, Mecca and Medina. The increasing tax burden and a decline in agriculture led, however, later on to a decline in the economic and political situation. Only under the dynasty of the Tulunid Governors (868 – 905) did the situation improve again. Cairo, including Old Cairo/Fustat with its numerous production facilities, developed in the following centuries into one of the most important commercial, social and theological cities of the Islamic world (ch. 14). Alexandria, previously so important, was now sidelined.

The Arabs brought a new religion to Egypt – Islam. The settlement of the country by Arabs (initially only as garrisons in the towns) happened gradually, and likewise Islamization (ch. 4). The old-established population of Egypt remained to a large extent Christian until the ninth/tenth centuries. Jews only reappear to modern scholars as an important group under the Fatimids (969 – 1171). This is evidenced by the documents of the Cairo Genizah, which give a deep insight into the general commercial and social life of Egypt at this period (ch. 18).

Whilst the earliest mosques in Alexandria and many smaller ones out in the country were converted churches (ch. 8), the first (and until 879 the only) Great Mosque in Egypt was the 'Amr-Mosque in Old Cairo/ Fustat, founded in 642, a new building appropriate for the needs of Islamic practice. Its layout was followed by later mosques. Many mosques have additional functions. Thus the al-Azhar (972) in Cairo remains a *madrasa* (theological school) to the present day. The veneration of persons seen as 'holy' – Christian, Jewish and Muslim (ch. 16) – produced a plethora of smaller mausoleums beside the great mosques housing tombs. The festivals in the country bordering the Nile also remained numerous, where even the great religious feast days of the Jews, Christians and Muslims had a relationship to the Nile. Here many old traditions lived on, reinterpreted and with new names (ch. 21). For Muslims, Egypt became an important transit country for the prescribed pilgrimage to Mecca (ch. 17). [GH]

154 World map from the *Book of Curiosities*

Egypt. *c.*first half of the 11th century; copied in the late 12th or 13th century
Paper. 32.4 × 29 cm
Bodleian Library, Oxford. MS.Arab.c.90, fols 23b–24a

Entitled *The Book of Curiosities of the sciences and marvels for the eyes*, this treatise is a compilation of earlier works including otherwise lost 9th–11th-century works by Muslim astronomers, geographers and travellers. Divided into 2 parts, the 1st half concerns celestial bodies with a focus on astrology and divination, while the 2nd concerns the earth. For the rectangular world map shown here, *Geography* by Claudius Ptolemy (see fig. 34) and the scholars commissioned *c.*830 by the Abbasid caliph Al-Ma'mun are cited as sources. North is at the bottom. At right are the Atlantic coasts of West Africa and the Iberian peninsula, and at left China. The Nile Delta is nearly in the centre while the southern sources of the Nile are at the top. The author's considerable knowledge of the Nile Delta and his use of Coptic vocabulary, as well as his recognition of the authority of the Ismaili Fatimid caliphs of Cairo, suggest that Egypt was the location of the work's production. This is the earliest rectangular world map to survive from before the Renaissance, and its graduated scale along the top is unique in the history of cartography up until the 14th century. [ERO]
Bib: Rapoport and Savage-Smith 2014

14 Cairo

Peter Sheehan

OLD Cairo, the area in and around the Roman fortress of Babylon on the east bank of the ancient Nile, presents an unbroken sequence of occupation from the sixth century BC to today. Following the Arab conquest of Egypt (AD 639–42), the fortress became the nucleus of Fustat, a new capital that would develop through cycles of decline and revival into the Fatimid metropolis of al-Qahira/Cairo, today the largest city in Africa and the Middle East. Old Cairo/Fustat is home to Jewish, Christian and Islamic monuments, and constitutes a unique backdrop against which to consider the major cultural transitions of Late Antiquity and a microcosm for many of the themes and topics explored in this book.

These transitions and the creation of the new metropolis took place within an ancient cultural landscape defined by three enduring topographical features – the Nile, the Red Sea Canal and the Muqattam Mountain (fig. 155). The strategic location of the city, at the junction of the Nile Valley, the Delta and a Nile crossing-point via the island of Roda, meant that the course of the canal through the city was complemented by ancient roads that shaped its development and directed the footsteps and lives of its people. The final element of this shared landscape was the city's cemetery, a place of quarries and legends located at the foot of the Muqattam Mountain and once sacred to the ancient Egyptian goddess Hathor. The cemetery is part of the *qarafa al-kubra*, a huge ancient funerary landscape that has followed the development of the city northwards. Today some of the tombs and mausolea dating from the tenth to the twelfth centuries in the southern *qarafa*, and from the Mamluk period in the northern *qarafa*, house the living in the so-called 'City of the Dead'. Together these elements fundamentally influenced the formation of the city, shaping the urban setting and representing components and waypoints of a 'sacred geography' that was shared by the diverse groups within it. Absorbing and co-opting earlier layers of this complex cultural landscape to new purposes was a constant feature, from the churches built within the Roman fortress through to the construction of mosques, shrines and tombs at key locations that were both demonstrations of political power and the focus of popular ceremonies and processions within the ceremonial space of the city.[1]

The rich variety of papyrological and literary sources for the metropolis has been supplemented by new insights into its foundation and development gained during recent archaeological work in Old Cairo/Fustat, itself a response to new urban pressures and rising groundwater caused by the city's continuing expansion in

modern times.[2] Phases of construction, abandonment and reconstruction revealed in the buildings of Old Cairo mirror the cycles of urban growth, decline and revival within the wider city. The material evidence for daily life, such as pottery, coins, glass and textiles, demonstrates continuity as well as the gradual changes brought about by new contacts and cultural interaction.

The transitions of Late Antiquity were rooted in earlier events, echoes of which are found in the archaeology of Old Cairo. Attempts at conquest beginning from 700 BC, first by the Assyrians and Babylonians, were followed by successful campaigns that led to periods of Achaemenid Persian rule (505–425 and 343–332 BC) and, hundreds of years later, Sasanian Persian rule (AD 619–29). Herodotus, writing in the 450s BC, paints a vivid picture of the intrigues and struggles for power between these great empires, together with the arrival of significant numbers of Greek-speaking traders in the seventh-century BC and, later, mercenaries and veterans. Ascribed by the ancient authors Diodorus Siculus (fl. 60–30 BC) and Strabo (*c*.63 BC–AD 23) to settlers from the great Mesopotamian city, a date of around 500 BC for Babylon in Egypt is supported by archaeological finds of wine *amphorae* and storage vessels, that indicate a trading centre with extensive contacts throughout the Levant and Aegean.[3] Babylon's foundation is therefore contemporary with the first successful cutting of the Red Sea Canal by the Persian 'Great King' Darius (522– 486 BC), linking the Nile valley to the Red Sea and ultimately the Mediterranean to India. Trade with Greek city-states, the foundation of Alexandria by Alexander the Great, and Ptolemaic rule in Egypt (323– 30 BC) brought Egypt firmly within the Hellenized Mediterranean world. After Augustus' defeat of Antony and Cleopatra at Actium in 31 BC, Egypt officially became a province of the Roman (later Byzantine) empire, with a special status as the granary of Rome (later Constantinople), supplied through the great port-city and capital at Alexandria (see ch. 5).

In AD 112 Emperor Trajan shifted the mouth of the Red Sea Canal to Babylon and built a great stone harbour at its entrance, several sections of which were revealed during recent archaeological work beneath the churches of Old Cairo. This was a defining moment in the city's history, for the canal and the route alongside it would remain determining features of the topography of the metropolis until the end of the nineteenth century. Even when the canal north of the city had gone out of use, the lake where it ended (Birkat al-Hajj) became the starting point for medieval pilgrimage caravans to Mecca (see ch. 17).

Around AD 300 Emperor Diocletian enclosed the harbour and entrance to the canal within the fortress of Babylon in the context of widespread military, political and cultural change taking place throughout the empire. The tetrarchic fortress was one of the largest and most impressive Roman structures ever built, containing baths, granaries and perhaps even an imperial palace.

The Arab conquest of Egypt, beginning from AD 639 and led by 'Amr ibn al-'As, took place in a political and military vacuum that was created by the struggles of the later Roman and Sasanian empires, resulting in the empire of early Islam that stretched from the Indus to Spain and turned the focus of its Egyptian province, ruled from a new capital at Fustat, away from the Mediterranean and once more to the East. The half-century after the conquest saw the land on higher ground located outside the range of the Nile flood divided among the settlers into tribal parcels.[4] This early staking of claims was followed from the 680s by spectacular expansion in the aftermath of the complex politics of the second Muslim *fitna* (civil war) and the Sunni-Shi'a schism. At the centre of this new urban project was a caliphal residence, and new central districts that were not based on tribal groups and included Jews, Persians and other non-Arab Muslims.

The expansion of Fustat revolved around two of the existing elements in the landscape – the Red Sea Canal and the fortress at Babylon – and involved a degree

156 Plan of Old Cairo

Map of Old Cairo today, with Roman fortress of Babylon (1), the Mosque of 'Amr ibn al-'As (2), the nilometer at the southern end of the Island of Roda (3), the archaeological area of Fustat (4) and the Ayyubid city wall (5), which was excavated in the early 20th century

157 Aerial photograph of Old Cairo

Looking towards the citadel in the north-east, this view shows the Roman fortress and the old course of the Nile (now the line of the modern Metro) and the 'Amr Mosque and the Fustat area in the north. The medieval city and the Qarafa cemetery can be seen behind them, bordered in the east by the Muqattam Mountain.

of planning and coordination that was a far cry from the 'picturesque disorder' that is sometimes presented.[5] The canal was revived to supply Arabia with grain; its entrance was shifted to allow the creation of the urban centre north of the fortress.[6] The old course of the canal within the fortress was filled in and converted to a road, while the entrance between the two round towers of the Roman fortress was blocked by a huge stone wall, parts of which can still be seen beneath the Greek Church of St George that now surmounts the northern tower.[7] The name Fustat probably derives from the Greek *phossaton* (ditch), and may have been related to the works carried out to bring the canal back into operation.[8] The city was also known as (Fustat-)*Misr*, a name linked to the Arabic word for 'camp', but probably derived from an ancient Semitic word for Egypt.[9]

The organization of space at the heart of the new city was dictated by the earlier layout of the Roman fortress in two parallel enclosures, either side of the old canal, each with a central colonnaded street leading north. Another important axis was the main east-west street bisecting the fortress and leading to a bridge across the Nile to Giza and Memphis – whose buildings were used to construct the new city – via the island of Roda and its shipyards. New archaeological evidence for the original size of the fortress suggests that the northern half, with its larger buildings and palaces, was integrated into the elite areas of the new city, arranged around an administrative and ceremonial space created by the enlarged Friday mosque of 'Amr and the governor's residence.[10]

Archaeological and textual evidence points to an influx of Egyptian Christians, called *qibti* (Copts) by Arabic-speakers, who played a central role in the construction of the new city and the administration of the new province.[11] Under the initial tolerance of Muslim rule, new churches were founded as the Coptic Patriarchate revived and resumed its 'tending of sacred space' after the dominance of the state-backed Chalcedonian Church in the sixth and early seventh century (ch. 3). This relationship was delicate and tended to break down periodically, and it was acutely sensitive with regard to foreign contacts with other Christian churches. It also came with conditions, in particular the involvement of Muslim authorities in the election and consecration of patriarchs of the Coptic Church.[12] Within the city the articulation of Christian and Muslim space is suggested by textual references as well as archaeological evidence for the construction of churches in the southern half of the fortress, including a new patriarchal church of Abu Sargha, where recent archaeological work has revealed a large colonnaded basilica with marble floors and evidence of painted wall plaster.[13]

Administratively and militarily the Arabs at first continued the Byzantine mechanisms for the government of Egypt, using an existing tax apparatus administered by the Christian elite and simply replacing the Byzantine garrisons at Alexandria, Babylon and Luxor.[14] These strategic locations had been used from the time of Diocletian to secure the province, levy customs and taxes, and control the movement of the population. The governor and his chief officials based in Babylon (the name Fustat only appears in papyri from the early eighth century) regulated finances, plus an army that was drawn from Arab settlers who were enrolled on the *diwan* (army lists) and therefore entitled to wages and supplies. The burden of a *jizya* (poll tax of two dinars) levied on the Christian population was increased by a *rizq* (subsistence allowance) for Muslims consisting of wheat, honey, oil and vinegar, and the annual provision of clothes including long embroidered woollen gowns.[15] Papyrus sources show the different hierarchies within this complex administration. Greek and Coptic continued to be used at least for a century, but Arabic was introduced immediately as an administrative language (see ch. 4 and ch. 23). The importance of this administrative apparatus is suggested by John the Deacon's eyewitness account of the calamitous events immediately preceding the

Abbasid conquest in 750, when Marwan II, the last Umayyad caliph, 'had burnt all the books and accounts of the Divans, so that they did not know the amount of the revenues, whether paid in cash or in kind'.[16]

The existing port facilities, along with the presence of an established customs point on the trade routes that developed around them, were crucial to the choice of Fustat and its development as a commercial *entrepôt* and trans-shipment point for the corn supply to Arabia via the Red Sea Canal.[17] The stepped quayside of the Roman riverfront remained in use until the Fatimid era, divided into different areas for different commodities and ships from Upper and Lower Egypt.[18] Al-Muqadassi, writing in AD 985, speaks of 'a great number of ships at anchor and under way', while al-Kindi, a hundred years earlier, hints at the journeys involved in transporting the material culture revealed by archaeology: 'all the cities of Egypt were reached by vessels which carried food, property and implements to Fustat'.[19] Early papyri dealing with the requisition of skilled and unskilled labour suggest a hive of activity along the riverfront, that was related to the commerce of the capital and the shifting of its shipyards to a location safe from the Byzantine fleet.[20]

Much of the southern and eastern part of the city was destroyed and abandoned during the Abbasid conquest of Egypt in AD 750, and the subsequent robbing out of these buildings provides the earliest archaeological evidence we have for the recycling of material by those distinctive figures of Cairo life, the *zabbaleen* (garbage collectors).[21] John the Deacon's vivid description of the burning of Fustat provides a contemporary Christian account of the extent of the destruction, and a valuable perspective on the social and economic workings of the metropolis that would have remained constant throughout the early centuries of its existence:

Meanwhile we saw flames ascending from al-Fustat, and we were informed that Marwan had set fire to the store houses of provisions and cotton and straw and to the surplus of barley … So all the people passed over to Al-Gizah and the Island and other parts, escaping in the boats; even the carefully guarded girls,

158 a–b Both sides of a re-carved marble panel
Egypt, found in Cairo. 500–650; re-carved 1470–1500
Marble.189.5 × 82 cm
Victoria and Albert Museum, London. A. 99-1930

Carved with a slim cross standing on a globe, this marble panel was probably used in a religious context, perhaps as part of a sanctuary screen for a church. The panel was repurposed about 1,000 years later when the reverse was carved with overlapping patterns – one of symmetrical cusped roundels and palmettes over another of arabesques – both of which were once gilded on a red ground. Only the circumstances of the panel's last phase of use in Cairo are known; it was built into a wall of a house near the Citadel where it had served as the backing for a small fountain. It was removed before 1930 when the street was widened. [ERO]
Bib: http://collections.vam.ac.uk/

who had never been outdoors, went away with their families, and the people left all their goods behind. And the caliph caused Misr to be set on fire from the south to the north until it reached the Great Mosque of the Muslims ... [22]

The core of Fustat around the fortress and along the river north of the great congregational Mosque of 'Amr ibn al-'As recovered, and continued to grow steadily to the northeast thereafter – gradually swallowing up the initially separate elite military or administrative centres of the cities al-'Askar and al-Qata'i', founded and developed under Abbasid rule (750–969), and those of the largely independent Tulunid (868–905) and Ikhshidid (935–69) dynasties. The close relationship between politics and landscape was continued by the siting of al-Qata'i' on the heights of Jebel Yashkur, dominating the entrance to the canal below. Ibn Tulun's palace and the magnificent congregational mosque that survives to this day became the latest venue for the expression and administration of power within the ceremonial and ritual space of the city.

Apart from the Arabs, the influx of new ethnic groups drawn to the rebuilt and culturally diverse city included at different times Berbers, Africans, Armenians, Turks and Andalusians, as well as Greeks and Syrians from the old Byzantine empire. The religious communities included Sunni and Shi'a Muslims as well as Jews and the various Christian denominations.[23] These demographics produced the pluralistic polyglot society that is reflected in early papyri and later in the Genizah documents (see ch. 18). It was a society that also melded vernacular and imported styles, and increasingly shared a common language of building, particularly in the areas of woodwork and stucco. However, the rich ethnic mix could also make the city a tumultuous place. Groups with intolerant ideas or a history of persecution fostered ethnic and religious tensions which had been present under the Umayyads and would resurface later under the Fatimids, but were most strongly felt during the period of direct Abbasid rule. Increasing Arabization of the administration and the population led to attempts to regulate contact between the different groups. Estimating the numbers involved is difficult, but the economic pressure of the poll tax certainly fuelled conversion to Islam, which was then further accelerated by edicts of the caliph al-Mutawakkil in AD 850 and 853 concerning renovated churches, sumptuary laws that required Christians and Jews to be identified by their dress, and the dismissal of non-Muslims from the administration. This legal discrimination would eventually lead to the fictitious rescript of 'Umar that falsely claimed these repressive measures went back to the early conquests (ch. 4).[24]

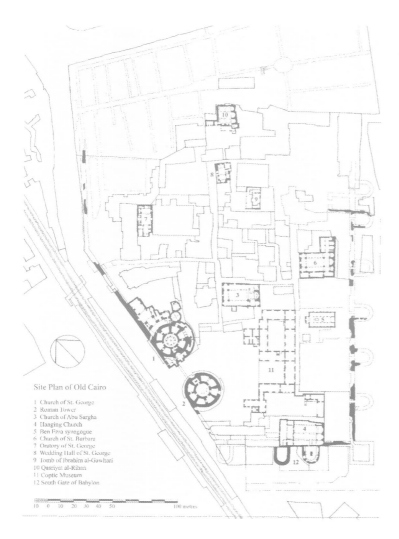

Site Plan of Old Cairo

1　Church of St. George
2　Roman Tower
3　Church of Abu Sargha
4　Hanging Church
5　Ben Ezra synagogue
6　Church of St. Barbara
7　Oratory of St. George
8　Wedding Hall of St. George
9　Tomb of Ibrahim al-Gawhari
10　Qasriyat al-Rihan
11　Coptic Museum
12　South Gate of Babylon

10　0　10　20　30　40　50　　　　　100 metres

159　Plan of Old Cairo

The Roman-period Fortress of Babylon – with its round gates and characteristic horseshoe-shaped towers – later enclosed medieval Old Cairo, including several churches and the Ben Ezra Synagogue

The conquest of Egypt by the Fatimids in AD 969 and the creation of the walled 'royal city' of al-Qahira to the north of the existing metropolis meant that, for the first time since Antiquity, Egypt and its capital became the centre of an empire ruling large parts of the Middle East, North Africa and Sicily, and trading with southern Europe through its Mediterranean ports and with South Arabia and India through the Red Sea (fig. 005). The imperial administration was centred in al-Qahira, but the continuing economic and political significance of Fustat and its port required the new rulers to reach out to both the elites and the general populace through programmes that combined ceremony and construction.

The city was also the centre of the Fatimid Shi'a-Ismaili caliphate. Minority rule over a sometimes hostile Sunni majority and substantial Christian and Jewish groups was generally achieved through consent and pragmatism, although repressive measures resurfaced under the caliph al-Hakim (996–1020). Religious debate between these groups flourished under the first two Fatimid caliphs, with one famous dispute regarding the power of faith to move mountains leading to the miracle of the Moving of the Muqattam and the salvation of the Christian community.[25] It is perhaps significant that this demonstration of the continuing relationship between belief and landscape preceded the rebuilding of churches in Fustat/Old Cairo, part of the major construction boom that took place there under the Fatimids. Many of the churches destroyed in 750 or neglected thereafter were restored, including the Church of Abu Sargha which was entirely rebuilt and furnished with a series of crypts that were probably intended for burials related to the shifting of the Coptic patriarchate to Old Cairo.[26] The conquest was accompanied by an influx of North African Jews. The revival of Fustat included the creation of a new Jewish quarter and the construction of at least two synagogues within the walls of the fortress, as testified to in the earliest documents of the Genizah archive.[27]

Both parts of the metropolis flourished under the early Fatimids, until the economic disasters and political turmoil of 'The Great Crisis' (1066–72) led to the final abandonment of Fustat for Cairo – a move sealed by the famous 1072 edict of the vizier Badr al-Jamali allowing its houses to be used for building material.[28] For a thousand years Fustat was a ruin field and a vast dumping ground, used for potteries, tanning and other noxious industries downwind of Cairo just to the north, but also the site of monasteries, mosques and tombs that grew up in this new desert at the edge of the metropolis. Even when the river shifted to the west and the port and economic life of the city moved north, the churches, mosques and synagogues of Old Cairo continued to be visited and revered by pilgrims and travellers of all three religions, drawn by the sacred associations of this ancient cultural landscape.

160 Oil lamp

Egypt, Fustat (?) 12th–13th century
Earthenware, glazed. 8.5 × 11.5 cm
Museum für Islamische Kunst, Staatliche Museen
zu Berlin. Inv. I. 3974

The lamp has a slightly waisted base, with a sturdy body, a funnel-shaped neck, a small handle and a long wick-holder, which is broken off at the end. This shape of lamp appears around the end of the Fatimid period and, with variations, remains the most widespread form of oil lamp in medieval Egypt. Many examples have been found in Fustat. [GH]

15 Mosques

Gisela Helmecke

161 Mosque of 'Amr, Qus

The modern interior of the 'Amr Mosque in Qus, Upper Egypt. On the right of the *mihrab* is the *minbar* erected in 1155.

OSQUE furnishings include architectural elements, decoration and equipment. The distinctive architectural element of a mosque is the *mihrab* (prayer niche),[1] located in the *qibla* wall (facing Mecca), usually prominantly. Built firmly into the wall, it is usually clad in stone, brick, stucco or ceramic. Wood was also used in the early medieval period – an ornate wooden *mihrab* was set up by the Fatimid caliph al-Amir (1101–30) in the al-Azhar Mosque in Cairo in the year 519 AH/AD 1125–26 – and also in other Fatimid mosques there were wooden *mihrabs*.[2]

The ornamentation of the interior and exterior walls, wooden ceilings, doors and windows are also part of the mosque's furnishings in the broadest sense. The inner walls of the Friday mosques of earlier periods in Alexandria and Cairo were decorated with mosaics under the Umayyads (seventh century and mid-eighth century). They must have resembled those in the Dome of the Rock and the al-Aqsa Mosque in Jerusalem, as well as the Umayyad Mosque of Damascus, with their different landscapes, city symbols and rich floral and ornamental decor. The walls were adorned with stone and stucco inscriptions, floral and ornamental patterned wood panels, as well as wooden bands of inscriptions. New constructions and the expansion and remodelling of existing mosques, regarded as a work of piety, were reflected in corresponding inscriptions (fig. 162).

Some architectural decoration was only temporary. The reasons for this lay in changed power relations, often coupled with new religious alignments. The Umayyad wall mosaics in the 'Amr Mosque in Old Cairo, for example, were eliminated under the Shiite Fatimids, and the Fatimid gold and silver inscription bands of the eleventh and twelfth centuries in the main mosques of Cairo were eliminated under the Sunni Mamluk Sultans of the fourteenth and fifteenth centuries. The choice of pious texts in the mosques was also determined by the religious alignment of the commissioner. Of particular value were the big wooden entrance doors. Whether simple or richly decorated with carvings, large doors were rescued when buildings were demolished, and incorporated into new ones. Doors were also donated, as can be seen from some of their inscriptions. The Fatimid caliph al-Hakim (996–1021), for example, donated to the al-Azhar Mosque a large wooden door with carving.[3]

162 Building inscription
Egypt, Cairo (?) 1098 (491 H)
Stone. 30 × 52 cm
Museum für Islamische Kunst, Staatliche Museen
zu Berlin. Inv. I. 6003

The text of the panel, written in angular
Kufic script, consists of 7 lines. The last of
these interrupts the middle of the beaded
border that frames the text. The outer
frame is formed by tendrils. The inscription
announces the founding of a mosque by Emir
Abu Mansur Khutlukh al-Afdali, one of the
followers of the distinguished and successful
Fatimid vizier and ruler al-Afdal (1094–1121).
A verse from the Qur'an (Sura 9.18) is given
at the beginning, according to which only
believers are allowed to support the mosque.
[GH]
Bib: RCEA 8 1937, no. 2867; Grohmann 2
1971, p. 58, pl. V/1

The most striking and largest piece of furnishing in a mosque is the *minbar* (prayer pulpit).[4] It is required for the Friday sermon and stands beside the prayer niche. Its introduction is attributed to the Prophet Muhammad, whose simple *minbar* with three steps is said to have been made by a Christian.[5] Initially reserved for the main (Friday) mosque in the governor's seat (in Cairo), from the middle of the eighth century prayer pulpits were provided in all provinces for their Friday mosques. These early pulpits were movable; they were brought in for the Friday sermon and then put away.[6] The medieval prayer pulpits of Egypt were usually made of wood, often with ornate exterior walls (fig. 161). Sometimes pulpits were exchanged for political or prestigious reasons. The pulpit donated to the 'Amr Mosque in Old Cairo by the Governor Qurra ibn Sharik, on behalf of the Umayyad caliph al-Walid I in 710, was in 378 AH/AD 988–89 replaced by a gilded one donated by the vizier Ibn Killis (died 991).[7] Ibn Killis was of Jewish origin, and after his conversion to Islam he rose to the highest office under the caliph. He was one of the most remarkable personalities of early medieval Egypt.[8] But after a reconstruction that enlarged the mosque, his pulpit was probably no longer prestigious enough – it was replaced by a new, 'larger' one when the Fatimid caliph al-Hakim had it taken in 1014 to the renovated 'Amr Mosque in Alexandria.

To determine prayer times, astrolabes were used in the main mosques and sundials were common. In the Mosque of Ibn Tulun in Cairo, there was a particularly precious sundial on the roof of the ablution house in the yard where Muslims washed before prayer. When it burned down in 986, the clock was lost. In other mosques sundials were carved on the pillars of the court arcades – such as the one that can still be seen in the Nasir Mosque (fourteenth century) in the Citadel of Cairo – or else they were simply carved into the walls.

163 Inlay panels with arabesque patterns

Egypt, Cairo. 1296
Wood. Each approx.18.5 × 14.5 cm
Museum für Islamische Kunst, Staatliche Museen zu Berlin.
Inv. I. 664, I. 633 and I. 661

Although these small polygonal panels date from
the Mamluk period, their densely carved arabesque
patterns are in the tradition of the best works of Fatimid
wood carving. The double ivory frame emphasizes the
exclusiveness of the pieces. They come from the *minbar*
of the Mosque of Ibn Tulun in Cairo, which was donated
by the Mamluk Sultan Lajin in 1296. After ascending
to power, Lajin ordered the dilapidated mosque to be
restored. While a reconstructed *minbar* has stood in the
mosque since 1910, the original inlay panels have been
scattered all over the world since the late 19th century.
There are over 90 pieces in the Victoria and Albert
Museum in London and 35 in the Museum of Applied
Arts in Vienna. There are 14 such panels in the Berlin
Museum, and the Louvre in Paris and the Metropolitan
Museum of Art in New York also have examples. All
were originally inserted in the basic framework of
narrow planks that formed the basis of the *minbar*. The
framework and panels, which were only held together
by tongue-and-groove joints, formed a unique overall
pattern of different stars and polygons. A few of the
framework planks are modern additions. [GH]
Bib: Heiden 2010

164 Inlay panel

Egypt, probably from Qus. First half of 12th century
Wood. 25 × 46.5 cm
Museum für Islamische Kunst, Staatliche Museen zu
Berlin. Inv. I. 2629

This elaborately carved panel displays an intricate
symmetrical pattern with fine detail. Pairs of
arabesque vine tendrils at the sides run in and out
of one another into the central ten-pointed star and
into the frame. The way the surface is completely
filled is a characteristic of Islamic art. In style it is
closely related to the panels of the *mihrab* from the
Mausoleum of Sayida Nafisa in Cairo, now in the
Cairo Museum of Islamic Art, and the *minbar* of the
'Amr Mosque of Qus in Upper Egypt, which is one
of the few Fatimid pulpits still standing in its place in
the mosque. Qus, an important hub for long-distance
trade, was largely Christian until the Fatimid period
and also had a Jewish community. The splendid
minbar was certainly intended as a clear sign of
Muslim supremacy. It was the gift of one of the
powerful men of the late Fatimid period, the vizier
Tala'i 'ibn Ruzzik. After coming into office in 1154
he ordered the renovation of the mosque and
presented it with the *minbar* in 1155. [GH]
Bib: Garcin 1976; Kaiser Friedrich II 2008, no. VI.39

165 Inscribed panel

Egypt. 10th century
Wood. Approx 9.5 × 21.5 cm
Museum für Islamische Kunst, Staatliche Museen
zu Berlin. Inv. I. 2629

This panel is part of a long Arabic inscription
frieze. It includes the words *wa-baraka* ('and
blessing'). The style of the script is known
as 'flowering Kufic', because of the many
floral elements – numerous small leaves on
short tendrils, which seem to merge into the
angular script. The origin and purpose of the
panel remain uncertain. It might have been
part of a piece of furniture, a door or a wall-
covering, and could equally well have started
life in a private or religious context. In religious
buildings the word *baraka* often precedes the
name of the person who commissioned the
building, to wish him God's blessing. [GH]

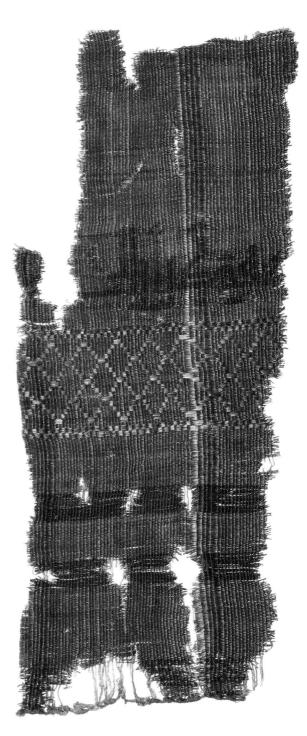

166 Fragment of a mat

Tabariya (Tiberias). Mid 10th century
Reed, hemp; partially dyed. 44 × 18 cm
Museum für Islamische Kunst, Staatliche Museen
zu Berlin. Inv. I. 68/63

Section from the under part of a small woven
mat, decorated with a band of diamond-shaped
lattice work, dyed red-brown stripes and an
inscription. The part of the inscription that has
been preserved says *fi-tiraz al-kh[assa]* ('in

the official *tiraz*'). Two complete mats in the
Benaki Museum in Athens and the Metropolitan
Museum of Art in New York show that the
fragment originates from the *tiraz* workshops
of Tabariya (Tiberias) on the Sea of Galilee.
The mats produced there were among the best
of their kind and were taken to Egypt – even
though very fine soft mats were also made in
Egypt, the best of them in Alexandria. [GH]
Bib: Helmecke 2012

Everything needed for the furnishing as well as for the maintenance of mosques was mostly provided by foundations (*waqf*) that were considered works of piety. These foundations for the great mosques were usually set up by the governor of the country or the caliph himself, but other members of the nobility – the court, the civil service, the merchant class, the military – also set up significant foundations. Women are also often recorded as endowing a *waqf*.

From the Fatimid era in Egypt, two foundation charters of the years 1009 and 1010 relating to donations by the caliph al-Hakim have been preserved, as well as reports of others.[9] The foundation document of the year 1010 primarily affects three mosques, of which only the al-Azhar Mosque still exists. It meticulously notes the distribution of income from each piece of property and estate for each item in the document. Everything that was needed in the mosque is listed here – besides the personnel expenses costs, we read about wax for large and small candles, lamp oil, lamp wicks, cleaning salt and replacement glass for the lamps of the candelabras, and fragrant smells (Indian aloes, camphor and musk are listed). Also listed are palm-fibre cords, hemp ropes, leather buckets, baskets, charcoals (for the burning of perfume and incense, and possibly for the portable stoves in the winter), brooms for cleaning, and two hundredweights of cloths for polishing the metal candlesticks.

Mats, woven in Egypt from hemp and reed, were the preferred material for the floor of the prayer room (fig. 116).[10] For the great mosques they were purchased in bulk, cut on site and placed in several layers. Particularly beautiful mats were laid out on top on feast days. Around the year 1000 these came mainly from the south Mesopotamian river island of 'Abadan.[11] Hakim's donation in 1009 lists 1,000 cubits of mats from 'Abadan. They should be available 'so that there is no shortage of mats'. Also purchased were 13,000 cubits of ordinary mats.

As in the churches and synagogues, there were large curtains in the mosques, usually on the doors and passages as well as forming dividers between men's and women's sections. On festivals and when the Fatimid caliph led the Friday prayers, mosques were decorated with precious textiles. In 1013, on its reopening after expansion and renovation, the al-Azhar Mosque was emblazoned with custom-made brocade curtains at its gates. The sumptuous decoration of the interior walls of the Hussein Mosque, with its precious silks and brocade hangings, was reported by

Ibn Jubayr in 1183. On such occasions the prayer pulpits were also decorated with fine cloths and mats. When the caliph said the Friday prayers, curtains decorated with Qur'anic verses were hung on either side of the *mihrab*. In front, silken carpets were laid.

Some items in the donation lists of al-Hakim refer to the lighting of the mosques, especially in the nights of the month of Ramadan and other holidays. Here several valuable pieces are mentioned. Three large silver chandeliers and thirty-nine silver candlesticks were to be used only in Ramadan. The copper and bronze chains on which the lamps and chandeliers were hung are mentioned separately. For the al-Anwar Mosque, founded by the caliph al-'Aziz and completed by his son al-Hakim, the caliph donated four large chandeliers and many candlesticks, all of silver. In 1013 al-Hakim placed a huge *tannur* (chandelier) in the 'Amr Mosque. It was so big that the doorposts had to be removed in order to bring it in.[12] Silver weighing 308 kg had been used for it. Silver and golden candlesticks with huge white wax candles (that looked like large columns, as Ibn Jubayr noted in 1183) often flanked the *mihrab* and stood around the shrines inside the mausoleums. These precious pieces illuminated the mosques only on feast days. Not mentioned in the documents are the ordinary ceramic oil lamps (see ch. 24), but glass is mentioned as a replacement for broken glass in lamps. This could refer – amongst others – to the glass insets in the traditional *polycandeloi* which were still used in the medieval period (see ch. 10). Other types of glass lamps were in the shape of a goblet or a cup (figs 167, 168). In all glass lamps the lamp oil floated on water. On holidays this water was coloured, thus creating coloured light effects.

Islam has no liturgical equipment, except, in the broadest sense, the Qur'an. Thousands of Qur'ans were donated for use in mosques. It is reported that in 1013

167 Candle holder (?)

Egypt. 9th–10th century
Glass. Height: 6.5 cm; diameter 13.3 cm
Museum für Islamische Kunst, Staatliche Museen zu Berlin. Inv. I. 1538

Small steep-sided bowl. The pinched decoration on the outside displays a frieze of simple palmettes and double vertical lines below a row of oval rings. The low ring on the base of the inside of the bowl may have served as a candle holder. [GH]

168 Oil lamp on a stand
Egypt. 9th–11th century
Glass. Height 20.5 cm; diameter 15.5 cm
Museum für Islamische Kunst, Staatliche Museen
zu Berlin. Inv. I. 2337

Hand-blown glass lamp with pressed-on
stand (stemmed glass); 3 rings pressed on to
the rim also allowed it to hang. This form of
lamp goes back to a type from Late Antiquity.
The lamp was filled with water and a layer of
oil, in which the burning wick floated. The wick
was kept in place by a wick-holder, usually
made of metal. The wick went out when the
oil was used up. Lamps of coloured glass
gave a particularly striking effect, sometimes
in combination with coloured water. [GH]

al-Hakim sent seven boxes with 1,298 Qur'ans of various sizes, some entirely written in gold, to the 'Amr Mosque,[13] and 814 Qur'ans to the Mosque of Ibn Tulun.

Boxes or small cabinets and shelves were used to store the Qur'ans, enabling multiple copies to be kept. Respect for the sacred word required careful handling of Scripture, so Qur'ans were (and are) given an additional protective cover, or were at least wrapped in a cloth. For the most precious copies of the Qur'an, elaborately crafted and richly decorated individual boxes of fine woods, expensive metal or ivory were made. Unfortunately, so far no box which can be dated to the period before 1300 has been clearly identified as a Qur'an container. The above-mentioned document of foundation of caliph al-Hakim of 1010 for the mosques in Cairo is not complete. It may therefore be that here also provision was made for protecting the Qur'ans possessed by the faithful.

The now common *rahla* (Qur'an stands) that look like folding chairs seem to have been introduced around the twelfth century. They were used generally as book stands, and could either have been kept in the mosque or used by the faithful for their own use.

16 Muslim Saints

Gisela Helmecke

ISLAM does not have saints in the Christian sense. The word for a holy person is *wali* (*waliya* in the feminine and *awliya'* in the plural). It actually means 'one who is under special protection' and 'friend', in the sense of God's friend. It is someone who is both guided by God and offers God worship and obedience.[1] Usually it is someone who, often from childhood, is a very pious, humble person blessed with miraculous powers. Many *awliya'* were also mystics (Sufis), founders of religious orders or brotherhoods.[2] One of the earliest Sufi saints was a woman living in Basra, in Iraq – Rabi'a al-'Adawiyya (died 801).[3]

In the rich literature on the ideas of the mystics a whole hierarchy of saints developed, though this was known only to experts.[4] In popular belief, a pious, often austere lifestyle and reports of a person's miraculous powers were sufficient for them to be considered saintly. Also, a 'madman' could be regarded as holy. Through the *baraka* (blessing) of the saints, people hoped for protection against all evils, a cure for diseases, and help to overcome infertility and indeed to combat all the perils of life. Many *awliya'* were patron saints of professions, brotherhoods or places. Several properties were often combined in a saint.[5] Accordingly, there were countless saints who were viewed only by those living in their proximity as saints, which meant they had a local character. Rural Egypt was covered with *qubbas* (small shrines) (fig. 169).

Some saints gained importance throughout all of Egypt. One, for example, is mentioned in the *tadhkirat al-awliya'* (Tales of the Saints) by Farid ad-Din 'Attar (died *c.*1221) – the Nubian Abu-l-Fa'id Thauban ibn Ibrahim al-Misri, known as Dhu-l-Nun al-Misri (ninth century).[6] Also thought to possess knowledge of hieroglyphs, Dhu-l-Nun is considered one of the most important early Sufis and a patron saint of physicians. Veneration of his grave in the cemetery of al-Qarafa al-Sughra, where the legal scholar al-Shafi'i (see below) is also buried, is attested from at least the twelfth century.[7] In the whole of Upper Egypt, 'Abd al-Rahman al-Maghribi al-Qanawi (died 1195), also a Sufi, is still revered – his grave is located in Qena.

Among the revered persons treated as saints, there are a number of figures from the family of the Prophet Muhammad). They were venerated everywhere and in every variant of Muslim belief. The prominent cults of Shiite saints supported by the Fatimids were therefore shared by the Sunni majority in Egypt. Many sanctuaries were built and ever more *mawlid* festivals commemorating the birthday of the saints were introduced. Many of these traditions were maintained in the following centuries or even extended (see ch. 21). It was believed that the power of blessing attributed to the

169 Qubba

Domed tomb of an unknown local saint.
Photograph taken by an unknown
photographer in the 1950s.

saints extended over and beyond their graves, to the shrines, mausoleums and mosques that were built over them. Merely by visiting such a building one could share in the power of this blessing, especially by touching. The sale and purchase of relics was common. In mausoleums, as in mosques, the donating of precious chandeliers and other pieces of equipment, and the installation of *waqf* (pious foundations) for maintenance of the building, were viewed as pious deeds.

The largest Shiite shrine in Egypt is the Hussein Mosque in Cairo, also revered by Sunnis. Built under the Fatimids in the twelfth century it houses a shrine in which the head of the grandson of the Prophet Muhammad – al-Hussein, who was murdered in 680 – is said to be preserved. It was kept in a silver casket, as reported by the traveller Ibn Jubayr who travelled from Andalusia in 1183. This casket stood in a precious large wooden box with extraordinarily beautiful carved calligraphy and ornamentation (fig. 171).[8] The shrine of 'Our Lord Hussein' (*sayyidna* al-Hussein) is still a centre of pilgrimage.[9] Another such pilgrimage centre is the shrine of al-Hussein's sister, Zainab (*sayyida* Zainab), which has existed in Cairo since the Fatimid era.[10]

The mausoleums of other female members of the family of the Prophet Muhammad have also remained centres of pilgrimage, especially for women. One mausoleum[11] contains the grave of Nafisa (died early 825), a great-granddaughter of the Prophet's second grandson al-Hasan.[12] Making thirty pilgrimages to Mecca, Nafisa was considered particularly religious and is credited with numerous miracles and extraordinary powers of blessing. Likewise, the conversion of Jews and Christians to Islam is attributed to her miracles, and forms part of her legendary repertoire.[13] Over the centuries she was given the status of a patron saint of Cairo, though only after the Fatimid era. Reports on the veneration of her grave begin in the tenth century shortly before the Fatimid conquest of Egypt, and then intensify in the Fatimid era, together with an intense official devotion to the tombs of the family of the Prophet.[14] In order to share in the power of its *baraka* (blessings), many people were

170 Hussein Mosque

View of the Hussein Mosque in Cairo as it is today. The mosque is situated in the Old Town district of Cairo, near the al-Azhar Mosque, and has been completely rebuilt over the course of the centuries. The shrine inside was part of the original Fatimid building of 1154. The minaret dates from the year 1237. On the left we can see one of the great furled umbrellas, opened on Fridays and festivals to provide shade for the many visitors. [GH]

buried near her grave, as is also the case with many saints' tombs. In the course of time, this produced an entire graveyard.[15]

The grave of Imam al-Shafi'i, the founder of one of the four legal schools of Islam, was already revered in Cairo in Fatimid times. Around the grave a mosque, a mausoleum and a *madrasa* (educational establishment) were built. The complex included 'baths and other facilities providing comfort', as Ibn Jubayr, who saw the expansion of the mosque under the Ayyubid Sultan Saladin, reported. Construction was personally supervised by Sheikh Imam Najm al-Din al-Khabushani. People such as this religious scholar, whose fame had reached Spain, were also credited with a great power to bless. Ibn Jubayr, along with his travelling companion, duly visited the great Sheikh 'in his mosque in Cairo in the narrow little room where he lives. He prayed for us, and then we left him. Among all the men of Egypt we saw none who could match him'.[16] In order to obtain as many blessings as possible, Ibn Jubayr and his companion – they were both on the pilgrimage to Mecca – also visited the tombs and grave mosques of various *sheikhs*, *imams* and members of the family of the Prophet in Cairo and in other places.

Despite various transformations, the belief in the efficacy of the holy, in whatever form, has survived up until today in broad swathes of the population of Egypt. The *mawlid* of Zainab in her mosque in Cairo, for example, lasts for several days and is one of the largest festivals of its kind in Egypt.

171 Wooden cenotaph

Egypt, Cairo, Hussein Mosque. 12th century
Museum of Islamic Art, Cairo. Inv. MIA 15025

Detail of the upper part of the front of the wooden cenotaph
from the shrine of the Hussein Mosque. It dates from the
12th century and its decoration is mainly composed of
inscriptions – appeals to God, and verses from the Qur'an.
The detail shows coffering and a large inscription in vertical
Kufic script above spiralling vine tendrils. The whole is
framed by narrower bands of cursive inscriptions on a spiral
background. Inscriptions can also be seen on the octagons
of the coffering. [GH]

17 Egypt and the Hajj

Venetia Porter

172 A treatise on the sacred direction to Mecca

Egypt. 12th century
Paper. 19 × 12.5 cm
Bodleian Library, Oxford. Marsh 592, fol. 88v

The *qibla* is here rendered as a red line from each of 4 cities. Labeled from right to left, the cities are Cairo, Jerusalem, Damascus and Aleppo. The Hajj route is represented by a red wavy line. Commencing from Cairo or Jerusalem, the routes meet at the Red Sea port of Aila (modern Aqaba, Jordan) before proceeding to Medina, at the left, and on to the Ka'aba in Mecca (represented by the square at top-left). The drawing is part of a treatise written by the Egyptian legal scholar al-Dimyati. [ERO]
Bib: Porter 2012, p. 110, fig. 75

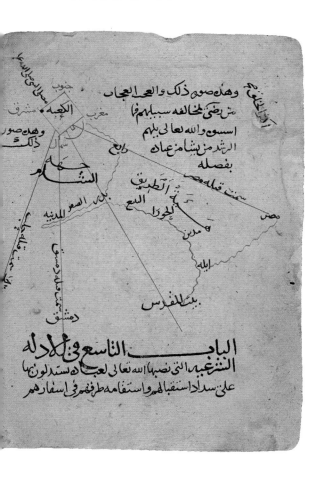

AS the fifth pillar of Islam, there is an obligation upon Muslims to make the pilgrimage known as Hajj to Mecca if they are able. It takes place in the 12th month of the Islamic calendar, Dhu-al-Hijja. As Islam uses a lunar calendar, it occurs at different seasons of the year. The rituals which take place between the 8th and the 13th of Dhu-al-Hijja include the *tawaf*, during which pilgrims will circumambulate the Ka'aba seven times, and will then perform a series of other rituals in and around Mecca.[1]

As the Muslim empire expanded, the pilgrims came from increasingly further afield.[2] Those seeking to go on Hajj from Egypt had several options as to which route to take. These routes were not all, however, simply for pilgrimage – they were also used for trade, or for military purposes, and were therefore affected by the geopolitics of the Red Sea region at different moments in time.[3] The most frequently used route from Cairo, which acted as the hub for pilgrims from not only Egypt but also from north and west Africa, started at Birkat al-Hajj outside the city (ch. 14). Continuing across Sinai to the port of Aqaba, the route then went down into the Hijaz to Medina and on to Mecca. This route was used in the early Islamic era up to the early twelfth century, for reasons outlined below, and again from the rule of the Mamluk Sultan Baybars (reigned 1260–77) who, with other sultans, built water installations and forts for the protection of pilgrims.[4]

A key trading post and port was Qulzum (Suez). The site of ancient Klysma, it had been connected by canal to the Nile and to Fustat (ancient Babylon). It was caliph 'Umar ibn al-Khattab (reigned 634–44), the second of the Rightly Guided Caliphs, who ordered that the canal, having silted up, should be dredged so that it could be used to send supplies of grain from Qulzum to the Hijaz. Taking the sea route from Qulzum to al-Jar for Medina (as did the traveller Nasir-i Khusraw on his second Hajj in 1048[5]) or to Jeddah for Mecca was a popular route for pilgrims who did not want to cross Sinai, and there is evidence of consistent but sometimes intermittent use of the port of Qulzum from the seventh until the nineteenth century.[6]

Crusader expansion at the beginning of the twelfth century meant that, between 1116 and 1187, a network of castles rendered the land routes between Egypt and Syria impassable and Muslim pilgrims from Egypt had to find alternative routes – the principal one being up the Nile and across the desert to 'Aidhab.[7] It has been suggested that the port of 'Aidhab was founded soon after the Islamic conquest of Egypt, as part of the campaign (led by 'Abdallah ibn Abi Sarh) to capture Aswan, and that the rise of the port-town in the ninth century can be attributed in part to the development of the Hajj.[8] In the late ninth century, Ya'qubi wrote that 'people sail from it ['Aidhab] to Mecca, the Hijaz and Yemen, and merchants come to it and carry [away] gold and ivory in boats'.[9] It continued as an active port well into the thirteenth century.

From soon after the conquest of Egypt in 639, there are references to Hajj in a variety of ways. The principal context is the offering of the textile known as *kiswa*. Made to cover the Ka'aba, it was replaced every year during Hajj in a tradition that existed before Islam, when the Ka'aba was the focus of a pre-Islamic cult. Following the death of the Prophet Muhammad in 632, the prerogative of providing the sacred cloth fell to whoever had suzerainty over the holy cities of Mecca and Medina. Since Egypt had been an important centre of textile production for centuries before Islam, it was logical that the same factories should be used by the Muslim rulers for this important task, and this was put into immediate effect by 'Umar ibn al-Khattab. Azraki, historian of Mecca, writing in about 859 said: 'Umar ibn al-Khattab covered the Ka'aba with *qubati* [Coptic] from the treasury. He used to write concerning it to Egypt [Misr] where it was woven for him, and then 'Uthman did the same after him.'[10] Serjeant identified the location of manufacture of these *qubati* cloths as the *tiraz* factories around Damietta (see focus 7). The practice of making the sacred textiles in Egypt continued thereafter until the twentieth century.[11]

As far as individuals going on Hajj is concerned, an early reference to the practice is in a papyrus document dating to between 705 and 709 (fig. 173).[12] This is an invitation to go on Hajj by Sahl ibn 'Abd al-'Aziz to 'Uqba ibn Muslim al-Tujibi, in which Sahl states that the caliph himself (Walid I, reigned 705–15) is asking people to go on Hajj but that he must pay for the cost of his own camels. Both these men are mentioned in other sources; 'Uqba is likely to be a deputy governor of Fustat. It demonstrates the early importance of going on Hajj and how key members of the ruling elite were being encouraged to make the journey, thereby setting an example to others.

The writings of two Hajj-going travellers, Nasir-i Khusraw and Ibn Jubayr, give us clear descriptions of the route and the experience of the journey. The Persian traveller Nasir-i Khusraw (died 1088) was an Isma'ili from present-day Tajikistan, whose intention, in addition to performing Hajj (which he did four times between 1047 and 1050), was to visit the Fatimid court in Cairo. It is his last Hajj in 1050 that is the most relevant in the present context, for he chose to take the Nile route that was becoming increasingly popular at this time. It was high summer, and sailing first to Asyut he then went on to Akhmim and Aswan via Qus. He describes how he remained at Qus for twenty days, 'because there were two routes from here, one through arid desert and the other by river, and we could not decide which way to take'. In the end he decides to take the river route to Aswan.[13] From there he undertook a punishing

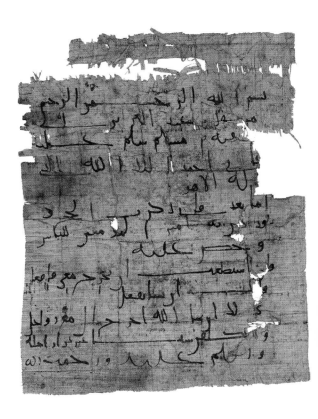

173 An invitation for Hajj

Egypt. 705–9
Papyrus. 24 × 20.5 cm
Oriental Institute Museum, University of Chicago.
Papyrus OI 17653

This is the earliest known documentary evidence for Hajj. The writer tells the recipient that the caliph – 'the commander of the believers' – has announced Hajj and that he should prepare to travel, his only concern being the rental of a camel to undertake the journey. The document demonstrates the caliph's role as leader and patron, mobilizing the elite probably in a series of caravans from the empire's capitals. The writer, Sahl ibn 'Abd al-'Aziz, was probably a son of the governor of Egypt, 'Abd al-'Aziz ibn Marwan (in office 684–705). The recipient is probably 'Uqba ibn Muslim al-Tujibi (died. *c*.737), who was later appointed deputy governor of Fustat (721). Both men are known from other sources to have transmitted Hadith. [ERO]
Bib: Sijpesteijn 2014

174 The Temple of Horus at Edfu

View of the Ptolemaic-period temple from the south-east, with the pylon rising dramatically over the Nile flood plain, c.1800. [ERO]

175 Arabic inscription at Temple of Horus at Edfu

On the eastern face of the girdle wall of the temple, in the uppermost register, is depicted the seated god Horus on his throne. The figure of the god was hacked out at some unknown point in time. The throne was used as a framing device by the anonymous pilgrim, who passed by in the 10th or 11th century and invoked the reader of his inscription to say a prayer for his safe return. [ERO]

fifteen-day journey across the desert to 'Aidhab, where he had to wait for three months for the right wind to take him to Jeddah.[14]

Although he does not mention it, Nasir-i Khusraw must have gone through Edfu, the dramatic ancient Egyptian site where, on the throne of the seated god Horus in the uppermost register on the eastern face of the girdle wall, is an Arabic inscription in Kufic script that has been ascribed to the tenth/eleventh century (figs 174, 175).[15] The stopping places along the Hajj routes of Arabia are full of the graffiti of pilgrims, and there is also evidence of such graffiti at sites around Aswan.[16] Through their texts, the travellers offer themselves to God's mercy, ask for protection on their journey or otherwise record their presence, sometimes with their names and the date they were there.[17] The Edfu text bears no name or date but touchingly states: 'In the name of God the Merciful [the Compassionate]. Remember me if I go away and say, may you return safely oh stranger. And we remembered you oh stranger and we said may God return you safely soon.'[18]

Ibn Jubayr took the Nile route in 1183, shortly after the fall of the Fatimid period in 1171 and in the early years of the reign of Saladin (reigned 1169–93). He went this way because of the disruption caused by the Crusader presence. His route differed from that of Nasir-i Khusraw, taken a little over a hundred years earlier, in that he went only as far as Qus (not Aswan). From there he took the desert route to 'Aidhab. Ibn Jubayr's account of his journey is highly evocative. He was travelling both as a pilgrim and a tourist, and his description of Akhmim is extremely detailed:

The most remarkable of the temples of the world talked of for their wonder is the great temple east of the city… the ceiling of this temple is wholly formed of slabs of stone so wonderfully joined as to seem to be one single piece… each slab has a different painting. Some are adorned with comely pictures of birds with outstretched wings making the beholder believe they are about to fly away; others are embellished with images of men, very beautiful to look upon and elegant in form… Within and without this great temple… there was hardly a space… which did not have an image or engraving or some hieroglyphic writing that is not understood.[19]

Once on the land road to 'Aidhab he describes how, while the more affluent pilgrims travelled in litters and played chess, poorer pilgrims rode their camels sitting on top of their luggage in the heat of the burning sun. They would stop at watering holes, sometimes for several days at a time. Eventually arriving at 'Aidhab, Ibn Jubayr describes disparagingly how the inhabitants treated the pilgrims: 'they load the *jilab* (boats) with them until they sit one on top of the other so they are crammed in a coop. To this they are prompted by avarice, wanting the hire… "ours is to produce the ships: the pilgrims to protect their lives". This is a common saying amongst them.'[20]

Going on Hajj was arduous; people fell prey to abuse, became sick and died. G.W. Murray, who visited 'Aidhab in 1926 noted: 'the most striking feature of the site, and a rather depressing one, is the disproportionately large size of the cemeteries compared with the smallness of the town'.[21] He had counted some 3000 graves. The cemetery at Aswan with its numerous graves, which probably included not only the inhabitants of this prosperous city but those who had come on Hajj,[22] also testifies to the huge toll that performing the spiritual journey of Hajj could take.

176 Battle between Arabs and Franks
Egypt, Fustat. 12th or 13th century
Painting on paper. 21 × 31.4 cm
British Museum, London. ME 1938,0312,0.1

Discovered at Fustat, this fragment depicts the siege of a town. The defenders, although wearing turbans, can be identified as Franks by their long shields. A Muslim warrior appears only in the upper right, recognizable by his round shield. The dramatic scene shows archers and equestrian soldiers as well as foot soldiers with lances. [GH]
Bib: Cat. Paris 2001, no. 62, p. 94

18 The Cairo Genizah

Esther-Miriam Wagner

THE Cairo Genizah is our name for the contents of a storeroom in the Ben Ezra Synagogue in Old Cairo/Fustat, that were discovered at the end of the nineteenth century. This most valuable treasure trove of manuscripts was amassed in a walled-off chamber. Jewish custom dictates that anything that may have the name of God written on it cannot be destroyed, and instead must be handled with care and either stored away or buried. Every medieval synagogue would have had a Genizah, but the Cairo Genizah is special in that its contents were never buried. Instead, members of the Jewish community placed their discarded writings into the Cairo Genizah over the course of hundreds of years.[1]

Thus, like a giant wastepaper basket, the Genizah has preserved all sorts of writing – alongside Bibles, religious works and prayer books are literary works (fig. 183), magical amulets, medical prescriptions, writing exercises (figs 178, 223) and other documents. Most of the material dates from the tenth to the thirteenth centuries, but some of the manuscripts are even older; they were possibly contained in a room previously used for storage, and transferred to the Ben Ezra Synagogue when the Genizah chamber was built. In addition to the medieval sources, there are also a large number of documents from the seventeenth to the nineteenth centuries. Marriage contracts, wills and divorce deeds of ordinary Jewish Egyptians were mixed up in the same heap of manuscripts as autographs of the important personalities of the time. Recommendation letters and answers to legal queries are written in the cursive Spanish hand of Maimonides, arguably the greatest Jewish thinker of all time, in addition to drafts of some of his most important works. His replies to legal issues raised by members of the Jewish community convey the picture of a very pragmatic leader, and are sometimes rather brief (fig. 179). Documents composed by the famous poet Judah ha-Levi are preserved in the Genizah, as well as correspondence in the hands of Isaac Luria, the 'father of contemporary Kabbala', and Joseph Karo, one of the great rabbinic authorities of Jewish law.

Not only Jewish texts were deposited. We also find a number of texts of Muslim provenance, such as pages with extracts from the Qur'an (fig. 224) and Islamic religious literature, documents and petitions from the Fatimid and Ayyubid chanceries, or books of a sci-

177 Deciphering the Cairo Genizah

After the polymath twins Mrs Lewis and Mrs Gibson introduced their Cambridge colleague Solomon Schechter to manuscripts they had acquired in the Middle East in 1896, he endeavoured to locate the source and acquire the bulk for study. Today the Taylor-Schechter Collection of the University of Cambridge holds about 140,000 manuscripts from the Cairo Genizah. Schechter (shown here at work in Cambridge) described the Genizah thus: 'It is a battlefield of books, and the literary production of many centuries had their share in the battle, and their *disjecta membra* are now strewn over its area.' [ERO]

178 School primer

Egypt, Old Cairo, Ben Ezra Synagogue. 11th century (?)
Vellum. 16.7 cm; 23.4 cm
Cambridge University Library, Cambridge. T-S K 5.13

This colourful children's Hebrew teaching aid is designed
to interest and delight children. It is one of a large number
of Cairo Genizah fragments depicting the world of children
through their scribbles and Hebrew writing exercises. Such
an early use of the *magen david* (star of David), together with
other Jewish symbols, makes this a particularly interesting
example. [EMW]

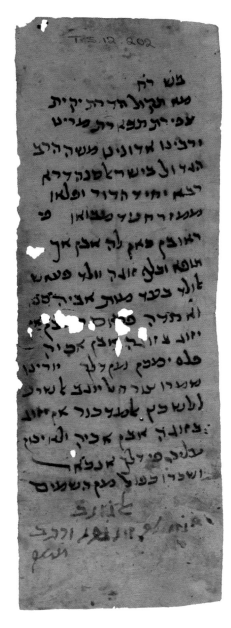

179 Response from Maimonides

Egypt, Old Cairo, Ben Ezra Synagogue.
12th century
Paper. 24.1 cm; 8 cm
Cambridge University Library, Cambridge.
T-S 12.202

In response to a question regarding whether
or not someone can marry his nephew's
widow, the great Jewish scholar Maimonides
replies: 'He is permitted to marry her'. [EMW]

entific and philosophical nature. Many of these last works are translations of Greek and Syriac texts, gathered under the Abbasids as part of the Greek and Syriac translation movement, where Muslim, Christian and Jewish scholars endeavoured to codify much of the existing knowledge in the world in Arabic. Christian texts were found among the Genizah sources too, although to a much smaller extent than their Jewish and Muslim counterparts. Some of these Christian texts, in particular those conserved as the lower layers of palimpsests, are extremely precious, such as Aquila's translation of the Hebrew Bible and leaves from Origen's *Hexapla*.

The Genizah contains thousands of documents from all walks of life – private and official letters, marriage and divorce documents, deathbed wills and documents from the Jewish chanceries. Thousands of legal documents detail business transactions and communal affairs. For the inter-communal relationships between members of the different faith communities, the business correspondence and documents are the most revealing sources (fig. 182). Trade can provide a platform in which members of different religious groups easily mingle, for the protagonists' religious backgrounds become secondary as economic self-interest outweighs confessional differences.

The Fatimid period was the economic heyday for the medieval Egyptian economy, and its trade networks spanned the entire Mediterranean.[3] The Genizah documents reveal that at the time extensive Jewish business networks were active from Syria and Persia via North Africa all the way to Spain. These Jewish networks often operated in partnerships with Muslims, whereas the members of the other Egyptian minority – Christians – are rarely mentioned as trading partners. This may be the reason why the Genizah is relatively silent on the topic of medieval Jewish-Christian relations, except for some amusing tales of Christian women, eager to convert when approaching the Jewish community in search of suitable husbands, or of an illicit love affair between a Christian doctor and a Jewish girl. It is only in late medieval documents that we hear about trade relations between Jewish Egyptian merchants and the Italians and Spanish, who came to dominate Mediterranean trade from the end of the eleventh century onwards.

Some Jewish traders had exclusively Muslim business associates.[4] We know of Muslim–Jewish partnerships concerning large sums of money, and there is ample evidence that Muslims acted as business agents for Jews and vice versa. These sorts of relationships would run in families, first with the father then with his sons. Jewish travellers carried consignments for Muslims, and in times of heavier custom payments for non-Muslims the same thing occurred the other way around. As much of the business was conducted on a personal basis grounded on trust, there had to be tight relations and even friendship between partners.

The writer of one letter, for example, recommends his Muslim business partners to a Jewish associate. He praises them as 'two distinguished, honourable and very trustworthy people', and asks his partner to take care of them, protect them and buy what they bring with them (T-S 8J19.24). If the Jewish partners send their wares with the Muslims, this will strengthen the writer's reputation. Introducing Muslim partners into a Jewish business network was therefore probably a common phenomenon.

Most of the correspondence was written in Hebrew script. With Jewish schooling based exclusively on the Bible, this was the alphabet they knew best (fig. 178). The language the traders spoke and wrote, however, was Arabic, which we call Judaeo-Arabic when it is written in Hebrew characters. While nearly all Jewish traders were literate in Hebrew script, many could also write Arabic. Nissim bin Halfon, a prolific letter writer in the Genizah, scribbled in the margin of one letter: 'I just wrote a letter to Ali b. al-Marabut, which is inside this letter of mine. But it is in Hebrew script. Give it to him and read it out to him, please!' (T-S 8J18.33). Thus the Jewish partner, able to read Hebrew script, would read the Arabic out to the Muslim partner in order to relay Nissim's message.

From legal queries, we know about workshops in which Muslims and Jews worked together. Such collaboration enabled them to keep the shops open on Friday, the Muslim day of prayer, and on Shabbat.[5] Muslim partners would even copy the day of rest from their Jewish partners – the shop's proceeds from Friday would go to Jews, whereas those from Saturday would belong to the Muslim partners. Although Friday is not a day of rest for Muslims, they would effectively have Fridays off in exchange for their Jewish partners' Sabbath rest.

Certainly, these inter-communal partnerships could cause friction. A legal document (fig. 182) details the problems of a Jewish silkweaver, who worked with Muslims and a Jewish convert to Islam, when the latter started a bullying campaign against his Jewish colleague. We have to bear in mind, though, that the reason for the production of a legal document in the Genizah sources or in any legal writing is typically to announce or solve a problem; peaceful coexistence tends to leave less of a trace in the legal records.

Business letters provide ample evidence about personal relations between Muslims and Jews. For example, a partner writes to the merchant prince Nahray bin Nissim that the government's finance director and the *qadi* ask about his well-being every day. In another letter (fig. 181), the writer describes how he will go into the house of a Muslim partner to congratulate him and his family on the occasion of a Muslim holiday. Business relations could thus spawn cordial personal relationships that bridged the cultural and religious divide.

180 Letter detailing revolt in Damascus

Egypt, Old Cairo, Ben Ezra Synagogue. 1050
Paper. 29.8 × 8.6 cm
Cambridge University Library, Cambridge.
T-S 13J26.13

This Hebrew letter was probably sent from the Jewish community in Damascus (officially under Fatimid rule) to the Jewish authorities in Jerusalem. It tells the story of how the Bedouin rose up and took control of Damascus. They then, in conjunction with the local mob, cut off the Jewish community's access to water, saying 'Why should the Hebrews drink from our water?', and introduced other harsh measures, such as unfair taxes. By appealing to the Fatimid government, and through the payment of bribes to the newly appointed governor, the water supply is restored and anti-Jewish measures against the community are reversed. [EMW]

181 A merchant's letter

Egypt, Old Cairo, Ben Ezra Synagogue. 1030
Paper. 20.5 × 18.2 cm
Cambridge University Library, Cambridge.
T-S 13J17.11

In this Judaeo-Arabic letter the writer, a merchant
called Kalluf bin Zechariah, reports to his business
partner, the merchant prince Joseph bin Jacob
Ibn 'Awkal, that he intends to visit a Muslim friend
and business partner to congratulate him on a
Muslim holiday. [EMW]

182 Legal document

Egypt, Old Cairo, Ben Ezra Synagogue. 12th century
Paper. 25 cm; 17.4 cm
Cambridge University Library, Cambridge. T-S NS J277

A legal document concerning a workshop in which
Muslims and Jews work together. [EMW]

183 Front and back of illustrated leaf of
Kalila wa-Dimna

Egypt, Old Cairo, Ben Ezra Synagogue.
c.13th–15th century
Paper. 31 x 24.2 cm
Cambridge University Library, Cambridge. T-S Ar. 51.60

Kalila wa-Dimna is a collection of originally Indian
inter-related animal fables called the *Panchatantra*,
translated into Persian and then into Arabic.
This leaf shows the fable of the lioness and her
cub. The presence of this in the Cairo Genizah
suggests that it was read in the Jewish community,
too. [EMW]

BELIEF AND PRACTICE ACROSS THE FAITHS

5

5 INTRODUCTION

IN the first and early second centuries, Jews in Egypt are barely visible in the archaeological record due to the bloody suppression of the Jewish uprisings by the Romans. Only towards the end of the third century do they seem to settle there again, even if in considerably smaller numbers than in Ptolemaic or Roman times. For centuries they lived unobtrusively and without significant conflicts within other populations in Egypt. The day-to-day needs were the same for all people in the country, and therefore also their material culture. Jews, Christians and Muslims shared – in addition to their common forefather Abraham (ch. 1) – a preference for certain saints and heroes. Thus the Archangel Gabriel (in Hebrew Gawriel, Arabic Jabra'il) is considered in all three religions to be the bearer of God's word and of other good news (ch. 19). Joseph, the Patriarch from the Old Testament, was particularly venerated because of his direct connection to Egypt (ch. 20). The shared experience of the Nile also found common expression in festivals (ch. 21).

For several centuries Greek was the official language; in the countryside Coptic, the final stage of the ancient Egyptian language written in Greek script, was spoken. Within Jewish communities, Hebrew and Aramaic were used. With the new religion the Arabs eventually also brought a new language and a new script to Egypt. Both were adopted gradually. Like the Christians, Jews eventually used Arabic as an everyday language, often using Hebrew script (learned from a young age) to write it, in what is known today as Judeo-Arabic (ch. 23). Thus the limits of languages attributed to respective religions – 'pagan'/Greek, Christian/

184 Wall painting with the three Hebrews in the fiery furnace and the martyrs Cosmas and Damian

Egypt, excavated near Wadi Sarga 1914.
c.6–7th century
Painting on stucco
86 × 144.5 cm
British Museum, London. EA 73139

The central narrative scene of this wall painting depicts the 3 Hebrews – originally labelled Ananias, Azarias and Mishael – in the furnace, together with an angel (Daniel 3:19–30). They wear characteristic 'Eastern' dress, with pointed caps and patterned leggings. The Coptic text below the scene names the probable donors and otherwise unattested Egyptian martyrs, probably represented by the floating busts to the right of the framed text: ['The 60 martyrs of Samalut. Their day the 12th of (the month) Mechir. Esurkene, the Little, my brother, Mena, the Little' (*SB Kopt.* 1.321).] Framing this scene and painted in a different style, the figures of the internationally renowned physician saints Cosmas and Damian stand in praying pose, dressed in tunics and coats and holding bags carrying their medical instruments, together with their brothers, shown standing between them and labelled Anthinmos, Leontios and Eupredios. The composition neatly layers 3 sets of figures representing salvation through faith in God, proto-martyrs from the Jewish Bible, local Egyptian and international Christian martyrs. [ERO]
Bib: Dalton 1916; Papaconstantinou 2001, pp. 131–32, p. 225; O'Connell 2014a, p. 133, figs 72–74

Coptic, Islamic/Arabic and Hebrew/Jewish – were permeable.

One cannot discern an abrupt break with the previous epoch when new cultures were being established – whether in the fourth century with the spread of Christianity in the countryside, where there was a multiplicity of gods, or in the seventh century with the takeover by the Arabs of an Egypt that had until then been ruled from Constantinople. Rather, a slow cultural change takes place. Many customs remained in existence – transformed, if at all, only gradually. In the medieval period Jews, Christians and Muslims could in principle

exercise any profession. Preferential treatment of certain professions had primarily social causes. Christian and Jewish craftsmen seem to have worked for Muslim clients, as well as the other way round. Joint use of workshops and commercial enterprises was not uncommon (ch. 26).

Independently of religious affiliations, the same forms and motifs were generally used for items of daily use (ch. 24). The 'neutral' iconography of Classical Antiquity – plants, animals, hunting scenes, ornamentation – remained the pattern for decoration of everyday objects. In the medieval period the Arabic script itself became an important aspect of visual culture.

Arabic calligraphy and new patterns were predominant from about the early ninth century. In spite of recurring bans, there are no differences in style of dress visible between the religious groups (ch. 25, see also focus 6). Remnants of old Egyptian ideas were mixed with Jewish, Christian and Muslim traditions (ch. 22). In funerary customs, traditional practices in a modified form were still maintained into the early Islamic period (ch. 27). Definite delimitations are however evident on the tomb stones, which show clear confessions of the respective faith (focus 10). In representations of Paradise there are common elements (ch. 28, ch. 29). [CF]

19 Archangel Gabriel: A Divine Messenger

Clara ten Hacken and Gertrud J. M. van Loon

185 Resist-dyed hanging depicting the Annunciation

Egypt, Akhmim. 6th century AD
Dyed linen. 55 × 68 cm
Victoria and Albert Museum, London. 723-1897

The Archangel Gabriel (centre) appears before the seated Virgin (left), identified by a Greek label as 'Maria', to announce that she will conceive and become the mother of Jesus Christ. The Annunciation is only briefly described in the Gospel of Luke (lines 26–38). Its iconography developed mainly from the apocryphal tradition, in which the Virgin is surprised by Gabriel while preparing threads to make the Temple veil. This textile fragment has been dyed blue using the resist-dye technique. The larger textile of which the fragment was a part was divided into individual scenes by borders and twisted columns, and may have been a wall hanging, probably depicting several scenes from the life of Jesus or Mary. [AM]
Bib: Kendrick 1922, III, no. 785, pp. 64–65, pl. XIX

ANGELS are members of the heavenly court. The Book of Daniel mentions two angels by name – Michael[1] and Gabriel[2] – and Raphael figures in the Book of Tobit. In the angelic hierarchy they are known as archangels, the first among the ranks, assigned special missions and closest to God.[3] They are God's servants and carry out his orders; they glorify him and participate in the heavenly liturgy. They guard his throne; on earth they are the guardians of mankind, teachers and mediators. Hence, they link heaven and earth and play an important role in Judaism, Christianity and Islam alike. Through time, the archangels acquired distinct characteristics and tasks and were a source of fascination and creative imagination.[4]

Michael is the chief angel, and Gabriel is second in rank and importance. His declaration 'I am Gabriel, messenger of God' (Luke 1:19) defines his role. From Yahweh to the prophet Daniel, from God the Father to the High Priest Zacharias and to the Virgin Mary, from Allah to the Prophet Muhammad, Gabriel conveys the words of the Most High. His name means 'Man of God', 'Power of God' or 'God has shown himself powerful'.[5] An incorporeal spiritual being, he reveals himself to mankind in the guise of a winged man radiating light and fire.[6] Anonymous angels in Jewish, Christian and Islamic scriptures were often identified with archangels known by name. One of the three angels visiting Abraham at Mamre to announce the birth of his son Isaac (Genesis 18:1–15) was seen as Gabriel.[7]

In Jewish tradition, Gabriel clarifies the apocalyptic visions given to Daniel (Daniel 7–12).[8] With Michael, Raphael and Suriel, he is assigned special functions in the heavenly court[9] and acts as intercessor of the righteous.[10] He is the angel of fire and, true to his name, the angel of power. Magic (amulets, invocations, curses, spells) and legend exploit his qualities to the fullest. His name is used in incantations; he saves the three young men, Hananiah, Mishael and Azariah, from the fiery furnace (Dan. 3:23–28); and he is sent to destroy the city of Sodom with fire (Gen. 19:24).[11] He helped Joseph[12] and taught him the seventy languages;[13] he is the angel of the summer and harvest.[14] Jewish art was largely aniconic because of the biblical prohibition of making graven images (Ex. 20:4),[15] and representations of the Archangel Gabriel have been hitherto unknown.[16]

In the Christian tradition, Gabriel stands with Michael near God's throne. This position makes him an intercessor of mankind, but primarily he is the angel of the Annunciation – the announcement of the imminent births of John the Baptist

186 Neck ornament depicting the Annunciation

From the area around Asyut, c.600
Gold. Diameter of necklace: 23.5 cm,
diameter of encolpion: 11.7 cm
Antikensammlung, Staatliche Museen zu Berlin.
Inv. 30219,506.506a

This large necklace is one of the most
magnificent pieces of jewellery from the
Asyut hoard (see pp. 75–76). The pectoral
fastened to the band is assembled from
a large imitation coin in the centre, with
smaller coins at the sides stamped with
the portraits of various 6th-century
emperors. Suspended from the pectoral
is an *encolpion*, with an Annunciation
scene at the centre, surrounded by a wide,
pierced frame decorated with lotus buds.
The Virgin Mary is seated in a basket chair
and gazing at the Angel Gabriel who is
foretelling the birth of Christ. His right
hand is raised in greeting, while in his left
he holds the sceptre with the cross. [CF]

and Jesus Christ.[17] He appeared to the High Priest Zacharias to tell him that he would have a child. Zacharias did not believe him and Gabriel demonstrated his might by striking him dumb until John was born. Shortly afterwards, he was sent by God to the Virgin Mary to announce the birth of Jesus Christ (Luke 1:8–38).

In Egypt, the archangels were highly venerated. Churches dedicated to them are known from the fourth century onwards,[18] and they were commemorated in the Synaxarium, the Calendar of Saints.[19] The Archangel Gabriel Church in Naqlun (Fayyum) has a legendary building history (see focus 6). Gabriel reveals himself as guardian of Aur, son of a magician and a princess, and tells him to build a church. Aur finally succeeds after Satan causes great delays.[20] Magical formulas, popular since ancient Egyptian times, often invoke Gabriel in spells for protection and healing.[21] Pictorial art mainly shows Gabriel in Annunciation scenes and, with Michael, he flanks the Virgin carrying her Child.[22]

In Islam[23] Gabriel is called Jabra'il.[24] Islamic commentators say Jabra'il revealed the Qur'an to Muhammad.[25] Therefore, the angel is regarded as keeper of the heavenly treasures. Jabra'il is recognized in two later angelic visions to Muhammad, and described as mighty in power and an honourable messenger.[26] In two other *suras* he is identified as 'our spirit'[27] and the 'holy spirit',[28] the power that strengthens 'Isa (Jesus), son of Maryam.[29] In the Hadith (reports of Muhammad's words and deeds) and *The Tales of the Prophets*, Jabra'il often plays a role as the messenger of Islamic beliefs, duties and values.[30] He frequently figures in legends based on biblical stories adopted by Islam – for example, when God wanted to create Adam, Jabra'il was sent to find clay to shape Adam's body.[31]

A post-Qur'anic narrative recounts that Jabra'il led Muhammad on a nocturnal journey from Mecca to Jerusalem and from there as far as the Seventh Heaven, before God's throne.[32] During this Night Journey, Muhammad had visions of hell and punishment and of the Garden of Paradise. In Islamic magic, tradition says Jabra'il uttered an incantation over Muhammad to cure him of illness.[33] Although human representations are absent in religious art,[34] literary manuscripts are often richly illustrated, showing Jabra'il as messenger and guide.[35]

187 The Angel Gabriel
Iraq, al-Wasit. 27 February 1280 (24th Shawwal 678 AH)
Paper, various inks, wash. 26.8 × 16.8 cm (text area)
Bayerische Staatsbibliothek, München. Hss Cod.arab. 464
fol 33r

The angel is depicted in lively movement. Only the nimbus and the wings characterize him as a higher being, whereas his clothing looks like that of contemporary Muslim mortals. This representation comes from the oldest known manuscript of the cosmography *Marvels of Creatures and the Strange Things Existing*, written by al-Qazwini (1203 – 83), and produced in his lifetime in the southern Iraqi city of al-Wasit. The associated text lists the qualities and descriptions of Gabriel, and gives stories about him. [GH]

20 Joseph: A Hero for Everyone?

Elisabeth Ehler

O NE of the most famous and popular stories in the three Abrahamic religions is the story of Joseph.[1] In the Jewish and Christian Bibles his tale is narrated in the First Book of Moses (Genesis 1:37-50). In the Qur'an, the twelfth sura is dedicated to Yusuf, who is also named as a prophet in Islam (e.g. Sura 6, verse 84).

Joseph is the second youngest of the twelve sons of Jacob. While he is still young, God reveals his will to him in dreams. He is his father's favourite and so hated by most of his brothers that they initially plan to kill him before deciding to sell him to traders who are heading for Egypt. The brothers pretend to their father that Joseph has died, soaking his clothes in the blood of a slaughtered animal (fig. 188).

Joseph enters the service of a court official and his wife. She is captivated by the attractive young man and tries to seduce him, but fails because of his steadfastness. Although Joseph has done nothing wrong, he is imprisoned because of the incident. In prison he interprets the dreams of two inmates. Since his prophecies come true, Joseph then interprets the dreams of the pharaoh. He prophesies that there will be seven fruitful years that will be followed by seven lean years. The pharaoh should therefore set up a wise man to save his country from ruin. Joseph is given the task. He orders food to be stored so that it can be sold to the people in lean times. Far away, his brothers suffer hunger too and they come to Egypt to buy food. Joseph does not immediately make himself known to them. Instead, he has property hidden in their luggage and makes it look as if they have stolen it. Accusing them of theft, he pretends he wants to enslave the youngest of them as a punishment, whereupon the older brothers offer themselves as slaves. But Joseph refuses, finally makes himself known as their brother, and absolves them of any guilt. The story makes clear that God has ordained everything according to his plan, so that neither revenge nor punishment are necessary.[2] Then Joseph has Jacob his father, and his family (the Israelites), brought to Egypt too.

Is Joseph a hero? A hero is characterized by boldness and courage; he does something for the sake of others. He can often draw on special abilities. Joseph turns trustingly to God at every low point in his life, and always experiences a turn for the better. Through his God-given ability to interpret dreams, he predicts the impending disaster and his wise actions save whole peoples from starvation.

No matter how heroic the deeds of Joseph may be, it is solely his unwavering trust in God that enables him to accomplish them. This conclusion underlies the Jewish, Christian and Muslim tradition. And yet they differ. The Jewish and

188 Roundel (orbiculus) with the Life of Joseph

Egypt, probably Akhmim. 7th–10th century
Linen and wool. 25 × 28.5 cm
Katoen Natie, Antwerp. Inv. KN 625

Depicted here is the dream cycle according to Genesis 37–50. The story begins in the central medallion, where Joseph is shown sleeping, with the sun, moon and stars above him, which are likened to his parents and brothers in the dream. Anti-clockwise from the top we can see further episodes from Joseph's life: Jacob sends Joseph out to his brothers in the field; a stranger shows him the way there; Joseph is thrown into the well by one of his brothers; Joseph is rescued from the well and a goat is sacrificed instead of him; Joseph is sold to a slave trader (the damaged scene at the bottom); Joseph's brother Reuben stands mourning by the empty well; the slave trader takes Joseph with him to Egypt; lastly Joseph is sold to Pharaoh's officer Potiphar. [CF]
Bib: De Moor et al. 2008, pp. 202–3; Fluck 2008, pp. 8–9

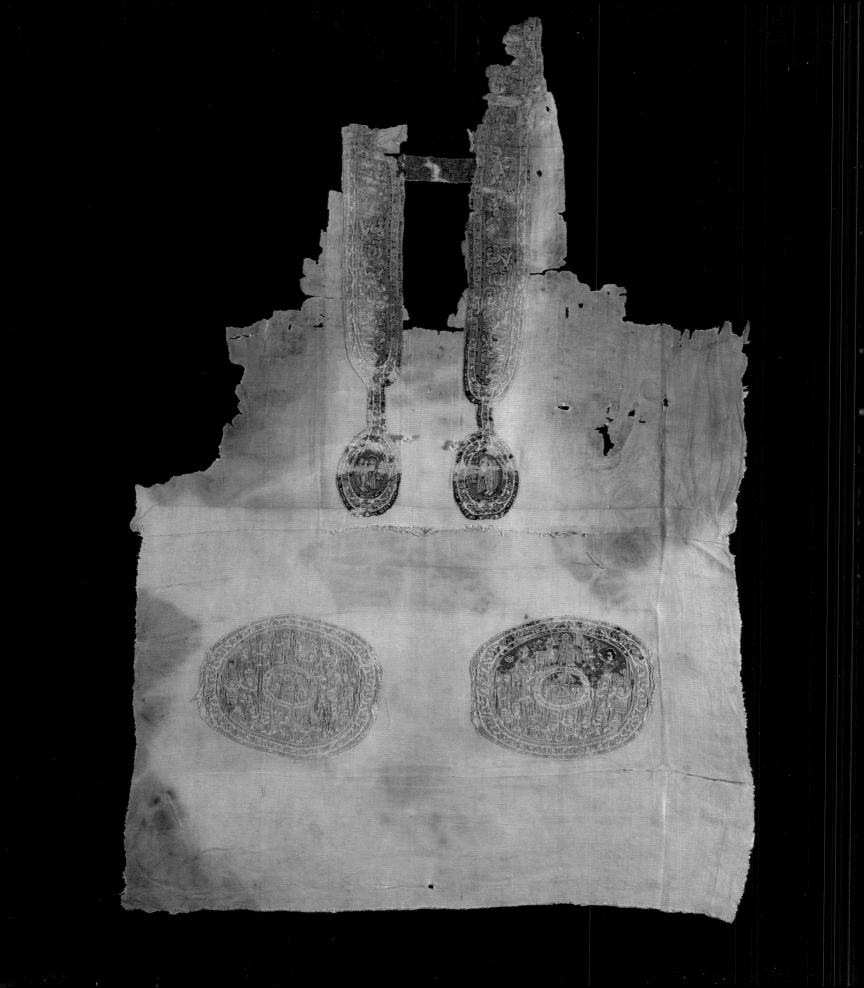

Christian Biblical story is like a folk tale, in which Joseph is held up as a wise and tactically minded Jew, who acts on his own behalf[3] without moralizing too much. In the Qur'anic story, in spite of some folkloristic features, Joseph (Yusuf in Arabic) is more clearly interpreted in moral terms.[4] Here we have more of a sermon or allegory,[5] culminating in the so-called prison sermon (Sura 12, verses 37–40) in which the morally righteous and staunchly faithful Yusuf confirms his basic commitment to his belief, to the God of Abraham, Isaac and Jacob (in Arabic Ibrahim, Ishaq and Ya'qub).[6]

In the Jewish and Christian scriptures, the Joseph story acts as a bridge between the patriarchal tradition and the Exodus tradition.[7] First, the patriarchal narratives set out the family relationships of the different tribes. This is followed by the Joseph story that tells of a Jewish influx into Egypt in which Joseph summons Jacob his father, with all his family (the Israelites), to the land of the Nile. This part of the story is needed so that, later on, Moses can carry out God's command to lead the Israelites out of Egypt into the Promised Land (Book of Exodus).

The stories about Joseph were often adopted and commented on by all three religions, with individual passages given different embellishments.[8] Thus, a Jewish-Hellenistic tale reports, inter alia, that the Egyptian woman Asenath first converts before Joseph will marry her.[9] In Islamic poetry it is primarily the love story between Yusuf and his beloved (who is simply called 'Woman of the Egyptian' – later Sulaika) that is recorded and most frequently illustrated in miniature paintings.[10] Already in the second to fourth centuries Jewish manuscripts seem to have been decorated with illustrations of the story of Joseph.[11] Especially in Late Antique textiles from Egypt, these episodes were among the most popular motifs c.500–1000 (figs 188, 189, 190).[12] This is probably due to people in Egypt identifying and commemorating events said to have happened in Egypt.[13]

Joseph, who through his exploits becomes a model for everyone who is forced to live abroad, proves that trust in God leads to a positive result for everyone.[14] Although Egypt is not to be the homeland of Israel, the Jewish-Christian tradition does not view it as the symbol of a sorrowful exile, but a country in which survival is possible and marrying foreign women is not wrong.[15] The Islamic tradition reveres Yusuf as a prophet and thus as a precursor of Muhammad. He is regarded as the epitome of virtue, wisdom and trust in God. These traits allow him to overcome all difficulties in his life, providing a model for Jews, Christians and Muslims, alike.[16]

189 Tunic with the Life of Joseph
Egypt, probably Akhmim. 7th–10th century
Linen and wool. 142 × 97 cm
Skulpturensammlung und Museum für Byzantinische Kunst, Staatliche Museen zu Berlin. Inv. 9109/9110

The story of Joseph is depicted almost exclusively on tapestry trimmings used to decorate tunics. These trimmings were produced as matching sets. The designs on the *orbiculi* (roundels) shown here are similar to those on the orbiculus on the previous page (fig. 188); individual scenes from the story can be seen in the *clavi*. [CF]

190 Tunic sleeve with the Life of Joseph
Egypt, probably Akhmim. 7th–10th century
Linen, wool. 26.3 × 33 cm
British Museum, London. EA17175

While the lower tapestry panel of this textile is simply adorned by birds and vegetal motifs, the main band shows a more complex iconography organized around the central scene of Joseph's Dream. The patriarch is lying down, surrounded by two human faces, and a group of small triangular shapes, perhaps stars (cf. fig. 188). The central medallion is framed by 4 peacocks (Christian symbol of resurrection) and by scenes repeated in diagonal on each side. One shows Joseph's brother selling him to the slave trader; the other shows Joseph being re-sold by the slave trader. The shape of this textile fragment, and the organization of its applied polychrome tapestry panels, indicates that it once adorned the sleeve of a linen tunic. [AM]
Bib: Kitzinger 1938; Nauerth 1978, p. 107 and pl. 28a

21 Festivals[1]

Mary Kupelian

THE extant evidence indicates that Jews, Christians and Muslims in Egypt shared many similarities in the celebration of festivals (see table below). Many festivals are connected to calendars and seasons. The Copts (Christian Egyptians) used a reformed version of the old Egyptian calendar which goes back to the Pre-dynastic period. Today they use it in their liturgy just as their ancient ancestors did. Both the ancient Egyptian and the Coptic calendars consist of 365 days and are connected to the Nile – the year starts in September when the Nile is around its highest level. The Nile shaped not only the everyday life of all inhabitants of Egypt but also their religious practices.[2]

Table: overview of calendars

EGYPTIAN CALENDAR			COPTIC CALENDAR			GREGORIAN CALENDAR		JEWISH CALENDAR (in 2015)		ISLAMIC CALENDAR (in 2015)	
Solar calendar			Solar calendar			Solar calendar		Lunisolar calendar		Lunar calendar	
Season	**Month**	**Days**	**Season**	**Month**	**Days**	**Month**	**Days**	**Month**	**Days**	**Month**	**Days**
Akhet (inundation)	Thoth	30	Akhet (inundation)	Thout	30	September/October	30	Tishrei	30	Muharram	30
	Pa-en-Ipet	30		Paopi	30	October/November	31	Marcheshvan/Cheshvan	29/30	Safar	29
	Hathor	30		Hathor	30	November/December	30	Kislev	29	Rabi' I	30
	Ka-Hor-Ka	30		Koiahk	30	December/January	31	Tevet	30	Rabi' II	29
										Jumada I	30
										Jumada II	29
Peret (sowing)	Ta-aabet	30	Proyet, Peret, or Poret (sowing)	Tobi	30	January/February	31	Shevat	30	Rajab	30
	Pa-en-mechir	30		Meshir	30	February/March	28/29	Adar	29	Sha'ban	29
	Pa-en-Amenhotep	30		Paremhotep	30	March/April	31	Nisan/Aviv	30	Ramadan	30
	Pa-en-Renenutet	30		Parmoute	30	April/May	30	Iyar	29	Shawwal	29
										Dhu-al-Qa'da	30
										Dhu-al-Hijja	29
Shemu (harvest)	Pa-en-Khonsu	30	Shomu or Shemu (harvest)	Pashons	30			Sivan	30		
	Pa-en-inet	30		Paone	30			Tammuz	29		
	Ipip	30		Epip	30	May/June	31	Av	30		
	Mesut-Ra	30		Mesore	30	June/July	30	Elul	29		
epagomenal days	Heriu-renpet	5	the little month	hepagomene/pekoui nebot/El Nasii (the little month)	5/6	July/August	31				
						August/September	31				

Compiled by Sara Rodríguez-Berzosa, based on a model by Gisela Helmecke and Cäcilia Fluck

Today (2015) we are in the year 1731 of the Coptic calendar. The Coptic New Year 1732 corresponds to 12 September 2015 of the Gregorian calendar, the 28 Elul 5775 of the Jewish calendar and the 28th Dhu al-Qa'da of the Muslim calendar. The official New Year's day of the Jewish calendar, 1st Tishrei 5776, corresponds to 14 September 2015. The beginning of the Muslim year, 1 Muharram 1437, is 14 October 2015.

**191 Roundel (*orbiculus*)
depicting nilometer**

Egypt. 430–640
Linen and wool. Diameter 13 cm
Département des Antiquités égyptiennes,
Musée du Louvre, Paris. AF 5448

This *orbiculus* is one of a pair sewn
onto the shoulders of a linen tunic
found in a burial at Antinoopolis. The
Nile god and his consort Euthenia
preside over the inundation of the river,
symbolized by the nilometer below
(shown as a green kiosk topped by a
red column). The crowned Nile holds
a cornucopia and an ear of grain while
his consort, personifying the prosperity
resulting from a successful flood,
holds a veil bearing fruit and a cup.
Surrounded by lotuses, an *erote* on the
left engraves the numbers IZ (17) and
IH (18) with a mallet and chisel – the
levels of an ideal flood. Another *erote*,
on the right, holds a bird captive. [MD]

Jewish festivals

As long as Jewish communities existed in Egypt (see ch. 2) they celebrated their main
feasts of Passover (commemorating the Exodus), Sukkot (the Feast of Tabernacles),
Hannukah (Festival of Light, celebrating the Temple's rededication in Jerusalem) and
Shavuot (commemorating the day when God gave the Torah to the entire nation of
Israel at Mount Sinai). They are mentioned in the writings of Philo (*c*.20 BC–*c*.AD 40).[3]
He also refers to pilgrimage and other local festivals of the Jews living in Egypt – for
example, the Alexandrian festival of the translation of the Septuagint.[4] This festival
best characterizes the process of defining Jewish identity in Egypt. It was celebrated
on Pharos Island in Alexandria's harbour. According to Philo, a large number of

non-Jews in Alexandria took part in Jewish festivals.[5] Information about local feasts associated with specific Jewish communities in the Egyptian *chora* (hinterland) is almost entirely lacking.

An exception is the veneration of the prophet Moses, who was especially popular in Egypt. Still in Islamic times many shrines existed to places at which he allegedly lived. These places were visited not only by Jews, but by Christians and Muslims alike into medieval times. The most well-known place of worship was the synagogue (Kanisat Musa) in Damwah/Dammuh in Giza. It was surrounded by Christian monasteries. People travelled to this place in the month of Adar (February) in spring. Moses' birth and death date was 7 Adar, and both were celebrated on 8 Adar. An edict of the Rabbi's Counsel from the early eleventh century is preserved among the documents of the Cairo Genizah (see ch. 18), which shows that at the pilgrimage festival in Dammuh the same amusing and partly excessive customs (see note 14) existed as at Christian and Muslim pilgrimage sites, customs which Jewish religious scholars also encountered. For the Jews the synagogue at Dammuh was also a pilgrimage centre, regarded as a substitute for the pilgrimage to Jerusalem.[6]

Nile festivals

Specific to Egypt were festivals that were connected to the Nile rising and falling during the year. The rising and flooding brought to the land the fertile silt necessary for agriculture. Thus the Nile festivals reflect the population's dependency on the

192 Censer with Nile landscape

Egypt. 3rd–4th century
Bronze. 7.5 cm, diameter 11.2 cm
Skulpturensammlung und Museum für Byzantinische Kunst, Staatliche Museen zu Berlin. Inv. 3/99

The bowl's walls are covered with typical scenes of Nile landscapes in relief. Between lotus blossoms and various creatures – including a bird, a crab and an octopus – are fishing *erotes* and a boy riding on a dolphin. [CF]

correct level of the Nile flood, the fertility of the land and the prosperity of Egypt. To measure the river's water level, nilometers were constructed at strategic points from ancient Egyptian times.[7] Today the festivals have become almost obsolete, due to the modern construction of the High Dam in Aswan to control the flooding of the Nile. Still remembered, however, is the celebration of the Nile rise at the beginning of September, called *semasia* by the Romans, and which is known in the second century. In the Islamic period the fulfilment of the Nile remained of major importance. Now called *wafa' al-nil*,[8] the feast kept its character as a combination of popular festivities and official duties of the ruler and the religious authorities. In the Fatimid period the caliph had to go to the nilometer (Arabic *miqyas*) on the island of Roda in Cairo to anoint it. When the water level reached 16 cubit marks, celebrations started and streets were decorated to welcome the caliph on his way to the nilometer.[9]

Christian festivals

Since the spread of Christianity in the Roman empire, Egyptian Christians, like their brothers and sisters in faith elsewhere, celebrated the main feasts of Easter, Pentecost and Christmas. From the beginning, the birth of Christ was celebrated in Egypt on 6 January (and is still today).[10] In the west it is connected to the visit of the Magi.

A new Christian festival culture had developed by the fifth century, with the veneration of Christian martyrs. The festivities mainly took place at the martyrs' shrines, and resembled earlier temple festivals (see ch. 13). In the fifth century Cyril (*c*.379 – *c*.444), the 24th Archbishop of Alexandria, admonished Christians for participating in Jewish festivals, a practice which therefore seems to have been common in his time.[11] A famous Christian festival was that of the Martyr (*'id al-shahid*), celebrated on 8 Pashons (16 or 17 May).[12] It is closely linked to the Nile cycle. Christians thought that the Nile would not rise unless a sacrificial object – a wooden casket containing the finger of a male Christian martyr from Egypt – was thrown into it. The priests of the Shubrah church near Cairo[13] coordinated the ritual that was believed to bring about inundation. People came from far and wide, pitched tents on the river banks, and shared singers and musicians. In the tenth century it was greatly celebrated; Christians and Muslims feasted in boats, on roofs and on the river banks wearing their richest clothes. *'Id al-shahid* continued only to the mid-fourteenth century.

One of the great Christian feasts in Egypt, also related to the Nile, is Epiphany, commemorating Christ's baptism.[14] It was celebrated on 11th of the Coptic month Tobi (18 or 19 January), after winter solstice. The Arabic name *al-ghitas* means 'submersion', reflecting the focal ritual performed during this festival – submersion into the Nile, as a rite of water purification. In the Islamic period it was still, at the time of the Fatimids, the most popular, merry and unrestrained Christian feast. It was celebrated by thousands of people who crowded the river banks. Muslims also participated in the entertainment aspects of this festival. Even the caliph himself

193 Engraved gem with Osiris standing before a nilometer

Egypt, provenance unknown. 3rd century
Heliotrope / jasper, dark green veined with red.
1.7 × 1.3 × 0.3 cm
Ägyptisches Museum und Papyrussammlung,
Staatliche Museen zu Berlin. Inv. 9800

To the right of a nilometer, on which there is only a suggestion of a scale, is the mummiform god Osiris with the Atef crown and flails depicted. The god and the nilometer stand on hastily carved and framed Greek letters IΛω , with a star between them. This image refers to the annual flooding of the Nile, shown springing from the leg of the god. On 1st Thoth, the day of the Nile festival, the arrival of the Nile was celebrated. In a more general sense this gem reflects the desire for fertility and renewal that is bound up with the regular cycle. [JHD]

sometimes came to observe these activities.[15] During the Fatimid era, popular festivals were sometimes allowed and sometimes restrained, mainly because of the excesses associated with them.[16] *Id al-ghitas* is still one of the most important Christian Nile feasts, but is now regarded as a solely religious event.

A similar popular festival was the annual feast of the first day of the Coptic year on 1 Thout (11 September). It coincided roughly with the highest level of the Nile, after which the falling of the water started and the agriculture cycle started again. In the Islamic period it was named *nayruz* (and remains so today), derived from the Persian name *nawruz*.[17] The festival was both a Christian event and an important official celebration feast under the Fatimids, in which gifts were given to officials and their families.[18] As a popular festival attended by Muslims as well, it was celebrated in that period with great splendour. The dyeing of eggs – which is still practiced at Easter – and the sprinkling of water, sometimes even of perfume, were among some of its rituals, and it had also carnevalesque elements.[19]

Muslim festivals

Following the Islamic lunar calendar (see table), the great Muslim festivals drift back each solar year by 11 to 12 days. One main feast is *'id al-adha* (or *'id al-kabir*), the feast of Sacrifice on 10 Dhu-al-Hijja – coinciding with the great pilgrimage Hajj (see ch. 17). It commemorates Abraham's sacrifice of his son Ismail (see ch. 1). Sheep, camels or cattle are sacrificed, and usually a third of the meat is given away for pious purposes. The second great feast is *'id al-fitr* (also *'id al-saghir*), the fast breaking on 1 Shawwal and the following days, after the fasting month of Ramadan. Just as in the rest of the Islamic world, both feasts have been characterized with special religious ceremonies such as public prayers, reciting the Qur'an, and the lighting and decoration of mosques and other religious buildings. Besides this, these feasts were also celebrated as popular festivals according to the usual customs in Egypt. This part of the Muslim festivals was also often joined by their Christian neighbours.

The most important festival that honours the Prophet Muhammad is *mawlid al-nabi*, the celebration of his birthday. It occurs on the third month of the Muslim lunar calendar.[20] According to historical sources, this day was celebrated in a wider scale only since Fatimid times. There was an official procession to the caliph's palace, and sweets and food were distributed to officials and to the people.[21] A description is given by the Andalusian traveller Ibn Jubayr (eleventh century). Generally, under the Fatimids (969–1171) – who sponsored the celebration of religious and public feasts – a remarkable range of feasts can be observed, which were abandoned in the following periods.

194 *Ampulla* in the shape of a fish

Egypt. 5th–6th century
Clay. 11 × 14.8 (lying down) × 4.6 cm (at the tail fin)
Skulpturensammlung und Museum für Byzantinische Kunst,
Staatliche Museen zu Berlin. Inv. 6002

Flasks in the shape of fish occur from early antiquity and were especially popular in late Roman times. The *ampulla* was filled through the fish's gaping mouth; 2 small handles are attached on either side of the mouth. The vessel can be stood on the tail fin. The fish is considered to be one of the oldest Christian symbols, but whether this is a Christian object or simply neutral is questionable. [EE]

195 'Interior of the nilometer, Island of Roda, Cairo' by Luigi Mayer, c.1800

Watercolour. 34.6 × 23.3 cm
Victoria and Albert Museum, London. SD.645

Roda Island, just opposite Fustat, was the location of the principle nilometer in Egypt from AD 715. If the level of the Nile reached 16–19 cubits, residents could be assured of a plentiful agricultural year, and the administration of the payment of tax. The watercolour shows the building constructed by the Abbasids and restored under both the Tulunids and Fatimids. The scale to measure the level of the Nile is marked on the central column. [ERO]

PARTE INTERIORE DEL MEKIAS O NILOMETRO
SITUATO ALLA PUNTA MERIDIONALE DELL'ISOLETTA DI RODDA.

As well as the *mawlid* of the Prophet Muhammad, there were also *mawlids* of the many Muslims 'saints' in Egypt (see ch. 15). Whereas Coptic Christians' feasts celebrate the day of a saint's burial as a second birth into everlasting life, the aim of the Muslim feasts is to honour the natural birth of the saint.

Nowadays, there are two important feasts which were celebrated by Christians and Muslims together. The first is of the Virgin, *al-adhra* in Arabic (Assumption Day), and the second is the feast of Abu Hajjaj in Luxor.[22] The Virgin holds an important cultural status amongst all Egyptians. Christians as well as Muslims often share her feast, commemorating the ascension of her body to heaven. The *mawlid* of *al-adhra* traditionally features both ecclesiastical rituals and popular festivals. Celebrations in major cities like Asyut, Minya and Sohag are usually large and colourful. Although there is no evidence about the origin of this feast, it is assumed that it has its roots in the time of the apostles and was celebrated in the sixth century.[23]

Many scholars regard the festivals of Abu Hajjaj as a continuation of the ancient Egyptian *Opet* festival, where the placement of the barque in a joyous procession from the Karnak to the Luxor temples was accompanied by celebrations in the season of flooding.[24]

One may conclude that the many common features of the Coptic Christian and Muslim festivals, which have been preserved for centuries, prove that deep, shared roots exist between the differing religions and customs in Egypt. Festivals are similar at their core, and it is difficult to determine how these traditions emerged and who has been influenced by whom.

22 Magic

Tonio Sebastian Richter

196 Amuletic pendant in the shape of a fish

Egypt. 12th–13th century (?)
Lead. Length 3.9 cm
Museum für Islamische Kunst, Staatliche Museen zu Berlin.
Inv. I. 6391

Cast in a mould, the amulet is decorated on
both sides, with large rings on the back and
3 small rings and pendant at the lower edge. In
the middle of the body on both sides there are
inscriptions in cursive Arabic script, on one side
bismillah (in the name of God) and on the other side
mashallah (as God wills) – these pious statements
are still popular today on amulets of all kinds. The
small, disc-shaped pendants each have a rosette on
both sides. Right up to recent times, depictions of
fish have been thought to ward off the 'evil eye'. They
were often seen individually in obvious places, and
also worn on chains together with other amulets and
pieces of jewellery. [GH]
Bib: Islamische Kunst 1984, no. 343

IN the Late Antique and medieval periods, the area of magic was a forum to bring different religions into contact and exchange.[1] Various reasons for the permeability of magical traditions can be surmised. Magical traditions are both conservative and accumulative, and they often have a subversive relationship to official religion. Magic, when seen as a technique for establishing realities beyond everyday experience, fostered a professional esteem for the 'Other', the 'Exotic'. Magic as science, and closely related occult sciences such as astrology and the study of precious stones and talismans (figs 196, 198), played a part in the international circulation of knowledge and its transfer between different cultures, languages and religious communities. Finally, the religions and magic of the Late Antique and medieval periods rested on one and the same ideological foundation – namely the cosmological and theological premises of Neo-Platonism.[2]

In First Millennium Egypt, ideas and motifs from linguistically and religiously distinct milieux came together in the magical tradition (figs 197, 200, 201, 202, 203).[3] Already the Graeco-Egyptian magical texts of the Roman period[4] integrated many Jewish or Judaizing elements into ancient Egyptian and Greek traditions.[5] As a striking example, magical 'poetics' owes to the Jewish tradition a highly productive format for creating names of spiritual powers – the name endings *-êl* and *-oth*.[6] The demonology of the *Testament of Solomon*, originally a Jewish text from Late Antiquity, had a long-lasting influence as a source of knowledge about types of demons and as a pattern of Christian and Islamic legends about Solomon (fig. 199).[7] In a Greek papyrus of the fourth century, the 'Eighth Book of Moses' made its appearance for the first time.[8]

In the London-Leiden Magical Papyrus (fig. 205),[9] a demotic Egyptian manual of magic from the third century AD, Yahweh is called upon to appear in the flame of a lamp:

> ... Reveal yourself to me here and now in the same shape in which you
> revealed yourself to Moses, the shape which you assumed on the mountain
> where you created the darkness and the light ... so that I may praise you in
> Abydos, so that I may praise you before Re [the names of further deities of
> ancient Egypt follow]...

The invocation is addressed to the God of the Torah who, according to the biblical testimony in Exodus (19:16–25),[10] is willing to appear to humans in a divine epiphany,

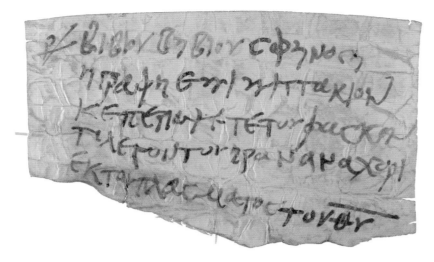

197 Exorcism amulet

Egypt, Fayyum. 4th–5th century
Papyrus. 6.8 × 11 cm
Ägyptisches Museum und Papyrussammlung, Staatliche Museen zu
Berlin. Inv. P 7977

The Greek text begins with a *staurogram* (cross monogram)
and a few magical words. This is followed by instructions to
drive out a demon from a person who is possessed. Notes
containing magical texts were usually folded, tied and then
wrapped up and left at or collected from the site of an oracle.
The papyrus fragment still clearly shows traces of the original
folds. [CF]
Bib: http://ww2.smb.museum/berlpap/index.php/06352/

198 Talisman roll

Egypt. 13th–15th century (?)
Paper, brownish-black and reddish ink. 86.5 × 9.5 cm
Ägyptisches Museum und Papyrussammlung, Staatliche Museen zu
Berlin. Inv. P 15210

This long, narrow roll of paper had been folded several times
so that it could be kept in a tubular amulet holder. There
is writing in brownish-black and red ink on the inside, and
it is divided into several sections. These contain prayers,
texts from the Qur'an, exorcism formulae and the names
of God, as well as 3 'pictures' composed entirely or partly
of characters, including a hexagram with the words *al-mulk
li-llah* ('the power is God's'), in the centre. The majority of
these Arabic texts are written in cursive letters without
vowels and without diacritical marks. The headings have
characters with vertical extended stems similar to Kufic
letters, and have a reddish tinge similar to two of the
'pictures'. [GH]

and therefore seems suitable for magically provoked divination – here, of course, as
one god among others from the ancient Egyptian pantheon!

While it may not be surprising that themes from a monotheistic religion can be
borrowed and used in a magic based on polytheism, borrowings in the other direction are also attested. Magical texts in the Coptic language[11] – partially continuing the
Graeco-Egyptian magical traditions in Christian Egypt – counteracted contemporary
anti-'pagan' polemic by telling *historiolae* (magical exempla) about ancient Egyptian
gods.[12] One magical text against stomach-ache, for example (the effectiveness of which
is based on a *historiola* about the divine child Horus, his impatient gobbling up of the
wrong sort of food, and his cry for help to his mother Isis), ends with the magician
saying: 'Every disease and every plague and every pain that are in the body of so-and-
so, son of so-and-so, should stop immediately: I am the one who calls; the Lord Jesus
is the One who provides the cure!'[13] So the divine realm of the ancient Egyptian
pantheon is at the last moment subordinated to the Christian saviour as the effective
healing power, and the 'pagan' spell receives its 'emergency baptism'.

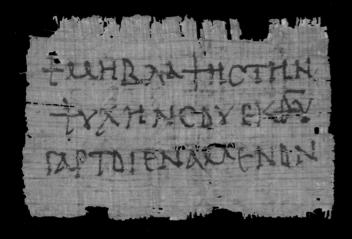

199 Christian oracle ticket

Egypt, al-Ashmunain (Hermopolis Magna).
4th–7th century
Papyrus. 3.8 × 5.6 cm
Ägyptisches Museum und Papyrussammlung,
Staatliche Museen zu Berlin. Inv. P 13232

'Do your soul no harm, for what has happened
is from God!' is the message of the Greek
saying on this oracle ticket. Such answers to
questions from those seeking advice have
been found in great numbers at places of
Christian pilgrimage; this oracle ticket is a
typical example. [CF]
Bib: http://ww2.smb.museum/berlpap/index.
php/03642/

200–201 Magical gems

Egypt. 2nd–3rd century
a) Haematite. 1.8 × 1.4 × 0.3 cm
b) Jasper / green with red veins. 3.1 × 2.2 × 0.62 cm
Ägyptisches Museum und Papyrussammlung,
Staatliche Museen zu Berlin.
a) Inv. ÄM 11918
b) Inv. ÄM 9850

On one side, the haematite gem (a) shows a
simplified representation of a locked uterus.
Gems with this symbol were used as spells in
courtship and also as a way to relieve pain when
giving birth. The following inscription is found on
the reverse: ΘΑΛΒΟΥ | ΘΑΛΒΑΑ | ΟΡΩΡΙΟ | ΥΘ.
Ορωριουθ is the formula that is almost always
cut into these stones and may mean 'light of
lights, original light'. The remaining letters should
probably sound like *ablanathanalba*.

The green jasper gem (b) has on one side
a depiction of a male deity, wearing a pleated
apron, similar to the Egyptian *shenti*. He holds
a long spear, with an open-mouthed snake
entwined around its shaft, and what is probably a
wreath with a ribbon. The headdress could be an
unusual depiction of an ancient Egyptian crown
with feathers, uraeus and headband. Behind the
figure, reading vertically, it says ΓΑΒΡΙΗΡ ΣΑΒΑΩ,
which can be interpreted as 'Gabriel – Sabaoth'.
The other side shows the god Anubis in a short,
belted tunic and long boots, holding two branches
in his right hand and a palm frond in his left. As
well as being a general symbol of victory, palms
imply a visit to the other world. The gaps on both
sides are filled with single letters and stars. [JHD]
Bib: a) Toelken 1835, p. 32, no. 132; Philipp 1986,
p. 112, no. 182, pl. 47
b) Toelken 1835, p. 449, no. 100; Erman 1899,
p. 379; Philipp 1986, pp. 96–97, no. 145, pl. 38

202 Amulet holder

Egypt. 2nd–3rd century
Gold. Length 3.5 cm, diameter 1.2 cm
Skulpturensammlung und Museum für Byzantinische Kunst,
Staatliche Museen zu Berlin. Inv. 23/72

This elaborately worked amulet holder consists of
a thin-walled gold tube with chased ornamentation.
On the front, surrounded by birds and fishes, are two
snakes, which can be identified by their different
heads as Isis and Serapis. Between them is a
small amphora. The underside is decorated with a
geometrical surface pattern. On the back is a laterally
reversed inscription in Greek, with a protective
formula. Holders of this kind were worn around the
neck on chains or on strips of cloth, as evidenced by
some mummy portraits. [CF]
Bib: Cat. Frankfurt 1999, p. 198, no. 105 (K. Parlasca)

203 A love spell to bind Ptolemais

Middle Egypt, probably Antinoopolis. 3rd–4th century
Jar: terracotta. 14.6 cm, diameter 11.9 cm
Tablette: lead. 11.2 × 11.1 cm
Figurine: terracotta with bronze nails. 9.6 × 4.2 × 7.2 cm
Département des Antiquités égyptiennes, Musée du
Louvre, Paris. E 27145 A, B and C

Misshapen at its mouth in production, the jar was
found containing the figure of a woman, bound
and pierced with spikes, and a rolled lead sheet
inscribed in Greek. It must have been placed in a
tomb. The inscription is a love charm, the script of
which is similar to that of the papyri of the 3rd and
4th centuries. A certain Sarapamon, son of Area,
here appeals to the spirit of a dead man, Antinous,
to ensnare the senses and the love of Ptolemais,
daughter of Aias and Origen. He intends to bind
her to him by depriving her of the ability to taste
food, to sleep, to feel anything or to enjoy the
pleasures of love. He invokes Greek, Babylonian
and Egyptian chthonic gods, such as Pluto, Kore-
Persephone, Ereshkigal , Adonis, Hermes-Thoth
and Anubis, and the spirits of those who died
prematurely and are still wandering. The whole
set of objects embodies a ritual known from a
large magic papyrus handbook now in Paris
(PGM IV) giving the recipe for a 'love spell to bind
the beloved'. It requires making a model in wax or
potter's clay, bound and in a kneeling posture, and
piercing it with thirteen needles while pronouncing
the magic formulas written on a sheet of lead.
[FGM]

Bib: Du Bourguet 1975, pp. 255–57; Du
Bourguet 1980, pp. 225–38, pls XXXIV–XXXVIII;
Kambatisis 1976, pp. 213–23

204 Curse

Egypt, Edfu. 10th century
Parchment. 33 × 15 cm
Département des Antiquités égyptiennes, Musée
du Louvre, Paris. Inv. E 14250

The Arab conquest of Egypt in the middle of
the 7th century brought profound changes
– a new calendar, and Arabic used as an
official language. Bilingual documents
(Coptic–Arabic) appeared but Christians still
used Coptic, especially in magical texts. This
piece of parchment from Edfu, purposely cut
in the shape of a blade, includes on both front
and back magical texts and drawings in black
ink. It is a curse meant to sow discord in a
couple, and is aimed at a certain man called
Sipa; the invocations are repeated to reinforce
their power. Carefully folded and placed in
a case, the sheet would then have been
deposited under the victim's head without his
knowledge. [FC]

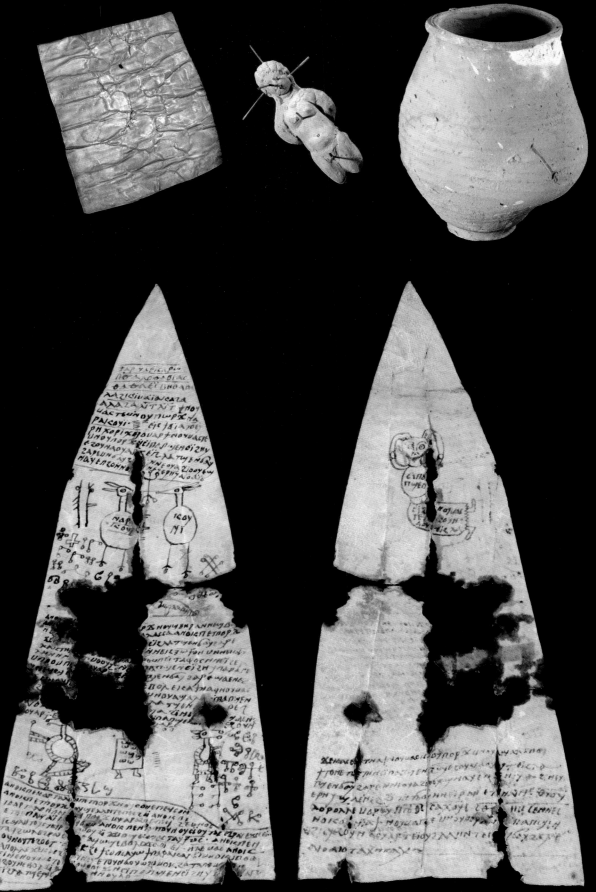

Works of Jewish magical literature of Late Antiquity such as the *Sefer Ha-Razim*[14] also assimilated the traditions of Graeco-Egyptian magic,[15] especially the tradition of incomprehensible signs of magical power that could be activated as *voces magicae* (magic words) or *charaktêres* (magic characters) (figs 204, 206, 207).[16]

Speaking and writing in many tongues was a prominent feature of Graeco-Egyptian magic.[17] Demotic Egyptian and Greek texts or textual parts could be compiled into bilingual sequences of spells and recipes in individual papyri.[18] We encounter the same phenomenon in a Heidelberg papyrus dating from the eighth century, comprising a collection of harmful spells relating to 'love', separation and other areas.[19] All the instructions are written in the Arabic script and language, while the magical words and utterances of invocation are formulated in Coptic. At one point, the linguistic and religious communities implied in the bilingual drafting of the text are even explicitly named, when a love spell needs to be written down: 'You write such things on gazelle parchment and bind it up in all your transactions, and if it is a Copt woman [*qubtiya*], tie it to the earring of her ear, and if it is a Muslim woman [*muslima*], at the top of the root of her neck (?).'

Islamic magic (*sihr*),[20] as a relatively recent branch of magical tradition, drew on older traditions.[21] For example, Arabic magic made use of the *charaktêres* and even

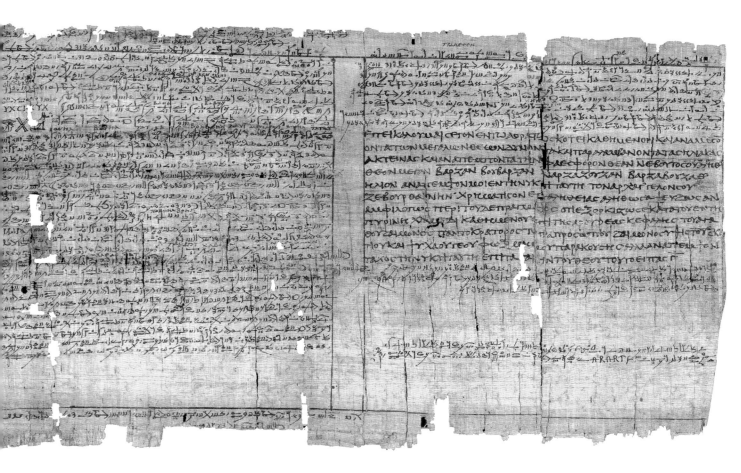

called them so – the Arabic *kalfatiriat* or *kalaqtiriat* is a transcription of the Aramaic *kalaqtiraia*, which itself is a transcription of Greek *charaktêres*.[22] Such tried and tested magical writing can still be found in Egyptian-Arabic spell books of the early twentieth century.[23]

The origins of the so-called 'seals' – seven symbols or letter-like signs, typical of Arabic magical texts and objects – have been traced back, not only by modern scholars but by medieval Arab writers such as al-Buni (died 1225),[24] to signs and emblems of power provided by Christian and Jewish traditions (figs 208, 209).[25]

Holy scriptures of the Jews and Christians such as the Torah, the Psalter[26] and the Gospels could, in Islamic magic, be named in the same breath as the Qur'an; thus in the spell for preservation known as the 'Talisman of the Washer-Woman', for example, we find the words: 'And by the Torah and the Gospel and the Psalter and the Qur'an: May you take the bearer of this my writing under your protection and your care...'[27]

Islamic magic, too, was familiar with the names of angels based on the long-standing traditional pattern (in Arabic ending in -*il*, from the Hebrew ending in -*el*), beginning with those of the archangels.[28] Islamic magic even knows and makes use of some Jewish names of God, which could co-occur together with the name of Allah

205 Section of the London–Leiden magical handbook (PDM XIV)
Egypt, said to be from the Theban Necropolis.
*c.*200–25
Section of a papyrus roll. 23.9 × 85.4 cm
British Museum, London. EA 10070/2

The so-called Theban Magical Library, comprising up to 14 papyrus rolls, sheets and codices, contained compilations of spells for various purposes or alchemical handbooks. Written in Greek, demotic Egyptian and Old-Coptic, they belong to the milieu of bilingual Egyptian temple priests in Thebes *c.*200–400. Spells invoke the names of deities or powers from Hellenistic, Egyptian, Mesopotamian, Persian, Jewish and Christian traditions – the more the better. Originally *c.*5 m long, one of the book rolls, the so-called London–Leiden magical handbook, contains spells for divination, curing fever, causing madness and desire, among others. The prescriptions are written in red ink and the instructions for achieving them are in black ink. One of the spells on the section of the papyrus shown here invokes the God of Moses among a roster of ancient Egyptian deities. [ERO]
Bib: Dielemann 2005; Bagnall 2009, pp. 83–86

206 Cloth with magical texts and signs

Egypt. 1024–1215 (radio-carbon dated)
Cotton, with painting and writing in ink. 248 × 123 cm
Skulpturensammlung und Museum für Byzantinische Kunst,
Staatliche Museen zu Berlin. Inv. 9993

This cloth, bordered on the long sides with double blue stripes,
has been preserved in its entirety. In the bottom quarter is
an ink drawing of a kind that is hitherto unique, consisting
of four squares which are subdivided from left to right into
25, 25, 16 and 20 fields and filled with letters. Between the
3rd and 4th squares is a drawing of a bird with a triangular,
cross-hatched body on a slightly curved base. The text below,
running parallel to the right edge, is indecipherable, except
for the abbreviation for the name of Jesus Christ and a few
onomatopoeic syllables. The arrangement of letters in squares
is reminiscent of magic squares with the palindrome Sator-
Rotas formulae. The bizarrely shaped bird figure in connection
with an incomprehensible inscription – possibly an encrypted
message – also suggests the magical nature of this cloth.
[CF]
Bib: Cat. Hamm 1996, p. 375, no. 427 (where it has revised
dating information)

207 Talisman

Egypt. 13th–15th century (?)
Paper. 5.5 × 8.6 cm
Ägyptisches Museum und Papyrussammlung, Staatliche Museen
zu Berlin. Inv. P 15138

The writing on the inside of this small rectangular paper, in
brownish-black ink, comprises 3 lines of Arabic in unvocalized
cursive script followed by a line of magical letters – so-called
charaktêres. Next come 3 very simplified figures with their
hands touching, surrounded by 'Coptic' letters, a Christogram
and Arabic words and numbers. The lower part has been
cut off. [GH]

208 Stamp

Egypt (?) 11th –12th century (?)
Agate. Height approx. 2.5 cm;
diameter approx. 4 cm
Museum für Islamische Kunst, Staatliche Museen
zu Berlin. Inv. VA 2951

The stone has been cut to form a ring with a
smooth surface. The stamp side is engraved
with a hexagram, with a religious phrase in
the centre. The hexagram is a variant of the
khatim Sulayman (seal of Solomon). The
inscription is in reverse, so that when stamped
it would appear correctly. This stamp could be
used, for example, for printing talismans. [GH]

209 Medallion with hexagram

Egypt. 11th –12th century
Glass. Diameter 2.6 cm
Museum für Islamische Kunst, Staatliche Museen
zu Berlin. Inv. I. 4075

The front of this small glass disc is engraved
with a round stamp containing a hexagram.
The hexagram has small rosettes in the
points and illegible characters in the centre.
In the Fatimid period, similar small discs with
inscriptions rather than symbols were used
instead of coins. Others bore religious and/
or magic symbols like this hexagram and
often had an eyelet, so they probably had
both decorative and magical functions. The
hexagram – like the pentagram (fig. 210) –
was regarded as the seal of Solomon, and
was considered to be a powerful sign by
Jews, Christians and Muslims alike. [GH]
Bib: Winkler 1930, p. 174, pl. 3/5; Islamische
Kunst 1984, p. 344

**210 Amulet pendant in the shape
of a hand**

Egypt, acquired in Cairo. 12th –13th century (?)
Lead. 6.1 × 2.7 cm
Museum für Islamische Kunst, Staatliche Museen
zu Berlin. Inv. I. 2152

With stamped ornamentation on both sides,
this cast pendant is furnished with 2 small
rings on the thumb and ring finger, and a large
ring at the top. Inscribed in cursive script on
both sides at the wrist are 2 favourite religious
formulae – *bismillah* (in the name of God)
and *mashallah* (as God wills). The back of the
hand is embellished with a pentagram inside
a double circle, accompanied by 2 branches
running out from a decorative band. The hand
is one of the oldest and most widespread
symbols of humanity; it has several layers
of meaning in the Islamic world. The primary
function of the form seen here, with its open
fingers, is to ward off and protect. The ancient
symbol of the pentagram, which in the Islamic
world is considered to be the seal of Solomon
(who, among other things, is regarded as the
master of demons), thus fits in with the other
elements of this little hand amulet to promise
the protection of God and ward off evil. [GH]

to reach the addressee of magical wishes – as in the sequence of names *Sharahya Adunai Asba'ut Al Shaddai*. This formulation is based on the Arabic transcription of the Hebrew names for God *Äh'jäh ashär äh'jäh* ('I am that I am', as in Exodus 3:14), *Adonai Sabaoth* ('Lord of Hosts'), and *El Shaddai* ('Supreme God', as in Genesis 49:25). Medieval Islamic scholars were well aware of the provenance of these names.[29] On the other hand the Arabic name for God, *Allah*, is used in a Coptic magical papyrus in Berlin.[30]

Jewish and Muslim traditions often seem to interact in the Arabic, Judaeo-Arabic and Hebrew magical texts that are among the finds from the medieval Jewish community of Fustat attested in the Cairo Genizah (see ch.18).[31] In this huge collection of documents, the script and language of Egyptian Christians, namely Coptic, does not appear at all – with the striking exception of a few magical texts.[32]

Despite these and other connections between Jewish, Christian and Muslim magical traditions in the Egypt of the Late Antique and medieval periods, they all, as a matter of course, had their own idiosyncratic features, starting with writing and language. So the beginnings of the four Gospels can act as a protective amulet only in Christian magic, and the beginning of Sura 1 (*al-fatiha*) and the throne verse (*ayat al-kursi*) from Sura 2 of the Qur'an occur only in Islamic magic. The phraseology, terminology and symbolism of magical texts have their own peculiarities, based on the religion in question and its written culture.

But the magician would be unconcerned by the question posed by Nathan, in Lessing's 1779 play *Nathan the Wise* (a plea for religious tolerance set in Jerusalem during the Third Crusade): 'How can I believe my fathers any less than you believe yours?' Lessing's ring parable centres on the heirs' difficulty in identifying their father's authentic ring among three similar ones, as an allegory for the impossibility of awarding to any of the Abrahamic religions the predicate of the only true one. The magician's solution would have been for him to *unite* all three rings in his hand!

23 Language and Writing

Arietta Papaconstantinou

LIKE today, past societies were pervasively multilingual, even within small territorial units. It is not easy to know how those societies spoke or wrote in their everyday lives, because most of the evidence we have from the First Millennium reflects learned written practice – law, literature, philosophy or various forms of scholarship. As a multi-lingual society, Egypt was no exception.[1] It is exceptional, however, in another way. The papyri found in its sands allow fascinating glimpses into the world of everyday language, with its diversity of registers and functions.[2] While they reflect written rather than oral practice, they cover a much wider linguistic range than what has come down to us through the formal manuscript tradition. Hundreds of thousands of letters, administrative and legal documents, receipts, lists and accounts have survived, allowing us to capture levels of communication that are inaccessible to us for most regions during the same period. Through such documents we can observe the varying degrees of formality and informality, competence and incompetence in written communication in a society that was economically active and culturally diverse.

The variety of texts and registers present in the papyri – from long, formal and informed administrative or legal documents, to formulaic economic documents such as accounts and receipts, to very basic private letters and notes – indicates that literacy was widespread, and necessary for a large number of functions. This literacy was of varying degrees. It was often functional, centred on arithmetic or the production of short, standardized documents, but a certain competence in the written word was an important feature of Egyptian society. Egypt has also preserved a large number of school exercises (fig. 213), documenting with some precision how this competence was acquired – from basic writing skills to the mastery of epistolary and

211 Reed pen holder

Egypt, Antinoopolis. 6th – 7th century
Leather and bronze. 20.8 × 6.9 cm
Département des Antiquités égyptiennes, Musée du Louvre, Paris.
Inv. E 21249

Very similar to the reed pen holder of the 'scribe' Pamias (Louvre, DAE inv. AF 5158), this one also comes from Antinoopolis (tomb C 494). Embossed into the leather is a figural depiction of a saint armed with a lance slaying a monster in the shape of a serpent, and an inscription. Such equipment was the prerogative of the scholar, in our case a senior official working in the city government in the Byzantine era. As such, it accompanied the deceased to his final resting place. Shaped like a trapezoidal sheath, it has cells at the top for reed pens and styluses. An ink pot was probably attached via riveted strips on the sides. [FC]

212 Three reed pens

Egypt. Date unknown
Reed. Length 19 cm (maximum)
Museum für Islamische Kunst, Staatliche Museen
zu Berlin. Inv. I. 8433 and 2 unnumbered

These pens are sharpened to a point and split at the tip at one end to allow the ink to flow, and cut off or specially shaped at the other. The reed pen (Greek *kalamos*, Arabic *qalam*) replaced the brush that had been used to write Egyptian scripts. It was the main tool of scribes writing in Greek, Coptic and Arabic. Lines of different thickness could be produced, depending on the sharpness of the point and the angle at which the reed was held. In the Islamic period, the grid pattern produced by applying the reed pen formed the basic unit for the system of proportions for Arabic script developed by Ibn Muqla in the 10th century, which included 6 styles of cursive script (*al-aqlam al-sitta*). These are still taught today. Reed pens were also used in ceramics workshops to draw the contours and details of coloured patterns, and similarly by other craftsmen for their preliminary drawings. [GH]

documentary formulae. The most widespread literacy was directly geared to professional needs (see ch. 26), as in most trades some degree of competence was necessary in order to function properly. Higher positions, of course, required higher degrees of competence – firstly in grammar and literature and, for the very top, rhetoric and philosophy, as well as more technical fields like medicine and law.

Egypt's conquest by Alexander the Great in the fourth century BC marked an important moment in its linguistic history. Greek became the language of power and administration, and remained so until it was replaced by Arabic in the early medieval period. Egyptian was never again used in that capacity. Throughout the Hellenistic period Egyptian was the majority language, used in legal documents, accounts, and letters. It was written in the script known as 'demotic', which showed a conservative tendency to keep Egyptian devoid of Greek vocabulary – which was certainly common in oral practice.

213 Student's punishment

Egypt, from Hermopolis (?) 3rd century
Wood, with writing in black ink.
17.5 × 37 cm
Ägyptisches Museum und Papyrussammlung,
Staatliche Museen zu Berlin. Inv. ÄM 13234

The first line written on the rectangular wooden tablet is a sentence set by the teacher, and the following 4 lines are the pupil's copy. The Greek exercise states: 'work diligently, my child, so that you will not be beaten.' [JHD]
Bib: Erman and Krebs 1899, p. 233; Erman 1899, p. 375; Ziebarth 1913, pp. 5–6, no. 12; Luft and Poethke 1991, p. 76. Further reading at: http://smb.museum/berlpap/index. php/03644/

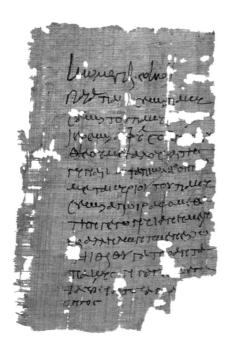

214 Announcement of the birth of a daughter

Egypt, Soknopaiou Nesos . Late 2nd – early 3rd century
Papyrus. 17.8 × 7.5 cm
Ägyptisches Museum und Papyrussammlung, Staatliche Museen
zu Berlin. Inv. P 25099

The priest Pakysis and his wife Tapiomis inform the
government official of Soknopaiou Nesos (Fayyum)
of the birth of their daughter. [CF]
Bib: Cohen 1996, pp. 385–98

215 Detail of a shawl with bilingual inscription

Egypt. Late 9th–early 10th century
Wool and linen. 119 × 57cm
Département des Antiquités égyptiennes, Musée du Louvre, Paris.
Inv. E 25405

The ends are criss-crossed with polychrome tapestry strips,
and fringed. The strips are flanked by two prophylactic
inscriptions, one in Coptic and one in Arabic, calling for
Christ's protection and 'full prosperity' for the owner and
client – a Christian named Raphael, son of Genarches.
A *tiraz* factory is also cited, under the control of the caliph,
located in Tutun (formerly Tebtunis), southwest Fayyum
(long renowned for its wool-weaving). [FC]

The Roman conquest introduced yet another language in the written record, namely Latin (see ch. 9). With no deliberate policy to promote it, however, except in very formal administrative or military documents and inscriptions, Latin did not spread in the country. It was often used in symbolic ways that evoked imperial power, as in fifth- and sixth-century Greek subscriptions in Latin characters that were intended to convey the authority of the individuals who wrote them.

In the Roman East, Greek was widely accepted as the uncontested lingua franca for day-to-day administration (see ch. 2, ch. 5, ch. 7). The introduction of a system of imperial and provincial tribunals that used Greek created the necessity for legal documents to be in that language. This practice robbed the Egyptian demotic of its principal terrain. At the same time, formal schooling in Greek had become common. With time, demotic script became restricted to religious and literary contexts. The brush, the traditional writing tool for Egyptian on papyrus, was replaced by the Greek pen.

By the end of the first century AD, everyday literacy among the Egyptian population was almost exclusively in Greek. As a largely oral language, Egyptian in the early empire underwent a linguistic and symbolic transformation. Its degree of normativity decreased and regional dialects became more prominent, while losing the redactional habits necessary for documentary production. The dominant Greek literacy amongst a largely Egyptian-speaking population led, by the end of the third century, to the adoption of the Greek script to write Egyptian words (ch. 22) and, little by little, the Egyptian language itself. This new form of Egyptian is known to us as Coptic, even though that term did not come into use until the eighth or ninth century.[3]

Coptic soon became the vehicle for the spread of Christianity along the Nile. The Bible and important patristic works were translated to make the Christian message accessible to Egyptian-speakers. In its earliest phase, the language contained about twenty per cent of Greek vocabulary – comprising partly administrative and theological terms, and partly everyday borrowings that must have happened over the centuries, but were kept out of demotic documents. In the fourth century, when Coptic took off in written documentation, it was still limited essentially to religious

216 Textile *tabulae* (squares) with the name of God

Egypt. 8th–9th century
Wool and linen. 6 × 6 cm
Département des Antiquités égyptiennes,
Musée du Louvre, Paris. Inv. AF 5941

These tapestry *tabulae* originally decorated a piece of cloth, either a tunic or a soft-furnishing, from which they have been cut out in modern times. The border of each *tabula* is red on an ecru background: this is a pattern of Vitruvian waves borrowed from ancient mosaic art. In the centre – in a round medallion on an ecru background, inscribed in a red square with an ecru dot outside at the corners – an identical inscription in blue-black stands out, in geometric Kufic Arabic script. It gives a shortened version of the name of God (Allah), the final vowel being accented with a red point. This inscription, whose economical style is like that of the calligraphy found on many Muslim monuments, dates it to soon after the Arab conquest in Egypt in the middle of the 7th century. [FC]

217 Textile *tabulae* with representations of animals

Egypt. 7th–9th century
Wool and linen. Each 13.5 × 13.5 cm
Skulpturensammlung und Museum für Byzantinische Kunst, Staatliche Museen zu Berlin. Inv. 9830

After the Arab conquest of Egypt traditional designs and compositions from Late Antiquity continued for centuries. Like the tapestry *tabulae* with the character representing the name of God in Arabic (fig. 216), these decorative trimmings are probably from a tunic or soft-furnishing. As is typical, they have an ornamental frame – here consisting of the so-called 'running dog' on the outside and loose tendrils – surrounding a medallion in a square with a figurative motif, which in this case is a hare. [CF]
Bib: Wulff and Volbach 1926, p. 51 (formerly ÄMP Inv. 11442/3), pl. 79

texts and private letters. Its perceived lack of sophistication made it the perfect instrument of monastic self-presentation, and in the anti-intellectual discourse developed in the early monasteries, Coptic, as a non-learned language, came to play a symbolically important role.

The trope that Coptic was 'simple' and closer to God than knowledge-cluttered Greek was to a large extent an illusion, and became increasingly difficult to maintain as textual production in the language rose. By the end of the fourth century the sermons of Abbot Shenoute were permeated with Classical rhetorical techniques, and the many other texts produced in Coptic show a strong awareness of Classical culture – unsurprisingly, since most of their authors had been schooled in it. By the sixth century the language had acquired a degree of prestige, making it acceptable to use even by the Hellenized provincial élites who previously adopted a purely Greek identity. The famous sixth-century lawyer and dilettante Dioscorus of Aphrodito (who read Menander, wrote much-maligned poetry, and composed rhymed petitions to the local governor in Greek) drew up legal documents for inhabitants of his town in Coptic – a first in the papyrus record. The sixth century saw a more generalized public use of the language, especially as it was now employed in inscriptions and sermons by bishops in urban contexts, rather than just in monastic settings.[4]

With the Arab conquest of 639–42, Arabic was gradually introduced to Egypt. Although there are Arabic papyri dating from as early as the conquest years, they only became common in the first half of the eighth century as a result of the gradual tightening of central control over the provinces under the Marwanids. Until then the administration of the Valley was largely carried out in Greek, while legal and other private documents were primarily in Coptic. This trilingual situation is reflected by the existence of numerous bilingual – and even trilingual – documents between the seventh and the eleventh century.

218 Board from a chest

Egypt, probably Old Cairo/Fustat. 9th century
Wood. 77 × 19 cm
Museum für Islamische Kunst, Staatliche Museen zu Berlin.
Inv. I. 4471

The upper part of the long side of a chest, this board
was connected to the missing lower part by the
insertion of wooden dowels. It is decorated with areas
of overlapping arcading on either side of a circular
medallion with an interwoven hexagram. Above it,
under a toothed frieze, is an Arabic inscription in a
Kufic script with low vertical strokes, which fits well
into the narrow space available. It shows Sura 112
of the Qur'an from verse 2, with only the last word
missing. The 1st verse and the 1st word of the
2nd verse must have been on the preceding short
side of the chest. This succinct Sura tells of the
uniqueness of God. Boards from similarly decorated
chests can be found today in various museums. They
are always about 40–45 cm in height, with short
sides measuring about 65 cm and long sides of
about 90 cm. A few of them are also inscribed
with Sura 112 of the Qur'an. [GH]
Bib: Strzygowski 1904, p. 311, fig. 88

220 Tyche of Constantinople

Egypt, Edfu. First half of the 7th century
Painted wood, with inscription. 37 × 18.6 × 0.7 cm
Département des Antiquités égyptiennes, Musée du
Louvre, Paris. Inv. AF 10878/10879

This fragmentary tablet, painted (with oil binder)
and inscribed, unites 6 contiguous pieces glued
together. It comes from the excavations of H. Henne
in 1921–22 at Tell Edfu, within an urban context. The
exceptional standing figure represents the Tyche
of Constantinople according to ancient custom –
namely, in the guise of a woman richly dressed and
adorned, wearing a crenellated crown and holding
a long staff (a sign of power and protection). It
symbolizes Byzantine imperial authority, personified
by the tutelary goddess of the city and identified here
as 'the beautiful and thriving one', a name given to it
by Constantine at its inauguration in 330. Another
text, prior to painting, is in Melkite Aramaic and
contains New Testament verses. [FC]

219 Beaker with inscription

Egypt. 9th–10th century
Glass. 8.1 × 8.5 cm
Museum für Islamische Kunst, Staatliche Museen zu Berlin.
Inv. I. 1539

Pincers were used to pinch the decoration on the outside
of this cylindrical, flat-bottomed glass vessel, while the
glass was still hot. The thick walls are divided into 9
sections by double comb-lines. In each one there is a
brief vertical inscription, the 1st word of which is Allah,
while the 2nd is illegible. Vessels of this kind, which have
no pre-Islamic models, were much used as drinking
vessels as evidenced by other inscriptions, but it is
also possible they were used as lamps. They are found
widely throughout the Near East, but the good state of
preservation of this glass points to Egypt. [GH]
Bib: Lamm 1929/1930, p. 68, pl. 18/11; Cat. Vienna
1998, no. 182; Vorsicht Glas 2010, no. 9

With its demise from the administration, Greek slowly disappeared from the
Valley. Egyptian continued to be spoken until the eleventh century, and probably
later in the south. Renewed economic prosperity under the Fatimids, however, and
the foundation of Cairo as a caliphal capital and international centre of learning, boosted the prestige and the utility of Arabic. Early in the eleventh century
the Coptic church adopted Arabic as its sole language of communication, a move
that eventually led to the general abandonment of Coptic in favour of Arabic by
Egyptian Christians.[5]

Egyptian, Greek and finally Arabic are the dominant languages in Egypt in
the First Millennium. Many other languages were also spoken in the country, and
there are written traces of various kinds, such as an Aramaic inscription on a reused
painted wooden panel (fig. 220). Of these, the only other language of power is
Pahlavi, introduced by the Persians when they conquered the country in the seventh
century (619–29). They left behind a large number of administrative texts in Pahlavi,
but the short-lived Persian presence did not leave time for the language to take root in
any form in Egypt, or to interact in any way with the languages already present.

221 Fatimid dinar of al-Mu'izz

Egypt, minted at Misr (Cairo). 973–74 (363 AH)
Gold. Diameter 1.8 cm, weight 4.09 g
Münzkabinett, Staatliche Museen zu Berlin.
Id.-Nr. 18246098

Fatimid gold coins typically have 3 bands
of inscription running round each side. The
Arabic script is an elegant Kufic. These gold
coins were issued in the name of the Fatimid
caliph Abu Tamim Ma'add al-Mu'izz li-din
allah (r. AD 953 –75 / 341–65 AH), whose
name and title appear in the inner circle on
the reverse side. The place and year of issue
are also shown on the reverse, in the outer
circle. On the front the inner circle contains
the Muslim confession of faith, while the outer
circle has a quotation from the Qur'an and
the middle circle praises 'Ali, the fourth caliph,
who was particularly admired by the Shiite
Fatimids and the son-in-law of the Prophet
Muhammad. This type of dinar of caliph
al-Mu'izz li-din allah is thought to be the Mu'zzi
dinar mentioned by historians, which was
famous for its high gold percentage. [GH]

The relatively limited presence of Hebrew in the written record does not
reflect the diachronic importance of the Jewish community. Here too, for most of
the period, Greek was the language of communication. Hebrew was known, at
least as a learned language, and several Roman and Late Roman inscriptions in
Hebrew are known. After the conquest, Judaeo-Arabic (fig. 222) seems to become the
language of transactions, and several documents from the end of the millennium are
preserved in the Cairo Genizah. The Genizah also contained texts in Hebrew and
Aramaic, most of which date from the eleventh century and after (see ch. 18).

Other languages have left fewer traces – Syriac was used in the monastery
of the Syrians in Sketis, but has also been found in documents from Kellis in the
Dakhleh Oasis; a fifth- or sixth-century Greek papyrus in Armenian script confirms
the presence of Armenians in Egypt; and graffiti in Nabatean and various Arabian
dialects on the routes of the Eastern desert show a continuing presence and interaction with the people of the neighbouring peninsula.

222 Judaeo-Arabic letter

Egpyt, Fayyum. 9th –10th century
Papyrus. 14.8 × 25 cm
Ägyptisches Museum und Papyrussammlung, Staatliche
Museen zu Berlin. Inv. P 105 99

Letter in Arabic language using Hebrew
characters, written on both sides, with additional
Arabic text on the back. [VL]

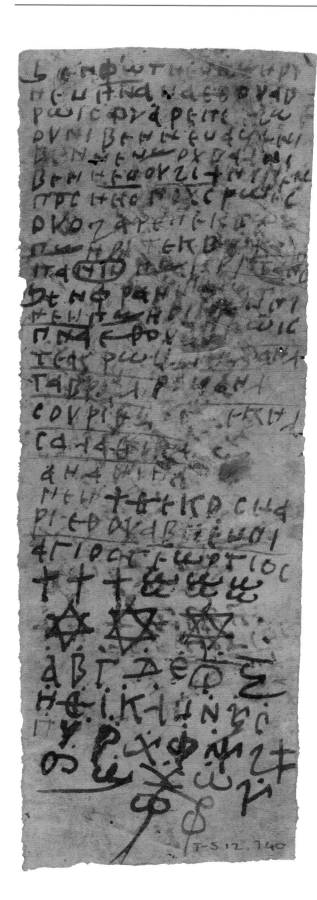

223 Coptic alphabet and prayer for protection

Egypt, Old Cairo, Ben Ezra Synagogue. 12th–13th century
Paper. 23 × 7.6 cm
Cambridge University Library, Cambridge. T-S 12.740

This amulet, written in the Bohairic dialect of Coptic,
contains a Christian magical prayer for protection
from dangers such as the evil eye. It displays a
remarkable number of spelling mistakes even in the
most common words and phrases, and ends with
three 6-pointed stars (so-called seals) and a Coptic
alphabet. The back contains another Coptic alphabet,
possibly written by another hand, which is partially
annotated in Hebrew letters – this being the most
remarkable feature of the piece. It seems to indicate
that Coptic magic was used in some way by members
of the Jewish community represented in the Cairo
Genizah documents. [TSR]

224 Text with extracts from the Qur'an

Egypt, Old Cairo, Ben Ezra Synagogue. c.12th–13th century
Paper. 17.1 × 24.9 cm
Cambridge University Library, Cambridge. T-S Ar. 51.62

This Judaeo-Arabic Genizah fragment contains Suras
1 and 2 from the Qur'an, followed by an interpretation
of omens for undertaking a journey. Since the text
was transliterated into Hebrew script, it can only
have belonged to a Jew. The Qur'an was said to have
magical properties by those working on magic and
divination even in Jewish circles, and we find, for
example, protective amulets with Qur'anic citations in
the Genizah, so it is possible that this transcoding of the
Qur'an happened in the context of someone working on
the production of magical or divinatory texts. [EMW]

24 Everyday Objects

Dominique Bénazeth

225 Base or stand

Egypt. 3rd–4th century
Limestone. 13 × 18 cm (max)
Skulpturensammlung und Museum für Byzantinische Kunst,
Staatliche Museen zu Berlin. Inv. 4135

This stone object is unusual in both its shape and in the
choice and combination of iconography. It is probably
a base on which to stand a vessel. On all 4 exterior
surfaces there is a suggestion of an architectural
structure which frames scenes relating to the function
of Isis as a fertility goddess. On the side shown here
she is crouching in a basket, with a lyre-playing Eros
striding towards her. The other sides depict couples
having sex, a youth with garlands of leaves and a large
bird, and a female dancer and a musician playing a flute,
with a pointed amphora on a stand and a sheaf of grain
beside them. [CF]
Bib: Cat. Berlin 2012, pp. 49–50, no. 27

226 Bes jar

Egypt. 2nd–3rd century
Fired grey marl clay. 11.5 × 7.7 cm
Skulpturensammlung und Museum für Byzantinische Kunst,
Staatliche Museen zu Berlin. Inv. 3537

This small, handled jug belongs to a group of ceramic
vessels popular in Egypt in the Roman period and Late
Antiquity. The front shows the grotesque face of the god
Bes with his tongue hanging out. Although Bes was not
one of the deities to whom temples were dedicated, he
played an important part in everyday Egyptian life as
a symbol for fertility and procreation. As such, he was
credited with protective powers beneficial for pregnant
women, women in labour and infants. [CF]
Bib: Cat. Berlin 2012, pp. 44–45, no. 23

WAYS of life can be identified and interpreted using texts, representations and objects that have survived in abundance due to the arid climate in Egypt.[1]

Child-birth had special importance; it was seen as proof of prosperity in a period when infant mortality was high. Depictions of coupling (fig. 225) and of protective spirits for women in labour (fig. 226) were charms intended to ensure successful births. The ancient veneration accorded to Isis and her son Harpocrates (see ch. 6) was widespread in the Roman period, not only in Egypt but also in the other provinces of the Roman empire, through the diffusion of Isaic cults (see focus 3). Their depictions probably influenced the iconography of the Virgin with the Christ Child at her breast or the Mother of God holding her son incarnate on her knees, as painted, in the medieval period, on the walls of churches (focus 5) and in illuminations of sacred texts.

In objects from everyday life one sees a mother carrying her child (fig. 228), as well as toys for boys (fig. 230) and girls (figs 227, 229). Dolls, some of which are dressed in very realistic miniature clothes, prepared future women for their role as mothers. To ensure that girls become adult and procreate in their turn, the dolls provide magical protection. This is attested to over the whole period under consideration, and for everyone, of whatever religious persuasion.[2] The message was expressed as a simple allusion on small household objects, like these lamps from the end of antiquity showing embryos (fig. 231), or else the frog, associated with the flooding of the Nile and hence with fertility (fig. 232).

227 Bone figure

Egypt. 7th–10th century
Bone, mud. 16.5 × 3 cm
British Museum, London. EA 65665

The figure is carved from a single piece of bone with
incisions marking out the features of the body. Such figures
have been found in a variety of domestic and funerary
contexts in Egypt. This example is rare for the survival of
hair represented by strings of mud-beads. [ERO]
Bibliography: cf. Cat.New York 2012, no. 134, pp. 193–94

228 Terracotta figurine of a mother and child

Egypt, probably from Abydos. 4th–6th century
Fired red clay, with a white base coat and painted with yellow ochre,
red-brown and black. 16.9 × 6.1 × 2.6 cm
Ägyptisches Museum und Papyrussammlung, Staatliche Museen zu
Berlin. Inv. ÄM 14371

The 3-dimensional effect of this flat terracotta figure is
mainly produced by the painting. It represents a woman with
her left arm around a child, who clings to her. The painted
clothing has been interpreted in various ways – it can either
represent a short-sleeved underdress and a white garment,
or a long-sleeved tunic with diagonal hatching indicating
parts of the underdress showing below its hem. This hatching
suggests a sitting position with legs apart. The angular
face of the woman is dominated by disproportionately large
eyes. The short diagonal strokes at the top of the head may
indicate either a wreath or plaited hair. [JHD]
Bib: Weber 1914, p. 151, no. 232, fig. 90; Kaiser 1967,
pp. 118-19, no. 1100 (with fig.); Philipp 1972, pp. 7–8, p. 15,
p. 33, no. 47a–b; Cat. Hamm 1996, p. 157, no. 125; Langener
1996, pp. 149–50, cat. KN 247

229 Doll

Egypt. 1st–2nd century
Linen, wool (dyed blue), human hair, jewellery of gold and leather
with gold leaf, painted red and black (face). 14.5 × 3 × 10 cm
Ägyptisches Museum und Papyrussammlung, Staatliche Museen zu
Berlin. Inv. ÄM 17954

The doll's torso is made of linen and filled with a flexible
material, while the head is framed by a coiffure of real, coiled
hair. This almost hides the face, with its large, almond eyes
and small mouth. The doll wears a poncho-like dress with
an embroidered neckline. The shorter underdress is made
of a very fine linen fabric. The doll's jewellery is unusual. The
earrings are made of real gold; the rings round her neck,
ankles and wrists are of leather covered with gold leaf. As
a result, this doll is one of the most luxurious of its kind and
would have belonged to a child from a wealthy family. The
hair invites comparison with women's hairstyles from the
time of the emperors Hadrian (117–38) and Antoninus Pius
(138–61). [JHD]
Bib: Kaiser 1967, p. 57, no. 604a; Bachmann and Hansmann
1988, pp. 38-39, fig. 44; Cat. Berlin and Munich 2004,
fig. 57; Fluck 2004, pp. 383–86, p. 399, figs 1–3; Fluck
and Finneiser 2009, pp. 46–48, no. 18, fig. 7

230 Toy horseman

Egypt. 4th–5th century
Tamarisk wood. 15.8 × 14.1 × 9.05 cm
Département des Antiquités égyptiennes, Musée du Louvre, Paris.
Inv.-Nr. E 27134

Toys on wheels were pulled along on a string or possibly also
pushed with a stick. The most common seems to be a man
on horseback. Both man and horse are represented in highly
stylized form. This example was probably intended to depict
the driver of a pair of horses. Toys of this kind were especially
popular with little boys in Late Antiquity. Examples came to
light in the children's graves at Antinoopolis. Easy to carry and
brightly painted, the toys may also have had a social function
of encouraging boys to become horsemen themselves. [CJ]

232 Frog lamp

Egypt, probably from Edfu. 3rd–4th century
Fired yellow-buff clay. 12.2 × 9 cm
Skulpturensammlung und Museum für Byzantinische Kunst,
Staatliche Museen zu Berlin Inv. 4975

This mould-made lamp depicts a warty toad in relief on the
upper side around the oil filling hole, facing the wick hole.
'Frog lamps' were widespread across Egypt, where frogs
symbolised fertility and the Nile inundation. They were also
associated with the cult of the frog- or toad-headed goddess
of birth, rebirth and fertility, Heket. [EE]
Bib: Wulff 1909, pp. 256–57, no. 1306; Cat. Hamm 1996, p.
224, no. 238a, cf. Cat. Hannover 1993, pp. 370–71, no. 352

231 Foetus lamp

Egypt, probably from Fayyum. 3rd–4th century
Fired pale grey marl clay. 3.3 × 7.2 × 8 cm
Skulpturensammlung und Museum für Byzantinische Kunst,
Staatliche Museen zu Berlin Inv. 10321

Two foetuses are depicted around the filling hole of this
mould-made lamp, their hands reaching toward a hoop
near the wick hole. Such lamps were widespread across
Egypt, where white clay lamps were sought after as
magical ingredients. The foetuses may represent birth,
rebirth and fertility. [EE]
Bib: Wessel 1957, p. 79; Cat. Hamm 1996, p. 221,
no. 234a–b, fig. S.221

Clay oil lamps were used for lighting the house, during festivals or in a funerary context. The top of the fuel chamber provided a surface for decoration, and was often stylized given the minute area available. From it one can often work out the religious persuasion of the owner. The candelabra with seven branches, an image of the gold lamp which illuminated the Temple at Jerusalem, is the Jewish *menorah* (fig. 236); whereas the cross and many inscriptions are explicitly Christian (10). Arabic inscriptions, from the time when the language was adopted in Egypt, provide a date for when the lamp was made (fig. 234). The type of lamp, and technique used in its manufacture, provide other dating evidence, due to a stylistic development from the Roman to medieval periods. The forms become rounded, a collar sometimes surrounds the pouring hole, and coloured glaze covers the clay material. Examples with two nozzles increased the light intensity. A proliferation of lamps on chandeliers enabled the illumination of larges areas such as churches (see ch. 10, figs 109, 115).

233 Oil lamp with Christian inscription

Egypt. 5th –6th century
Fired red clay. 6.2 × 10.4 × 11 cm
Skulpturensammlung und Museum für
Byzantinische Kunst, Staatliche Museen zu Berlin.
Inv. 9518

The Greek inscription on this ornate lamp
with relief decoration reads 'the holy and
consubstantial Trinity. Amen' (ΗΑΓΙΑ ΚΑΙ
ΟΜΟΦΥΣΙΟϹ ΤΡΙΑΔΟϹ ΑΜΗΝ). This is a
conscious statement of the trinitarian
doctrine of the consubstantiality of God
the Father and God the Son, which was
officially asserted in the 4th century,
contrary to the teachings of Arianism. [EE]
Bib: Cat. Hamm 1996, p. 225, no. 241, fig.
S. 225

234 Oil lamp

Egypt. 8th –9th century
Fritware. 4 × 9.6 cm
Museum für Islamische Kunst, Staatliche Museen
zu Berlin. Inv. I. 6077

The upper part of this flat, drop-shaped lamp
with its compact handle is decorated with
relief for which a model was used. A branch
motif connects the space between the filling
hole on the top and the wick hole at the
front. On the sides is a pattern of intersecting
arches, and around the filling hole is an Arabic
inscription in angular Kufic script, referring to
the maker of the lamp. Other lamp inscriptions
from this period contain poetic contemplations
on light or religious references to the lamp as
the light of God. [GH]

235 Oil lamp

Egypt. 10th –11th century
Fired clay, glazed. 5.5 × 10.5 cm
Museum für Islamische Kunst, Staatliche Museen zu
Berlin. Inv. I. 6348

Standing on 4 small feet, this box-shaped lamp
has a rounded back, 2 mouths for the wicks, a
cylindrical filling hole and a disc-shaped handle.
A model was used for the floral relief decoration
on the sides and top. This type of lamp is only
known from Egypt. [GH]

236 Oil lamp with *menorah*

Egypt, said to be from Alexandria. 3rd –4th century
Fired orange-brown clay. 8.7 × 5.9 cm
British Museum, London. BEP 1886,0623.2

This mould-made pottery lamp has a raised base
with a handle and two fill-holes. The discus is
decorated with a *menorah*, flanked by an ear of
wheat and fruit. The *menorah* is by far the most
common Jewish symbol on lamps from Egypt,
whereas scenes from the Book of Daniel and
other Jewish narratives occur on lamps elsewhere
in North Africa. [ERO]
Bibliography: Bailey 1988, Q2063, p. 251, fig. 38,
pl. 44

Besides lamps, crockery played a major role in the home. In a hot country like Egypt, containers to store water were essential. The walls of clay water storage vessels were porous to ensure the water's freshness through evaporation. Large ceramic jars were placed on stands decorated with Christian motifs and, later, in Islamic style (figs 237, 238). The jars themselves were often decorated with images typical of the Roman and then Late Antique periods, whilst filters from the Islamic period depict animals, geometric designs or decoratively styled Arabic script (figs 239, 240, 241, 242). Filters functioned to prevent insects and impurities from polluting the liquids. The water was decanted using buckets. Copper-based alloys, like brass and bronze, were more expensive than ceramic. Only rich houses could possess metal objects, sometimes decorated and inscribed with the name of the owner (fig. 243).

Large earthenware jars were used for storing food. Very beautiful vases with necks of varying diameter contained liquids or solids (fig. 270). Exquisite decoration made tableware valuable in any era, whether painted (ch. 18, fig. 245) or decorated with relief elements (focus 8). The magnificent Fatimid bowls with metallic lustre painting depict individuals from court scenes and festivals or religious practices (focus 8). Others adopted, with a new style, the Late Antique repertoire, interlinking designs depicting plants and animals, birds, hares and fish (figs 244, 271). This bestiary is found again on a series of clay seals, using in diagrammatic form the hare, gazelle or lion. Other seals have an Arabic inscription (fig. 250). Wooden examples enabled the printing of geometric motifs or again, more by implication, a religious symbol like the *menorah* or the cross (figs 248, 249). The application of such seals to bread that has been blessed and is distributed to Christians after divine service is known to this day, but no doubt one could use them in other circumstances too.

237 Water stand

Egypt, Wadi Sarga. 7th–8th century
Limestone. 35 × 74 × 38.5 cm
British Museum, London. EA 1788

Originally carved from a single block of limestone, this water stand is decorated with foliate designs on either side of a stylized lion-face spout. Connected by channels, 3 shallow circular recesses are carved into the top of the stand. The outer 2 would have held large earthenware water jars, condensation from which would have flowed to the central recess before flowing through the spout. It was found at the Monastery of Apa Thomas at Wadi Sarga, a c.600–800 settlement located in and around earlier, Pharaonic gallery quarries. [ERO]
Bibliography: Dalton 1921, p.12, fig. 6

238 Water jar stand

Egypt. 12th–13th century
Marble. 40 × 57 × 37 cm
British Museum, London. ME 1988,1107.1

This stand, carved from a single block, is supported on 4 curved legs. It is polygonal in structure, with a shallow basin at the front, and is richly decorated with reliefs. Within architectural framing elements are lions and fantastical beasts as well as Arabic inscriptions in decorated angular Kufic script. Stands of this kind, which are known almost exclusively from Egypt, would have held large water jars. [GH]

239 Water jug with filter

Egypt. 10th–12th century
Fired clay. 16 cm, diameter 7.8 cm (neck opening)
Museum für Islamische Kunst, Staatliche Museen zu Berlin. Inv. I. 1930

Made of fired clay, this jug is similar in shape to the jug with
thumb support (fig. 247). At the top of the neck-opening
is a filter, depicting a long-legged water bird on a pierced
background. Jugs made of porous clay are ideal containers
for water in warm climates, because the water is kept cool by
evaporation. Filters also help to control evaporation and keep
out dust at the same time. Such fine jugs with elaborately
patterned filters (see figs 240–42) were also mass-produced
for export, as proven by the discovery of a jug with the same
water bird in the wreck of a ship that sank in the bay of Serçe
Liman, on the west coast of Turkey, in the 11th century. [GH]
Bib: Museum für Islamische Kunst 1971 and 1979, no. 330;
Wasserwelten 2010, no. III.5

240 Filter with inscription *man haff taff* (Whoever opens it will find it full)

Egypt. 10th–12th century
Fired clay. Diameter 5 cm
Museum für Islamische Kunst, Staatliche Museen zu Berlin. Inv. I. 42/65

241 Filter with ornamental pattern

Egypt. 10th–12th century
Fired clay. Diameter 6.5 cm
Museum für Islamische Kunst, Staatliche Museen zu Berlin. Inv. I. 1849

242 Filter with elephant

Egypt. 10th–12th century
Fired clay. Diameter 6.4 cm
Museum für Islamische Kunst, Staatliche Museen zu Berlin. Inv. I. 6831

Filters inserted into the necks of fired clay water jugs (see fig.
239) were common throughout the Mediterranean world, but
these extremely elaborately decorated filters with their variety
of patterns were produced only in early medieval Egypt. There
are geometric and vegetal patterns, animals such as the birds
and elephants shown here, mythical beasts, inscriptions and,
more rarely, even human figures. Similar or identical patterns
indicate that they were mass produced from models. There is
very little religious symbolism to be found on these everyday
objects; even the inscriptions are most often short, general
aphorisms. Hundreds of these filters have been found in the
medieval rubbish heaps of Old Cairo and other cities. They were
clearly intended for slightly more prosperous households, where
people could afford to pay more for better crockery. [GH]

243 Container

Egypt. 11th century
Copper alloy. Height 11.5 cm, diameter 29.5 cm
Museum für Islamische Kunst, Staatliche Museen zu Berlin.
Inv. I. 3679

This large, circular container stands on 3 small feet.
The lid is attached to the body by 2 hinges and a catch,
all of which end in long points. It is engraved with an
inscription in angular Kufic script around the rim and a
plaited pattern. Containers of this kind were intended
for anyone of any faith who could afford an expensive
metal vessel. The inscription offers good wishes 'to the
owner' (*li-sahibihi*). [GH]
Bib: Museum für Islamische Kunst 1971 and 1979, no.
307; Islamische Kunst 1984, no. 238

244 Platter

Egypt, Akhmim (produced in Aswan). *c.*600
Fired red clay, painted. Height 5.5 cm, diameter 48.5 cm
Skulpturensammlung und Museum für Byzantinische Kunst,
Staatliche Museen zu Berlin. Inv. 6637

The central field of this platter, which has been
re-assembled from a number of fragments, is painted
with a lotus blossom with a tendril growing from it, a
hare looking toward a bunch of grapes, and a fish. The
images appear to be connected by chains as if they
had to be kept together. The double circle surrounding
them strengthens this impression. Outside the central
medallion are diagonal groups of rectangles made by
single brush strokes. Produced in Aswan, many plates
of this kind have survived, but for the most part the
decoration tells us little about their use. [EE]
Bib: Cat. Stuttgart 1984, p. 188, no. 156; Cat. Hamm
1996, p. 170, no. 151, fig. p. 170

245 Painted storage jar

Egypt, probably Fayyum (produced in Aswan).
5th–6th century
Fired red clay, painted. Height 26.5 cm, diameter 23 cm
Skulpturensammlung und Museum für Byzantinische Kunst,
Staatliche Museen zu Berlin. Inv.- Nr. 3500

This large vessel is decorated with a tendril composition
of animals and birds. The *guilloche* bands and other
decoration are typical for Late Antique pottery. Each of
the eight tendrils of the frieze is occupied by an animal.
From left to right are a 1-horned, a 2-horned and a
hornless antelope, 2 birds, a horse and 2 lions. Most
of the animals look back anxiously to the lions. On the
rear body of one of the lions is a Greek cross in a circle.
Its meaning in this composition is unclear. The vessel's
decoration and the vessel itself are well executed. Its
size suggests that it functioned as a container. [MK]
Bib: Wulff 1909, cat. no. 1509, p. 286, fig.S. 286; Cat.
Berlin 2012, 23–25, no. 7

A beautifully adorned table had to have decorated glassware. Surviving goblets, flagons, jugs and glasses show splendid creative achievements, with an evolution of forms and decoration from the beginning of Late Antiquity to the Islamic period (fig. 247).

The everyday objects recall ancient customs from life beside the Nile. Over more than a millennium a stylistic development is perceptible, in the techniques used and the decoration. If certain objects are specifically Egyptian (frog-shaped lamps, stands for earthenware jars) or show Pharaonic deities (Bes, Isis, Harpocrates), others adopt a style that is generally part of the larger Byzantine (metal lamps) or Islamic worlds (decorated ceramic). Trade and travel favoured the circulation of objects and fashions in the countries of the Middle East. In this context Jews, Christians and Muslims follow the same models, which generally do not assert their religious identity. Only a few symbols, such as the *menorah* and the cross, or inscriptions make it possible to attribute a given object to these believers.

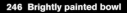

246 Brightly painted bowl

Egypt. 11th century
Fired clay, glazed. Height 6.3 cm, diameter 24 cm
Museum für Islamische Kunst, Staatliche Museen zu Berlin.
Inv. I. 1747

Unglazed on the outside, this deep bowl has a circular
base and a flat rim. The inside is painted with slightly runny
coloured glazes. The shape, colours and patterns are typical
of the ceramics that have been found in large numbers in
the Fayyum (which was still largely inhabited by Christians
in the Fatimid period), and are therefore known as Fayyum
ceramics. However, finds have also been made in Lower
Egypt and it is now thought possible that they were also
produced in Fustat. The bright range of colours on these
ceramics, including a strong violet and a light blue, was
almost unique at that time and looks very modern today. [GH]
Bib: Museum für Islamische Kunst 1971 and 1979, no. 300

247 Jug with thumb support

Egypt. 11th–12th century
Glass. Height 14.3 cm, diameter 9 cm
Museum für Islamische Kunst, Staatliche Museen zu Berlin.
Inv. I. 2204

This small hand-blown jug has a separate circular base and
a pontil mark on the bottom. The compressed globular body
merges into a slightly funnel-shaped neck. The attached handle
is folded over at the top to form a thumb support, which has
then been pinched. Jugs of this shape were very popular and
were also widespread outside Egypt. They were also made
in ceramics (see fig. 239) and in metal. The greenish colour
suggests that this one was produced in Egypt which, like the
Syrian coast, was a major centre of Islamic glassmaking at the
time. Glassware was exported from both Syrian and Egyptian
glassworks, as demonstrated by the finds from a ship which
sank in the 11th century in the bay of Serçe Liman on the
west coast of Turkey, the cargo of which included glass jugs
of this shape. [GH]
Bib: Islamische Kunst 1984, no. 11; Vorsicht Glas 2010, no. 32

248 Stamp with a cross

Egypt, probably from Akhmim. Uncertain date
Fired red clay. Diameter 7.9 cm
Skulpturensammlung und Museum für Byzantinische
Kunst, Staatliche Museen zu Berlin. Inv. 3530

The raised surface of this stamp shows a cross,
surrounded by a Greek key-pattern border. The lower
part of the jagged edge of the stamp is damaged.
Here there is a thicker place in the border, which
could be either a kind of handle or stand, or possibly
damage from fire. It is doubtful whether the stamp
was ever used, as the narrow, notched handle on the
back is almost impossible to get hold of. To the side
of the handle are roughly engraved palm fronds. [EE]
Bib: Wulff 1909, p. 277, no. 1435, pl. LXX; Cat.
Hamm 1996, pp. 178–79, no. 166a, fig. S. 178

249 Stamp with a *menorah*

Egypt, probably from Ashmunain. Uncertain date
Wood. Height 2.8 cm, diameter 5.8 cm
Skulpturensammlung und Museum für Byzantinische
Kunst, Staatliche Museen zu Berlin. Inv. 3654

The main surface of the stamp is engraved with the
image of a *menorah* standing on a tripod. At the
sides of the candlestick are 2 characters, whose
meaning is uncertain. They might be the Greek
letters *iota* and *sigma*, which could be understood
as an abbreviation of the name of Jesus and point
to its use as a bread stamp in the Egyptian church.
However, a more likely interpretation is that they
represent a *shofar* (ram's horn) and an incense
burner, which would suggest it was used to mark
kosher bread. The back of the stamp, which has
slight damage to the surface with the impression of
a palm branch engraved on it, argues in favour of
the latter interpretation. The palm branch (*lulav*) is
one of the symbols most often appearing with the
menorah. [EE]
Bib: Wulff 1909, p. 99, no. 316, pl. XII; Cat. Frankfurt
1961, no. 69, fig. 32; Cat. Karlsruhe 2013, p. 318,
no. 201

250 Stamp with Arabic inscription

Egypt. 9th–11th century
Fired clay. Diameter 7.3 cm
Museum für Islamische Kunst, Staatliche Museen zu Berlin.
Inv. I. 1081

This stamp has a curved handle on the back made of
red clay and covered with a thin beige-coloured slip.
It has an engraved inscription, consisting of 2 Arabic
words in angular Kufic script in negative: *kull hani'an*,
'Eat healthily!' Inscriptions like this could be used
in all households of whatever religious persuasion.
The stamping of flat bread was common in Egypt
from the Roman period on. In the Byzantine period
it is found mainly in the ecclesiastical setting, where
the communion bread was stamped with Christian
symbols. This practice was also adopted in everyday
life, when other motifs appeared, and it was not
restricted to Christians. Ornamental bread stamps are
sometimes still in use today, for instance in Morocco,
Syria and as far away as Central Asia. [GH]
Bib: Kühnel 1939, p. 53, fig. 1f; Das Staunen der
Welt 1995, no. 9

25 Clothing and Soft Furnishings

Amandine Mérat

251 Red tunic
Egypt. *c.*670–870
Linen, wool, appliqué. 131 × 209 cm (including sleeves),
131 × 124 cm (excluding sleeves)
Victoria and Albert Museum, London. Inv. 291–1891

This adult tunic is a rare survival of an almost complete
coloured woollen garment. The decoration of the bands
and medallion ornaments – applied and sewn, and possibly
supplied by a specialist tapestry workshop – mainly
comprises floral devices, birds and figures of uncertain
identification. In Arabic, Allah can be read in the shoulder-
bands. One letter is missing – perhaps the weaver was not
familiar with the word. Using the word Allah was common
at that time, both for faith and purely decorative purposes;
this tunic could have been equally worn by a Muslim, a
Christian or a Jew. [AM]
Bib: Kendrick 1922, III, fig. 620, pl. IV; King 2004,
pp. 246–67, fig. 21; Pritchard 2006, p. 92.

IN the First Millennium the most basic item of costume worn in Egypt – in the various religious communities and by men, women and children alike – was the tunic (figs 251, 253).[1] It is depicted on the mummy portraits dating from the first centuries AD (ch. 27), and came with the Romans to Egypt where, following the fashion that held sway throughout the empire, it promptly became the rule.

Mostly made of linen, sometimes of wool, the tunic was woven in the form of a large cross. Usually a vertical warp-weighted loom was used. The finished woven tunic was folded along the horizontal axis and sewn together at the sides. Men and children could wear the tunic short or long. For women it was ankle-length so as to completely cover the legs (fig. 253). The tunics came with or without sleeves, and they could be belted at the waist as required. In Late Antiquity they were richly decorated. Patterns in tapestries, sometimes directly woven into the basic weave and sometimes applied (sewn into) and, more rarely, embroideries in different shapes and sizes, accented the shoulders, the neck and the knee or wrist areas. Here Roman and Eastern traditions met.[2] Motifs on the *clavi* (long bands), *plastrons* (neck-opening ornament) and wrist bands – as on the *tabulae* (squares) and *orbiculi* (roundels) decorative elements – came in many varieties. The decoration upon them ranged from simple stripes to figurative motifs of flora and fauna, from simple geometric designs to complex interlaced ornamentation. Motifs from the world of the Nile can be found,

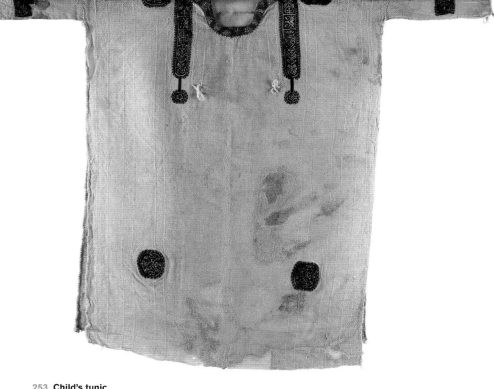

252 *Kohl* tube decorated with figure of Tyche

Egypt. 5th–6th century
Tamarisk wood. 21.1 × 7 × 5.6 cm
Département des Antiquités égyptiennes,
Musée du Louvre, Paris. Inv. E 17211

Decorating this *kohl* container, Tyche stands between two columns. The figure has an elongated torso and is dressed in a fine pleated tunic and a draped cloak. Wearing a *kalathos*, she holds in one hand a cornucopia while the other pulls back a fold of her cloak. This personification of Fortune promised success and prosperity to the owner of the object. The container itself (not shown) is in the shape of an *amphora* with a tapered body, striated and topped by a high cylindrical neck decorated with chevrons. Propped up by a support, it is set against a carved background of stylized foliage. Leather straps holding a plug were probably attached to the handles. Traces of *kohl* prepared on a galena base, as a blackish residue, remain inside. [MD]

253 Child's tunic

Egypt. 5th–6th century (?)
Wool; collar: braided weave, added and sewn on.
68 × 89 cm (with sleeves)
Département des Antiquités égyptiennes, Musée du Louvre,
Paris. Inv. E 26248 (F 74; AC 282)

The tunic, a piece of cloth woven in one piece and sewn on the sides, is a unisex garment worn by children and adults. Tapestry decorations – *clavi*, *orbiculi* and *tabulae* – are either an integral part of the fabric, or are formed separately and then stitched on. They are placed on the shoulders, sleeves, necklines and hems of garments. Especially common are decorative motifs based on plants, usually highly stylized, and geometric decoration, usually in a purple colour at this time. This child's tunic demonstrates these features. The *clavi* with pendants depict plant motifs in an overlapping sequence, ending in palmettes. The arm bands and *orbiculi* on the shoulders and skirt contain abstract flowerings. [CJ]

254 Tapestry decoration with *menorah*

Egypt. 5th–7th century
Linen, wool. 24.5 × 24 cm
Département des Antiquités égyptiennes, Musée
du Louvre, Paris. Inv. AF 6139

The central motif of this tapestry shows
a 7-branched candelabra with 3 feet and
a central shaft, from which 6 side candle-
holders project. Approaching the base are
2 small figures, flanked by branches. The
geometric figuration is surrounded by a
square, the black lines of which are broken at
the corners and in the centre of each side to
form a kind of star. Its points end in 8 small
medallions enclosing a stylized animal (hare
or cat, and bird) and a full cup (left). Finally,
the intervals are full of stylized figures that
seem to be dancing. One of them is bringing
an object (a basket or a lantern). The motifs,
made with wool threads, have been largely
eaten away by insects, although the woven
linen parts have survived. Nevertheless, the
medallion, intended to decorate a tunic, is
of interest because representations of the
menorah rarely survive on textiles from Late
Antique Egypt. [DB]

as well as figures and stories from Classical mythology such as genre depictions of
shepherds and hunters. These motifs were widely popular and were worn by all,
regardless of their religious affiliation.

In the first centuries AD religious motifs were rare, limited mainly to signs
and symbols such as the cross. Jewish motifs were extremely rare (fig. 254).[3]
Although Judaism prescribed rules for the use of certain qualities of fabric that are
mentioned in the sources, these were apparently not produced and so cannot have
been worn.[4] From the fifth century, on the other hand, stories from the Christian
Old and New Testaments such as scenes from the lives of David or Joseph (figs 188,
189, 190) were depicted on the tunics. From about the same time we find in Egypt
a type of costume with flared sides, influenced by Persian cavalry garb. Later the
galabiya (long costume for everyday wear, still generally worn in Egypt today) shows

255 **Fragment of a child's dress**
Egypt, probably from Upper Egypt. 12th–13th century
Linen, silk. 50 × 59 cm
Museum für Islamische Kunst, Staatliche Museen zu Berlin. Inv. I. 1035

When opened out the cut of this small dress is clear – a rectangular central panel with a long slit down the chest, with wide sleeves and sloping side panels attached to it under a narrow cross-strip. This type of garment remained in use throughout the Near East until recently. This linen tunic, embellished with rows of fine ornamental pattern-darning in brownish-black and red silk, was probably the child's best dress. The striking rows of triangles along the hem of the garment and around the front opening could possibly be interpreted as types of defensive and protective amulets. Infant mortality was high; the protective signs on this dress, which was found in a grave, could not protect the child from an early death. [GH]
Bib: Kühnel 1927, p. 59, pl. 35

256 **Base of a bowl with a figure**
Egypt. 11th–12th century
Fritware, decorated with lustre. Diameter 101.5 mm
Museum für Islamische Kunst, Staatliche Museen zu Berlin. Inv. I. 1856

The figure, only a fragment of which remains, is wearing a dress that fastens tightly at the neck and a long, striped overdress with long, wide sleeves. The edges of the dress overlap at the front of the upper body and are held in place by a girdle made up of several sections that hang down. The fine, striped pattern of the dress has been picked out of the lustre background using a *qalam* (reed pen), and looks in places like pleating. Pale decorative bands with inscriptions, known as *tiraz* bands, can be seen on the upper arms. [GH]

similar features (figs 255, 256). This type of dress is composed of different pieces of fabric, cut out and sewn together. In the Islamic period these garments were decorated using the greatest variety of techniques, both with geometric patterns and with simplified figurative and floral motifs, as well as with Arabic inscriptions – a real innovation (see focus 7). The type of the classic tunic with straight sides gradually disappeared towards the end of the First Millennium. But it continued in monastic clothing (fig. 130).

We get a good idea of clothing in Islamic times from the dowry lists of Jewish women that have survived among the documents of the Cairo Genizah (see ch. 18),[5] and even from a book of etiquette for high society in the tenth century.[6] In this period many more textiles-types were coming from other parts of the world to Egypt, and silk in particular was gaining in importance.[7]

258 Embroidered cap

Egypt. c.9th–10th century
Linen, silk. Height 8.5 cm, diameter 16 cm
Museum für Islamische Kunst, Staatliche Museen zu Berlin.
Inv. I. 1995.5

Both the crown and the band of this round cap have several
layers, and are densely embroidered in different coloured silk
threads. This style of cap indicates it was produced in the
early medieval period; from around the 13th century people
preferred caps tailored from a number of sections. Small caps
like these were worn by children and adults of both sexes,
indoors as well as out. The head-covering was completed with
a length of fabric placed over the cap or wound around it (in
the case of a turban), especially outdoors. [GH]

259 Lustreware fragment depicting headgear

Egypt. 11th–12th century
Fritware, lustre painted. Length 7.3 cm, diameter
6.7 cm
Museum für Islamische Kunst, Staatliche Museen zu
Berlin. Inv. I. 43/64.129

The face of a young man is framed by curls,
and he wears a richly decorated turban.
His serene, contemplative expression is
characteristic of this type of painted ceramic.
[GH]

257 Hairnet

Egypt, Crocodilopolis/Arsinoë. 5th century
Linen, wool. 31 × 47 cm (unmounted)
Skulpturensammlung und Museum für
Byzantinische Kunst, Staatliche Museen zu Berlin.
Inv. 17/2010

Hairnets made using the sprang technique
are the typical head-covering for women in
Late Antiquity. They are made of wool or linen
or a mixture of both materials, and they can
be rectangular in shape or conical, as here,
with a variety of decoration. Sprang is a type
of knotting that produces a stretchy fabric
and is therefore extremely suitable for making
head-coverings. The knotting technique
produces many different mesh patterns. [CF]
Bib: Cat. Berlin 2010, pp. 81–82, no. 51

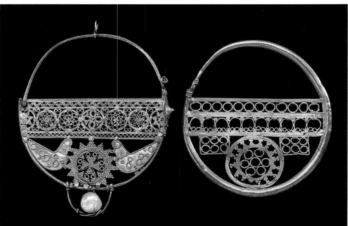

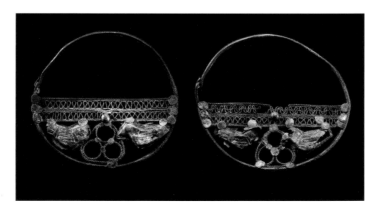

260–261 Gold and silver earrings

Egypt. 6th–7th century (a, c); 7th–8th century (b)
Gold (a–b), silver (c), pearl (a)
Museum für Islamische Kunst, Staatliche Museen
zu Berlin. Inv. I. 1986.52 and I. 2333 (a, b)
Skulpturensammlung und Museum für
Byzantinische Kunst, Staatliche Museen zu Berlin.
Inv. 9725 (c)

This type of earring, with only the lower part of
the hoop being decorated, was common in the
whole Eastern Mediterranean region in the
period of the Islamic expansion. The upper left
example and the lower pair show the use of
one model for different materials and different
quality depending on the wealth of the client.
Both have a pair of birds flanking a medallion.
The golden earring shows an elaborate
and carefully executed ornamentation with
different wires, granulation and small discs,
and has an additional pearl. Cross shapes
recall contemporary Christian-Byzantine
decoration and indicate a Christian wearer.
The upper right earring shows the further
development of this earring type in the Islamic
period. The absence of Christian symbols may
indicate a Muslim or a Jewish wearer. [GH]

262 Child's sock

Egypt, Antinoopolis (excavated 1913/14).
200–400 (radiocarbon-dated)
Wool. 5.5 × 12.5 cm
British Museum, London. EA53913

The big toe is separated from the other toes of this left-foot child's stripy sock, indicating that the original pair was designed to be worn with sandals. The excavation documentation confirms that it was indeed found together with a sandal (BM EA 53915). It has been made in *naalebinding* – a single needle-looping technique – starting from the toe upwards (each toe being made separately before being joined), and finishing with the sole of the heel and the heel itself. [AM]
Bib: Pritchard 2013, pp. 34–55; O'Connell 2014c, no. 14 (p.473); De Moor, Fluck, Strydonck and Boudin (forthcoming)

To complement their costumes people sometimes wore a mantle or a shawl, as well as all sorts of headgear that differed with gender and age.[8] In Late Antiquity women often covered their heads with a sprang hairnet (fig. 257), or with a veil to which, on the part framing the face, a beading or wreath of coloured wool was attached (focus 9, fig. 302).[9] In the Islamic period rectangular cloths were used by women as headgear. Men, meanwhile, wore hats in various forms; for children, the most common headgear was the hood. Most of these forms of headgear changed little in the Islamic period, but some, like the sprang hairnets, disappeared completely. A new feature is the turban, a piece of cloth wrapped around a skullcap into various forms (figs 258, 259).

The same applies to footwear. From the second century onwards socks produced by a single needle-looping technique (*naalebinding*) were widespread; they were mostly made of coloured wool, often with separation between the big toe and four other toes (fig. 262). They are attested into the fifth century. By the tenth to eleventh centuries knitted one-piece socks and stockings were worn, of the kind still familiar today, both displaying great variety. Footwear made of leather, straw or raffia could be worn by men, women and children (fig. 263). There were closed, often slipper-like shoes, and sandals, both also in many different forms. The financial position and social status of the wearers, both male and female, dictated the material and design of their footwear. The most precious shoes were perfumed, and decorated with silk, gold-gilding and precious stones (fig. 264). In most cases, however, people went barefoot.

263 Pair of child's shoes

Egypt. 5th–6th century
Leather. 1.5 × 6 × cm
Skulpturensammlung und Museum für Byzantinische Kunst, Staatliche Museen zu Berlin. Inv. 2009

The soles and uppers of this pair of child's shoes are made of the same brown dyed leather. Rounded where they surround the toes, each toecap has a small round scroll on it made from a narrow band of leather. On the instep is a 'cockscomb' decoration in the shape of a heart. It is bordered with a narrow band made from a rolled-up strip of red leather, which also runs round the entire upper edge of both shoes. Similar shoes have been found in Akhmim and Antinoopolis. A few examples closely resembling this child's shoes have recently been radiocarbon-dated to the period 420–600. [CF]

264 Pair of gilded shoes

Egypt, probably from Akhmim. 4th–5th century
Leather with gilding and embroidery, linen and silk thread
26 × 7 × 8 cm
Victoria and Albert Museum, London. 837&A-1903

These leather women's shoes were made by the common shoemaking technique of turning, which consists of sewing together the upper and sole before turning the shoe inside-out, thus protecting and concealing the sewing on the inside. This pair has been extensively embellished with gold leaf to create a disc-shaped motif on the top enclosing 8 smaller circles, themselves decorated with embroidered stars. The embroidery thread is possibly silk. Said to have come from a Christian female burial in Akhmim, this pair of shoes is testimony to the Christian belief that death is not an end but a step before resurrection, for which people wished to present themselves in their finest clothes. [AM]

265 Hanging with the story of Jonah

Egypt. 320–420
Linen, wool. 119 × 210 cm
Département des Antiquités égyptiennes, Musée
du Louvre, Paris. Inv. E 26820

This large fragment of a hanging, structured
in registers, is characterized by shimmering
colours and a relief effect obtained by the
technique of weft loops. On the lower level,
beasts stand on either side of a Tree of
Life. At the top biblical symbols and scenes
exalt the resurrection of Christ. In the centre
2 columns flank a handled cross with an
imposing hoop. On the left a peacock, facing
a donkey, holds in its beak an identical cross
while on the right are 2 episodes from the
Jonas cycle. The prophet emerges from the
mouth of the sea monster in the attitude of a
person praying, sheltered by the gourd vine.
The iconography of the piece suggests that it
decorated the walls of a church or a monastic
space. [MD]

Textiles played a central role in the
interiors of homes, where they took on different functions and displayed a repertoire
of images as wide ranging as the motifs
on the garments. The fabrics used for furnishing included curtains and drapes that
were installed on windows or door frames,
or which served to separate two different
areas from each other (fig. 114). Hangings
could decorate the walls just like paintings, while rugs lay on the floor resembling
mosaics of which they were meant to be
the woven equivalents. Furthermore, there
were tablecloths on the tables, and blankets
and pillows on the beds and benches.[10] The
textiles deployed in houses changed little in
the Islamic period. Most changes were in the decoration – in the early period, it often happened that only Arabic inscriptions were used as a sign of the new era. In the Fatimid
period curtains, hangings, cushions and floor coverings were decorated with patterns similar to those on clothing.

Such soft-furnishings in the Roman through to the Fatimid periods comprised large
rectangular pieces, often covered with knots or equipped with loops. They were usually
made of linen and wool, more rarely cotton or silk. Patterns were, as with clothing, embroidered, made in tapestry or brocaded. Textiles were often decorated with scattered patterns
distributed over the entire surface of the fabric, or with strips, squares and medallions sym-
metrically arranged on the rectangle. These patterns could be of a purely ornamental
nature, or consist of figurative and abstract motifs, and they gave the interiors a colourful
and welcoming touch.

However, a considerable number of domestic textiles in Late Antiquity had more
complex ornaments in the form of images from Classical mythology or the Christian
Old and New Testaments. They were part of a long tradition, gradually changing in style
and, in the Islamic period, adding new features such as Arabic script. Purely religious
symbolism was rarely found in everyday life, but occurred primarily in the realm of
worship (ch. 9, 10, 16, fig. 265). In the eleventh to twelfth centuries everyday clothes for
Christians, Jews and Muslims were basically the same (with the exception of the periods
in which dress codes were enforced). The differences in clothing resulted primarily from
social standing.

FOCUS 7 TIRAZ TEXTILES

Gisela Helmecke

IN the Muslim world, textiles played a greater role than in Europe – in home decor, clothes, in wage and tax administration, and as objects of investiture. The massive quantities of luxurious fabrics in particular were due to the system of *tiraz* (official workshops) that primarily served the needs of the caliphal courts. This system had precursors in both Persian and Byzantine empires, but in the Islamic empire reached a hitherto unattained perfection. The monopoly of the *tiraz* was possessed by the state – primarily the caliph himself. Having responsibility for the *tiraz* was one of the chief offices of state. Under the Umayyads in the eighth century, in some places there already existed two types of workshop – the *tiraz al-khassa* (for the caliph and court alone), and the *tiraz al-'amma* (more general workshop that was also accessible to a wider clientele).

In Egypt, outside Cairo there were several places in the Nile Delta where *tiraz* workshops were found – Tinnis, Dimyat (Damietta), Dabiq, Shata, Abwan, Tuna, Alexandria and others. Many were already known for their textiles in pre-Islamic times. This also applies to Fayyum with Tutun and the capital Medinat al-Fayyum and to Upper Egypt with al-Bahnasa, Taha, Ashmunain, Asyut and Akhmim. In all these places, weavers and textile workers were predominantly Christians until the tenth century.

266 Tiraz fragment
Egypt, probably produced in Tinnis or Cairo. 975–96
Linen, silk. 18 × 26 cm
Museum für Islamische Kunst, Staatliche Museen zu Berlin. Inv. I. 6407

This fragment, with part of a large *tiraz* inscription, is from a loosely woven fine linen and silk tapestry. It is copied from a model by an expert calligrapher, written in an impressive decorated Kufic script which was introduced in this form under al-Muti'bi-llah, the last Abbasid caliph to rule over Egypt. The inscription states the name of the 5th Fatimid caliph, al-'Aziz bi-llah (975–96). During his reign the Fatimid caliphate was extended and stabilized, the al-Azhar mosque and university was founded, and Jews and Christians also achieved high offices. [GH]

267 Tiraz fragment
Egypt, produced in Fayyum. 9th century
Wool, linen. 10.5 × 36 cm
Museum für Islamische Kunst, Staatliche Museen zu Berlin. Inv. I. 6441

On this fragment of a decorative border, a simple ornamental framework encloses a repeated statement of faith: *al-mulk li-llah* (The power/supremacy is God's). The script appears in pairs of normal and mirror-writing, *al-mulk* always in white, *li-llah* in colour. The style of the script, with its letter stems like small trees and the small birds and geometrical elements scattered in between, is characteristic of work from the Fayyum Oasis, which was largely inhabited by Christians until well into the Fatimid period. [GH]
Bib: Helmecke 2006, p. 188, no. 5, fig. 41; Fluck and Helmecke 2014, p. 254, fig. 18.31

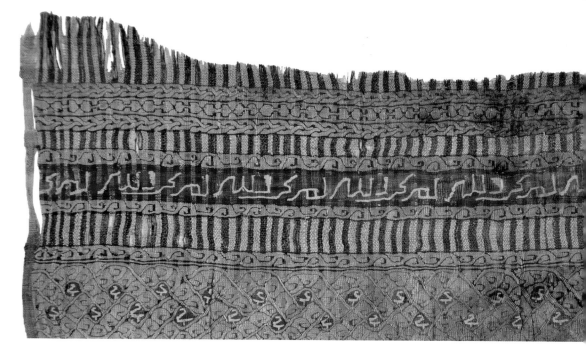

268 Fabric fragment

Egypt. 11th–12th century
Linen, silk. 21.5 × 32.5 cm
Museum für Islamische Kunst, Staatliche Museen zu Berlin.
Inv. I. 3128

This fragment is of an end of a narrow woven strip that may have been used as a sash, shawl or turban. Three decorative stripes in red and gold silk and others in natural-coloured linen are worked into the blue and white striped linen background. On the wide stripe is an interlacing pattern that forms medallions with swan-like birds, and a brief statement in white, slightly cursive Arabic script on a red ground is repeated in one of the narrower stripes. The religious text *nasr min allah* (help from God) refers to a passage from the Qur'an (Sura 61, verse 13), which goes on to say *wa-fath qarib* (and victory very near). It is one of the most popular inscriptions from the late Fatimid period (12th century). [GH]
Bib: Kühnel 1927, p. 31

269 Tiraz fragment (above)

Egypt (produced in Iran or Iraq). 10th–11th century
Cotton, silk. 18.5 × 40 cm
Museum für Islamische Kunst, Staatliche Museen zu Berlin.
Inv. I. 13/64

The long, embroidered inscription on this fragment (not completely preserved) praises God and invokes blessings on the Prophet Muhammad and his family, followed by pious wishes for the caliph (name not preserved). The script, a angular Kufic, is characterized by tall stems and a bottom row of arcs, both elements having a function here that is to some extent purely decorative. Like the cotton fabric, this style of writing and the chain-stitch technique point to the eastern part of the Islamic world. The fine, soft cotton fabrics produced there were in demand everywhere, as is evidenced by this fragment from an Egyptian grave. [GH]
Bib: Islamische Kunst 1986, no. 42; Niewöhner 2006, p. 200

The identification of all pieces of cloth coming from these workshops by so-called *tiraz* inscriptions was obligatory. Official *tiraz* inscriptions usually contained the name of the reigning caliph (fig. 266). They were therefore considered to be insignia, similar to the mention of the caliph in the Friday prayer, on the state seal, and on coins. Correct and complete inscriptions, in full accordance with protocol, contain the caliph's full name, including his title, as well as the place and year of manufacture and the type of workshop.[1] They are often found, however, in abbreviated versions. Because of this information, *tiraz* inscriptions are historically important documents, but they also fascinate due to the beauty of their calligraphy.

The inscriptions produced in the workshops of Cairo and the Nile Delta were initially embroidered as single lines with silk on linen ground, and appeared in angular kufic script.[2] In the tenth century *tiraz* inscriptions were made mainly in tapestry that had been practised in Egypt from ancient Egyptian times. Fine natural-coloured or bleached linen and coloured silk threads were used for decoration. This technique and the fine silk material available at this time in the workshops of Cairo and the Nile Delta, and later also in Upper Egypt,[3] allowed a clear rendition of fine details in the smallest area. Thus true textile masterpieces were produced in Egypt, following instructions provided by master calligraphers. From the twelfth century inscriptions in cursive script also appeared, which gradually displaced the kufic inscriptions. While initially the tapestry inscriptions, like the embroidered ones, stood alone, they were increasingly accompanied by separate ornamental trimmings (fig. 268), until these merged with the inscription. At the end of this process there are ornamental stripes in which writing is used purely for decoration and is finally no longer legible. In addition to the indigenous *tiraz* textiles, some from other parts of the Islamic world have also been found in Egyptian tombs.

Tiraz inscriptions were attached to curtains and other textile furnishings, but hardly any have survived. They also decorated garments, mainly in the upper sleeve area and as edge trimmings, as well as the ends of turbans. Many medieval Arab and Persian miniatures include robes with these bands of writing. Since fine Egyptian fabrics were also much sought-after in Europe until the fourteenth century, we can see garments with *tiraz* bands in Italian paintings from the thirteenth to the fifteenth century.[4]

26 Professions and Crafts

Alain Delattre

BY the fourth century AD, wine had largely replaced beer as the staple beverage of choice in ancient Egypt, while colourful wool or wool-decorated garments had replaced the previously, largely plain, linen.[1] Despite such cultural changes, the agricultural infrastructure of Egypt was not otherwise dramatically altered from earlier times. Produce, materials and goods that were once destined for Rome and, later, Constantinople were, post-conquest, instead sent east to the caliphal capitals and the Hijaz.

Agriculture is by far the most important and well-known economic sector in ancient economies – especially in Egypt, where the climate and the flood of the Nile made the land particularly fertile and productive. Throughout the year the major part of the population in the countryside undertook agricultural tasks such as ploughing, sowing and harvesting arable land, but also maintaining the irrigation system consisting of dykes and hydraulic machinery, which was essential to the development of land. All these operations were carried out according to a strict timetable.[2] Wheat, barley, vegetables and grapes were the most commonly grown crops. The processing of agricultural products such as flour, wine or oil was sometimes made within the agricultural property, sometimes in specialized units, or at the place of consumption. It required the manufacture of containers – bags for dry goods, ceramics for liquid food (fig. 270). In production units, animal husbandry was also practised, mainly chickens, pigs and cattle. The proximity of the Nile, channels or lakes also allowed fishing. Distribution of agricultural products was done through an efficient transport system. For shorter distances, muleteers and camel drivers brought the products to the place of consumption or centralization, while boats were preferred for long-distance transport.[3]

Crafts also played a significant role in the Egyptian economy. Greek sources of the Graeco-Roman period show the existence of no less than 800 skilled occupations in craft and trade.[4] Indeed, the numerous documents from the Cairo Genizah show that during the medieval period there was a high level of specialization and labour division, not only in the great industries but also in smaller handicrafts.[5]

Professional craftsmen are well attested in the sources, but craftsmanship in the domestic area is more difficult to bring to light. The best-known industry is the textile sector, which required a large and highly diversified workforce, dealing with the different stages of production from the cultivation of flax, to spinning and to the manufacture of clothing itself (ch. 25). The building sector required various sorts of specialized work – brick manufacturers, quarrymen, carpenters, masons, architects and so on. The smith's activity was essential at all levels of the economy. Painters and sculptors were only required for the most important buildings.

Besides production, many services are attested in the Egyptian economy. People in charge of transport have already been mentioned. There were also various merchants as sellers of wine, oil, vegetables, salt, salted fish products, textiles etc. (although producers sometimes marketed their own production themselves). In addition there were various administrative functions within the central government, as well as at the district and village levels, such as officials and secretaries, not to mention the army. The scribes are well attested in our documentation, and usually knew both Greek and Coptic, and later Coptic and Arabic (see ch. 23). Lawyers, bankers, businessmen, physicians, artists and school teachers complete this overview of professions in Late Antique Egypt. During the first centuries of Arab rule, medicine was mainly in the hands of Christian and Jewish physicians; some of them were attached to the army and navy.[6]

In the Roman and Late Antique periods the workforce was organized in associations, colleges or corporations, which brought together members of the same profession.[7] Family business often determined the choice of profession, with experience usually passing from father to son, but some professional mobility still occurred, as evidenced by many apprenticeship contracts.[8]

With the development of Christianity, a new kind of production unit appeared during the fourth century – monasteries.[9] Typologically we can distinguish two types of monks, either leading a more solitary life (anchorites) or a communal one (coenobites) (see ch. 11 and ch. 12). The anchorites worked essentially in domestic crafts, especially the production of ropes, mats and baskets.[10] This repetitive activity allowed the balancing of work and prayer; it required little equipment and could

270 Liquid container

Egypt. 5th – 7th century
Fired white clay, painted. Height 37.5 cm, diameter (base) 6.5 cm, diameter (top) 4.2 cm
Skulpturensammlung und Museum für Byzantinische Kunst, Staatliche Museen zu Berlin. Inv. 3504

Earthenware vessels are practical containers for water or wine because clay allows continuous evaporation through the surface, which cools the contents. The decoration of this vessel is divided into 2 registers. The upper part is decorated with simple paintings, concentric circles, floral motifs and a stylized fish – one of the most common designs in Late Antique Egyptian art. On the back an interlaced palm branch and spiral circle pattern can be seen. In the centre of the vessel runs a stripe, framing a wavy line cursorily painted to separate the 2 registers. The lower register is left plain. The use of black paint on a light colour is typical for pottery produced between the 5th and 7th centuries. [MK]
Bibliography: Wulff 1909, cat. no. 1527, pp. 289–90; Cat. Hamm 1996, p. 169, no. 149

be accomplished by a single monk. Conversely, in bigger monasteries, diversification of activities was important. *The Lausiac History* (419–20) tells of the variety of crafts and economic activities in the Pachomian monasteries: 'they work at every kind of craft and with their surplus output they provide for the needs both of the women's convents and the prisons.'[11] The text lists the monks' activities – weaving baskets or working on the land, in the garden, at the forge, in the bakery, in the tannery, in the scriptorium, or in the carpenter's, fuller's or shoemaker's workshop. The work met the needs of the monastery. Surplus could be sold, and may have been allocated to the exercise of charity. Archaeological remains provide further illustration of the economy of monasteries. In the seventh-century monastery Deir Anba Hadra, near Aswan, its walled space encloses the church, the cells, the refectory, the kitchen, an oven and also some economic facilities, such as a wine press, an oil press, vats to extract salt or decant water, and stables.

271 Platter

Egypt (produced in Aswan). 7th century
Fired red clay, painted. Height 5 cm, diameter
55 cm
Skulpturensammlung und Museum für
Byzantinische Kunst, Staatliche Museen zu Berlin.
Inv. 3355

The Nile played an important role as a lifeline for Egypt; depictions of Nilotic animals and plants are therefore extremely common on ceramics such as this platter. Here fish are arranged in the circular central area. – 2 of them follow the circular form, a 3rd moves in the opposite direction, and the 4th occupies the middle of the circle. This fish is linked to one of the others by a kind of chain (see fig. 209), while 2 of the fish seem to be chained to the innermost of 3 ornamental bands running round the edge of the central area. These 'chains' may possibly be a reference to the way fish were caught in the Nile. [EE]
Bib: Wulff 1909, p. 294, no. 1565

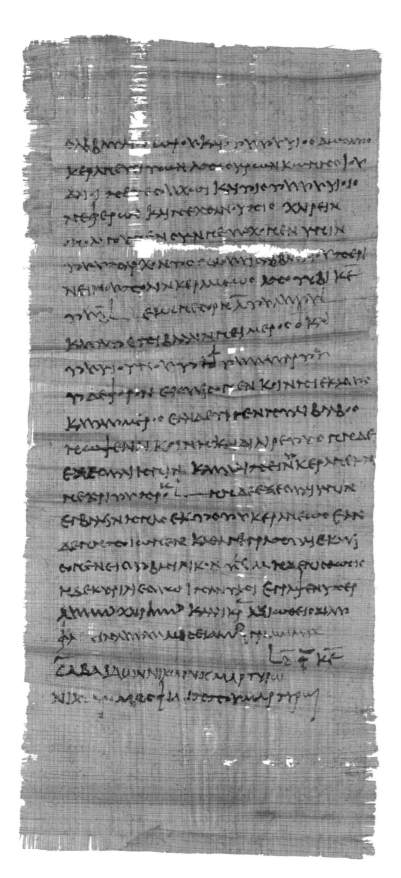

272 Partnership contract (BGU 6 1282)

Egypt, Fayyum. 2nd–1st century BC
Papyrus. 32.3 × 135 cm
Ägyptisches Museum und Papyrussammlung,
Staatliche Museen zu Berlin Berlin. Inv. P 11641

The subject of this contract is the joint
use of a pottery by a craftsman named
Petesuchos and his sons and the Jewish
potter Sabbateios and his son. The contract
sets out the conditions and punishments for
non-compliance. The partners declare their
agreement by signing it. The document is
evidence of the contact between members
of different faith communities in everyday
life. [CF]

The arrival of the Arabs did not affect the economic landscape of Egypt greatly. In pursuit of territorial expansion the new Islamic state demanded the requisition of workers skilled in maritime activities (sailors, caulks etc.).[12] At the same time the Arabs recruited skilled workers for major construction projects outside Egypt and in the Levant (including the Dome of the Rock in Jerusalem, the Great Mosque of Damascus, and the Castle of Mshatta – the façade of which has been in Berlin since 1904), and even in Arabia.[13] One can also see occupations reappearing during the Islamic period, for example with merchants connected to the slave trade which had declined in Late Antiquity but became important again in the post-conquest era.[14]

In addition, the new authorities from time to time imposed restrictions on the movement of people, which in some ways makes all trade more complex. We see in a papyrus from the Theban region, dating from the first half of the eighth century, that three monks have to ask for a passport to go to the Fayyum in order to sell their production of ropes.[15] Difficulties such as these prompted monks to diversify their activities. The archives of Frange (early eighth century), living in a hermitage in a Theban tomb, show that he worked as a weaver, but also as a copyist of books and as a bookbinder.[16] The excavations have brought to light a loom in the courtyard of the tomb, as well as binding material and reed pens.

FOCUS 8 LUSTREWARE

Gisela Helmecke

IN the rubbish heaps of Old Cairo/Fustat, hundreds of sherds were found which had a shimmering layer of gold paint on them. Intact vessels have also survived, but in much lower numbers. The earliest examples of this ceramic 'lustreware' came from Iraq, where this technique was apparently invented. Most of the lustreware pottery found in Fustat and in other places in Egypt dates to the Fatimid period (969–1171). For the Persian traveller Nasir-i Khusraw (1004–*c*.88), who in the time of the Fatimid caliph al-Mustansir spent three years in Egypt, the lustre painting looked like '*buqalamun* [sea silk] because, depending on which way you turn it, the colour changes'.

The extremely wide range of painting on this type of ceramic conveys something of the almost entirely lost painting of the Fatimids. Although figural images were generally avoided in Islamic religious art they were not uncommon, especially in the court settings and in the houses of rich people of all confessions in that period.

On the vessels appear lush plants and ornamental patterns, Arabic inscriptions (fig. 273), and numerous animals – various birds, fish (fig. 274), gazelles, hares, horses and even giraffes – as well as fantastical animals. Especially impressive are the numerous figurative representations. Before the eye of the beholder unfolds a world of luxury and pleasure – musicians, both male and female, dancing girls, revellers, riders, hunting scenes, cockfighting, cruises and scenes from fabulous stories. The faces, with their big eyes and small mouths, different hairstyles and headdresses, are intriguing (fig. 275). The masters worked with a fine brush or reed pen for drawing and details, and a wide brush for the larger patterns, the fillings and the decoration on the outside, which typically consists of simple strokes, sketchy scribbled circles and a thin coating of dots.

The technique of lustre painting is expensive, very time-consuming and requires great care. Silver and copper oxides and the finest clay as medium are the main ingredients,

273 Fragment of a bowl with writing
Egypt. 10th–11th century
Fritware, lustre decoration. Diameter 26.5 cm
Museum für Islamische Kunst, Staatliche Museen zu Berlin. Inv. I. 43/64.54

This half of the side-wall of a bowl is about 6.5 cm wide. The outside is decorated with roughly painted double rings and brush strokes, while the inside has an inscription in so-called flowering Kufic script. It repeats the word *baraka* (the Arabic word for blessing, a concept that was understood as God's blessing by all faiths). It is one of the words most often used in inscriptions, and was an element of the good wishes that are found on many objects from the Islamic world. [GH]

applied to a ready-fired glaze. The early glazes were white, but later on colourless glazes were used on white or coloured backgrounds. In a second firing – in a reduced atmosphere at red heat, in small, divided capsule-type kilns – reduction produced pure metal compounds, which fused with the glaze to form a very thin covering. The remaining earthy parts were brushed off after cooling. Only if there were enough metal components, and the temperature was right, did a full gold lustre develop. Under-firing or too short a length of time in the kiln led to a wan, non-reflective lustre with poor durability, while over-firing led to a dark reddish appearance. The masters controlled the temperature with small sherds whose lustrous colour indicated the state of the process. As the same temperature could not always be achieved everywhere in the kilns, the lustre could assume many different shades, from bright gold yellow, via light and dark shades of brown, to dark red. One bowl (fig. 276) shows this very clearly. It was

274 Base of bowl with fish
Egypt, probably Old Cairo/Fustat. 12th century
Fritware, lustre decoration. Diameter 10 cm
Museum für Islamische Kunst, Staatliche Museen zu Berlin. Inv. I. 1411

A vividly drawn fish is seen above tendrils of vegetation. Its scales are depicted by cross-hatching, while its pale belly is detailed with hatching and dots. Marine and freshwater fish were an important food source for all levels of Egyptian society. The fish could also be interpreted as Christian, as it is a symbol for Jesus. [GH]

275 Fragments depicting people
Egypt. 11th–12th century.
Fritware with monochrome lustre decoration. Diameters between 15 and 6.5 cm
Museum für Islamische Kunst, Staatliche Museen zu Berlin. Inv. I. 188; I. 1925; 1904,218; I. 43/64.109; I. 43/64.129; I. 43/64.130; I. 43/64.189

The faces of Egyptian men and women from the Fatimid period are brought to life on numerous lustreware bowls. Although only fragments remain, the vivid drawing and fine detail of these examples fascinate the modern viewer. Each one of the very different painted faces, always turned slightly to one side, has a different expression. In some, the eyebrows are drawn together. Some of them are bare-headed, while others have their heads covered. The hairstyles vary slightly, though all have curls at the sides, and one of the figures has a moustache and beard. [GH]
Bib: Hussein 1981, fig. 217; Türkis and Azur 1999, no. 250

276 Jar with fish

Egypt. 10th–11th century
Clay or fritware, lustre decoration. Height
33 cm, diameter (base) 14 cm, diameter
(opening) 10.5 cm
Victoria and Albert Museum, London.
Inv. C.48-1952

This complete round body vessel is
decorated by 4 registers, divided by
simple lines. In the lower zone is a
plaited band, in the middle a frieze of
heart-shaped palmettes, and above
appears a frieze of fish. The narrow
neck is decorated with a zigzag band
with points. (CF)

277 Fragment of a bowl with a bird

Egypt. 11th century
Fritware, lustre decoration. Height 7 cm, diameter
24.5 cm
Museum für Islamische Kunst, Staatliche Museen
zu Berlin. Inv. I. 43/64.162

Roughly painted on the exterior with
circles and lines, this is a rounded bowl
with flattened rim. A 4--pointed shape fills
the interior, at the centre of which is a bird
surrounded by spiral tendrils of foliage.
The bowl broke during firing. The varying
temperatures in the different parts of the
kiln caused the lustre decoration on each
fragment to turn a different colour and
bleed in places. This bowl clearly shows
the difficulties of the firing process, and
also that variations in the tone of the lustre
decoration depend less on differences in the
composition of the lustre than on different
firing temperatures and/or varying conditions
in the kiln. [GH]
Bib: Türkis and Azur 1999, no. 252

broken during the firing of the lustre, perhaps
due to improper stacking; the parts fell into
different spots in the kiln, and in each fragment
the lustre took on a different hue.

Mainly because they were expensive to
make, lustreware pieces were luxury objects
(figs 277, 278). They were made to order.
Representations of priests, for example,
show that some of the clients for these items
were Christians (figs 117, 118). The artisans
themselves belonged to all three religions.
Lustreware ceramics were also offered on the
market. The market supervisors were required
to check every single piece, as people sometimes
tried to sell inferior articles by placing them in
packs of well-done pieces.

The production of lustreware was linked
to an urban culture, and limited to a few centres.
When, at the end of the eleventh century, Egypt
was plagued by civil unrest, famine and crop
failure, the producers of luxury tableware surely
also suffered. Some masters probably gave up
their profession, others left the country and
went to Syria, and some perhaps even ventured
into Persian territory. For it was at about this
time that the first lustreware appeared in that
part of the world. Egyptian masters doubtless
played an important role in the flourishing of
this art, especially in Iran, where it experienced
another great creative period in the twelfth and
thirteenth centuries.

278 Bowl with hare

Egypt. 10th–11th century
Fritware, lustre decoration. Height 8.5 cm,
diameter 27.5 cm
Museum für Islamische Kunst, Staatliche
Museen zu Berlin. Inv. I. 35/64

This bowl is painted on the exterior
with simple brush strokes and 4 circles.
Sloping sides lead to a circular base,
on the inside of which is a hare with
a leaf in its mouth, facing left. On the
sides, radiating from the base, are 4
pairs of leaves resembling candelabra
alternating with 4 palmettes of leaves.
The hare was already a widespread
motif in pre-Islamic times and was seen
as a symbol of fertility. In the Fatimid
period (969–1171) it was still one of
the most popular animal motifs. One of
the palmettes contains the signature
of the master *al-baitar*. By placing his
name in the pattern on the visible side
he was probably following the practice
of one of the most famous masters
of lustre decoration, Muslim ibn
al-Dahhan. [GH]
Bib: Museum für Islamische Kunst
1971 and 1979, no. 273; Schätze der
Kalifen 1998, no. 142

27 Burial Practice

Cäcilia Fluck and Gisela Helmecke

279 Funerary mask of a woman
Egypt, probably Tuna el-Gebel. 3rd century
Stucco. Height: 33cm
Roemer-und-Paelizaeus-Museum, Hildesheim. Inv. 574

This is the surviving upper part of the lid of a
sarcophagus with the bust of a woman. She is dressed
in a tunic and mantle, which were worked into the upper
part of the lid. Her neck is bejewelled with 3 striking
necklaces; her head is raised and painted. The soft,
regular features of her face are dominated by large
eyes, further emphasized by dark, thick eyebrows. Her
coiffure, with the hair pinned up and a ring of hair on the
top of her head, is first seen in images of Tranquillina,
the wife of Gordian III. This means that the mask cannot
have been made before the year 240. [CF]
Bib: Kayser 1967, p. 42, p. 118

FROM ancient Egyptian times onwards, it was the wish of the Egyptians to preserve their bodies intact for the afterlife. The custom was adopted by the Ptolemies, of Greek origin, and by the Romans, who ruled the country after the death of Cleopatra in 30 BC; and it was continued by the Christians.[1]

Artificial mummification, with removal of the brain and internal organs, was less often performed in the Roman period. Corpses continued to be wrapped in shrouds and elaborate bandaging. A special feature of the Roman period is the gilding of the body or certain body parts. The anthropoid coffins of the pharaonic era gave way in the Ptolemaic period to stucco or cardboard masks that only covered the head and upper body. They were increasingly given more individual traits, and indicated contemporary fashions and hairstyles (fig. 279). In the first century AD a new type developed – mummy portraits painted on wood (figs 281, 282, 283) and enveloped in the mummy cloth. They are attested until about the fourth century. From Roman times painted shrouds have also been preserved. They replaced coffins or masks and display nearly life-size portraits of the dead, often between the gods Osiris and Anubis, surrounded by traditional scenes from the ancient Egyptian cult of the dead (fig. 280).

Between the time of embalming and the actual burial, quite a long period could elapse. The prepared corpses were probably temporarily stored in chapels in the area of the necropolis and not, as the historian Diodorus (first century BC) assumed, in the house of the bereaved.[2] To avoid confusion during transport to the chosen burial site, little mummy labels were attached to the body with the name of the deceased, his or her profession, home town and age. Sometimes they also contained small messages to the undertaker to ensure that the funeral went smoothly.[3]

In general, cemeteries from previous eras located outside settlements were reused. Their layout and equipment depended on local geological conditions. Some burials are found in mausoleums, chapels and in *hypogea* (underground chambers) or shafts, others are carved into rock or consist of simple *fossae* (pits) in the sandy desert ground, sometimes covered with small brick vaults or stone slabs. Significant Roman grave sites include Kom el-Shugafa (Alexandria), Terenouthis/Kom Abu Billu in the Eastern Nile Delta and Tuna al-Jabel (Hermopolis). A feature of the design of the tombs and the decor of the gravestones is a mixture of Roman stylistic elements with traditional Egyptian representations of the death and resurrection of Osiris.

280 Shroud of a young man between Osiris and Anubis

Egypt, Saqqara, 170–180
Linen, painted. 240 × 129 cm
Ägyptisches Museum und Papyrussammlung, Berlin.
Inv. ÄM 11651

The shroud shows the deceased standing between figures of the ancient Egyptian gods Osiris and Anubis, who guide the dead into the netherworld. The bearded young man is wearing a tunic with dark stripes. In his left he holds a garland; with his right he is offering a flask to Osiris. Between the heads of the approximately life-size figures, at a smaller scale, Anubis is depicted behind Osiris lying on a litter and Thoth is depicted in a kneeling position with a balance and a bowl in his hands. [CF]

281 Portrait of an older woman

Egypt, Fayyum. 2nd century
Tempera on wood. 35 × 21.5 cm
Antikensammlung, Staatliche Museen zu Berlin. Inv. 31161, 20

Among the many surviving mummy portraits from Egypt, depictions of older people are rare. If they show people at the age they died, this either means that only a few lived to old age or that only those who died young were honoured in this way. The woman here has slightly wavy grey hair, wrinkles on her forehead and, unlike the portraits of younger women, she wears no jewellery. [CF]
Bib: Borg 1998, p. 100, fig. 123

282 Mummy portrait of a woman with gold jewellery

Egypt, Hawara. Late 1st century
Wood, wax painting (encaustic). 32.5 × 21.8 cm
Ägyptisches Museum und Papyrussammlung, Staatliche Museen zu Berlin. Inv. ÄM 10974

This portrait comes from W.M.F. Petrie's excavations in Hawara, Fayyum. It shows a young woman with her head turned slightly to the right. Her round face is dominated by her bushy eyebrows and widely spaced eyes. She is gazing in the direction in which her head is turned. Her black curly hair is bound on top of her head with an ochre band. She has a dark violet mantle draped over her left shoulder. Beneath this we can glimpse what appears to be two underdresses – one depicted in colour, the other only recognizable by the gilded net-like fabric. The three-dimensionally modelled, gilded jewellery consists of earrings with little balls and large discs hanging from them and a narrow, dark, textile band with a lunula pendant. Her hairstyle is typical of the fashion prevalent around AD 70. [JHD]
Bib: Schäfer 1910, p. 87, no. 147, fig. 84; Parlasca 1966, p. 120 notes 177, 226, nos 90, 250–51; Parlasca 1969, p. 44, no. 67, pl. 17.1; Borg 1996, p. 31, pp. 96–97, p. 166, p. 169; Cat. Frankfurt 1999, p. 115, no. 16, fig. S. 117

283 Mummy portrait of a young man with a beard

Egypt, Hawara (Fayyum). Late 1st century
Wood, wax painting (encaustic). 43.5 × 23 × 2 cm (including mount)
Ägyptisches Museum und Papyrussammlung, Staatliche Museen zu Berlin. Inv. ÄM 19722

This painted panel from Heinrich Brugsch's excavations in Hawara shows a young man with a youthful downy beard and a long triangular-shaped head. His large eyes, looking straight at the viewer, and his slightly open mouth create the impression of a combination of awareness and astonishment. His hair is short, black and curly. He is wearing a mantle pulled high around his neck over a white tunic. Most of the mummies with painted panel portraits have been discovered in Fayyum. [JHD]
Bib: Möller 1919, p. 3, pl. 7; Parlasca 1966, p. 33, note. 116, no. 5; Parlasca 1969, p. 38, no. 42, pls. 11, 4; Doxiadis 1995, p. 126, p. 135, p. 139, p. 197, no. 37, fig. 197 (S. 54); Borg 1996, p. 70, p. 91, p. 98, p. 106, p. 154, p. 192, pl. 3 (image taken before conservation); Borg 1998, pp. 38–40, fig. 45; Cat. Frankfurt 1999, p. 115, no. 14, fig. p. 114

Also dated to Roman times is one of the few well-known Jewish cemeteries of ancient Egypt. It is located in Leontopolis (Tell al-Yahudiya), about 20 kilometres north-east of Cairo. Here the Jewish high priest Onias IV is said to have founded, in around 170 BC, the only temple to Yahweh outside Jerusalem. It existed until the Jewish Revolt in AD 71 (see ch. 2, ch. 5).[4] The temple has not been archaeologically identified, but the existence of Jews in this place is attested by grave inscriptions from the first century BC to the first century AD (fig. 284).[5] According to excavator F. Ll. Griffith, at Tell al-Yahudiya there were three adjacent cemeteries with hundreds of Jewish graves of different types – square pits; pits about three metres deep, opening into an elongated cavity; rectangular tombs, carefully cut into the rock; tombs with a groove for a locking plate; and subterranean, mostly undecorated chambers with symmetrical niches, so-called *loculi*, also familiar from Jerusalem, Jericho and Qumran.

Elsewhere there will also have been Jewish cemeteries wherever Jewish communities were established.[6] It is probably from these that various *ossuaries* (small stone boxes) and smaller objects come, such as lamps with depictions of the *menorah*, grapes and palm branches, now in possession of the Graeco-Roman Museum in Alexandria and the Egyptian Museum in Cairo. They suggest that in Roman times the Jews in Egypt were also buried in accordance with their own contemporary tradition.[7] Their dead were wrapped in linen and, equipped with grave goods, initially buried in a family grave. After some time the bones were collected and placed in an ossuary, which was then kept in a separate area in the family tomb.[8]

With the increasing Christianization of Egypt during the third century, 'pagan' funeral practices gradually changed. Preserving the body and supplying it for the afterlife, now connected with the Christian belief in resurrection, remained essential. To ensure this, funeral arrangements were made during one's lifetime and ensured by testamentary agreements (fig. 101).[9]

The elaborate mummification of the Roman period gave way to ever more practical and inexpensive methods. The bodies of the dead were washed, treated with a natron mixture and occasionally dusted or sprinkled with fragrant essences, such as incense, oils or resins. Then they were wrapped in their tunics, laid on cushions and covered with cloths; body cavities were stuffed with rags. Usually the bodies were stabilized with a board under the back, which often followed the outline of the body, or with simple slats. Finally, the bodies were tied up into bundles with bands of cloth, often wound in complicated and elaborate patterns as in the centuries before (fig. 144). A special kind of binding seems, as far as our current understanding suggests, to have arisen at the end of the fourth century, limited to the Middle Egyptian regions. Here several mummies were found with a construction over their heads, shaped like a gable roof and made from textiles and palm leaves (fig. 285).[10] The tradition of the technique of binding a mummy, known since ancient Egyptian times, was still alive in the seventh to eighth centuries in the form of the mummies of monks from the Theban monasteries.

From the fourth century onwards, clothes played an important role in preparations for the funeral. The deceased often wore several tunics, coats, shawls and head coverings on top of each other (see ch. 25). Usually the garments were not specially made for the funeral, but had previously been worn in everyday life, as suggested by traces of wear and tear, and repairs.[11] Depending on their wealth, the deceased were also provided with accessories such as sandals, shoes and boots, jewellery and combs, as well as everyday objects including clay lamps and small vessels, votive offerings and toys or equipment from professional life (fig. 211), and even reading matter (*codices*), loosely inserted into the bindings.[12] The ancient Egyptian custom of equipping the deceased with wreaths of blossoms or garlands for eternity was maintained, as can be judged by the finds in quite a number of graves (focus 9).

Excavations and the rich archaeological material that they have revealed have highlighted the importance of the late Roman and early Christian necropoleis of Arsinoe and Fag al-Gamus in Fayyum, Saqqara, al-Hiba, Qarara, Kom el-Ahmar in Sharuna and Antinoopolis in Middle Egypt, Panopolis (Akhmim) and Western Thebes

284 Stela of Iohannes

Egypt, Tell al-Yahudiya. *c.* 25 BC–AD 50.
Limestone. 55 × 22 × 11 cm
Département des Antiquités égyptiennes, Musée du Louvre, Paris. Inv. AM 1475

Stela from Tell al-Yahudiya are characterized by a gable design with a suggestion of a pediment on the upper part and below it a recessed rectangular field with an inscription in Greek. This contains the name of the deceased, typical funerary formulae, the date of death and also in a few places brief lamentations or exhortations to the bereaved to mourn for the departed. The lower part is not decorated and was evidently anchored in the ground. [CF]
Bib: Bernand 1992, pp. 117-18, no. 68

285 Head of a mummiform burial from Qarara

Typical triangular structure over the head of a body from the cemetery at Qarara. [CF]

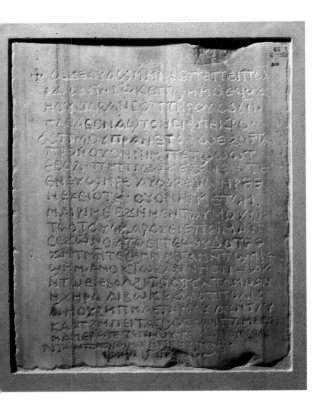

286 Funerary stela with a lament for the dead (*SB Kopt.* I 464)

Egypt, probably Antinoopolis. 8th century
Marble. 54 × 46cm (case)
British Museum, London. Inv. EA 900

The inscription commemorates a deacon
named John, from the city of Kos (modern
Qus), who died on the 13th of the month of
Paophi (or 11 October) in the 3rd indiction
year. In this inscription of 21 lines the
deceased is mourning himself. This type
of stela with a lament for the dead was
produced in the region of Antinoopolis in
the 8th century. [CF]

in Upper Egypt, as well as al-Bagawat, Dush and al-Deir in the Kharga Oasis. The burial sites of this period do not differ fundamentally from those of the preceding period. The habit of occupying already existing tombs was retained, as well as the rituals of commemoration in the cemeteries; these services were, much later, moved into the churches. For this purpose existing meeting-places near the graves were reused or buildings were constructed, sometimes equipped with fixed tables and benches for the funeral feast, as in Saqqara,[13] Antinoopolis and al-Bagawat.

'Pagan' and Christian burials can in principle often be distinguished from one another only when they are connected to a monastery or can be identified by certain grave goods – such as crosses, psalm books, Christian symbols and motifs related to the afterlife, or grave inscriptions (figs 286, 287, 288, 289, 290, 291, 292, 293, 294). The inscriptions are written in the regional dialect and contain an invocation to God and Jesus Christ and the name of the dead man or woman. Sometimes the age of death or the date of death is also stated, as on Roman and Jewish grave stelae. But longer texts with litanies, prayers and salutations to the living are also attested. And although Church Fathers and prominent monks such as Shenoute (ch. 7, ch. 11) opposed the practice, lamentations for the dead were also offered (fig. 286) – a custom already found in ancient Egyptian times and also in the Jewish treatment of the dead.[14]

Islam also rejects lamentations for the dead. Nevertheless, this custom persisted among Muslim Egyptians. It is commonly practised even today in rural areas. Under Muslim rule little changed concerning Christian burials. In Fayyum, for instance, the traditions of Late Antiquity were still to be found in the Fatimid period. At the same time, one can see how, as the Christians became a minority, they adjusted to a society in which Muslims were now the majority. This is shown by the excavations in the area of the Monastery of the Archangel Gabriel in Naqlun (see focus 6).[15] By 2011 about 200 tombs from the pre-Islamic sixth to seventh centuries had been found. About 500 graves of different types and quality, containing men, women and children from the Fatimid to the Mamluk period (eleventh to the fourteenth centuries) were also found, mainly in cemetery A (see focus 6).[16] Some of the burials from this period contained biers or latticed *qafas* (crates) made from the ribs of palm fronds. Most of the corpses lay in wooden coffins, mostly consisting of boards nailed together. Biers, containers and coffins were covered with mats, and sometimes also with baskets[17] and funeral palls that were knotted with ropes. Sometimes the containers were also wrapped in mats. The dead lay on their backs; their heads, pointing westwards, lay on pillows that were sometimes specially made and filled with aromatic herbs.[18] Similar plants were also placed around the bodies. The traditions of Late Antiquity continued in this type of bedding for the dead, as well as in the clothes they wore (typical costumes of the day, with covered heads and usually without shoes) and, to some extent, in the grave goods accompanying them. In one of the richer burials from the period around 1100, one woman even wore a wreath of leaves around her head, recalling much earlier practice.

But the costume changed – many Christian dead now wore the same clothes as their Muslim neighbours. While most garments were simple and unadorned, the more decorated bore the ornamental *tiraz* bands characteristic of the Fatimid period, as well as purely Muslim inscriptions. Perhaps the blessing that resided in the name of God (even the Muslim God), and in the name of a caliph (to which a certain power of blessing, *baraka*, was always attributed), was thought to be helpful to a dead Christian on his or her way into the afterlife. Other deceased persons, however, were dressed in special tunics for the dead.[19] These consisted of coarse linen, were very large and simply cut, both long-sleeved and sleeveless, and hastily stitched together. Sometimes they were used as burial shrouds (figs 295, 296). Almost all the dead were wrapped in these or similar shrouds (including those made of leather), which were sewn together at the sides and tied around the ankles with a string.

Among the burial shrouds, some were embroidered with pseudo-inscriptions in Arabic. Some did not show any signs of wear. Apparently they were made just for this purpose and were clearly of local origin. Presumably they were also produced for Muslims, since the inscriptions, accompanied by general invocations of God, were so neutral that they could be used both for Christians and for Muslims. In some children's tombs, crosses were painted on the shrouds.[20] Only a few burials in this cemetery A from this period at Naqlun were in brick vaults.

Muslim burial regulations also include washing the dead body, wrapping it in a shroud and burying it in a cemetery. According to the Hadith (the recorded traditions of the Prophet Muhammad), burials should be simple – an unadorned shroud, immediate burial, no coffin and no grave stone or anything of that kind. The dead person must be accompanied on his or her last journey, and at every action prayers are to be said,[21] so that the deceased will be properly prepared to await the Day of Judgment.[22] Despite the sustained efforts of religious scholars and pious rulers, however, many old habits were retained: 'The devil has so deceived the majority of the common people that they follow the old traditions,' was one eleventh-century view.[23]

The *qabr* (grave) of a Muslim could take a great variety of forms. The dead person was usually just placed in a pit, and the place marked with simple earth or stone heaps, bricks, stone slabs or grave stelae (*shahid*) (figs 297, 298). In contrast to Christian burials, the Muslim dead were buried on their sides and with their faces towards Mecca. The grave of an important person, or one who was respected and revered as holy, was particularly marked. Sometimes such a person was buried in his or her own house and only later transferred to the graveyard. They often had a tomb outside the cemetery, too. There were many small *qubba* (square-shaped tombs with domes), but also larger mausoleums and grave mosques to which the faithful made pilgrimage to gain *baraka* (blessing) (see ch. 21). The large grave mosques of Egypt are among the most important architectural monuments of the Islamic world.

Comprehensive documentation of the Muslim burial of the dead in Egypt in this

Overleaf

287 Funerary stela of Theodoros and Kosman
Egypt, probably Fayyum. 8th century
Limestone. 73.7 × 36.4 × 9.4 cm
Skulpturensammlung und Museum für Byzantinische Kunst,
Staatliche Museen zu Berlin. Inv. 1/66

The formulaic inscription 'May they rest in the bosom of Abraham and Isaac and Jacob', the motif of the cross, and especially the names of the deceased 'Theodoros and Kosman' show that this stela is a Christian grave stela. The inscription, written in the Fayyum dialect of Coptic, runs across the central field of the stela over a Greek cross. The engraved spandrels also have inscriptions on them. The central field is framed on either side by 2 columns with palm fronds and crosses on them. The top of the frame depicts an architrave formed of laurel leaves, with an arcade of laurel leaves above it. The arched field created by this is filled by a shell. [EE]
Bib: Cat. Stuttgart 1984, p. 191, no. 161; Cat. Hamm 1996, p. 121, no. 70, fig. S. 121

288 Upper part of a funerary stela
Egypt. 6th–7th century
Limestone. 22.5 × 33.5 × 11.5 cm
Skulpturensammlung und Museum für Byzantinische Kunst,
Staatliche Museen zu Berlin. Inv. 4730

The round arch gable originally crowned a Christian funerary stela, the bottom of which does not survive. The gable bears a wreath, finely carved in low relief, enclosing a deeper-set monogram cross with a loop. Instead of leaves, the wreath is covered with angular and rounded shapes imitating decoration with precious stones and beads. Running down from the wreath to form waves on either side are 2 ribbons. The wreath symbolizes victory and refers to Christ's resurrection of the dead. To the left and right of the wreath the gable is very smooth and retains traces of the original painting. [EE]
Bib: Wulff 1909, p. 40, no. 90; Cat. Hamm 1996, p. 122, fig. 71

289 Funerary stela of Besa
Egypt. *c.*5th–8th century
Limestone, red pigment. 60 × 44 × 13cm
British Museum, London. EA 937

Commemorating a Christian man with an ancient Egyptian theophoric name Besa, this stela was re-carved from a Ptolemaic-period temple relief depicting the falcon god Horus and fragmentary hieroglyphic text, 'He of Behdet, lord of the sky' (not shown). [ERO]

290 Funerary stela of Pleinos
Egypt. *c.*5th–6th century
Limestone. 62 × 39 × 8 cm
British Museum, London. EA 679. [ERO]

Bib: Hall 1905, p.140; Badawy 1978, fig. 3.207, p.218

291 Funerary stela of Jacob
Egypt. *c.*6th–7th century
Limestone, pigment. 56.3 × 38.2 x 5.5 cm
British Museum, London. EA 1801 [ERO]

Bib: Beckwith 1963, no. 128 (p.56, pl.128); Badawy 1978, fig. 3.210, p.219

292 Side panel of a chest

Egypt. 6th–8th century
Tamarisk wood. 71 × 87.8 × 2.5 cm
Skulpturensammlung und Museum für Byzantinische Kunst, Staatliche Museen zu Berlin. Inv. 3598-3601

This side panel was part of a chest that once contained a coffin or a mummified body. Fitted into their original positions in a modern frame are 4 panels, carved in relief. Besides ornamental interwoven bands, a tendril, hunting scenes and animal fights, the decoration includes motifs relating to the afterlife, such as the tree of life or eagles with outspread wings with a cross held in their beaks or worn around their necks. In funerary art the eagle is understood as a symbol of the salvation of souls, while the tree of life symbolizes Paradise. [CF]
Bib: Cat. Hamm 1996, pp. 138–39, no. 100; Cat. Schallaburg 2012, pp. 290–91, no. IX.19

293 Stela commemorating Pachomius

Egypt, said to be from Saqqara. 6–7th century
Limestone. 57 × 44 × 14 cm
British Museum, London. EA 1533

Bib: Cat. Paris 2000, no. 11 (p.43)

294 Funerary stela of Sophrone (right)

Egypt. 6–7th century
Limestone. 82.5 × 41 × 4 cm
British Museum, London. EA 1790

Bib: Wessel 1963, no. 85 (p.114), where 'Edfu' is attributed findspot

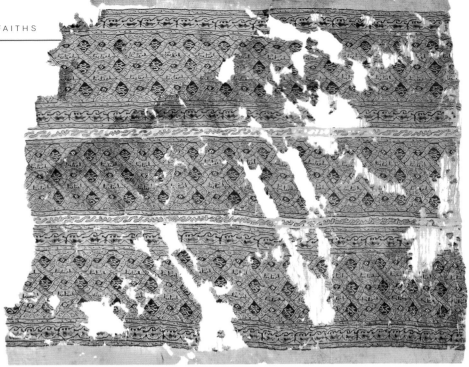

295 Textile fragment

Egypt. 11th–12th century
Linen, silk. 49.5 × 48 cm
Museum für Islamische Kunst, Staatliche Museen
zu Berlin. Inv. I. 3139

Part of a fine linen cloth with a broad band
of tapestry in silk and natural-coloured linen.
This consists of stripes filled with a repeating
pattern of plaited bands. In the resulting
medallions and spaces are stylized hares and
pseudo-inscriptions in red. A brief statement
in a distorted angular and in a cursive Arabic
script is repeated in the hems of the stripes.
The pious text *nasr min allah* ('help from God')
refers to a passage from the Qur'an (Sura 61,
verse 13), which continues with *wa-fath qarib*
('and victory very near'). This was one of the
most popular inscriptions in the late Fatimid
period (12th century). [GH]
Bib: Kühnel 1927, p. 29, pl. 12

296 Textile fragments

Egypt. 11th–12th century
Linen, silk. Approx. 13 × 16 cm
Museum für Islamische Kunst, Staatliche Museen
zu Berlin. Inv. I. 3117

These fragments are of fine linen with
coloured selvages and a patterned stripe
of the finest silk and double linen thread.
This is an example of a purely ornamental
tiraz band, consisting of a plaited band
forming medallions, filled with running hares,
small birds and small, 3-frond palmettes.
Recumbent 'S' shapes can be seen on the
hemline strip. [GH]
Bib: Kühnel 1927, p. 26, pl. 11

period still needs to be compiled, analysed and interpreted. It can be documented only rather sketchily so far through archaeological finds, since the opening of Muslim graves is, for religious reasons, not permitted. One of the few exceptions, carried out by Roland-Pierre Gayraud between 1985 and 2005, is the investigation of the remains of the grave complex of the Fatimid rulers in Qarafa al-Kubra (the Great Cemetery) on the plateau of Istabl 'Antar to the southeast of Cairo.[24] Built on an older site dating to the Abbasid period, the complex was occupied by Fatimid burials from *c.*973 to the end of the eleventh century. Many features found here are probably due to the fact that this site was used by the Fatimid family, or the 'house'[25] of the Fatimids, as a cemetery. There were different types of tombs, with group and individual burials.[26]

Surprisingly, in the brick or stone vaults, excavators discovered numerous coffin burials. Normally in Muslim burials, no coffins are used. So far, coffins have been found only in Istabl 'Antar and in the grave openings in the al-Hadra al-Sharifa mausoleum in the 'Ayn as-Sira cemetery in Cairo. Most coffin burials were in individual graves. The coffins were made of planks, and some had iron decorative strips on their covers.[27]

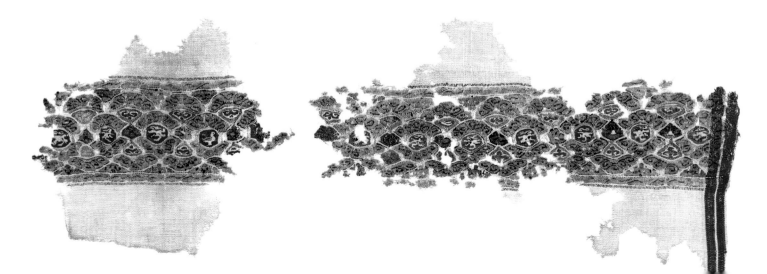

Some shrouds had *tiraz* inscriptions on them. These grave cloths were wound in such a way that the lines of writing on the fabric cover the place of the eyes. The burial of one white-bearded man (his beard had been dyed with henna) in a special tomb (grave 49) has been investigated more closely. He was wrapped in three shrouds, then in a mat, and was eventually placed in a wooden coffin, of which only remnants remain. Between the lower and the middle cloth there was still a layer of cotton wool. Each of the three cloths bears different *tiraz* inscriptions, dating to between 320 AH/AD 932 and the end of the eleventh century.[28] The upper cloth was the oldest. It showed no signs of wear and still had its original finish – it had been carefully preserved for some fifty years until it was finally used as a shroud.

Some coffins contained more than one person.[29] Most multiple burials, however, did not involve coffins. In addition, an *ossuary* was found in which the skeletons dated from older burials from the Abbasid era.

In the now cleared parts of the 'Ayn as-Sira cemetery in Cairo, the ordinary graves were also coffinless. Conversely, in the Muslim cemetery at Kom el-Dikka in Alexandria, many grave superstructures had been built from stone, more rarely brick, with the tombs being dug into the earth.[30] The fragments of ceramic and glass vessels, oil lamps, gaming pieces and bronze coins found in the vicinity of the graves also point to the traditional custom of frequent cemetery visits. In early medieval Egypt these visits to the tombs on certain days, especially on the fifteenth day of the Muslim month of Sha'ban, were accompanied by music and other forms of merriment. They were repeatedly denounced as un-Islamic and forbidden, but could not be eradicated. Here, as in other Muslim cemeteries of Egypt, grave stones have been preserved on which the often very beautiful calligraphic inscriptions provide information about the deceased and their beliefs (see focus 10).

297 Funerary stela of Abu-l-Fawaris Ahmad ibn al-Hasan al-Khwarizmi

Egypt, probably Cairo. Dated April–May 858 (*al-muharram* 244)
Limestone. 61 × 36.5 cm
Museum für Islamische Kunst, Staatliche Museen zu Berlin.
Inv. I. 25/68

The dense, 14-line inscription in Kufic script on this gravestone is broadly chiselled out of the hollowed-out ground. The edge that has been left forms the frame. The inscription says that God provides all consolation and compensation for every loss, and that the death of the Prophet Muhammad was the greatest misfortune. The deceased's confession of faith is followed by his name and date of death. The part of his name al-Khwarizmi suggests that he or his ancestors originated from the Khorezm region of modern Uzbekistan, possibly the Karakalpak people, who were horse-breeders there until recent times. The dead man's cognomen or personal name (*laqab*), Abu-l-Fawaris ('father of riders'), would fit this interpretation. [GH]
Bib: Museum für Islamische Kunst 1971 and 1979, no. 6; Islamische Kunst 1985, no. 347

298 Panel with inscription

Egypt. End of 10th to 11th century
Marble. Height 45.7 cm, diameter 65 cm
Museum für Islamische Kunst, Staatliche Museen zu Berlin.
Inv. I. 4466

This panel probably originated from a cenotaph. There is a plain frame around the inscription which is broken at the left side. The inscription is from verse 18 of the Sura 3 of the Qur'an. It shows some of the so-called flowering Kufic (visible in one letter with a leaf), and the so-called plaited Kufic, which has knotted and plaited letters (left). This panel is a reused tombstone of the early 10th century, whose carved inscription is preserved at the back. Similar panels also made from tombstones are in the British Museum and in the Museum of Islamic Art in Cairo. [GH]
Bib: Kühnel 1942 and 1947, fig. 14; Grohmann 2 1971, p. 193, fig. 222

FOCUS 9 FLOWER GARLANDS FOR THE DEAD

Marina Heilmeyer

IN Egypt, the custom of adorning the dead with branches and leaves is found at least as far back as the Middle Kingdom. In the extremely dry climate of Egypt, the garlands and bouquets with which the dead were crowned for their journey to the afterlife have been excellently preserved in the tombs.

Since the excavations of the nineteenth century, several scientists have also taken an interest in this specific form of historical evidence. Thanks mainly to the botanist and explorer of Africa, Georg Schweinfurth (1863–1925), the Berlin Museums possess a rich collection of plants left as grave goods in Egypt. The flower garlands of the pharaohs of the New Kingdom found in these collections have often been described.[1] The finds from the Greek and Roman period in Egypt, on the other hand, have remained almost unknown hitherto. They date from the second to third centuries AD, and were for the most part found in the excavations in Hawara in Fayyum in the years 1893–97 (fig. 299).[2] They are well-preserved individual flowers, petals, bouquets and fully preserved garlands that could perfectly easily be identified botanically.[3]

These finds differ significantly from the aforementioned floral decoration of pharaonic times, both in the technique used to bind the plants and in the way they were put together. Of course, since the period in which the garlands for Ramses II (died 1213 BC) had been woven, the selection of flowers in the gardens of Egypt had changed. Especially after the conquest of the country by the Ptolemies, many new plants came from the western parts of the Mediterranean to Egypt, among them the previously unknown rose (fig. 300), myrtle, marjoram and the rose-

of-heaven. But this in itself does not explain the difference between the flower arrangements from ancient Egypt and in the Roman period tombs of Fayyum. The most striking feature is the change in colour. Red, pink, orange and violet dominate the selection of flowers[4] – yellow[5] plays only a minor role and blue,[6] so popular and iconic at the time of the pharaohs, has almost completely disappeared. The reason for this cannot lie in the seasonal or regional availability of the plants. Over and above the general symbolism of floral decoration in the cult of the dead, the change expresses the new cultural and religious ties between different parts of the population of Fayyum in the second to third centuries.

It is worth taking a closer look at some of the plants used for the bouquets and wreaths. Particularly remarkable are the many garlands that were plaited from red and pink rose petals or rose leaves. The Roman naturalist Pliny in *c*.AD 50 still thought of these as representing the highest degree of luxury.[7] They were usually *Rosa sancta*, a variety of *Rosa gallica*. The earliest document for the use of this rose as a decoration for mummies comes from Fayyum in 220 BC.[8] The young woman in question was adorned with seven garlands of flowers, five of which were made of rose petals. In addition to the general importance of such rose garlands as a precious and fragrant gift symbolizing life, they are reminiscent of ancient descriptions of Aurora, goddess of the dawn, who at break of day 'opens the purple gate of her rose-filled hall'.[9]

The rose, an attribute of the goddesses of Greek and Roman mythology, was the most common grave offering in imperial Rome. However, the rose was not (as in Egypt) used to

299 Flower garland
Egypt, Hawara. 2nd–3rd century
Roses. 7.5 x 5 x 26.5 cm
Botanischer Garten und Botanisches Museum, Berlin. Inv. 298.

This flower garland of cultivated roses (*Rosa sancta R.*) comes from a Roman grave in Hawara in Fayyum. [MHe]

300 Reconstructed rose garland
This garland has been reconstructed after an original from Hawara, which is now in the Ägyptisches Museum und Papyrussammlung, Staatliche Museen zu Berlin (ÄMP Inv. 14276). The rose petals are threaded on strips of papyrus pith (*Cyperus papyrus*). [MHe]

adorn the mummified body of the dead, but was wrapped as a wreath or garland around the gravestone (fig. 301) or scattered on the altars like a rainfall of flowers.[10] The rose remained bound to the western cultures of the Mediterranean. Although it was also native to Phoenicia, it was not only unknown to the pharaohs, but played no role in the Bible or later in the Qur'an.[11]

Alongside the plants, green leaves and branches with which the dead were adorned, there were also plants that people needed for their diet, or those whose evergreen foliage or aromatic fragrance symbolized immortality, eternity and God's power. Over the centuries, particular favourites were the leaves of grapes, willow and olive – all plants that are explicitly mentioned in the texts of the Bible or the Qur'an. On one hand, this continuity is clearly seen in floral grave offerings from Fayyum; on the other hand, plants newly introduced into Egypt were incorporated into these traditions and partially replaced those which had hitherto been customary, such as celery (*Apium graveolens*).[12] Thus, the mummy of

301 Mummy portrait of a woman
Egypt, Fayyum. 1st half of 3rd century
Tempera on wood. 40.5 × 21 cm
Antikensammlung, Staatliche Museen zu Berlin. Inv. 31161, 48.

Dressed in a lilac tunic and a shawl of the same colour, the
woman holds a garland of pink flowers, which might well be
roses. Garlands of this kind were typical funerary gifts in the
Roman period. [CF]

Leukyone from the cemetery of Antinoopolis[13] is
wearing a wreath of leaves of evergreen citron (*Citrus
medica*), which came to the Mediterranean from India
via Persia *c.*300 BC. The citron (*Citrus medica var. etrog*)
possessed great symbolic importance in the Jewish
religion from 135 BC.[14] Radiocarbon analysis of this
mummy was carried out recently to determine its
age. The body dates to the seventh to ninth centuries,
while one of the wreaths dates to the seventh century.
Even in a tomb of the Fatimid period a wreath of
flowers has been found (see ch. 27). The custom of
burying plants with the dead is thus attested even after
the Arab conquest.[15] It is possible that the so-called
'bourrelets', wreaths that were made of thick multi-
coloured wool yarns and usually attached to veils, were
textile imitations of such wreaths. Many of them had
been found in female graves in Antinoopolis (fig. 302).

Among the floral grave offerings from Fayyum,
the high proportion of garlands woven from green
marjoram (*Origanum majorana*) is cause for surprise.
With this highly fragrant herb, the boundaries between
its magical significance and its medical benefits in the
realm of religious practice are blurred. Among the
Greeks, who brought this plant to Egypt, marjoram
(or hyssop) was viewed as a means of promoting deep
sleep and relaxation and the scent could also protect
you from disease. Marjoram was, moreover, seen
as a mysterious herb, able to prevent
the clotting of blood in sacrifices.
Therefore, Moses advised the Israelites
to use sprays of marjoram when, in the
night before the Exodus from Egypt,
they marked the doors of their houses
with the blood of sacrificial lambs.[16]

Red and green, rose and
marjoram are here being used as just
one example of change and continuity
in funeral rites, as can be seen from
the finds from Egypt now in modern
museum collections. Although divorced
from their original context, they
nonetheless document the love of
fragrant wreaths and bright colours
that people wanted to present to the
dead, for their journey into the afterlife.

302 Wreath headdress
Egypt. 5th–7th century
Linen and wool. 88 × 6 cm
Département des Antiquités égyptiennes, Musée du Louvre, Paris. E 32654

Wreath headdresses of padded rolls appear to be a special feature of female
costume in Antinoopolis in Late Antiquity. There are 2 types – a tapered
envelope shape stuffed with wool and, as shown here, a version where the
volume is made entirely of the fabric. The latter has been created by a chain of
linen threads, twisted together using small bars, with woollen threads wrapped
around it in a way that produces curls. The natural linen base is punctuated by
red and purple bands, and dotted with the same colours with the addition of
green. This roll was probably sewn to the middle of the long edge of a linen
mantle, to be wrapped around the neck or face of the dead woman. [MD]

FOCUS 10 EARLY ISLAMIC TOMBSTONES FROM ASWAN

Mahmoud Hawari

303 Muslim cemetery at Aswan

THE Islamic tombstones from the seventh to the twelfth century, especially the Fatimid ones (tenth to twelfth century) in Aswan in Upper Egypt reveal a high standard of craftsmanship and aesthetic splendour, which gained them an important status in the study of Islamic history and art. They are regarded as documents for tracing the development of Arabic calligraphy,[1] as well as important sources for social history. Their inscriptions provide the name of the deceased and their date of death and, sometimes, other valuable information such as their title(s), profession, place of origin and to which class they belonged – for example 'Habiba, daughter of 'Ali, son of Ahmad, son of 'Ubaid Allah, the potter from 'Idfu [Edfu]'.[2] And sometimes it is also evident to which branch of Islam they belong.

Although the traditional Sunni Islam has prohibited commemoration of the dead, graves of many Muslims are marked by upright slabs or stelae (Arabic *shahid*) and/or flat rectangular superstructures (cenotaphs). The tombstones are made of different materials, depending on local availability.[3] While early Islamic tombstones from Cairo are largely carved from limestone and marble, Aswan stelae are carved in the region's local material, sandstone.[4] It is not certain when inscribed tombstones were first introduced in Islam, but a few rare examples dating to the first two centuries of Islam survive beginning from 174 AH /AD 790.

Throughout the first centuries of Islam until the first half of the eleventh century, the town of Aswan developed into an important Islamic political, trade and learning centre in Upper Egypt, reaching prominence in the Fatimid period.[5] It was a major station on the Hajj route to the holy cities of Hijaz, particularly for pilgrims from North Africa.[6] The large cemetery of the city, with its impressive monuments, is known by scholars as the Fatimid cemetery, although it actually contains tomb monuments dating to the Umayyad and Tulunid dynasties, as well. From 2006 to 2014 it has been the subject of conservation and study of the German Archaeological Institute, under the direction of Philipp Speiser.[7]

About 1,500 intact tombstones and about 500 fragments of tombstones were brought from Aswan to Cairo in the late nineteenth century, and others were found during excavations in the 1960s.[8] Today they are held by the Aswan Museum, the Islamic Museum of Cairo, and in other museums around the world.[9] A group of twenty-five stelae from Aswan that are now in the British Museum date from between 252 AH/AD 866 and 420 AH/AD 1029. Sixteen of them have been briefly published.[10]

Aswan stelae share features with other contemporary Islamic stelae from elsewhere in the Islamic world. The earliest tombstones were inscribed in a simple Kufic script, which from the late eighth and early ninth century was increasingly embellished with foliate terminals and plaited letters, including various decorative devices, such as a hook, arc or palmette[11] ('flowering Kufic', 'knotted Kufic'). The stems of the beveled angular letters evolved into a floral ornament, often set in a surging scroll ground. The calligraphy is characterized by clarity of the letter forms and spacing between the lines and the words. Terminals of the upright letters and some initial and final letters are wedge-shaped. In some instances upper and lower corners of the wedge extend out to form petals. Sometimes the decoration of the apices of letters, consisting of half palmettes, or two or three lobed leaves, might extend over whole words.[12]

The purpose of the inscriptions on tombstones was two-fold – to record the name of the deceased, and to bear witness to his or her faith. Each inscription begins with the *basmalah* (invocation of God). Usually this is followed by a set of introductory phrases, either in the form of familiar Qur'anic verses – *hamdalah* (thanks to God), the *tasliya* (benediction on the Prophet Muhammad), Hadith (a tradition of the Prophet Muhammad) – or sometimes a freely composed phrase or invocation. The Qur'anic verses mainly deal with judgment and resurrection. Two of the most popular verses are the so-called Throne Verse (Sura 2:256), stating God's dominion over heaven and earth, and the final chapter (Sura 112), about God's uniqueness and the denial of the Trinity. Additional phrases or statements were also included; the most common of these is the *shahada* (profession of faith), which is meant to be said by the deceased. The name of the deceased comes next with his or her genealogy, titles, and sometimes profession and place of origin. The name is usually preceded by the phrase *hadha qabr* (this is the grave of). The date of his/her death, often precise, mostly follows the name.[13]

304 Tomb stela of a woman from Aswan named Fatima

Egypt, Aswan. 1052 (443 AH)
Sandstone. 64 cm (with base) × 42 × 17 cm
British Museum, London. Inv. ME 1887,0402.1437

The 9-line Arabic text is carved in angular Kufic, with some letters terminating in either wedge-shaped terminals or split leaves – which is characteristic of monumental scripts of this period. According to the inscription the deceased is Fatima, daughter of Ja'far, son of Muhammad the dyer, who died on 13 August 1021 (Sunday the first of *jumada I* in the year 412 AH). Abiding by a typical formula the inscription begins with the *basmallah* followed by the 4 verses of Surah al-Ikhlas (Sura 112), commonly used on tombstones from Upper Egypt, North Africa and Hijaz in Arabia. God's blessings are then called upon the Prophet Muhammad and his family, followed by the name of the deceased and the date she died. [MH]
Bib: Wright 1887, pp. 332–33, no. 4

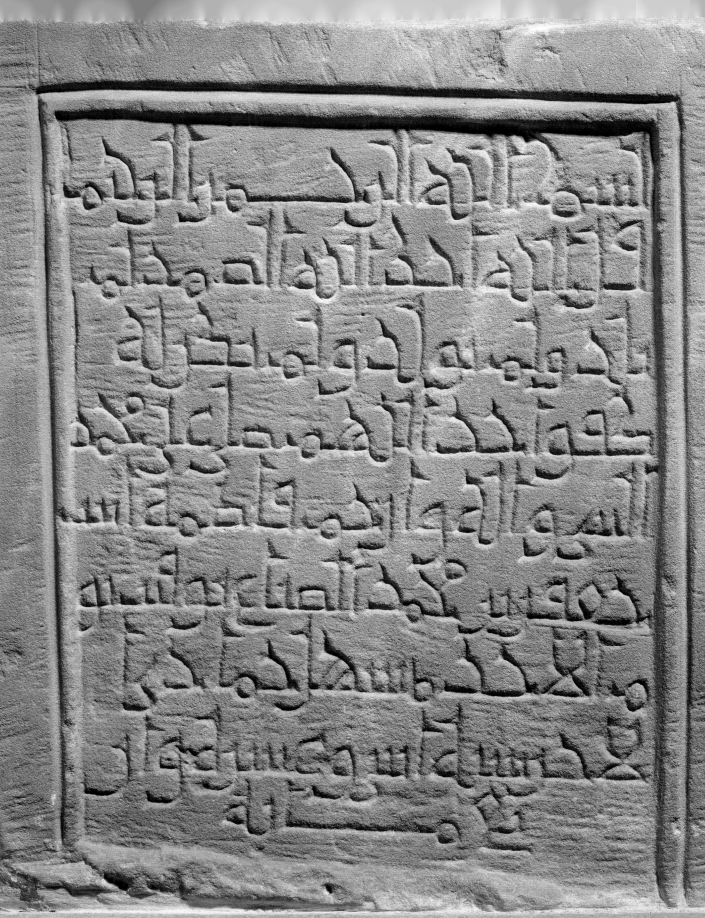

28 Jewish and Christian Visions of Paradise

Jürgen Tubach

WHEN the Hebrew Bible was translated into Greek, in the third century BC in Alexandria, the Greek loanword *paradeisos* (Latin *paradisus*) was chosen as the equivalent of the Hebrew word *gan* (garden) in the creation story (Genesis 2:8 and onwards). The word was borrowed from Old Persian and had been known to the Greeks since Xenophon (430/25–355 BC). It goes back to the Avestan *pairidaeza* (circular, completely self-enclosed rampart or wall), and refers to a fenced garden that, in the time of the ancient Persian empire of the Achaemenids (539–330 BC), lay next to the palace or was part of the domain of the Great King. Such a garden included a large number of trees and wild animals; the Assyrian kings already had similar gardens next to their residences. In the Greek text of the Bible the Persian loanword *pardes* occurs only in later writings, designating either a garden park with trees (Song of Solomon 4:13; Ecclesiastes 2:5) or a forest (Nehemiah 2:8). The word initially had no religious significance. Only through the translation of the Septuagint (the Greek translation of the Bible), did the term 'paradise' start to refer to the place where the first human couple lived. It returns in apocalyptic writings, as the name of the eternal abode of the blessed, in accordance with the idea that the beginning and end times correspond to one another, or that at the end of times the primordial state will be restored. The translators could not imagine God, the Creator of the universe, planting a garden as if he were an ordinary Greek planting a garden behind his house or near the city. Just like the Great Kings of Old Persia, God could only be the owner of a vast garden, a *paradeisos* in fact.

The way Paradise was imagined in Judaism corresponded entirely to the biblical model of the creation story. With the advent and development of Christianity in the first centuries AD, the Garden of Eden was thought of as the abode of particularly prominent figures from the Old Testament such as Abraham. Enoch and Elijah went straight to Paradise – it is said that they did not die, but were taken up (Genesis 5:24; II Kings 2:1–18). The primeval Paradise, the Garden of Eden, is hidden and will appear only at the end of time. According to the rabbinic view, the Garden of Eden already existed before the creation of the world (Pesahim 54a). It is located at the right hand of God, while Hell is on his left (Midrash Tehillim 90:12 [on Psalm 90:3]). The pious, who have led a life according to the law and its prescripts, enter Paradise either immediately after death or after the resurrection and God's judgment; here they sit and feast (Baba Batra 75a) at golden tables under shady canopies (Ta'anit 25a). In

Paradise there are also four streams, from which flow oil, balsam, wine and honey. However, many rabbis – such as Abba 'Arika, known as Rab for short (c.160–247), one of the most important scholars of Babylonia – rejected such earthly notions of Paradise (Berakhot 17a).

From the second century AD onwards, the religious world of Egypt underwent a rapid paradigm shift, for which the existing Jewish communities had already paved the way (see focus 1 and ch. 2). At the beginning of the Roman empire many more Jews lived in Egypt than in the actual mother country of Judea and Palestine. There were repeated revolts against Rome. In particular, the Second Jewish Revolt under Andreas Lukuas (115–17) damaged the reputation of the Jewish community – something from which Christian communities benefited in the subsequent period. The number of Christians continued to grow, so that Egypt was largely Christian in the fourth and fifth centuries (see ch. 3 and ch. 5).

In the second century, and to some extent even earlier, an effervescent and colourful spiritual movement took hold of the Christian communities. It is seen as part of the phenomenon of Gnosticism (see focus 2). Gnosticism was virtually the New Age movement of antiquity, and spoke mainly to the elites in the cities. The message for this 'new era' was that humans are not creatures lost and abandoned in the vastness of space and simply vegetating on earth. Rather, there slumbers in them a bright spark, part of the eternal, uncreated divine light that comes from a sphere that lies beyond the visible heaven of the fixed stars. The ultimate goal of human existence, the meaning of life, is to return to the heavenly homeland from which the immortal soul comes and is detained on earth as in a prison. The hope for salvation did not involve any return to the Garden of Eden in Genesis, especially as Adam's heavenly soul had been lured down into an earthly, transient body. Gnosticism was imbued with a very intellectual and sometimes elitist atmosphere, and so it barely spoke to the illiterate rural population. As early as the third century, the movement had lost much of its momentum.

The fourth century witnessed a new departure. Christianity was on the way to becoming an established state religion with all its privileges, but at the same time some believers withdrew from this 'brave new world'. A longing for a life of fulfilment, leaving behind the familiar paths of the humdrum everyday routine, now also started to affect the masses. This new movement was monasticism (see ch. 11). With its emergence, a biblically imbued piety entered the scene. Many Egyptians who requested to be admitted to a monastery first had to learn to read and write, so that they could read individual texts of the Bible in Coptic, and memorize them. Both the Old and New Testaments were translated from Greek (see ch. 3 and ch. 23). The Bible was being translated into individual Coptic dialects from the second

305 Bread stamp

Egypt, 12th–13th century
Fired clay, unglazed. Diameter 7.2 cm
Museum für Islamische Kunst, Staatliche Museen zu Berlin. Inv. I. 6740

The front side of this stamp depicts in bas-relief a date palm with 4 clusters of dates. Triangles appear on both sides of the trunk. On the back is an arched handle. Dates, leaves and the wood of the date palm were commonly used in Egypt by all classes of population for food, housing and equipment. The date palm is also mentioned in the Qur'an. [GH]
Bib: Kühnel 1939, p. 54, fig. 2e; Das Staunen der Welt, no. 9

306 Lamp with a palm tree

Egypt, Luxor. 5th–6th century
Fired clay. 11.5 × 6.6 × 3.8 cm (with handle)
Skulpturensammlung und Museum für Byzantinische Kunst, Staatliche Museen zu Berlin. Inv. 4951

This lamp belongs to a group produced in North Africa. The smooth handle, the body and the broad spout, which is damaged around the blackened wick hole, are of a single piece. The discus, which has two filling holes, is decorated with a palm tree in low relief, and there are geometrical patterns running over the shoulders. Palm trees are generally considered to be a symbol of life, because they turn the desert green. In Judaism their branches are a symbol of independence as, after the recapture of the Temple at Jerusalem, the Jewish people praised God with palm branches (2 Maccabees 10:7). At Sukkot it is customary to decorate the huts with palm branches. In Christianity the palm is a reminder of Jesus' entry into Jerusalem (Mark 11:1–10), when palm fronds were strewn before him. This event led up to Christ's passion, which reaches its climax in his victory over death. [EE]
Bib: Wulff 1909, pp. 247–48, no. 1244, pl. LX; Cat. Paderborn 1996, p. 189, no. 49.2

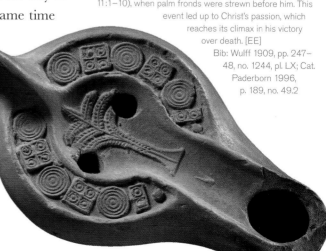

or third century onwards. Thinking was henceforth dominated by the world of the Bible, and not by the religion of ancient Egypt.

According to ancient Egyptian ideas, humans were made up of a body along with the *akh*, *ba* and *ka* (three parts of the soul), the *rn* (the person's name) and the *sw.t* (their shadow). They needed to be protected from any hurt in this world and in the Hereafter. The other world, the underworld, was thought to be located in the west where the sun goes down – a mythical, hidden land (Amenti). At first, only the pharaoh could look forward to a pleasant post-mortem life, travelling in the bark of the sun god across the sky until he reached the underworld in the west at sunset and, after crossing through it, reappearing in the morning in the eastern sky. As the belief in Osiris grew in importance, the idea arose that the world beyond, partly conceived as a mirror image of the earthly world, could not be reached without judgment being passed on the ethical conduct of the deceased during his lifetime. Osiris, or sometimes the Sun God, presided over this court of death.

With Christianization, a new view of the human condition came to prominence. The idea that there were three different parts to the soul was dropped. The *ka* and *ba* disappeared. The *akh*, the transfigured soul, was demoted in the vocabulary of two Coptic dialects to become a synonym for demon. Under the influence of Greek philosophy, Judaism and Christianity moved to a two- or three-part anthropology (body, soul, spirit). For the term 'soul', the word *psyche* was borrowed from the Greek.

Any continuity with ancient Egypt was preserved only insofar as the idea that death, as a complete end, was just as unimaginable as it had been earlier. The Christian idea of life in the heavenly world or kingdom of God differed significantly from the afterlife as envisaged in ancient Egypt. One major difference was that, in the Christian afterlife, earthly hierarchies were not maintained. In the funeral prayer, God was entreated to send the 'angel of light' to meet the soul of the deceased and protect it from the demons lurking on the road to the heavenly realms, so that it could safely enter the 'Paradise of joy', where it could then eat from the 'Tree of life' (Genesis 2:9) and rest 'in the bosom of our father Abraham' (Luke 16:23; see ch. 27, fig. 287). The pious hoped to enter into Paradise immediately after death, just as Jesus promised the crucified thief at his right hand – 'today you will be with me in Paradise' (Luke 23:43).

The pious must have wished to die in the midst of their assembled family, like Joseph the Carpenter. In the story of that name, perhaps from the fourth century, Jesus tells of the death of his adoptive father. When the soul (*psyche*) of Joseph becomes aware that death, along with its entourage – consisting of the Underworld (Amenti), the devil (*diabolos*) and the Decans – was lurking at the door to seize it, it becomes agitated. Because of Jesus' presence, death and its companions could not enter the death chamber. Jesus asked his heavenly Father to send a host of angels down from the celestial realm to bring Joseph's soul to heaven. Only after Jesus had stepped outside the door could Abbaton (the angel of hell/the underworld) take Joseph's soul

from his body. The two Archangels Michael and Gabriel now laid the soul on a silken cloth, kissed it and floated with it up to heaven, where the angels sang a hymn of praise that ceased only once Michael and Gabriel had arrived in heaven. The presence of the angels prevented the soul becoming the victim of predatory demons. What this meant was that, before the soul could reach the transcendental divine dwelling-place – or heaven – it needed to pass through the individual planetary spheres and the fixed stars, with their demonic guardians. The body of Joseph was wrapped in cloths by the two angels, and Jesus said a prayer that commanded it not to decay. Joseph's body was to remain unchanged until the Day of Resurrection (this corresponded to the ideals of ancient Egypt). Prayer replaced earthly methods of preserving the body. Devout Christians hoped that angels would also preserve their souls from harm.

Apart from a few figures of the Christian Old Testament (such as Abraham, Enoch, Elijah and Moses), both the righteous and the unrighteous went to the underworld. Christ descended to them after his death on Good Friday (I Peter 3:19 and 4:6; cf. John 5:25), before he was resurrected on Easter night, and preached the Gospel of salvation to the dead. Christ's Descent into the Underworld, also known as the Harrowing of Hell, is described in detail in the section of the Gospel of Nicodemus

307 Wall painting depicting Adam and Eve in Paradise

Egypt, Tebtynis. 11th century
Wall painting. 72 × 219 cm
Coptic Museum, Cairo. Inv. 3962

Surrounded by luxuriant vegetation symbolizing the Garden of Eden, in the right half of the composition Adam and Eve are shown standing peacefully under the tree of knowledge of good and evil. Eve is handing Adam the forbidden fruit, while the serpent twines around the tree. In the next scene they are both covering their nakedness with fig leaves. Adam is pointing to Eve with his right hand. A striking feature is his disproportionately long, outstretched index and middle fingers. This depicts the scene after they had eaten the forbidden fruit (Genesis 3:8–12). [JT]

308 Tapestry with *crux ansata*

Egypt. 4th–5th century
Wool and linen. 16.5 × 12 cm
Skulpturensammlung und Museum für
Byzantinische Kunst, Staatliche Museen zu
Berlin. Inv. 9212

This fragment, depicting a *crux ansata* (cross
with a handle) with a monogram cross in its
loop, was probably part of a hanging. The motif
corresponds to the ankh, the ancient Egyptian
symbol of life. Egyptian deities often hold this
ankh symbol in their hand, which earned it
the Latin name of *crux ansata* because the
loop can be used as a handle. In Christian
times it appears mainly on grave monuments.
In combination with the monogram of Christ
it symbolizes eternal life and the idea of
resurrection. [JT]

that bears the same name. Here, on Holy Saturday, Christ frees all occupants of the underworld. Holding Adam by the hand, he leads the righteous to Paradise, where they are received by the Archangel Michael. The description of Paradise as a place of peace and tranquillity, where cooling waters flow, is based on biblical statements. In Paradise the new (or heavenly) Jerusalem is located, as described in detail in the Book of Revelation (ch. 21, cf. Hebrews 12.22–24, Galatians 4:26), with various allusions to the story of Paradise in Genesis. However, it did not have the same resonance in the Nile valley as it did in other regions of Christendom. The Apostle Paul, in his second letter to the church at Corinth (12:2-4), describes how he was caught up into the third heaven, which he identified with Paradise.

In the Christian art of Egypt, the first human couple is occasionally depicted. A mural from church C of the ancient town of Tebtunis in the Fayyum is a scenic representation of Genesis 3, which depicts the tasting of the forbidden fruit and the expulsion from Paradise (fig. 307).

From ancient Egypt comes the *crux ansata*, also known as the Coptic Cross (fig. 308). It is shown to the left. The corresponding hieroglyph means *ankh* (life, life force). As a symbol it can be presented by the gods to the pharaoh, or held to the nose to provide the eternal breath of life or permanent vital energy. In Christian times the ankh symbol appears together with the cross on grave reliefs, and also in textile art (figs 4, 24, 120, 121, 290). It symbolizes eternal life, and the cross points to the resurrection (see ch. 27). If on monuments (particularly grave stelae) we find eagles and peacocks, the symbolism associated with them is borrowed from the Graeco-Roman world. Originally from India, the peacock was promoted to the sacred animal of Zeus/Jupiter's wife Hera/Juno, while the eagle is linked to Zeus/Jupiter, and later also connected to the Sun God. In the Roman empire the peacock acts as *psychopomp* (guide of the soul), and carries the empress seated on its back up to heaven, as evidenced in coins. Similarly, with the help of the eagle, the soul of the late emperor is carried to heaven. Apotheosis (deification) in principle happened only after death. In a Christian context the eagle is a mediator between heaven and earth, serving as a *psychopomp* and protecting from evil powers (cf. ch. 27).

In Christian art Paradise is represented as a garden idyll with vines and peacocks, which goes back to older models of Roman garden landscapes. In the Christian context, the peacock turned into a symbol of resurrection and eternal bliss. Vines on monuments are a legacy of Graeco-Roman art. Originally they are linked to Dionysus, the god of wine, but can occur also in other contexts. As a symbol of Paradise they were also included in Islamic art.

One deeply rooted idea, that goes back to the early epochs of ancient Egypt and persisted into Christian times, was the fear of having to eke out an arduous existence in the world beyond with some kind of physical handicap. In Christian times there was still a belief that there was a connection between the resurrection

309 Hanging with eagle

Egypt, probably Antinoopolis. 5th–6th century
Linen and wool. 113 × cm
Skulpturensammlung und Museum für Byzantinische Kunst,
Staatliche Museen zu Berlin. Inv. 6811

In the middle of a scattered pattern of roses and overlapping
rows of leaves and buds, arranged in a curve, is a large figure
of an eagle. Its wings are outstretched and its tail feathers
spread. Its head is turned to the left and in its beak it holds a
garland of flowers. Around its neck is a string of pearls. In Late
Antiquity depictions of eagles are very frequently associated
with the cult of the dead. According to ancient Egyptian tradition,
it was the ba-bird or 'soul bird' that would reanimate the dead
body. The eagle served a similar purpose in a Christian context,
as it was considered a symbol of Christ's ascension and thus
of the resurrection and the salvation of all souls. The garland
or wreath in the mouth of the eagle was a symbol of victory in
Roman triumphal art and, in a Christian context, also symbolizes
the conquest of death. [CF]

Bib: Cat. Hamm 1996, p. 299, no. 339

body and the earthly body at the time of death. The body should
have all its limbs and be undamaged, which is why mummification persisted into the seventh century and probably beyond
(see ch. 29). Abbot Shenoute (see ch. 11) of the so-called White
Monastery (Monastery of Shenoute) (see ch.11; ch. 12 and
focus 5) tried to reassure those listening to his sermons that anyone who had lost an eye (or other body part) would not appear
misshapen in Paradise, since (in the words of St Paul) the person receives a 'spiritual body' at the resurrection (I Corinthians
15:44). On the other hand, he threated the monks that any who
transgressed the vow they had sworn before God would, like
Moses, see the Promised Land, but not enter it. Rather, God
would cast them body and soul into the flames of hell where
they would be destroyed. In many lives of the martyrs, a theme
from the Osiris myth was often added. Similarly to the body
of Osiris the body of the martyr was fragmented, but later
re-assembled and restored by Michael, another angel or Jesus.
It was the representatives of the Roman state who were seen as
agents of destruction, such as Seth.

Belief in the resurrection was expressed in I Corinthians 15, in which no
limits are placed to God's omnipotence. Once this had become generally established, all measures to preserve the lifeless body were abandoned. Among the ideals
fostered by the hermits' colonies was the view that the *homo perfectus* (the perfect man
who lived according to the commandments of God) experienced a taste of his final
fate already in this world. The *vita angelica* (angelic life) could in principle be realized
only in the desert. The ancestors of this hermit ideal were the prophet Elijah, John
the Baptist and Jesus himself, as it was believed that he spent time in the desert before

310 Fragment of a tapestry with a peacock

Egypt. 3rd–4th century
Linen and wool. 39 × 43 cm
Skulpturensammlung und Museum für Byzantinische Kunst,
Staatliche Museen zu Berlin. Inv. 9715

This multi-coloured tapestry in a kind of looped pile follows
the artistic tradition of late Roman models. The peacock and
branches are depicted in a naturalistic way, and are notable
for their rich spectrum of colour and the fine nuances created
as one shade blends into the next. Like the eagle and the
grapevine, the peacock is also an iconographic motif that
borrows its meaning from its origins in Classical antiquity. The
hard flesh of the peacock was seen as a symbol of immortality
and thus became a part of grave art. It is one of the few
figurative motifs that are also found on Jewish monuments. [CF]

Bib: Effenberger and Rasemowitz 1975, pp. 241–54, pl. 31, 1–3

252

311 Decorative panel

Egypt, Cairo. 7th century
Pine. 13.5 × 73.5 cm
Museum für Islamische Kunst, Staatliche Museen
zu Berlin. Inv. I. 4469

A band of ornamental vine tendrils runs inside
the profiled long edge of the panel, which
is decorated with rows of small triangles.
The cone-shaped bunches of grapes fit
perfectly into the narrow space. This relatively
naturalistic representation is still in the
mainstream of the Hellenistic-Late Antique
tradition. Similar designs are also known from
textiles. The indigenous Egyptian craftsmen,
who were at first mainly Christian, continued
working in the old way for their new Muslim
clients. Changes came in only gradually. [GH]
Bib: Ettinghausen 1933, p. 18, fig. 12

312 Fragment of hanging with vine tendrils

Egypt. 4th–5th century
Linen and wool. 66 × 19 cm
Skulpturensammlung und Museum für
Byzantinische Kunst, Staatliche Museen zu Berlin.
Inv. 9067

The extremely carefully executed vine tendrils,
with bunches of grapes hanging from them,
were probably a structural element in a larger
hanging or cover. From the winding main vine
come thin twigs with precisely detailed, filigree
leaves and grapes in delicately nuanced
colours with effects of light and shade.
The vine as aniconographic motif emerged
from Classical antiquity. It was an important
attribute in depictions of the mystery cult of
the god Dionysus. It then became one of the
most popular motifs of funerary art. However,
its use as a symbol of Paradise is only one
of the many levels of meaning of the vine in
Judaism, Christianity and Islam. [CF]
Bib: Cat. Hamm 1996, p. 334, no. 382

313–314 Two decorative fittings

Egypt, Cairo. 7th–8th century
Bone. 9.6 × 5.7 cm, and 9.7 × 4.5 cm
Museum für Islamische Kunst, Staatliche Museen zu Berlin.
Inv. I. 5894, I. 5922

These slightly curved covers are made from long bones, with holes bored in them for wooden dowels to fix them in place. Both have similar patterns, comprising vine tendrils issuing from a base or a vase, in one case supplemented by a pair of palm fronds. The flat reliefs are surrounded by smooth frames. The pieces show that vine tracery, which in Egypt is associated with symbols of Paradise, was also popular on small objects that are more commonly used in private life. These pieces originating from the early Islamic period are very little different from their early antique and Byzantine predecessors. [GH]
Bib: Wulff 1909, nos 622 and 637, pls 27 (I. 5894) and 28 (I. 5922)

appearing in public. Only in the desert can one increase one's spiritual experience and attain perfection. Should the hermit succeed in resisting the constant attacks of the devil and his demonic companions, he is honoured with a very exceptional privilege – the hermit is served by angels. This is clearly described in the *Life of Onuphrius* (actually the travel memoirs of a certain Paphnutius in idealized form). In the desert Onuphrius reached such a degree of perfection that an angel provided him with bread every night, just as ravens fed Elijah at the brook Cherith (I Kings 17:6). On Saturdays and Sundays he celebrated the Last Supper, the elements of which were also provided by a heavenly messenger who supplied all hermits in the desert in this way. When hermits are entirely consumed by the desire for another world, their souls can even be swept up into heaven.

The last stop in Paphnutius' journey is an oasis that is like a magical garden, described like an earthly Garden of Paradise, with numerous fruit trees (cf. Genesis 2:9; 2:16; 3:3). Paphnutius meets four brothers from Oxyrhynchus, who have long lived there. Before the angel appears, bringing them supper, a sweet fragrance tells of his coming. Paphnutius would like to stay, but the angel commands him to return to his brothers in Egypt. Paphnutius experiences his seven-day stay with the four brothers as a kind of anticipation of his sojourn in Paradise, the Garden of Eden. The sweet scent given off by the fruit trees is identical to that which precedes the appearance of the angel. It is a sign of the presence of heaven. Their earthly Paradise is a foretaste of what is to come – re-entry into the Garden of Eden. One almost gets the impression that the brothers' fruit garden is, so to speak, a reflection of the primordial Paradise. As God once walked there in the cool of the evening (Genesis 3:8), now an angel appears in the evening. As a sign of God's reconciliation with the world, he offers the brothers his gift.

29 Judgment Day and Paradise in the Qur'an

Michael Marx

THE idea of Judgment Day, human reward and punishment after death, is an important theme in the Qur'an, a text that contains God's revelations to Muhammad in the form of a book. The Qur'an is made up of 114 Suras (chapters) which are more or less arranged according to their length (rather than according to the order of their proclamation), and dating from between 610 and 632. If one keeps in mind that the Prophet appeared in 610, first establishing a community in Mecca and then being forced to leave this old Arab place of pilgrimage to build up a first polity in 622 in the oasis Yathrib (Medina) about 350 km north (taking on the role of judge and military leader), it is not surprising that the Qur'an itself mirrors the different phases characterizing the establishment of a polity. To name just a few topics, in their historical order, this includes the request to believe in one god, a creator and judge; warnings of judgment day and the call upon people to vow to one god; the message of biblical prophets and Arab men of god/envoys (whose descendant is the Prophet himself); being rejected by the people of Mecca and establishing a polity; the dispute with the Jewish community of Medina; the reprimanding of the community's members; judicial regulations (inheritance, criminal law, law of obligation etc.); and the war against the community's enemies.

The call upon the people to profess to one god – who either rewards or punishes them for their deeds – is a recurrent theme in the Qur'an, although changing during the twenty-three years of proclamation by the Prophet. They include topics that we also find in the Jewish and Christian traditions and that partly go back to the ancient Near East (Mesopotamia, Egypt, Iran); the belief that humans live on after death is recorded in the Mesopotamian cuneiform inscriptions. The story of Gilgamesh visiting the world of the dead mentions the gods living in a garden. They have a book which records the deeds and lives of every past and present human being, and forms the base for their judgment. A former and very similar idea is the belief in the 'book of life' in the Jewish tradition that contains the names of 'the righteous'. In ancient Egypt the people believed in life after death as well. The soul was weighed after death and the one that was found to be too light was punished, whereas the good one was rewarded. Also ancient Iranian beliefs contain the idea of reward and punishment after death and even Plato (died 428/27 BC) speaks about the good souls going to the right side of heaven and the bad ones to the left, before being led on downwards. Plato does not describe in detail the place in which the souls shall live

eternally. The Book of Isaiah (Isaiah 66:24) mentions a garden for the righteous. Apart from the Bible there is the Book of Enoch (27:1), before AD 70, referring to a garden and Gehenna. In the Hebrew Bible itself, these two places are not yet regarded as places in the hereafter that correspond to heaven and hell.

The gospels mention a Lord who judges (Matthew 24:42, for example), who arrives unexpectedly. These texts give little information about heaven and hell, as described by the later Christian tradition. Judgment Day is one of the central themes in the Gospel of John which describes in detail the end of the world/doomsday – earthquakes and other catastrophes announce the end of the world, and are followed by the return of Jesus Christ as a judge. Sura 81 and other early Meccan Suras describe similar signs of doomsday, although not mentioning the return of Christ. The Qur'an focuses on the single human being, having to take responsibility for their own actions and being judged by a register that was created for every single person (88:10). The ancient Near Eastern way of thinking – the idea of souls being weighed and the 'book of life' – lives on in the tradition of Islam and Christianity. Meccan suras occasionally mention the scale as the instrument of divine judgment (7:8/9,

315 Prayer panel with throne verse
Egypt. c.1000
Wood. 23.4 × 169 cm
Museum für Islamische Kunst, Staatliche Museen zu Berlin. Inv. I. 1/80

This little panel shaped like a small *mihrab* contains 2 bands of inscription in decorative Kufic script. They show the popular 'Throne Verse' from the Qur'an (2:255). It is considered to be especially rich in blessings because it emphasises the omnipotence of God. Small panels of this kind are only known from the Fatimid period and are characteristic of the Shiite branch of Islam. Most of them contain prayers or appeals to the Prophet Muhammad, to 'Ali or the Shiite imams. Some have been found in graves under the head of the dead person, perhaps intended to help them to arise on Judgment Day. [GH]
Bib: Museum für Islamische Kunst 1979, no. 679; Brisch 1983

21:47, 23:102,103, 101:6/8) – a perception that is not mentioned in Medina anymore. Merely God's knowledge forms a judgment's basis. In Christian tradition it is the Archangel Gabriel who appears on Judgment Day with a scale in his hands.

In mid- and late Meccan suras the portrayal of Judgment Day is often followed by a description of heaven and hell (52:21). In Sura 44 the secluded and pleasant garden is the abode of the blessed, who enjoy the fruit and wine at a banquet surrounded by virgins and youths or young boys. The garden is decorated with luxurious fabrics. Both paradise and hell are described in earthly categories and terms, although this is occasionally modified by the statement that no living person can grasp the joys of paradise. There are springs in paradise, called *kautar* (108:1), *salsabil* (76:18) and *tasnim* (83:27), shady trees (56:28–30), fruits, grapes (23:19; 36:34) and pomegranates (55:68). This paradise's climate – eternal shade (13:35) – is mild (76:13). Its inhabitants live in peace (56:26), God is praised (35:34) and there is no false talk (88:11). The blessed live without fatigue (15:48; 35:35), trouble and work (35:34–5). He who is pious and righteous will be rewarded through fruit and meat (52:22), nectar scented with musk, mixed with the water of the springs (83:25–7) and pure wine (76:21), that does not intoxicate. Dark-eyed virgins (44:54; 52:20; 55:72; 56:22), gazing humbly (55:56) and that are flawless (56:34–5), along with youths as cupbearers (52:24, 56:17–19) stand to serve the blessed. There are couches (56:15; 76:13; 83:23; 88:13), pillows and carpets (55:76), the blessed are dressed in fine silk (22:23) and brocade (76:21), golden bracelets, pearls (22:23) and silver (76:21). The Qur'anic descriptions are pursued in the exegetic literature and expanded when it comes to describing sensual pleasure, as is the inhabitant's language – according to some exegetes into Arabic.

This very sensual description of paradise was often the subject of interest in Christian-Islamic polemics, for example in the writings of the Christian-Arabic scholar 'Abd al-Masih al-Kindi (ninth century), who deemed these descriptions inappropriate. Some years ago Christoph Luxenberg tried to demonstrate that the Arabic term for the virgins of paradise (*hur 'ain*) originally stems from a Syrian-Aramaic word meaning grapes. Luxenberg's assumption that the virgins of paradise do not coincide with the Christian idea of paradise, and that the original Syrian-Aramaic text included the word grape, was only accepted by a very small number of scholars. The fact that the Huris are mentioned in the pre-Islamic wine-poems by Arabic poets such as al-A'sha does also not support the theory of its new interpretation. Numerous descriptions of paradise – such as the shady garden, the fruits, and especially the grapes of the heavenly feast – can also be found in the so called 'anthems of paradise' by the Syrian church father Ephrem (306–73). It is striking here that the grapes are clearly described in a sexually connoted language.

Rational movements within Islam have resented these depictions of paradise, in which the material culture of the time of proclamation is so clearly expressed. In

Islamic mysticism for example, the direct experience of God is the most important aspect; for other exegetes, experiencing sensual pleasure is merely an allegoric description. Many modern scholars and reformists, such as Muhammad 'Abduh (died 1905) or Muhammad Rashid Rida (died 1935), have refused the sensual descriptions of heavenly paradise. These scholars hold the view that within the text these virgins of paradise are contrary to other Qur'anic statements, such as in Sura 43 which says that the blessed will live in paradise together with their wives (43:70). Medinan Suras, that were proclaimed when the Prophet was already head of the Islamic polity, do not contain any sensual descriptions of the joys of paradise. Here paradise is only mentioned as a reward for the righteous – as a garden with streams of water running through it. In Islamic architecture gardens and parks represent the heavenly garden of paradise. The Islamic gardens with their water installations can therefore be seen as a way of foreshadowing the heavenly gardens to the believers.

It has become clear that Judgment Day, as well as the descriptions of heaven and hell, are based on Jewish and Christian beliefs, which themselves carry ideas originated in the ancient Near East. The first Islamic polity in Mecca and Medina was most probably acquainted with these concepts in their Late Antique context. Life after death, judgment, retribution and punishment all have become central theological themes of every Islamic school and orientation (Sunnis as well as the Shia). The sensual description of shady gardens of paradise, with luxurious and expensive equipment, with food, fruit, wine and the fulfilment of sexual desires, forms part of the suras of Mecca.

After 622 – the year of emigration to Yatrib (Medina) – paradise is depicted as much less colourful. The suras proclaimed during the period of Medina merely mention a garden for the pious, which is not described in further detail. It is not surprising that the way paradise was depicted in Meccan Suras was problematic in Medina. In Medinan Suras men and women are often directly addressed in the text – which is contrary to Meccan Suras. Here the main focus is the righteous men living in paradise together with their wives. Even modern Qur'anic exegesis distances itself from the idea of the fulfilment of sensual desires, and emphasizes more abstract notions of heavenly reward. Christian paradise is also seen more matter-of-factly in modern times; the pictures of paradise and hell by Hieronymus Bosch are rarely emphasized by theologians of the large Christian confessions. Apparently in Mecca the depictions of the joys of paradise were in order, which then changed in Medina. The fact that Islamic exegesis – a discipline represented by male scholars for hundreds of years – has refined sexual ideas (found in Meccan Suras) is unsurprising. Exegetes also often focus on understanding god in a mystical way, and claim that it is not humanly possible to grasp the extent of joy one will feel in paradise. Each and every time-period describes the hereafter using its own criteria – this has not changed since ancient Egyptian times.

EPILOGUE
Jewish, Christian and Muslim Heritage in Modern Egypt

Sebastian Elsässer

WITH the boom of the colonial economy in the global 'era of free trade'[1] in the second half of the nineteenth century, Egypt experienced immigration from the entire Mediterranean. From then on, for several generations non-Muslim foreigners played an economically and culturally influential role, even though they accounted for no more than one to two per cent of the total population.[2] Christian religious communities of Middle Eastern origins[3] and European missionary societies pioneered the introduction of modern educational institutions and social services. The most significant foreign 'colonies' were those of the Greeks, Italians, Levantine Christians, Armenians and Jews. The Jewish religious community, indeed, had a small proportion of long-established Arabic-speaking Jews, as the Harat al-Yahud (Jewish street) in Old Cairo still testifies,[4] but immigrants from the Mediterranean dominated economically and culturally. Under their leadership, the Jewish community experienced one last heyday in the early twentieth century.

The Egyptian national movement of the early twentieth century demanded an end to British sovereignty over Egypt, and turned against the legal privileges enjoyed by foreigners and their economic and political domination. In addition to the Egyptian Muslims (over ninety per cent of the population), nationalists considered the Arabic-speaking and long-established religious minorities, such as the Jews and the Coptic Christians (six to seven per cent of the population), as part of the Egyptian nation.[5] Egyptian nationalism and its propagation of the ideal of a peaceful and harmonious co-existence of the monotheistic religions on Egyptian soil ('unity of Cross and Crescent') had, since the independence of Egypt in 1922, created a bond of unity between Christians and Muslims (fig. 316).

Some nationalists also propagated, in a secularist manner, the separation of religious and national affiliation: *al-din li-llah wa-l-watan li-l-jami'* (religion belongs to God, the Fatherland belongs to everybody!). But central elements of the premodern order were retained in the Egyptian nation-state, despite some innovations in the legal and institutional area – a family law that differentiated and discriminated by religion; the autonomous status of non-Muslim religious communities, particularly the Christian churches; and the general dominance of Islam as the majority religion

جمال بدوى

مسلمون وأقباط

من المهــــد إلى المجــــد

with simultaneous control of Islamic institutions and dignitaries by the state.[6] This complex religio-political arrangement has been a recipe for religious and social conflict up until today.[7]

First, the rise of Egyptian nationalism and other national movements in the region heralded the gradual decline of cosmopolitan minorities. By the late 1920s continuous emigration had begun, which gradually accelerated, and culminated between 1956 and the early 1960s in the context of the Suez War and the nationalization and socialization policy ('Arab socialism') of the Nasser regime.[8] Thus the Christian presence in Egypt was essentially reduced to the Copts, while the Jewish presence, apart from a few architectural remains, almost completely disappeared.[9]

Both Islam and Coptic Christianity experienced a revival in the second half of the twentieth century, in the course of which religious offices and institutions were reformed and modernized, enabling the men of religion to recover much of their lost social and political influence. While on the Coptic side the reforming popes Cyril VI (1959–71) and Shenoute III (1971–2012) restored the authority of the Church and the papacy, and ensured that the Coptic Orthodox Church would take comprehensive care of believers in all areas of life,[10] there was on the Islamic side no central institution and authority. Bureaucratic and cumbersome state Islam, whose representatives in any case had a credibility problem in the eyes of many Muslims because of their submissive attitude toward the regime, could after the 1970s hardly keep up with dynamically evolving Islamist movements such as the Muslim Brotherhood and Jama'a Islamiya.[11] Independent preachers, such as Sheikhs

316 Egyptian nationalism in the 20th century

Representation of the national unity of Muslims and Christians on a book jacket. Author Gamal Badawi; artwork Helmy El Touni.

317 Cross and crescent

The message of Muslim–Christian unity is conveyed in post-revolution street art stencilled on a wall in Zamalek, Cairo. The Arabic below the image states 'It's our Egypt, all of us'.

Sha'rawi and Kishk, set themselves up as a third force between Islamists and government, and achieved immense popularity. The educated public came under the influence of 'Islamic intellectuals' who brought Islam back into the centre of public debate. At the individual level, many Christians and Muslims took a conservative turn inwards. Religious differences and the claim to be sole possessors of the truth again became more important than the great similarities between religious communities.

The causes of this religious turn were varied. The inner process of renewal of the different religions made them newly and increasingly attractive for the educated elites who, of all groups within the population, had become the most secularized in their lifestyle and their world view and moved away from traditional religiosity. Belief in progress and optimistic expectations for the future, that came to a peak with the brilliant initial successes of the Nasser regime in the 1950s, continued for some time to favour cultural secularization, which now included wider sections of the middle class, and especially women. But belief in the rapid rise of Egypt into an economic and political power on the regional, if not the global scale, came to an abrupt end in 1967 with defeat in the Six-Day War. Since then, the Egyptian nation-state has been in a chronic state of crisis as to its identity and legitimacy. An unbridgeable gulf opened up between the three 'major objectives' of Egyptian nationalism – progress, development and national greatness – and the reality of the regimes of Anwar al-Sadat and Hosni Mubarak, which were mainly characterized by stagnation and the pragmatic desire on the part of the rulers themselves to maintain power.

How to manage the rapid demographic and social change, which began as early as the 1930s, has been the overwhelming issue of Egyptian politics up until today. The Egyptian population doubled between 1930 and 1963, and again by 1994. The large cities, especially Cairo and Alexandria, grew even faster thanks to migration from the countryside. From the 1960s onwards the state found it increasingly difficult to guide the uncontrolled growth of the cities and provide the growing population with basic public goods – drinking water, electricity and roads, security and justice, education and health, and economic prospects. For more and more Egyptians (especially the educated middle classes), religious networks and communities assumed some of these tasks. Today, they look after not just economic and social security, but also create meaning in a political and social context characterized by disorientation and a 'might is right' mentality.

At the same time, new conflicts have been sparked over the social role of religion. The demand for new places of worship that comes with population growth continues to lead to conflict between Christians and Muslims, in which the minority often feels disadvantaged.[12] The situation is similar as regards people who change religion, as they often arouse fierce resistance amongst those they have 'forsaken', especially if the converts are young unmarried women, generally regarded as immature and vulnerable. The last decade has been marked by ever more explosive religious tensions that have sometimes led to armed conflicts, sometimes to pogroms against the Coptic minority, especially in rural Upper Egypt. The social forces that seek reconciliation and equality, and adhere to the patriotic ideal of the harmonious coexistence of Egyptians of all religions (fig. 316), have so far proved too weak to overcome the religious polarization of Egyptian society. The future alone will show whether in Egypt, under the conditions of the twenty-first century, genuine religious coexistence is still possible, or whether the country through the emigration of the Copts – which is already happening, in the view of some observers – will sooner or later become entirely Muslim.

Notes

PART 1: THE THREE RELIGIONS IN EGYPT

Introduction

1　Dating systems for the three religions are different. This publication uses the system most widely used in the German and English speaking worlds, with the acknowledgement to the reader that this necessarily priviliges a Christian system.

2　Escaping famine, Abraham (Genesis 12:10–20); the sons of Jacob: (Genesis 42:1–5); Joseph's opportunity (Genesis 41:14–57); Moses leading his people from slavery (Exodus:1.1–15.21); false refuge (Jeremiah: 42.9–45.28); refuge for the holy family (Matthew 2:13, 20); Pharaoh in the Qur'an (e.g. 2.49).

1 The Role of Abraham in Judaism, Christianity and Islam

1　Bauschke 2007; Bauschke 2008; Bauschke 2014; Behr, Krochmalnik and Schröder 2011; Böttrich, Ego and Eißler 2009; Chilton 2008; Firestone 1990; Greiner, Janowski and Lichtenberger 2007; Hinterhuber 2009; Kratz and Nagel 2003; Kuschel 1994; Kuschel 2007; Mühling 2011; Mythos Abraham 2009; Paret 1971; Thalmayer 2001.

2 Judaism

1　See the *Letter of Aristeas*.

2　However, next to a 2nd-century BC papyrus of Deuteronomy from Egypt, the oldest manuscripts of the Septuagint come from the Judaean Desert, showing a need for these Greek texts in Judea in a pre-Christian context.

3　See, for example, Manetho's *Aegyptiaca*, partly preserved by Flavius Josephus in his *Contra Apionem*.

4　See Philo's *In Flaccum* and *De Legatione*.

5　Authorship and dates are debated. For discussion, see Metzger and Murphy (eds.), *The New Oxford Annotated Bible with Apocrypha and Deuterocanonical Books* (New York: Oxford University Press, 1994), AP 285, AP 57.

6　Josephus, *Jewish War* 2.487–498; 7.368.

7　Josephus, *Jewish War* 7.409–419.

8　Josephus, *Jewish War* 7.421–436.

9　*CPJ* 160-229; *O. Heerlen BL* 345; see also Heemstra 2010, pp. 13–20.

10　The Third Jewish Revolt, or Bar Kokhba (132–35), was localized in Judea and thus does not concern us here.

11　Frederiksen and Irshai 2006, p. 1004, note 86.

Focus 1 The Jewish community at Elephantine

1　The Berlin archaeologist and philologist Otto Rubensohn undertook systematic excavations for papyri on behalf of the Royal Museums of Berlin from 1906 onwards. His work and that of his co-workers over three excavation seasons was highly successful: the papyrus find was complemented by numerous other documents found in situ in Elephantine, including *ostraca*, now in the papyrus collection of the Egyptian Museum of the National Museums in Berlin (Lepper 2012).

2　For an overview, see Porten and Yardeni 1999.

3　See Porten 1969 and Lepper 2012.

3 Christianity

1　Luz 2002, p. 183.

2　For the quoted references see Lüdemann 1987 – this does not relate to Egypt directly, but suggests the early presence of Christianity in Egyptian Nubia, at Egypt's southern frontier.

3　Roberts 1979.

4　Lührmann 2000, p. 12; on the later dating cf. Bagnall 2009, p. 12.

5　Thus rightly Harnack as early as 1924, p. 707.

6　Frey 2012, Markschies 2012.

7　Schröter and Bethge 2012; Markschies 2012, p. 681; Lührmann 2000, pp. 26–31 and pp. 106–31.

8　Löhr 1996 and Markschies 1992.

9　Meyer 2007.

10　Eusebius, *Church History* II 16:24; for the legendary status of the account, see Pearson 2006, p. 336.

11　Harnack 1924, pp. 707–13; Pearson 2006.

12　Eutyches of Alexandria, *Annals*, PG 111, 982 D: '*Ille autem factus patriarcha tres constituit episcopos. Et primus fuit hic patriarcha Alexandrinus qui episcopos fecit*'.

13　Guyot and Klein 1993, pp. 124–25.

14　Guyot and Klein 1993, p. 373.

15　Eusebius, *Church History* VIII 9:3.

16　Brakmann 1994, p. 11.

17　On the theology of Clement and Origen as well as the Trinitarian debates and the position of Athanasius, see Dünzl 2006.

18　Dassmann 1999, pp. 71–101.

19　Müller 1969, pp. 118 ff.

Focus 2 Gnosticism and Manichaeism

1　At a 1966 colloquium 'Gnosticism' was defined as a name for just these systems. 'Gnosis' was defined as referring to a 'knowledge of divine mysteries, which is reserved for an elite' and is not limited to any one historical period (Bianchi 1967: XXIX–XXXII; Colpe 1969). Usually, in German (see for example Rudolph 1990), but also in ancient texts (see Markschies 1991), the term 'Gnosis' is used for the aforementioned ideological systems (see also Hengel 1976, Filoramo 1990, pp. 142–147). For an introduction to the topic see Richter 2008 and 2012.

2　Mortley and Colpe 1981. On the mythical systems arising in the Christian period, in contrast, see Colpe 1981.

3　For a good overview, see Rudolph 1990, pp. 352–79, Lieu 1992 and Böhlig 1995.

4　Lieu et al. 2012.

5　On the texts from Nag Hammadi see Schenke et al. 2001–2003; on Medinet Madi see Böhlig 1994, pp. 133–45; on Kellis see for instance *P. Kellis* V and, with texts also in Greek and Syriac, Gardner 2007.

6　These include the codices Askewianus, Brucianus and Papyrus Berolinensis (see the overview in Böhlig 1994, pp. 241–42).

7　On the many different apocrypha, see Markschies and Schröter 2012; Schneemelcher 1999.

8　See the overview in Böhlig 1995.

9　See Hengel 1976, pp. 556–60; Markschies 1991, pp. 869–70.

10　Richter 1997, esp. pp. 32–55.

11　Hengel 1976, p. 565.

12　Speyer 1981, pp. 144–46.

13　Koenen and Römer, 1988, see also the entire Codex at http://www.uni-koeln.de/phil-fak/ifa/NRWakademie/papyrologie/Manikodex/bildermani.html (last accessed 6 September 2015); Richter 1998, p. 2; for the edition of the Psalm book see at http://www.uni-muenster.de/IAEK/forschen/kop/mani/index.html (last accessed 6 September 2015).

4 Islam

1　Ibn 'Abd al-Hakam, *Futuh*, p. 56.

2　See also the Byzantine attacks on the Syrian coast throughout the 7th century (Foss 2010, p. 82).

3　Kister 1989.

4　Morelli 1998 and 2001.

5　Palme 2007.

6　Sijpesteijn 2007, pp. 444–48.

7　In the bilingual Greek-Arabic papyrus dated 22 AH / AD 643, the Greek and Arabic can be compared (Grohmann 1952, pp. 113–14). The Greek and Coptic version is a simple 'in the name of God', which was, however, already used in the pre-Islamic period in Egypt.

8　Sijpesteijn 2014.

9　Hanafi 2010.

10　This text, referred to in Kraemer 1958, p. 159 and Ragheb 2013, p. 715, no. 39, is being prepared for publication by Robert Hoyland.

11　See also Donner's argument that a distinctive Muslim identity only arose towards the end of the 7th century (2010, chapter 2).

12　Robinson 2005.

13　Sijpesteijn 2013, text 8.

14　Abbott 1967.

15　Loebenstein 1982.

16　For *hadith*, see for example Yazid b. Abi Habib (died 745) and al-Layth b. Sa'd (died 791) (Tillier 2011). For history, see Ibn Lahi'a (died 790) and al-Layth b. Sa'd (Kennedy 1998, p. 63).

17　Ibn Ishaq, born in Medina *c.*704, came to Alexandria when he was about 30 years old. Ibn Hisham, born in Basra or in Fustat of Basran descent, studied in Egypt.

18　He arrived in Egypt in 814, cf. El Shamsy 2013.

19　Sijpesteijn 2011.

20　Kennedy 1998, pp. 65–68.

21　Sijpesteijn 2014.

22　Kennedy 1998.

23　See for example the successful partnership of Egypt's governor 'Amr b. al-'As and the governor of Syria (639–60), later caliph, Mu'awiya (reigned 660–80). In later periods too the two provinces were united under one rule. See for example the Fatimids (969–1171) and the Mamluks (1250–1517).

24　Frantz-Murphy 2001.

25　Khan 2007.

26　Khan 1994.

PART 2: ROMAN EGYPT

5 Alexandria

1　The Ptolemaic inscriptions are collected by Bernand 2001; those of the Roman period by Kayser 1994. Both omit gravestones, and there is no corpus for Late Antiquity.

2　Empereur 1998 is a good guide to these discoveries, although much has been found in the succeeding years. Tkaczow 1993 summarizes what was known of the city's topography up to that date. McKenzie 2007 gives a comprehensive study of Alexandria's landscape and buildings throughout the Hellenistic, Roman and Late Antique periods.

3　Fraser 1972 is the standard work on the Ptolemaic city.

4　McKenzie 2007 surveys the available information.

5　For Alexandrian citizenship see Delia 1991.

6　Harker 2008 discusses the so-called 'Acts of the Alexandrians' and their relationship to the conflict with the Jewish population.

7　See Jördens 2009 for a comprehensive study of the prefect and his administration.

8　See McKenzie 2007, pp. 177–78.

9　Bagnall 2002 discusses the fate of the Alexandrian library.

10　For a general survey of Late Antique Alexandria, see Kiss 2007. A detailed study concentrating on topography and social conflict is Haas 1997.

11　See Davis 2004.

12　For the Melitian schism see Hauben 2012.

13　McKenzie 2007, p. 242.

14　Rodziewicz 1984 publishes the most interesting habitation and craft quarter of Late Antique Alexandria, at Kom el-Dikka; more production facilities have been found in recent excavations there.

15　For the Indian trade see Sidebotham 2011, Tomber 2008.

16　Fraser 1972 is the fundamental work on the cultural life of Ptolemaic Alexandria. On the library see Bagnall 2002.

17　Empereur 1998; Goddio *et al.* 1998.

18　For a readable synthesis see Modrzejewski 1995.

19　Davis 2004 gives an account of the bishops of the Alexandrian church from the earliest Christian community to the Arab conquest.

20　See Nirenberg 2013 for this fundamental characteristic of Christian discourse.

21　Haas 1997, pp. 302–4, relying largely on the church historian Socrates and on the late chronicle of John of Nikiu. Clearly this episode is to be seen in the context of the struggles for Christian dominance involving the prefect and the bishop.

22　Derda, Majcherek, and Wipszycka 2007 publish the auditoria and discuss education in Late Antique Alexandria.

6 Religion in Roman Egypt

1 From this point of view too, in Alexandria, in contrast to the other trends documented in Egypt, we find singular phenomena that are not highlighted separately here (see ch. 5).

2 Comparable representations with a cape can be found on the mummy masks, shrouds, coffins and funeral steles. Thus, this depiction of Osiris resembles that of Sokar-Osiris on the apex end of the mask (Parlasca and Seemann 1999, cat. 206c) and on the foot of the coffin of Teuris (Kurth, 1990, Scene II, Pl. C, 1), Steles: Abdalla, 1992, and also inter alia, in plates 4b, 5, 7, 8, 10a, 11b, cat. 8, 11, 14–16, 18, 23 and many others; Bernand 1992, cat. 86, 87, 88, 91, 93–95, plates 48, 49, 52, 54, 55 (documents from Roman times); Cat. Marseille 1997, 148–49, cat. 168. Shroud and corresponding mask from Meir (2nd quarter 2nd century AD; 125–35 AD): Parlasca and Seemann 1999, pp. 93-94, p. 313, cat. 206i. For coffins and a mask see Kurth 1990, pp. 33–35, fig. 12 (Cairo CG 33134 – JE 33144) plates 5–8; p. 9, 1–3n and Cat. Marseille 1997, p. 163, cat. 187. For a coffin (2nd century AD) from Tuna el-Gebel see: Kessler and Brose 2008, pp. 28–29, p. 31, p. 101. The cloak of Osiris is typical of representations from the 3rd century BC and after. For more details see Abdalla 1992, p. 111; Kaplan 1999, p. 32; Kurth 1990, pp. 47–50.

3 See for example Langener 1996; for caution on the direct borrowing of the iconography of Isis nursing and the Virgin and Child, see Török 2005, p. 272.

4 This period covers Dynasty 27 (525–402 BC) to the reign of the Emperor Caracalla (co-regent 198–211; sole emperor 211–17). Kaper 2003, p. 33. The only known temple dedicated to Tutu is in Kellis, the modern Ismant el-Kharab, in the Dakhleh Oasis.

5 We cannot here debate the origin of the god Serapis's name, which stems from Osiris-Apis or, much more probably, Apis.

6 Alvar 2008, Beck 2006, Clauss 2012. For a Mithreum excavated in Memphis, see Strzygowski 1940a, pp. 9–11, figs 4 and 5 (Inv. 7259 and 7260). A relief showing Mithras (ÄMP Inv. 12639) was in storage at the Ägyptisches Museum in Berlin until WWII (now missing).

PART 3: LATE ANTIQUE EGYPT
Introduction

1 Bagnall 1995, pp. 85–89; Clarysse 1995.
2 MacCoull 1989; Fournet 1999.

7 Religious Violence in Late Antique Egypt

1 For example Hahn 2004; Gaddis 2005; Sizgorich 2009; Athanassiadi 2010; Shaw 2011. This characterization has now also reached the general public through the 2009 film *Agora*.

2 For example Bremmer 2011; Kippenberg 2011; Juergensmeyer et al. 2013.

3 Mayer 2013; Bremmer 2014.

4 See the studies collected in Hahn, Emmel and Gotter 2008 and Lavan and Mulryan 2011.

5 The idea of widespread religious violence in Late Antique Egypt has been particularly persistent, for example see Frankfurter 1998 and Sauer 2003, but see now Dijkstra 2008. Given the emphasis on interactions between religions in this book, I shall leave aside here inter-sectarian Christian violence, for which see for example Isele 2010, esp. pp. 113–92 on Alexandria.

6 On the date of the incident – between 16 June 391 (the date of an edict by Theodosius I forbidding sacrifice and the access to temples at Alexandria; *Codex Theodosianus* 16.10.11) and 8 April 392 (when the governor Evagrius who was involved in the incident was out of office) – see Burgess and Dijkstra 2013, pp. 96–102.

7 Eunapius, *Lives of the Sophists* 6.10–11; Rufinus, *Church History* 11.22–25, 27–30; Socrates, *Church History* 5.16–17; Sozomen, *Church History* 7.15, cf. 7.20; Theodoret, *Church History* 5.22.

8 Rufinus, *Church History* 11.27; Sozomen, *Church History* 7.15.

9 McKenzie, Gibson and Reyes 2004, pp. 107–10; McKenzie 2007, p. 246. On the reuse of temples in Late Antique Egypt, see Dijkstra 2011a and 2011b.

10 On this codex and its date, see Burgess and Dijkstra 2013, with pp. 88–89 on the image of Theophilus on top of the Serapeum.

11 See ch. 23 of this volume.

12 Emmel 2008. A later incident, dating to the time of Cyril of Alexandria (412–444), is Shenoute's raid on idols in a nearby village, which he himself reports in his work entitled *Only I Tell Everyone Who Dwells in this Village*.

13 El-Sayed 2010. The temple was incorporated in the adjacent nunnery, also part of Shenoute's monastic network, from the early 5th century onwards. Blocks from the temple, among many others, have been found reused as *spolia* in the huge church of the Monastery of Shenoute, see Klotz 2010.

14 López 2013, esp. pp. 102–26 (ch. 4).

15 Procopius, *Persian Wars* 1.19.27–37.

16 Bernand 1969, pp. 251–68, nos 200–04.

17 Nautin 1967, reiterated for example by Hahn 2008.

18 Dijkstra 2008 and 2015.

19 I would like to thank Jan Bremmer and Geoffrey Greatrex for comments on an earlier draft of this contribution.

Focus 3 An Icon of Mary in Alexandria?

1 Merkelbach 2001.

2 Starowieyski 1989; Peltomaa 2004.

3 See Effenberger (forthcoming) with further references.

4 Deckers 1982.

5 Price 2008.

6 Rondot 2012; Matthews 2005 and 2006.

7 *P.Lond.Copt.* II 162. The text is in Worrell 1923, pp. 249–321 (Coptic text),

pp. 359–80 (English translation); Müller 1954, pp. 195–99 (text paraphrase); Orlandi 1981, pp. 110–20 (Italian translation).

8 Orlandi 2008, p. 74, see also Orlandi 1981, p. 96, p. 108.

9 McGuckin, 1994, p. 5.

8 Sacred Architecture

1 Gros 1996, 235–59, figs 284–309; and Ward-Perkins 1994, pp. 447–68, especially pp. 449–52, figs 1–2.

2 Perles 1905, pp. 619–28, especially 620–21.

3 References in Grossmann 2002, pp. 21–22.

4 Grossmann 2005.

5 De Vries Mzn 1981, pp. 15 and 28–32.

6 Majcherek 2007, especially pp. 17–21, figs 4 and 9.

7 With the exception perhaps of the Constantinian Church of Orléansville, Grossmann 2013, especially pp. 316–18, fig. 2.

8 McKenzie 2007, pp. 282–85, fig. 470.

9 Schwarz 1966.

10 Grossmann 2002, pp. 455–57, fig. 73.

11 Grossmann 2002, p. 47, fig. 80.

12 Grossmann and al-Taher 1997.

13 Bonnet et al. 2006.

14 Grossmann 1989, pp. 97–135, plan 4–5. For the eastern church: Grossmann 2002, pp. 490–91, fig. 104.

15 Grossmann 2002, pp. 90–93.

16 Grossmann 2002, pp. 511–12, fig. 130.

17 Deichmann, Feld and Grossmann 1988, pp. 47–53, figs 25–26.

18 Grossmann 1980, pp. 75–86, fig. 12.

19 Bénazeth and Hadji-Minaglou 2008.

20 Grossmann 1990, pp. 151–59, figs 3–5; also Grossmann 1980, pp. 86–111, fig. 27.

21 Creswell 1969, pp. 165–96, fig. 90.

22 Creswell 1969, pp. 181–96.

Focus 4 Living with the Monumental past

1 *HM* 18.3; Russell 1980, p. 102; cf. Ibn Jubayr (d. 1217); Broadhurst 1952, p. 46.

2 For his seminal work on architectural reuse in Late Antiquity, see *inter alia* Deichmann 1975. For the disjunction between the literature and archaeology for temples 'converted' into churches in the Mediterranean, see Caseau 1999; B. Ward-Perkins 2003; Lavan and Mulryan 2011.

3 Bagnall 1993, pp. 261–68; Grossmann 2002a, pp. 43-48; Dijkstra 2011.

4 For the Caesareum temple and its orientation, see McKenzie 2007, pp. 177–78. For the church, see p. 240 and pp. 406–7 note 25; p. 242 and p. 407 notes 34–36. For the Serapeum in Alexandria, see ch. 7 in this volume.

5 For example, at Ashmunein, Dendera, Atripe, Luxor, Karnak, Medinet Habu, Deir el-Medina, Esna, Aswan, Philae and Qasr Ibrim (O'Connell 2014, pp. 12–14).

6 For Luxor Temple churches, see McKenzie 2007, pp. 314–15, fig. 522. For the example of the Roman fort at Babylon later enclosing (medieval) churches and a synagogue, see ch. 14.

7 O'Connell 2007, pp. 239–40. For example, at Qubbet el-Hawa and Deir Anba Hadra at Aswan, Edfu, Kom el-Ahmar/Hierakonpolis, Abydos, Akhmim/Panopolis, Naga ed-Deir, Rifa, Asyut, Meir, el-Amarna, el-Bersha, el-Sheikh Said, Sheikh 'Ibada/Antinoupolis, Speos Artemidos and Beni Hasan, el-Bahnasa/Oxyrhynchos, Kom al-Ahmar/Sharuna and Saqqara (O'Connell 2014, pp. 9–12).

8 O'Connell 2007, 2010.

9 Godlewski 1986. For an overview of Bishop Abraham's correspondence, see Krause 1991, pp. 400–401.

10 For the church treasure, see Krause 1994; Bénazeth 2001, nos 309–315 (pp. 375–90). For the Hermonthis/Ermont diptych, see Crum 1908. For the painted portrait, see Krause 1971; Fluck 2010.

11 O'Connell 2007.

12 Quibell 1909, p. 106, pl. 34.1 and, *in situ*, 15.3; Thomas 2000, p. 13.

13 Quibell 1909, p. 105. For the reuse of Late Antique sculpture from recent, Late Antique tombs, see Severin 1982.

14 Quibell 1909, p. 112 and pl. 52.

15 For a catalogue of sculptures later incised with crosses on the forehead and elsewhere, with full bibliography and a survey of interpretations of the practice, see Kristensen 2012. The head of Germanicus is cat. no. A10 (p. 55) and discussed pp. 39–40.

16 For tattooing slaves, prisoners and religious devotees, see Jones 1987. For tattoos as the 'seal of baptism', marking the individual as a 'slave of God,' see Elm 1996.

17 Török 2005, pp. 271–72.

18 For the reuse of ancient Egyptian building material in medieval Egypt, see Heiden 2002, pp. 257–75, plates 30–31. Behrens-Abouseif 2014.

19 McKenzie 2007, p. 258 and p. 412, notes 189–92.

20 For Late Antique perceptions of earlier statues and their display in Christian contexts, see Mango 1963, esp. pp. 59–64; and Kristensen 2012, pp. 44–52.

9 Synagogues

1 Modrzejewski 1995, p. 91; Fine 1996, p. 25; Levine 2005, pp. 91–92.

2 Hachlili 1988; Fine 1996; Meyers 1996; Levine 2005.

3 Ma'oz 1995, pp. 194–95.

4 Levine 2005, pp. 91–93; McKenzie 2007, p. 184.

5 Hachlili 1988, pp. 182–83; Levine 2005, pp. 93–94, 145–62, 343–47. The authors note that in the synagogues from Roman-Byzantine Palestine no archaeological evidence for a raised central platform has been retrieved; furthermore, in some synagogues one or two raised stone platforms or podiums were built in front of a niche or an apse on the wall opposite the entrance or against the Jerusalem-orientated wall. In the case of wooden structures no traces would have survived.

6 Hachlili 1988, pp. 193–94; Levine 2005, pp. 93, 347-51.

7 Levine 2005, pp. 91–92, 337–38.

8 Modrzejewski 1995, pp. 88–94; Feldman 1996, pp. 50–51; Levine 2005, pp. 82–87.

9   Embassy 133; Levine 2005, pp. 88–89.
10   Hachlili 1988, pp. 166–87, 272–80;
     Levine 2005, pp. 351–56. Several forms
     were unearthed in excavations: a shrine
     of stone with columns and pediments, a
     half-circular or rectangular recess at the
     end of the hall, an apse in the Byzantine
     period (the latter probably influenced by
     church architecture).
11   Hachlili 1988, pp. 236–56; Levine
     2005, pp. 358–60, 602–4.
12   Such mirror plaques with the depiction of
     the Torah Shrine and glass inlays, dating
     from the Byzantine period, were hung on
     walls to ward off the evil eye. In the
     collection of the Institute of Archaeology,
     The Hebrew University of Jerusalem,
     provenance unknown, size 35 x 25 cm;
     Hachlili 1988, pl. 34; Cat. New York
     1996, pp. 164–65, cat. no. 40, pl. XXI.
13   Hachlili 1988, pl. 53.
14   Hachlili 1988, pp. 268–72; Levine 2005,
     pp. 230–36.
15   Hachlili 1988, pp. 221–23, 285–316,
     368–69; Levine 2005, pp. 210–36,
     242–49, 618–23. For detailed analysis
     and interpretation of the significance of
     the figural mosaic floor decoration see
     Weiss 2005.
16   McKenzie 2007, pp. 240–42.
17   See the discussion in Levine 2005,
     pp. 135–73, 623–24.
18   Le Quesne 2001, p. 80; for the location
     see the plans in Lambert 2001a, p. 22,
     fig. 2 and p. 205, fig. 7.1.
19   Lambert 2001b, p. 34; Le Quesne 2001,
     p. 86.
20   Le Quesne 2001, p. 81.
21   Lambert 2001a, pp. 80, 82, fig. 3.2. The
     synagogue is not on a strict east-west
     axis. The author rejects the tradition,
     referred to by Arabic historians, that the
     Ben Ezra Synagogue was originally a
     church, as it is unsubstantiated.
22   Le Quesne 2001, p. 85; Ben-Sasson
     2001, p. 213.
23   Goitein 1964; Ben-Sasson 2001, pp.
     214–15; the inventory manuscript is
     illustrated in fig. 7.2 on p. 215.
24   Ben-Sasson 2001, pp. 220–22, figs 7.4,
     7.7–7.10.
25   The panel is in the collections of the
     Walters Art Gallery, Inv. 64.181, and the
     Yeshiva University Museum, Inv.
     2000.231. At both museums it was
     exhibited in 2003, 'Threshold to the
     Sacred: The Ark Door of Cairo's Ben
     Ezra Synagogue', curated by A. Landau
     and J. Wisse; see www.yumuseum.
     tumblr.com/ArkDoor. (Last accessed 6
     September 2015.)
26   In case the double colonnade of the
     Great Synagogue refers to the ground
     and upper floors, it should not be
     interpreted as evidence for the
     existence of separate seating for
     women, see Hachlili 1988, pp. 194–96;
     Levine 2005, pp. 342–43, 504–5.
     Levine concedes that the function of the
     upper floors is not clear, but on the basis
     of rabbinic writings a multi-functional
     use appears most likely: a place for

festive meals and study, for court
proceedings or the residence of the
hazzan (the synagogue official).

10 Churches
1   Bolman 2006, pp. 76-91.
2   Bénazeth 2013, p. 10, fig. 6.
3   De Moor and Fluck 2009, particularly
     pp. 32–35, pp. 44–47, pp. 145–79.
4   Xanthopoulou 2010.
5   Xanthopoulou 2010, pp. 281–316.
6   Helmecke 1999; Cortopassi 2010, pp.
     95–99.
7   Bénazeth 2011.

11 Hermits and monks
1   Nagel 1966.
2   For more detail about this development
     see Richter 2004 with further
     bibliographical information; see also
     Richter 2010.
3   Bartelink 1994; Brunert 1994.
4   Rubenson 1990; Khosroyev 1995.
5   Goehring 2007 402–3; van der Vliet
     2000.
6   Horn 2013.
7   Schulz and Ziemer 2010.
8   Vivian 1993.
9   Goehring 1999; Wipszycka 2009.
10   Judge 1977.
11   Elm 1994.
12   Krause 1998, p. 154; Wipszycka 2009,
     pp. 206–12.
13   Bacht, 1983, pp. 9–63.
14   For a good overview, see Wipszycka
     2009.
15   Leipoldt 1964; for Shenoute's
     importance see Emmel 2008.
16   Emmel 2008a; Hahn 2013.
17   Goehring 2007.
18   Apollonopolis Heptakomias Mikra/Sbeht
     in Middle Egypt: Timm 1985, pp. 1433–
     38.
19   Krause 1998, pp. 124–27.
20   For an overview of modern
     developments, see Gerhards and
     Brakmann 1994.
21   Hodak 2013.

12 Monastic Architecture
1   For a good example of such a tomb on
     the West Bank of Thebes, see Górecki
     2008, pp. 225–36.
2   Winlock and Crum 1926.
3   See Guillaumont 1991. Hundreds of
     settlements were excavated here by
     French and Swiss archaeologists.
4   Innemée 2000, pp. 126–28.
5   White and Hugh 1932, pp. 327–29.
6   White and Hugh 1932, pp. 232–34.
7   See Quibell 1912 and Grossmann
     1971–1980. Excavated at the beginning
     of the 20th century by J.E. Quibell, and
     by P. Grossmann 1970 to 1975.
8   Excavated, though only for a small part,
     at the beginning of the 20th century by
     French archaeologists. See Clédat
     1904–1906 and Torp 2006, pp. 9–11.
     Since 2001 excavation has been led on
     the site by the Institut Français
     d'Archéologie Orientale, together with
     the Louvre.
9   Severin 1991, p. 365.
10   Schulz-Flügel, E. (ed.), Rufinus, Historia
     Monachorum sive de Vita Sanctorum

Patrum, Berlin and New York, 1990.
11   Grossmann 2002, pp. 546–52.
12   Rousseau 1999, pp. 81–83.
13   Grossmann 2002, p. 293.
Focus 5 Monastic Wall Paintings
1   Bolman ed. 2002 and Bolman ed.
     forthcoming 2015.
2   Bolman 2007.
3   Bolman 2006.
4   For a rare example of female saints, see
     Chapel 1 at Bawit (Palanque 1906, pl. XI).
5   Bolman 2012.
6   Bolman, Davis and Pyke 2010.
7   Bolman in Grossmann and Abdal-Fattah
     2009, pp. 35–37, pl. 8b.
8   Davies 2012, p. 12, p. 22, fig. 6. At the
     time of publication, archaeologists from
     the Yale team hypothesized that the figure
     in the wall painting was St Mercurius.
     Following further study and reconstruction
     of the extant fragments, the figure is now
     thought to be another equestrian saint
     – St Claudius.

**Focus 6 Monastery of the Archangel
Gabriel, Naqlun**
1   Mokbel 1966; Wipszycka 2009, pp. 66–7.
2   Ten Hacken 2004. Documents that could
     dispel the murkiness surrounding the
     origins of the Naqlun establishment are
     lost. Surviving texts leave no doubt that
     the two medieval traditions are little more
     than literary creations with no anchoring
     in the history of the hermitages.
3   See reports published annually in the
     journal Polish Archaeology in the
     Mediterranean (PAM).
4   Godlewski 2011a.
5   van der Vliet 2000, pp. 319–27.
6   Godlewski and Czaja-Szewczak 2009.
7   Godlewski 2012, pp. 201–5; Helmecke
     2012, unpublished report.
8   Godlewski 2000.
9   The term 'monophysite' is used
     advisedly, see ch. 3, this volume.
10   Czaja-Szewzcak 2004, pp. 159-64.
11   It was visited, for example, in the 17th
     century by J.M. Vansleb, who included it
     in a journal of his travels (Vansleb 1678,
     pp. 166–67). In the early 20th century
     some houses for visitors were added
     outside the monastery walls.

13 Jewish and Christian Pilgrimage
1   On monks as loci for charms, see
     Frankfurter 2003; on statue, see for
     example the colossal Min statues in the
     Ashmolean Museum (Inv. 1894.15 c, d,
     e). In general, see Frankfurter 1998b,
     pp. 13–18.
2   See for example Stewart 1991;
     Betteridge 1992.
3   Pseudo-Anasthasius, Homily on the
     Virgin, 96 (see Lefort 1958, p. 36).
4   Kerkeslager 1998, pp. 123–46
5   Kerkeslager 1998, pp. 214–22. Shared
     shrines: e.g. Albera and Couroucli 2012.
6   Kugel 1990, pp. 125–55.
7   Kerkeslager 1998, pp. 222–25.
8   Frankfurter 1993, 1994.
9   Athanasius, Festal Letter 42, tr. Brakke
     1998, pp. 479–80; see also Frankfurter
     2010.
10   Lefort 1954.

11   Baumeister 1972.
12   Brakke 2006.
13   Behlmer 1998; see Brown 1982 and
     Frankfurter 2003.
14   Frank 2000.
15   Winlock and Crum 1926; Brooks
     Hedstrom 2007.
16   See Timbie 1998; Behlmer 1998;
     Lubomierski 2008; Bolman et al. 2010.
17   Papaconstantinou 2001, p. 308.
18   See Montserrat 1998 and Gascou
     2006, with Papaconstantinou 2001,
     pp. 203–4, pp. 122–28, pp. 53–56.
19   See Frankfurter 2005 and Luijjendijk
     2014.
20   Grossmann 1998.
21   Bangert 2010; Vikan 2010.

PART 4: MEDIEVAL EGYPT
14 Cairo
1   Sanders 1994.
2   Sheehan 2010; Gayraud 1998; Kubiak
     1987; Scanlon 1972; Butler 1884.
3   Sheehan 2010, pp. 32–33.
4   Kubiak 1987, p. 65.
5   Akbar 1989, p. 22.
6   Trombley 2009.
7   Sheehan 2010, p. 52.
8   Power and Sheehan (see web sources).
9   Sheehan 2010, p. 2; Casanova 1901,
     p. 189.
10   Monneret de Villard, Feb 1924; May
     1924, p. 82; pp. 87–88.
11   Gayraud 1991, p. 66.
12   Swanson 2010, p. 10; Coquin 1974, p. 98.
13   Sheehan 2010, pp. 88–92.
14   Sijpesteijn 2009, p. 121.
15   Foss 2007, p. 17.
16   Evetts 1910, p. 188.
17   Sheehan 2012.
18   Kubiak 1987, p. 118 and p. 166, n. 49.
19   Fahmy 1950, p. 48.
20   Foss 2007, p. 9; Kubiak 1987, p. 105;
     Fahmy 1950, p. 37.
21   Gayraud 1991, p. 61.
22   Kubiak 1976, p. 63.
23   Den Heijer 2008.
24   Swanson 2010, p. 34.
25   Swanson 2010, pp. 48–51.
26   Sheehan 2010, pp. 92–96
27   Reif 2000; Lambert 1994; Goitein
     1967–88; Worman 1905.
28   Denoix 1994, p. 54.

15 Mosques
1   See Fehérvári 1993.
2   The wooden mihrab of al-Azhar and the
     foundation inscription (also in wood), as
     well as other wooden mihrabs, are now
     in the Museum of Islamic Art in Cairo.
     Following the bombing of the police
     station opposite the museum in
     January 2014, its condition is currently
     unknown.
3   In the 20th century it was placed in the
     present Museum of Islamic Art in Cairo.
     Its current state is unknown, following
     the bombing of the police station
     opposite the museum in January 2014.
4   See article J. Pedersen and J.
     Golmohammad, 'Minbar 1 and 2',
     Encyclopaedia of Islam 7, Leiden and
     New York 1993.

5   According to other sources it was made by a 'Byzantine' (see J. Pedersen, 'Minbar 1', *Encyclopaedia of Islam* 7, Leiden and New York 1993).

6   The Andalusian Ibn Jubayr reported from Mecca in 1184 that there was a similar pulpit that could be moved on four iron-rimmed wheels. Some portable *mihrabs* have survived to modern times (placed in the current Museum of Islamic Art in Cairo in the 20th century, their condition is unknown following the bombing of the police station opposite the museum in January 2014).

7   Halm 2003, p. 194 (after Maqrizi).

8   Lev 1981, pp. 287–49; Fischel 1937 and 1969, pp. 45–68; Al-Imad 1990, pp. 80–96; Halm 2003, p. 91 and pp. 119–22.

9   Halm 2003, 198-200; Walker 2012, pp. 149–51.

10 Helmecke 2013.

11 Today it belongs to Iran and is especially known for its oil refineries.

12 'In the presence of the Caliph it was hung to the cheers of the people and the sound of horns' (Halm 2003, pp. 194–95).

13 Halm 2003, p. 94.

16 Muslim Saints

1   Radtke 2002; Schimmel 1995, p. 284.

2   For an overview of Sufism, see *tasawwuf* in *Encyclopaedia of Islam*, new ed 11, Leiden 2000.

3   Smith 1928/2010.

4   Schimmel 1995, pp. 284–302.

5   For the veneration of saints in Islam, a fundamental study is still Goldziher 1890.

6   Ebstein 2014; Muslim Saints 1983; Ibn Arabi 1990; Schimmel 1995, 71–76; Attar 2002, pp. 99–115.

7   Ebstein 2014, p. 570, n. 46.

8   In the 20th century this was placed in the Museum of Islamic Art in Cairo.

9   According to another tradition, the head of al-Husain is buried in the Umayyad mosque of Damascus. The shrine there is also the object of great veneration.

10 Zaynab also has a much-visited shrine in Damascus.

11 A first building, about whose appearance nothing is known, was built by the Abbasid governor of Egypt, 'Ubaidallah. The Fatimid construction was founded in 1089 and enlarged in 1138. Four sections of the building with inscriptions can now be found in the Museum of Islamic Art in Cairo (Ragib 1977, pp. 27–28 and pp. 31–32).

12 This is what is claimed by the majority of the sources, who call her Nafisa bint al-Hasan bin Zayd bin al-Hasan bin 'Ali bin Abi Talib (Ragib 1976, p. 71).

13 Ragib 1976, pp. 79–80.

14 Ragib 1977, p. 28.

15 On this cemetery and the historical and legendary people buried in it, see Ragib 1977, pp. 49–55.

16 Ibn Jubayr, 1985, p. 30.

17 Egypt and the Haaj

1   Haleem 2012, pp. 27–52.

2   Qur'an 3: pp. 96–97.

3   Le Quesne 2013, p. 74.

4   'Abd al-Malik 2013, p. 52 ff.

5   Kennedy 2012, p. 114.

6   Le Quesne 2013, p. 75 and table 1 for a summary of the main period of pilgrimage traffic from Qulzum and the other ports.

7   Peters 1994, p. 90; 'Abd al-Malik 2013, p. 52. The Sinai route only resumed its pre-eminent position following the rule of the Mamluks in 1250.

8   Le Quesne 2013, p. 76; Peacock 2008, p. 32 ff.

9   Peacock 2008, p. 32 ff. The enigma of 'Aidhab as discussed in this article is that there is no archaeological evidence to support the presence of a major port; Peacock suggests the port could have been located at Halaib, 20 km south.

10 Serjeant 1942, p. 64.

11 Serjeant 1942, p. 64; Nassar 2013, p. 175 ff. There are *tiraz* fabrics inscribed with the word *kiswa* that Serjeant believed were destined for the Ka'ba, but there is some debate about this because the term also means clothing, garments, attire. Porter 2012, pp. 259–60.

12 Sijpesteijn 2014. I am grateful to Petra Sijpesteijn for allowing me to see this article before publication. For Islam in Egypt, see ch. 4 in this volume.

13 Nasir-i Khusraw/Thackston 1986, p. 64.

14 Kennedy 2012, pp. 110–122. Nasir-i Khusraw /Thackston 2001, p. 66

15 Effland, von Falck and Graeff 2009, pp. 9–11.

16 Documenting the graffiti in this area is an ongoing DAI project directed by Sebastian Tonio Richter: 'Deir Anba Hadra. Epigraphy, Art and Architecture in a medieval monastery on the west bank of Assuan'.

17 See for example: Thenayian 1999, pp. 162–269; al-Kilabi 2009.

18 The text was preliminary published in Kurth et. al 2004, p. 675 and again in Effland, von Falck and Graeff 2009, pp. 9–11. I am extremely grateful to Andreas Effland for drawing this to my attention. This is my translation from the Arabic. Later travellers went through Edfu including Abu-l-Hasan al-Shadhduli (b. 1196) in 1258 and Ibn Battuta in 1326 and 1332. See Ibn Battuta/Gibb vol. 1, p. 68 and vol. 2, p. 414.

19 Ibn Jubayr/Broadhurst 1952, p. 54. Nasir-i Khusrow also mentions Akhmim, where he saw 'huge edifices that would amaze anyone who saw them', p. 63.

20 Ibn Jubayr/Broadhurst 1952, p. 65.

21 Peacock 2008, p. 36 citing Murray 1926, pp. 235–40.

22 Björnesjö 2013, p. 10. See also Hawari in this volume.

18 The Cairo Genizah

1   For the discovery of the Cairo Genizah, see Hoffman and Cole 2011.

2   A good introduction to the various sources preserved in the Cairo Genizah can be found in Reif 2000.

3   Goldberg 2013 provides a good overview of medieval trade in the Mediterranean.

4   For an analysis of the interreligious business relations between Muslims and Jews, see the 'Symbiosis' section in Goitein 1971, pp. 289–99.

5   Goitein 1971, p. 296

PART V: BELIEF AND PRACTICE ACROSS THE FAITHS

19 Archangel Gabriel

1   Dan. 10:13, 10:21, 12:1.

2   Dan. 8:15–27, 9:21.

3   The number of archangels varies. Jewish and Coptic (Egyptian Christian) literature mention four (Michael, Gabriel, Raphael and (S)Uriel) or seven archangels (the remaining three have various names). Seven archangels are mentioned in the Jewish Books of Enoch and in the New Testament Book of Revelation (1:4) (Wright 2010, p. 329; Müller 1959, pp. 8–62; Aranda Pérez 1991, p. 1135. On the Books of Enoch, see Ben Dov 2013). In Islamic tradition, there are four archangels: Micha'il, Jibril, Israfil, the angel of the resurrection and 'Izra'il, the angel of death (Webb 2001; Zotenberg 1958, vol. 1 pp. 30, 171; vol. 3, p. 213).

4   Wright 2010; Müller 1959; Webb 2001.

5   Michl 1962.

6   Wright 2010, p. 329; Müller 1959, pp. 36–37, 40; Webb 2002, p. 278

7   Michl 1962, col. 241; Rothkoff in Ginsberg, Rothkoff and Dan 2007, pp. 168–69; Wright 2010; Müller 1959, p. 41; Müller 1962, pp. 71, 87–88; Ginzberg 1909–1938, vol. 1, p. 240; Zotenberg 1958, vol. 1, pp. 172–74.

8   Ginsberg in Ginsberg, Rothkoff and Dan 2007, p. 168. On Daniel's apocalyptic visions, see DiTommaso 2010, pp. 514–15.

9   Descriptions of the heavenly court are found, for example, in the Books of Enoch (Wright 2010, p. 330; Ben Dov 2013).

10 Wright 2010, p. 329; Michl 1962, col. 240.

11 Bohak 2010, p. 546; Ginzberg 1909-1938, vol. 1, pp. 241, 255.

12 Ginzberg 1909-1938, vol. 2, pp. 10, 11, 17, 127.

13 The total number of languages of the world was set at seventy, see Ginzberg 1909–1938, vol. 1, 62; vol. 2, p. 72.

14 Ginzberg 1909–1938, vol. 4, p. 268; Michl 1962, col. 240.

15 Cf. Ex. 20:4.

16 Hellenistic influence introduced animals, birds and figures into decorative geometric patterns. Byzantine mosaic synagogue floors sometimes show biblical scenes. A fragmentary scene in the floor mosaic of the synagogue of Sepphoris (5th to 7th century) might represent the visit of the three angels to Abraham (Hachlili 2010; Piccirillo 2010).

17 Müller 1959, pp. 36–37; Aranda Pérez 1991.

18 Zanetti 1994, pp. 325–26. The History of the Churches and Monasteries in Egypt attributed to the priest Abu 'l-Makarim (mainly compiled between c.1160 and 1187; Den Heijer 1996, pp. 77-80; Zanetti 1995; Ten Hacken 2006, pp. 185-95. Translations: Evetts and Butler 1895; Abuna Samuel al-Suryani

1992) mentions 26 churches dedicated to the archangel Gabriel. It is noteworthy that the majority of these churches was located in the Fayyum and in Middle Egypt. Churches dedicated to the archangel Michael and/or Raphael were often built nearby.

19 Gabriel was commemorated on 13 Hatur (9 November), 22 Kiyahk (18 December), 30 Baramhat (26 March), 13 Bauna (7 June), and 26 Bauna (20 June) (Müller 1959, p. 38; Aranda Pérez 1991, p. 1137; Zanetti 1994, pp. 344–48; Papaconstantinou 2001, pp. 68–69).

20 Ten Hacken 2004, pp. 340–43. At present, the 10th-century Church of the Archangel Gabriel is part of the Monastery of the Archangel Gabriel in Naqlun (Van Loon in Gabra and Van Loon 2007, pp. 202–7, with extensive bibliography).

21 For example Kropp 1930–1931, vol. 2, pp. 31, 59–60, 90–91, 104–5 etc.; Meyer and Smith 1994, pp. 51–52 (no. 29), 55–56 (no. 36), 83–90 (no. 43), 101 (no. 54), etc.

22 There are numerous examples of both themes, see e.g. Zibawi 2003, pp. 54–56, 62–63, 69, 89–90; Gabra and Van Loon 2007, pp. 76, 206, 282.

23 Compare Pedersen 1965 and Macdonald and Madelung 1991.

24 Webb 2002; see also Webb 2001.

25 Qur'an, Sura 26:193–95; and Zotenberg 1958, vol. 2, pp. 390–96.

26 Qur'an, Sura 53:5–18; 81:19–25.

27 Qur'an, Sura 19:17.

28 Qur'an, Sura 16:102.

29 Qur'an, Sura 2:87, 253; 5:110

30 Thackston 1978, for example pp. 43, 326–29. See also Webb 2002.

31 Zotenberg 1958, pp. 72–73; see also Ginzberg 1909–1938, vol. 1, pp. 54–55; and Gen. 3:19.

32 Qur'an, Sura 17:1; 67:3; 53:1–18. See Sells 2001.

33 Fahd 1966, p. 179; Sachau and Schwally 1905–1940, vol. 2-2, pp. 14–16.

34 Department of Islamic Art 2001.

35 For example a miniature of the Archangel Gabriel in a manuscript of The Wonders of Creation and the Oddities of Existence (c.1375–1425, Egypt/Syria), compiled c.1270 by Zakariya Qazwini.

20 Joseph: A Hero for Everyone?

1   Wimmer and Leimgruber 2007, p. 139.

2   Wimmer and Leimgruber 2007, p. 136.

3   Schweizer 2014, p. 735.

4   Schweizer 2014, p. 735.

5   SKD 1996, p. 1007.

6   Wimmer and Leimgruber 2007, p. 130.

7   Weimar 1996 col. 997.

8   Wimmer and Leimgruber 2007, p. 124.

9   Wills 2002, pp. 121–62.

10 Wimmer and Leimgruber 2007, p. 138.

11 Raspe 1996 col. 999.

12 Concerning the story of Joseph depicted on textiles, see Vikan 1979; for further evidence, Fluck 2008.

13 The narrative material has also inspired modern artists such as Georg Friedrich Händel, Richard Strauss, Thomas Mann

and Andrew Lloyd Webber. An Iranian television series entitled *Joseph, the Prophet* directed by Farajullah Salahshur aired in 2008, and quasi-theatrical performances on the theme take place today in Egypt (personal communication, Gisela Helmecke, September 2014).

14 Wimmer and Leimgruber 2007, p. 137.

15 Zenger 2007, p. 683.

16 Bearman et al., 2002.

21 Festivals

1 The author thanks Cäcilia Fluck, Friederike Seyfried and Gisela Helmecke for their consultation, discussion and editing of the text.

2 Krauss 1985; Parker 1950.

3 For Jewish festivals according to Philo's writings see Leonhardt 2001, pp. 18–100; see also Heinemann 1931, pp. 97–154. For Jewish festivals and pilgrimage see Kerkeslager 1998, pp. 99–228.

4 Kerkeslager 1998, p. 215.

5 Kerkeslager 1998, pp. 215–22; Borgen 2014, pp. 77–78.

6 Kraemer 1999.

7 The oldest nilometer on Elephantine Island was probably constructed in the Middle Kingdom (1800 BC). This and the nilometer on Roda Island in Cairo still exist. They were used until modern times. For nilometers see Popper 1951; for the nilometer on Elephantine Island, see Seidlmayer 2001. For the importance of the Nile and the agricultural seasons in Islamic times see also Halm 2003, esp. pp. 45–78.

8 Lutfi 1998, pp. 269–73.

9 For the procedure of the feast, and of the opening of the chanel in Fatimid times, see Halm 2003, pp. 62–68.

10 Förster 2007.

11 Lasser 2010, p. 149.

12 Shoshan 2006a, pp. 561–62; Lutfi 1998, pp. 263–68.

13 Today Shubra is a part of Cairo.

14 Lutfi 1998, pp. 259–63. This feast coincides with a seasonal transition shortly after winter. The Copts attached special religious significance to the feast, for it commemorated the sacred baptism of Christ. Hence it is considered the second most important Coptic religious festival after the Nativity.

15 See Halm 2003, pp. 141–42.

16 Descriptions of the entertainment include the public performances of musicians and singers of both sexes and of jugglers. Besides the many harmless and joyful customs that took place, excessive wine and beer drinking in public is mentioned (we read of both drunken men and women). Often there were riots and affrays, resulting even in death. See Langner 1998, pp. 28–62; Halm 2003, pp. 139–146, 310.

17 Al-nawruz was originally celebrated in pre-Islamic Persian territories and is still celebrated today. It is connected with the vernal equinox, and therefore celebrated in March. The reason for its arrival in Egypt is unknown. However, it could be the result of Persian rule of ancient

Egypt or an adaptation from the Roman era (see Shoshan 2006b, pp. 559–60).

18 Cuffel 2013, pp. 117–8.

19 Shoshan 1993, pp. 42–9; Lutfi 1998, pp. 273–80.

20 For a discussion of the historical origins of the mawlid ceremony, see Kaptein 1993, pp. 48–67; Katz 2007, pp. 1–3.

21 Gabra 2004, pp. 145–50; Gibb and Kramers 1974, p. 365; compare also Langer 1983, p. 34.

22 Abu Hajjaj (Abu Haggag) was a Sufi sheikh. Born in Baghdad in 1150, he moved to Mecca before finally settling in Luxor, where he died in 1243 or 1245.

23 This opinion is according to one of the monks in Dair al-Muharraq in Assyut.

24 Brewer and Teeter 1999, pp. 188–89.

22 Magic

1 See, most recently, the thematic and research overview by Frenschkowski 2009; see also Graf 1996; Meyer and Smith 1994; Meyer and Mirecki 1995. For working definitions of 'magic', itself a polemical and negative term in antiquity, see these same works.

2 See Edson and Savage-Smith 2004, esp. pp. 22–29, and for a complex picture of shared and separating features, Burns 2014, pp. 140–159.

3 When the concept of syncretism was developed in the 20th century to designate an era in the history of religions, particularly the religious developments in the Hellenistic-Roman Mediterranean, Graeco-Egyptian magic was seen as its epitome.

4 Betz 1996; Brashaer 1995; Dieleman 2005; Graf 1996; Ritner 1993; Ritner 1995.

5 Bohak 2008, pp. 196–209; Dieleman 2006, pp. 278–80.

6 Bohak 2008, pp. 197–201; Bohak 2011; Fodor 2004, pp. 137–38.

7 On the Testamentum Solomonis, see Bohak 2009, pp. 179–82; Busch 2006; Johnston 2002; an Islamic version is in Winkler 1930, pp. 57–65. On the Ethiopian 'Mirror of Solomon' see Löfgren 1972.

8 PGM XIII 1-734; see also Betz 1996, pp. 172–89. On Moses in Graeco-Egyptian magic see Gager 1972 and 1994; Graf 1996, pp. 12–14. On the 'supernumerary' books of Moses in the Western European tradition of magic books in the modern era see Bachter 2004, Daxelmüller 1993, Davies 2009.

9 PDM xiv, i.e. BM EA 10070 + P.Leiden I 383 r col. 5, lines 1–34 (T.S. Richter 2005, no. 94, pp. 116–18 and pp. 167–68; Bohak 2008, pp. 196–201).

10 Another allusion to the Divine Revelation at Sinai is in PGM XII, lines 92–96.

11 On magic texts in Coptic see Kropp 1930/1931; Meyer and Smith 1994; Pernigotti 2000; and van der Vliet 2014.

12 See Frankfurter 1995 and 2009.

13 P. Berl. P. 8313 r col. II and v – BKU I, 12 (T. S. Richter 2002 and 2005, no. 99, pp. 124–25 and pp. 172–73).

14 Rebiger, Schäfer et al., 2009.

15 Bohak 2008, pp. 170-75, p. 179.

16 Frankfurter 1994; Bohak 2003 and Bohak 2008, esp. p. 195, p. 218, Fig. 3.9, pp. 258–64, pp. 270–74; Dieleman 2005, pp. 96–101. On the *charaktêres* see also Winkler 1930, pp. 150–67.

17 Dieleman 1996, pp. 47–144.

18 So for example in PDM xiv, 675-694 / PGM XIVc, 16-27, where the instructions are in demotic script and language, but the invocation is in Greek (Dieleman 2005, pp. 130–38, 314–15).

19 P. Heid. inv. Arab. 500 + 501 (Bilabel and Grohmann 1934; fig. in Untermann 2011, p. 30).

20 Ullmann 1972, pp. 359–426; Fahd 1997.

21 Goldziher 1894; Fodor 2004; Vajda 1948; Winkler 1930.

22 Ibn Wahshiyya (10th century) attributes this script to a Coptic sage called Kalfatir (Canaan 2004, pp. 167–69).

23 Henein and Bianqys 2009.

24 Al-Buni, Shams al-ma'arif, after Winkler 1930, p. 80, see also Pormann and Savage-Smith 2007, pp. 147–49.

25 Bohak 2008, p. 272; Winkler 1930, pp. 55–149; Canaan 2004, pp. 169-70.

26 The Psalter was particularly popular in protective magic. Psalm 91 (Psalm 90 in the Greek and Coptic Bible), one of the most prominent psalms in Jewish magic (Rebiger 2003 and 2010), was no less popular with those who wore Christian amulets (Judge 1987 and Delattre 2006).

27 Winkler 1930, pp. 10–14.

28 Fodor 2004, pp. 137–38; on angels in Judaism and Islam see Rebiger 2007 and Macdonald 1991.

29 Vajda 1948, pp. 387–86; Winkler 1930, pp. 30–36.

30 P. Berl. P 5744 (Beltz, 1983, p. 63), line 2: 'In the name of Allah'; line 4: *troh nalla* 'the spirit of Allah'.

31 Bohak 2008, p. 219.

32 For example: the strip of paper in Cambridge University Library, T-S 12.207 + T-S AS 207.54, a binding spell written partly in Arabic (albeit in Coptic script), partly in Coptic (Crum, 1902, p. 329; see also Kropp 1930/1931, vol. II, pp. 242–43; Meyer and Smith 1994, pp. 197–99; Pernigotti 2000, pp. 78–79); the (unpublished) paper strip T-S 12.740, the formula of a protective spell written in Coptic; and P. Lond.Copt. I 524, a protective spell written on parchment for a woman and her child. See also Bohak 1999 and Bohak 2008, p. 219. In the (unpublished) paper manuscript in Cambridge University Library T-S K1.56, Coptic letters and words are used along with magical letters and the 'seals' as a kind of strange magical marks.

23 Language and Writing

1 Adams, Janse and Swain 1980; Neumann and Untermann 1980; Ceresa-Castaldo 1991; Campanile, Cardona and Lazzeroni 1988; Blanc and Christol 1999; McMullen 1966, pp. 1–17.

2 Papaconstantinou 2010; Fournet 2009, pp. 418–51.

3 Richter, T.S. 2009, pp. 403–14.

4 Papaconstantinou 2008, pp. 77–88.

5 Papaconstantinou 2007, pp. 273–99.

6 For bilingual inscriptions from Roman or Late Roman period in Egypt, see W. Horburry and D. Noy, *Jewish inscriptions of Graeco-Roman Egypt* (Cambridge 1992), nos 15, 16, 118, 119, 133.

24 Everyday Objects

1 Bénazeth 2014.

2 Documents from the *Genizah* bear witness to it: Reif 2013, p. 65.

25 Clothing and Soft Furnishings

1 See Pritchard 2006, esp. pp. 45–115.

2 Rutschowscaya 2012b, pp. 119–20.

3 See du Bourguet 1964, 370, G74 (text mistakenly under G73).

4 http://www.academia.edu/1534149/ Union_Yarn_and_Union_Fabric_-_ abstract (Nahum Ben Yehouda).

5 Stillman 1988.

6 Ibn al-Wašša' 1984. This book was indeed written in Baghdad, but one can assume similar conditions in the upper classes in Egypt.

7 For accessories, see, Pritchard 2006, pp. 117–27, Rutschowscaya 2012b, p. 120 and for example Cat. Lyon 2013, pp. 136–39, fig. 34. For jackets and shawls, see De Moor and Fluck 2011. For headgear, see Pritchard 2007, pp. 129–45.

8 Cat. Lyon 2013, pp. 206–10, figs 66 and 67. Hairnets were popular especially from the mid-5th to mid-7th century. De Moor et al. 2014. Radiocarbon dating of linen hairnets in sprang technique. BMSAES 21: 103–20. http://www.britishmuseum.org/ research/publications/online_journals/ bmsaes/issue_21/de_moor_et_al. aspx).

9 Rutschowscaya 2012a and De Moor and Fluck 2009.

10 I thank Cäcilia Fluck and Gisela Helmecke for their help and the information on the Genizah texts, and on textile production in the medieval period.

Focus 7 Tiraz Textiles

1 Bierman 1998; Stillman and Sanders 2000; Helmecke 2006.

2 The type of embroidery technique used means we can determine specific places (Kühnel and Bellinger 1952).

3 Islamic Egypt had become part of an empire that also included areas of traditional raw silk production such as Syria and some Persian provinces: knowledge of sericulture thus spread rapidly through the empire.

4 See Klesse 1967.

26 Professions and Crafts

1 For professions and crafts in Graeco-Roman Egypt, see Rathbone 1991; Bagnall 1993; Ruffing 2008; Gibbs 2012. For wine replacing beer by the 4th century, see Bagnall 1993, p. 32; for wool pp. 33–34. For medieval Egypt in the Genizah documents, see Goiten 1967.

2 Rathbone 1991, pp. 260–62.

3 Adams 2007.

4 Ruffing 2008.

5 Goiten 1967.

6   Goiten 1967, p. 73; Le Coz 2006. Some physicians were famous, such as Maimonides (1135 or 1138–1204).
7   Carrié 2012.
8   Wipszycka 2009.
9   Historia Lausiaca 32, p.12.
10 Fikhman 1974.
11 Schiller 1932, no. 3. The monastery must have had connections with the Fayyum to do a journey of more than 500 km.
12 Boud'hors and Heurtel 2010.

Focus 8 Lustreware
1   Jewish masters appear in the documents from the Cairo Genizah (Goitein 1, 1967, p. 92, pp. 110–111).
2   Made from long silky filaments secreted by pen shells, sea silk has a shimmering hue and is a rare, precious fabric. For quotation, see Khosrou 1993, p.100.

27 Burial Practice
1   Good overviews of funeral rites in Graeco-Roman and Christian Egypt: Horak 1995, pp. 39–71; Bénazeth 2000, pp. 105–7; Grossmann 2002, pp. 315–47; Krause 2003, pp. 33–44; Dunand and Lichtenberg 2006, pp. 72–93 and 123–30; Dunand 2007, pp. 163–84; Willburger 2007, pp. 228–53; Gessler-Löhr, Grabbe, Raab and Schultz 2007, pp. 254–77.
2   Lembke 2004, pp. 57–58.
3   Harrauer 2003, pp. 26–27; such mummy labels are attested until the 5th / 6th centuries and sometimes inscribed with Christian formulas: see Torallas Tovar 2013, pp. 15–26.
4   Naville 1890; Petrie 1906, pp. 19–27.
5   Griffith 1890, esp. pp. 51–53, plates III–IV, XVI (below); Leibovitch 1942, pp. 41–47; Bernand 1992, pp. 116–20, plates 42–43; Horbury and Noy 1992, esp. pp. 51–182, nos. 29–105; Hachlili 1998, pp. 263–64.
6   Jewish cemeteries of the Ptolemaic and early Imperial periods have been found in Alexandria: Goodenough 1953, pp. 62–63; Hachlili 2005, p. 264. Jews again settled in Oxyrhynchus, for example, in the 3rd century, after the conquest of Egypt by Queen Zenobia of the Palmyrene Empire (c.240–72/73). They left written documents in Hebrew and had close ties to Palestine (Bowman, Coles, Gonis, Obbink and Parsons 2007, p. 177 and p. 180).
7   For an ossuary belonging to Nicanor the Alexandrian, a man from a prominent Alexandrian family and found in Jerusalem, see BM ME 1903,0715.1
8   Hachlili 2005, pp. 447–516; Popović and Zangenberg 2013, pp. 88–89. On ossuaries, Jewish grave stones and grave goods from Egypt, see Goodenough 1953, figs 113, 863, 864, 923–26, 931, 935 (erroneously located in Rome, Berlin Obj. 188 in this volume), 936, 937, 959; on Jewish inscriptions from Egypt: Horbury and Noy 1992.
9   Krause 2003, pp. 34–35.
10 Mummies of this form were found in, for example, Lisht and Dahshur, Fag el-Gamous, Deir el-Qarabin, Kom el-Ahmar/Sharuna, Karara, Naqlun and

Antinoopolis: see summary in Gessler-Löhr, Grabbe, Raab and Schultz 2007, esp. pp. 256–57 and p. 265, note 8. On Dahshur see Cortes 2012, pp. 78–80, p. 84; on Naqlun Godlewski and Czaja-Szewcak 2008, Zych 2008.
11 Fluck 2004, p. 208; Gessler-Löhr, Grabbe, Raab and Schultz 2007, p. 256. An exception is several tunics from the cemetery of Karara: Huber 2013, pp. 12–21.
12 Numerous examples from Antinoopolis in Lintz and Coudert 2013, pp. 175–253.
13 Site 1823, which was initially interpreted as a church, is however clearly a mausoleum surrounded by porticoes: Grossmann 2002, pp. 319–20.
14 For example, on some stelae from Tell el-Yahudieh: Leibovitch 1942, pp. 41–42 (Cairo Egyptian Museum, JE no. 65909) or pp. 44–46 (Cairo Egyptian Museum, JE 65911).
15 Godlewski in PAM since 1986.
16 Zych 2005.
17 Lyzwa-Piber 2011.
18 Czaja-Szewczak 2011.
19 Czaja-Szewczak 2003, p. 108.
20 Godlewski 2003; Helmecke 2005; Czaja-Szewczak 2011; Godlewski 2011.
21 These rules are mentioned in the Qur'an (Sura 9, verse 84 / 85).
22 An overview of the religious precepts and practice in Egypt to modern times can be found in Massignon 1958.
23 Thus the Hanbali legal scholar Abu'l-Faraj ibn al-Jawzi (1116–1200).
24 See the excavation reports by Gayraud in the Annales islamologiques and Gayraud 1999.
25 The 'house' also included servants and slaves.
26 The largest mass burial contained 27 people. Most multiple burials included both female and male remains: this finding has yet to be explained.
27 Gayraud 1999, p. 460, fig. 14.
28 *Tiraz* cloths were also found among the shrouds at the grave openings in the mausoleum of al-Hadra aš-Šarifa in the 'Ayn as-Sira cemetery around 1930 (Yusuf 1999, p. 315).
29 In one of the tombs three coffins were found with several skeletons in very poor condition (Gayraud 1999, p. 462, fig. 15). Gayraud assumed these were the bones of the Fatimid leaders that had been brought along in coffins when the Caliph al-Mu'izz entered Egypt in 973.
30 Kulicka 2011.

Focus 9 Flower Garlands for the Dead
1   Most recently: Germer 2011.
2   In the Egyptian Museum of Berlin are 30 of these objects; 53 are in the Botanic Garden and Botanical Museum of the Free University of Berlin.
3   Heilmeyer and Lack 1997.
4   This colour scale was provided by following plants: red: ashwagandha or winter cherry (Withania somnifera); red

and pink: rose (Rosa sancta); pink: lotus (Nelumbo nucifera), henna (Lawsonia inermis), rose-of-heaven (Silene coelirosa), great willowherb (Epilobium hirsutum); orange: pomegranate flower (Punica granatum); purple: cockscomb (Celosia argentea).
5   Yellow: acacia (Acacia nilotica), helichrysum (Helichrysum stoechas), feverfew (Chrysanthemum coronarium).
6   Blue: Blue water lily (Nymphaea coerulea).
7   Gaius Plinius Secundus, Natural History, 5 vols, book XXI, ch. 38, p. 174 on rose wreaths: 'People's extravagance went so far that they valued only those which consisted entirely of petals'.
8   Mummy from Fag el Gamous, Cairo, Museum G 127 c. See Hamdy 2003, pp. 82–83.
9   Ovid, Metamorphoses, 2.112.
10 Ovid, Fasti, II.533.
11 Moldenke 1952, p. 151; Löw 1934, vol. 3, p. 195; Batanouny 1993.
12 Amarna, see n. 1.
13 BGBM, no. 47, Antinoopolis, grave of Leukyone.
14 Heilmeyer and Schirarend 1996, pp. 34–36.
15 For the clothes of the dead completely different data were obtained. According to the analyses they dated to the 4th–5th centuries. So far, no plausible explanation for these fluctuations in date has been found. See Lintz and Coudert 2013, pp. 208–10, no. 52.
16 Exodus 12:22; Löw 1934, vol. 2, p. 98; Moldenke 1952, p. 161.

Focus 10 Early Islamic Tombstones from Aswan
1   Grohmann 1957, p. 196. BM ME BM 1887,0402.1442: Wright 1887, no. 9, pp. 338–39.
2   Blair 1998, pp. 45–46. 'Sect' refers here to one of the four schools of law of Sunni Islam.
3   Blair 1998, p. 196.
4   Blair 1998, p. 196. Over 4000 stelae from Cairo and Aswan were published in the catalogues of the Musée Arabe du Caire: Hawary and Rached 1932–1938, vols I and II; Wiet 1936–1942, vols II, IV-X; 'Abd al-Tawab 1977 and 1982. Other important corpora of Islamic tombstones include: a series of 260 tombstones from the Red Sea islands of Dahlak, opposite Eritrea (began in the middle of the 9th century), published by Schneider in 1983. A chronological catalogue of 85 inscribed tombstones from Bab al-Saghir, a cemetery outside Damascus, was meticulously published by Moaz and Ory in 1977. Among the numerous museum collections of stelae that are published are the Museum of Fine Arts in Boston by Miles (1957); Dar al-Athar al-Islamiyyah in Kuwait by al-Zayla'i (1989); Cat. Louvre by Bittar (2003).
5   Björnesjö 2013, p. 9.
6   Le Quesne 2013, pp. 74–77, pl.1; see also ch. 17, this volume.

7   Björnesjö 2013, Speiser 2013.
8   Speiser 2013, pp. 219– 20.
9   Björnesjö 2013, pp. 9–10, note 8.
10 BM ME 1887,0402.1, 1887,0402.1434-1442, 1445–1449, 1889,0420.1, 1889,0420.6. Wright, W., 'Kufic tombstones in the British Museum', *Proceedings of the Society of Biblical Archaeology*, 17th Session, 1887, pp. 329–49.
11 Blair 1998, p. 198.
12 Grohmann 1957, p. 183, pp. 198–99, fig. 12; Blair 1998, p. 198.
13 Blair 1998, p. 198.

28 Jewish and Christian Visions of Paradise
1   According to the legendary tradition of the Letter of Aristeas (2nd century BC), 70 to 72 Jewish scholars translated the Pentateuch, the five books of Moses, at the suggestion of King Ptolemy II. Philadelphus (285–46 BC). This translation by the 70 scholars (Latin septuaginta) was then deposited in the famous library of Alexandria.
2   Zuri 1918; Felten 1972; Raphael 2009; Bronner 2011.
3   Amentet is the personification of the realm of the dead that lies in the west. Although she can be identified with Isis or Hathor, she is not worshipped as such. In Coptic, the term is a proper name, which is always used without the article, and corresponds to the Greek Hades. The Greek transcription is amenthes.
4   Lycopolitanic ih and Bohairic ih.
5   In the Acts of Pilate that survive in Coptic (Acta Pilati, in the first part of the Gospel of Nicodemus) his name is Dysmas (chapters 9 and 10).
6   The Decans are groups of stars that appear heliacally every ten days, at dawn just before sunrise – hence the name Decans (from *dekanos* in Greek, *decurio* in Latin, *decanus* in Late Latin), meaning 'tenths'. During this time the sun sets some ten degrees further back on the ecliptic (zodiakos), divided into 360 degrees. There are 36 groups in total. The doctrine of the Decans comes from Egypt and plays a role in astrology (the Graeco-Roman period), as each sign of the zodiac was divided into three Decans.

EPILOGUE
Jewish, Christian and Muslim heritage in Modern Egypt
1   Osterhammel and Petersson 2003.
2   Courbage and Fargues 1992.
3   Cf. Philipp 1985.
4   Krämer 1982.
5   Elsässer 2014.
6   Pink 2007.
7   Krämer 1982; Philipp 1985.
8   Beinin 2005.
9   Guirguis and van Doorn-Harder 2011.
10 Abdo 2000; Bayat 2007; Sullivan and Abed-Kotob 1999.
11 Elsässer 2014; Iskander 2012; Tadros 2013.

Bibliography

Abdalla 1992
Abdalla, A., *Graeco-Roman Funerary Stelae from Upper Egypt*, Liverpool.

'Abd al-Tawab 1977 and 1982
'Abd al-Tawab, A., *Stèles islamiques de la nécropole d'Assouan* I (nos 1–150), II (nos 151–300), Textes Arabes et études islamiques, Institut Français d'Archéologie Orientale, Cairo 1977 (I) and 1982 (II).

Abbot 1937
Abbot, N., *The Monastery of the Fayyum*, Chicago.

Abbott 1967
Abbott, N., *Studies in Arabic Literary Papyri* II, Qur'anic Commentary and Tradition, Chicago.

'Abd al-Malik 2013
'Abd al-Malik, S., 'The Khans on the Egyptian Hajj Routes in the Mamluk and Ottoman Periods', in Porter, V. and Saif, L., *The Hajj Collected Essays*, London, pp. 52–64.

Abdo 2000
Abdo, G., *No God but God. Egypt and the Triumph of Islam*, New York.

Adams 2002
Adams, J.N., 'Latin in Egypt', in Adams, J.N., *Bilingualism and the Latin Language*, Cambridge, pp. 527–641.

Adams 2007
Adams, C., *Land Transport in Roman Egypt. A Study of Economics and Administration in a Roman Province*, Oxford.

Adams, Janse and Swain 1980
Adams, J.N., Janse, M. and Swain, S. (eds.), *Bilingualism in Ancient Society. Language Contact and the Written Text*, Oxford.

Ahlwardt 1887
Ahlwardt, W., *Verzeichnis der arabischen Handschriften* 1, Die Handschriften-Verzeichnisse der königlichen Bibliothek zu Berlin 7, Berlin (reprint Hildesheim and New York 1980).

Ahrens 1997
Ahrens, D. (ed.), *Licht durch die Jahrtausende. Die Lampen-Sammlung Karl-Adolph Mummenthey im Städtischen Museum Simeonstift Trier*, Trier.

Akbar 1989
Akbar, J., 'Khatta and the Territorial Structure of Early Muslim towns', *Muqarnas: An Annual on Islamic Art and Architecture* 6, pp. 22–32.

Albera and Couroucli 2012
Albera, D. and Couroucli, M. (eds.), *Shared Sacred Spaces in the Mediterranean*, Bloomington.

Albersmeier 2002
Albersmeier, S., *Untersuchungen zu den Frauenstatuen der ptolemäischen Ägypten*, Aegyptiaca Treverensia, Mainz.

Alcock 1983
Alcock, A., *The Life of Samuel of Kalamun by Isaac Presbyter*, Warminster.

Al-Imad 1990
Al-Imad, L.S., *The Fatimid Vizierate, 969–1172*, Islamkundliche Untersuchungen 133, Berlin, pp. 80–96.

al-Souryany 1992
al-Souryany, S., *Abu al Makarem: History of the Churches and Monasteries in Lower Egypt in the 13th century*, Cairo.

Alvar 2008
Alvar, J., *Romanising Oriental Gods. Myth, Salvation and Ethics in the Cults of Cybele, Isis and Mithras*, Religions in the Graeco-Roman World 165, Leiden and Boston.

Andrews 1990
Andrews, C.A., *Ancient Egyptian Jewellery*, London.

Aranda Pérez 1991
Aranda Pérez, G., 'Gabriel, Archangel', in *Coptic Encyclopedia* 4, pp. 1135–37.

Athanassiadi 2010
Athanassiadi, P., *Vers la pensée unique. La montée de l'intolérance dans l'Antiquité tardive*, Paris.

Attar 1983
Attar, F., *Muslim Saints and Mystics. Episodes from the Tadhkirat al-Auliya ('Memorial of the Saints')*, translated by A.J. Arberry, London.

Attar 2002
Attar, F., *Muslimische Heilige und Mystiker*, Munich.

Bachmann and Hansmann 1988
Bachmann, M. and Hansmann, C., *Das große Puppenbuch*, 5th ed., Leipzig and Munich.

Bacht 1983
Bacht, H., *Das Vermächtnis des Ursprungs. Studien zum frühen Mönchtum* 2: Pachomius – der Mann und sein Werk, Würzburg, pp. 9–63.

Bachter 2004
Bachter, S., 'Grimoires and the Transmission of Magical Knowledge', in Davies, O. and de Blécourt, W. (eds.), *Beyond the Witch Trial: Witchcraft and Magic in Enlightenment Europe*, Manchester, pp. 194–207.

Badawy 1978
Badawy, A. *Coptic Art and Archaeology: The Art of the Christian Egyptians from the Late Antique to the Middle Ages*. Cambridge, MA.

Bagnall 1993
Bagnall, R.S., *Egypt in Late Antiquity*, Princeton.

Bagnall 1995
Bagnall, R.S., *Reading Papyri, Writing Ancient History*, New York.

Bagnall 2002
Bagnall, R.S., 'Alexandria: Library of Dreams', in *Proceedings of the American Philosophical Society* 146, pp. 348–62.

Bagnall 2009
Bagnall, R.S., *Early Christian Books in Egypt*, Princeton.

Bagnall 2011
Bagnall, R.S., *Everyday Writing in the Graeco-Roman East*, Berkeley.

Bagnall and Cribiore 2006
Bagnall, R. and Cribiore, R., *Women's Letters from Ancient Egypt, 300 BC–AD 800*, Ann Arbor.

Bailey 2008
Bailey, D.M., *Catalogue of Terracottas in the British Museum. Ptolemaic and Roman Terracottas from Egypt*, London.

Bamberger, Gutmann, Marmorstein et al. 2007
Bamberger, B.J., Gutmann, J., Marmorstein, A. et al., 'Angels and Angelology', in *Encyclopaedia Judaica* 2, new ed., pp. 150–61.

Bangert 2010
Bangert, S., 'The Archaeology of Pilgrimage. Abu Mena and Beyond', in Gwynn, D.M. and Bangert, S. (eds.), *Religious Diversity in Late Antiquity*, pp. 293–327.

Bartelink 1994
Bartelink, G.J.M., *Athanase d'Alexandrie. Vie d'Antoine*, Sources Chrétiennes 400, Paris.

Basilios 1991
Archbishop Basilios, 'Heaven', in *Coptic Encyclopedia* 4, pp. 1214–15.

Basilios 1991
Archbishop Basilios 1991, 'Paradise', in *Coptic Encyclopedia* 6, 1900–1.

Batanouny 1993
Batanouny, K.H., *Dictionary of the Plants of the Holy Qur'an*, Kuwait.

Bauer and Strzygowski 1905
Bauer, A. and Strzygowski, J., *Eine alexandrinische Weltchronik. Text und Miniaturen eines griechischen Papyrus der Sammlung W. Goleniščev*, Vienna.

Baumeister 1972
Baumeister, T., *Martyr Invictus. Der Märtyrer als Sinnbild der Erlösung in der Legende und im Kult der frühen koptischen Kirche*, Münster.

Bauschke 2007
Bauschke, M., *Der jüdisch-christlich-islamische Trialog. Wissenschaftliche Studie*, Munich.

Bauschke 2008
Bauschke, M., *Der Spiegel des Propheten. Abraham im Koran und im Islam*, Frankfurt am Main.

Bauschke 2014
Bauschke, M., *Der Freund Gottes. Abraham im Islam*, Darmstadt.

Bayat 2007
Bayat, A., *Making Islam Democratic. Social Movements and the Post-Islamist Turn*, Stanford.

Bearman et al 2002
Bearman, P., et al (ed.), 'Yusuf', in *Encyclopaedia of Islam*, 2nd ed., 2002 / Brill Online, 2014: http://referenceworks.brillonline.com.549439870two.erf.sbb.spk-berlin.de/entries/encyclopaedia-of-islam-2/yusuf-COM_1369.

Beck 1957
Beck, E. (ed.), *Des heiligen Ephraem des Syrers Hymnen de Paradiso*, Corpus Scriptorum Christianorum Orientalium 174, Scriptores Syri 78, Louvain.

Beck 2006
Beck, R., *The Religion of the Mithras Cult in the Roman Empire. Mysteries of the Unconquered Sun*, Oxford.

Behlmer 1998
Behlmer, H., 'Visitors to Shenoute's Monastery', in Frankfurter 1998a, pp. 341–71.

Behr, Krochmalnik and Schröder 2011
Behr, H.H., Krochmalnik, D. and Schröder, B. (eds.), *Der andere Abraham. Theologische und didaktische Reflektionen eines Klassikers*, Berlin.

Behrens-Abouseif 1998
Behrens-Abouseif, D., *Islamic Architecture in Cairo. An Introduction*, Studies in Islamic Art and Architecture 3, Leiden, New York, Copenhagen and Cologne.

Behrens-Abouseif 2014
Behrens-Abouseif, D., 'Between Quarry and Magic: The Selective Approach to Spolia in the Islamic Monuments of Egypt', in Payne, A. (ed.), *Dalmatia and the Mediterranean: Portable Archaeology and the Poetics of Influence*, Leiden and Boston, pp. 402–25.

Beinin 2005
Beinin, J., *The Dispersion of Egyptian Jewry*, Cairo.

Beltz 1983
Beltz, W., 'Die koptischen Zauberpapyri der Papyrussammlung der Staatlichen Museen zu Berlin', *Archiv für Papyrusforschung* 29, pp. 59–86.

Ben Yehuda
Ben Yehuda, N., Union yarn (*mischgespinst*) and union fabric (*mischgewebe*) in Antiquity: http://www.academia.edu/1534149/Union_Yarn_and_Union_Fabric_-_abstract. (Last accessed 6 September 2015.)

Bénazeth 2000
Bénazeth, D., 'Les coutumes funéraires', in Cat. Paris 2000, pp. 105–6.

Bénazeth 2000a
Bénazeth, D., 'Un catalogue général du Musée Copte. Les objects de métal', *Cahiers de la Bibliothèque copte XII – Études coptes VII*, pp. 74–58.

Bénazeth 2011
Bénazeth, D., 'De l'autel au musée. Quelques objets liturgiques conservés au Musée Copte du Caire', in Eaton-Krauss, M., Fluck, C. and van Loon, G.J.M. (eds.), *Egypt 1350 BC–AD 1800. Art Historical and Archaeological Studies for Gawdat Gabra*, SKCO 20, Wiesbaden, pp. 35–52.

Bénazeth 2013
Bénazeth, D., 'L'église de l'archange Michel à Baouit', in Boud'hors, A. and Delattre, A. (eds.), *Selected Papers from the ICCoptS 9 (Cairo 2008)*, Journal of Coptic Studies 15, pp. 3–20.

Bénazeth 2014
Bénazeth, D., 'Objects of daily life', in Gabra, G. (ed.), *Coptic Civilization*, Cairo, pp. 195–214.

Bénazeth and Hadji-Minaglou 2008
Bénazeth, D. and Hadji-Minaglou, G., 'Baouît', *Bulletin de l'Institut Français d'Archéologie Orientale* 108, pp. 403–11.

Ben Dov 2013
Ben Dov, J., 'Enoch, Books of (1, 2, 3 Enoch)', in Bagnall, R.S., Brodersen, K., Champion, C.B., Erskine, A. et al. (eds.), *Encyclopedia of Ancient History*, London, pp. 2416–18.

Ben-Sasson 2001
Ben-Sasson, M., 'The Medieval Period: The Tenth to Fourteenth Centuries', in Lambert 2001, pp. 201–23.

Bergmann 1977
Bergmann, M., *Studien zum römischen Porträt des 3. Jhs. n. Chr.*, Bonn.

Bernand 1969
Bernand, É., *Les inscriptions grecques et latines de Philae* II. *Haut-et Bas-Empire*, Paris.

Bernand 1992
Bernand, É., *Inscriptions grecques d'Égypte et de Nubie au Musée du Louvre*, Paris.

Bernand 2001
Bernand, É., *Inscriptions grecques d'Alexandrie ptolémaïque*, Cairo.

Betteridge 1992
Betteridge, A., 'Specialists in Miraculous Action: Some Shrines in Shiraz', in Morinis, A. (ed.), *Sacred Journeys. The Anthropology of Pilgrimage*, Westport, pp. 189–209.

Betz 1996
Betz, H.D., *The Greek Magical Papyri in Translation, Including the Demotic Spells*, 2nd ed., Chicago and London.

Bianchi 1967
Bianchi, U. (ed.), *The Origins of Gnosticism. Colloquium of Messina 13–18 April 1966*, Leiden.

Bierbrier 1999
Bierbrier, M.L., 'The Acquisition by the British Museum of Antiquities Discovered During the French Invasion of Egypt', in Davies W.V. (ed.), *Studies in Egyptian Antiquities: A Tribute to T.G.H. James*, British Museum Occasional Paper 123, pp. 111–13, plates 26–31, London.

Bierman 1998
Bierman, I.A., *Writing Signs: The Fatimid Public Text*, Berkeley, Los Angeles and London.

Bilabel and Grohmann 1934
Bilabel, F. and Grohmann, A., 'Nr. 123. Zauber gegen eine ungetreuen Liebhaber', in *Griechische, koptische und arabische Texte zur Religion und religiösen Literatur in Ägyptens Spätzeit*, Veröffentlichungen aus den badischen Papyrus-Sammlungen 5, Heidelberg, pp. 328–44.

Bittar 2003
Bittar, T., *Pierres et stucs épigraphiés*, Louvre, Département des arts de l'Islam, Paris.

Björnesjö 2013
Björnesjö, S., 'The History of Aswan and its Cemetery in the Middle Ages', in Raue, D., Seidlmayer, S.J. and Speiser, P. (eds.), *The First Cataract of the Nile, One Region – Diverse Perspectives*, Deutsches Archäologisches Institut Abteilung Kairo, Sonderschrift 36, Berlin, pp. 9–13.

Black 1985
Black, M., *The Book of Henoch*, new English edition, Leiden.

Blair 1998
Blair, S., *Islamic Inscriptions*, Edinburgh.

Blanc and Christol 1999
Blanc, A. and Christol, A., *Langues en contact dans l'Antiquité. Aspects lexicaux*, Nancy.

Blümel 1933
Blümel, C., *Römische Bildnisse. Katalog der Sammlung antiker Skulpturen, Staatliche Museen zu Berlin*, Berlin.

Bohak 1999
Bohak, G., 'Greek, Coptic, and Jewish Magic in the Cairo Genizah', *Bulletin of the American Society of Papyrologists* 36, pp. 27–44.

Bohak 2003
Bohak, G., 'Hebrew, Hebrew, Everywhere? Notes on the Interpretation of *Voces Magicae*', in Noegel, S., Walker, J. and Wheeler, B. (ed.), *Prayer, Magic and the Stars in the Ancient and Late Antique World*, University Park, PA, pp. 69–82.

Bohak 2008
Bohak, G., *Ancient Jewish Magic: A History*, Cambridge.

Bohak 2009
Bohak, G., 'The Jewish Magical Tradition from Late Antique Palestine to the Cairo Genizah', in Cotton, H.M., Hoyland, R.G., Price, J.J. et al. (eds.), *From Hellenism to Islam. Cultural and Linguistic Change in the Roman Near East*, Cambridge, pp. 321–39.

Bohak 2010
Bohak, G., 'Divination and Magic', in Collins, J.J. and Harlow, D.C. (eds.), *Eerdmans Dictionary of Early Judaism*, Grand Rapids and Cambridge, pp. 543–47.

Bohak, Harari and Shaked 2011
Bohak, G., Harari, Y. and Shaked, S. (eds.) 2011, *Continuity and Innovation in the Magical Tradition*, Jerusalem Studies in Religion and Culture 15, Leiden.

Böhlig 1994
Böhlig, A. 'Die Bedeutung der Funde von Medinet Madi und Nag Hammadi für die Erforschung des Gnostizismus,' in Böhlig, A. and Markschies, C. (eds.), *Gnosis und Manichäismus. Forschungen und Studien zu Texten von Valentin und Mani sowie zu den Bibliotheken von Nag Hammadi und Medinet Madi*, Beihefte zur Zeitschrift für die neutestamentliche Wissenschaft, Berlin and New York, pp. 113–42.

Böhlig 1995
Böhlig, A., *Die Gnosis. Der Manichäismus*, Zürich (revised reprint of 1980 edition).

Böklen 1902
Böklen, E., *Die Verwandtschaft der jüdisch-christlichen mit der persischen Eschatologie*, Göttingen.

Böttrich, Ego and Eißler 2009
Böttrich, C., Ego, B. and Eißler, F. (eds.), *Abraham in Judentum, Christentum und Islam*, Göttingen.

Bolman 2006
Bolman, E.S., 'Veiling Sanctity in Christian Egypt: Visual and Spatial Solutions', in Gerstel, S.E.J. (ed.), *Thresholds of the Sacred. Architectural, Art Historical, Liturgical, and Theological Perspectives on Religious Screens, East and West*, Washington, D.C., pp. 73–104.

Bolman 2006a
Bolman, E.S., 'The Newly Discovered Paintings in Abu Serga, Babylon, Old Cairo. The *Logos* Made Visible', *Bulletin of the American Research Center in Egypt* 190, pp. 14–17.

Bolman 2007
Bolman, E.S., 'Depicting the Kingdom of Heaven: Paintings and Monastic Practice in Early Byzantine Egypt', in Bagnall, R.S. (ed.), *Egypt in the Byzantine World, 300–700*, Cambridge and New York, pp. 408–33.

Bolman 2009
Bolman, E.S., 'Remarks on the Wall Paintings in the Ante-chamber of the Hypogeum', in Grossmann, P. and Abdal-Fattah, A., 'Qasimiya: Report on the Survey Work from June 17 to June 19, 2003', *Bulletin de la Société d'Archéologie Copte* 48, pp. 27–44.

Bolman 2012
Bolman, E.S., 'The White Monastery Federation and the Angelic Life', in Cat. New York 2012, pp. 75–77.

Bolman 2016
Bolman, E.S. (ed.), *The Red Monastery Church: Beauty and Asceticism in Upper Egypt*, New Haven.

Bolman, Davis and Pyke 2010
Bolman, E.S., Davis, S.J. and Pyke, G., 'Shenoute and a Recently Discovered Tomb Chapel at the White Monastery', *Journal of Early Christian Studies* 18, pp. 453–62.

Bommas 2005
Bommas, M., *Heiligtum und Mysterium. Griechenland und seine Ägyptischen Gottheiten*, Mainz.

Bonnet 1952
Bonnet, H., *Reallexikon der ägyptischen Religionsgeschichte*, Berlin and New York.

Bonnet et al. 2006
Bonnet, C. et al., 'L'église tétraconque et les faubourgs romains de Farama à Péluse (Égypte – Nord-Sinaï)', *Genava* 54, pp. 371–84.

Borg 1996
Borg, B., *Mumienporträts. Chronologie und kultureller Kontext*, Mainz.

Borg 1998
Borg, B., 'Der zierlichste Anblick der Welt...', *Ägyptische Porträtmumien*, Mainz.

Borgen 2014
Borgen, P., Philo. 'An Interpreter of the Laws of Moses', in Seland, T. (ed.), *Reading Philo: A Handbook to Philo of Alexandria*, Grand Rapids, pp. 75–101.

Bothmer 1971
Bothmer, H.-C. von, 'Die Illustrationen des "Münchener Qazwini" von 1280 (cod.Monac. arab.464). Ein Beitrag zur Kenntnis ihres Stils' (dissertation), Munich.

Boud'hors and Heurtel 2010
Boud'hors, A. and Heurtel, C., *Les ostraca coptes de la TT 29. Autour du moine Frangé*, Brussels.

Bouras and Parani 2008
Bouras, L. and Parani, M.G., *Lighting in Early Byzantium*, Washington, D.C.

Bowman, Coles, Gonis and Parsons 2007
Bowman, A.K., Coles, R.A., Gonis, N. and Parsons, P.J. (eds.), *Oxyrhynchus. A City and its Texts*, Egypt Exploration Society 93, London.

Brakke 1998
Brakke, D., 'Outside the Places, Within the Truth': Athanasius of Alexandria and the Localization of the Holy', in Frankfurter 1998a, pp. 445–81.

Brakke 2006
Brakke, D., *Demons and the Making of the Monk*, Cambridge.

Brakmann 1994
Brakmann, H., 'Die Kopten – Kirche Jesu Christi in Ägypten', in Gerhards and Brakmann 1994, pp. 9–27.

Brashaer 1995
Brashear, W.M., 'The Greek Magical Papyri. An Introduction and Survey; Annotated Bibliography (1928–1994)', in *Aufstieg und Niedergang der Römischen Welt* II.18.5., Berlin and New York, pp. 338–684.

Bremmer 2011
Bremmer, J.N., 'Religious Violence and its Roots. A View from Antiquity', *Asdiwal* 6, pp. 71–79.

Bremmer 2014
Bremmer, J.N., 'Religious Violence between Greeks, Romans, Christians and Jews', in Geljon, A.C. and Roukema, R. (eds.), *Violence in Ancient Christianity. Victims and Perpetrators*, Leiden, pp. 8–30.

Brewer and Teeter 1999
Brewer, D.J. and Teeter, E., *Egypt and the Egyptians*, Cambridge.

Bricault and Versluys 2010
Bricault, L. and Versluys, M.J. (eds.), *Isis on the Nile. Egyptian Gods in Hellenistic and Roman Egypt, Proceedings of the IVth International Conference of Isis Studies, Liège, November 27–29, 2008*, Religions in the Graeco-Roman World 171, Leiden and Boston.

Bricault and Versluys 2012
Bricault, L. and Versluys, M.J., *Egyptian Gods in the Hellenistic and Roman Mediterranean. Image and Reality between Local and Global*, Mythos. Rivista di Storia delle Religioni, supplement 3, Caltanissetta.

Brisch 1983
Brisch, K., 'Beobachtungen zu einer kleinen Holztafel mit Mihrab', in Knopp, W. (ed.), *Einblicke – Einsichten – Ansichten. Aus der Arbeit der Staatlichen Museen SMPK*. Jahrbuch Preußischer Kulturbesitz, Sonderband 1, Berlin, pp. 59–69.

Broadhurst 1952
Broadhurst, R.J.C., *The Travels of Ibn Jubayr: Being the Chronicle of a Mediaeval Spanish Moor Concerning his Journey to the Egypt of Saladin, the Holy Cities of Arabia, Baghdad the City of the Caliphs, the Latin Kingdom of Jerusalem, and the Norman Kingdom of Sicily*, London (reprint 2011).

Bronner 2011
Bronner, L.L., *Journey to Heaven. Exploring Jewish Views of the Afterlife*, Jerusalem and New York.

Brooks Hedstrom 2007
Brooks Hedstrom, D.L., 'Divine Architects. Designing the Monastic Dwelling Place', in Bagnall, R.S. (ed.), *Egypt in the Byzantine World, 300–700*, Cambridge, pp. 368–89.

Brown 1982
Brown, P., 'The Rise and Function of the Holy Man in Late Antiquity', in Brown, P., *Society and the Holy in Late Antiquity*, London, pp. 103–52.

Brunert 1994
Brunert, M.-E., *Das Ideal der Wüstenaskese und seine Rezeption in Gallien bis zum Ende des 6. Jahrhunderts*, Münster.

Bucking 2007
Bucking, S., 'On the Training of Documentary Scribes in Roman, Byzantine and Early Islamic Egypt: A Contextualized Assessment of the Greek Evidence', *Zeitschrift für Papyrologie und Epigraphik* 159, pp. 229–47.

Budge 1914
Budge, E.A.W., *Coptic Martyrdoms*, London (reprint 1977).

Budge 1922
Budge, W.E., *British Museum. A Guide to the 4th, 5th and 6th Egyptian Rooms, and the Coptic Room*, London.

Burgess and Dijkstra 2013
Burgess, R.W. and Dijkstra, J.H.F., 'The "Alexandrian World Chronicle", its Consularia and the Date of the Destruction of the Serapeum (with an Appendix on the praefecti augustales)', *Millennium* 10, pp. 39–113.

Busch 2006
Busch, P., *Das Testamentum Salomonis. Die älteste christliche Dämonologie kommentiert und in deutscher Erstübersetzung*, Texte und Untersuchungen zur Geschichte der altchristlichen Literatur 153, Berlin and New York.

Butler 1884
Butler, A.J., *The Ancient Coptic Churches of Egypt* 1, Oxford.

Calament, Eichmann and Vendries 2012
Calament, F., Eichmann, R. and Vendries, C., 'Le luth dans l'Égypte byzantine. La tombe de la 'Prophétesse d'Antinoé' au musée de Grenoble', *Orient Archäologie* 26, Deutsches Archäologisches Institut – Orient Abteilung, Berlin.

Campanile, Cardona and Lazzeroni 1988
Campanile, E., Cardona G.R. and Lazzeroni, R., *Bilinguismo e biculturalismo nel mondo antico. Atti del colloquio interdisciplinare tenuto a Pisa il 28 e 29 settembre 1987*, Testi linguistici 13, Pisa.

Canaan 2004
Canaan, T., 'The Decipherment of Arabic Talismans', in Savage-Smith 2004, pp. 125–77.

Carrié 2012
Carrié, J.-M., 'Les associations professionnelles à l'époque tardive. Entre *munus* et convivialité', in Carrié, J.M. and Testa, R.L (eds.), *'Humana sapit'. Études d'Antiquité tardive offertes à Lellia Cracco Ruggini*, Turnhout, pp. 309–32.

Casanova 1901
Casanova, P., 'Les noms coptes du Caire et localités voisines', *Bulletin de l'Institut Français d'Archéologie Orientale* 1, pp. 139-224.

Caseau 1999
Caseau, B., 'Sacred Landscapes', in Bowersock, G.W., Brown, P. and Grabar, O. (eds.), *Late Antiquity: A Guide to the Postclassical World*, pp. 21–59, Cambridge, MA.

Castiglione 1975
Castiglione, L., 'Zwei verschollene Reliefs aus der Römerzeit', in *Mitteilungen aus der Ägyptischen Sammlung VIII – Festschrift zum 150 jährigen Bestehen des Berliner Ägyptischen Museums*, Berlin, pp. 465–72.

Cat. Arles 2003
Charron, A. (ed.), *La mort n'est pas une fin. Pratiques funéraires en Égypte d'Alexandre à Cléopâtre*, Musée de l'Arles antique, *28 septembre 2002–5 janvier 2003*, Arles.

Cat. Berlin 1999
Gipsformerei der Staatlichen Museen zu Berlin (ed.), *Ägypten. Freiplastik und Reliefs*, Katalog der Originalabgüsse Heft 1/2, Berlin.

Cat. Berlin 2006
Das Museum für Byzantinische Kunst im Bode-Museum, Munich, Berlin, London and New York.

Cat. Berlin 2010
Finneiser, K., Linscheid, P., and Pehlivanian, M., *Georg Schweinfurth. Pionier der Textilarchäologie und Afrikaforscher*, Berlin.

Cat. Berlin 2012
Mietke, G., Ehler, E., Fluck, C. and Helmecke, G., *Josef Strzygowski und die Berliner Museen*, exhibition catalogue, Bode-Museum, Staatliche Museen zu Berlin, 19 Oct. 2012–20 Jan. 2013. Wiesbaden and Berlin.

Cat. Berlin and Munich 2004
Ägyptisches Museum Berlin and Staatliches Museum Ägyptischer Kunst München (eds.), *Ritual oder Spiel? Puppen aus Afrika und Ägypten*, Berlin and Munich.

Cat. Chicago 2015
Vorderstrasse, T. and Treptow, T. (eds.), *A Cosmopolitan City: Muslims, Christians, & Jews in Old Cairo*, The Oriental Institute of the University of Chicago, Chicago.

Cat. Frankfurt 1961
Synagoga. Jüdische Altertümer, Handschriften und Kultgeräte, exhibition catalogue, Historisches Museum Frankfurt am Main, Frankfurt am Main.

Cat. Frankfurt 1999
Parlasca, K. and Seemann, H. (eds.), *Augenblicke, Mumienporträts und ägyptische Grabkunst aus römischer Zeit*, exhibition catalogue, Schirn Kunsthalle Frankfurt, Munich.

Cat. Frankfurt 2005
Beck, H., Bol, P.C. and Bückling, M. (eds.), *Ägypten, Griechenland, Rom. Abwehr und Berührung*, Städelsches Kunstinstitut und Städtische Galerie, 26 November 2005– 26 February 2006, Tübingen and Berlin.

Cat. Hamm 1996
Ägypten, Schätze aus dem Wüstensand. Kunst und Kultur der Christen am Nil, exhibition catalogue, Gustav-Lübcke-Museum, Hamm, Wiesbaden.

Cat. Karlsruhe 2013
Imperium der Götter. Isis Mithras Christus. Kulte und Religionen im Römischen Reich, exhibition catalogue, Badisches Landesmuseum, Karlsruhe, Darmstadt.

Cat. Kuwait 1989
Al-Zayla'i, A.B., *Tombstones in Dar al-Athar al-Islamiyyah*, Kuwait.

Cat. London 1994
Buckton, D., *Byzantium: Treasures of Byzantine Art and Culture from British Collections*, London.

Cat. London 1997
Walker, S. and Bierbrier, M. (eds.), *Ancient Faces. Mummy Portraits from Roman Egypt*, exhibition catalogue, The British Museum, London.

Cat. Lyon 2013
Calament, F. and Durand, M. (eds.), *Antinoé à la vie, à la mode. Visions d'élégance dans les solitudes*, exhibition catalogue, Musée des Tissus, 1er Octobre 2013–28 Février 2014, Lyon.

Cat. Marseille 1997
Margerie, A. de (ed.), *Égypte Romaine l'autre Égypte*, Marseille, Musée d'Archéologie Méditerranéenne, Centre de la Vieille Charité, 4 avril–13 juillet 1997, Marseille.

Cat. Munich 1989
Dannheimer, H. (ed.), *Spätantike zwischen Heidentum und Christentum*, exhibition catalogue, Archäologische Staatssammlung München, vol. 17, Munich.

Cat. Munich 2004
Wamser, L. (ed.), *Die Welt von Byzanz – Europas östliches Erbe*, exhibition catalogue, Archäologische Staatssammlung and Museum für Vor- und Frühgeschichte, Munich and Cologne.

Cat. New York 1978
Weitzmann, K. (ed.), *Age of Spirituality. Late Antique and Early Christian Art, Third to Seventh Century*, exhibition catalogue, Metropolitan Museum of Art, New York.

Cat. New York 1996
Fine, S. (ed.), *The Emergence of the Synagogue in the Ancient World*, exhibition catalogue, Yeshiva University Museum, New York, New York and Oxford.

Cat. New York 2000
Waker, S. (ed.), *Ancient Faces*, British Museum Press, London.

Cat. New York 2012
Evans, H.C. and Ratliff, B. (eds.), *Byzantium and Islam: Age of Transition, 7th–9th Century*, exhibition catalogue, The Metropolitan Museum of Art, New York.

Cat. Paderborn 1996
Stiegemann, C. (ed.), *Frühchristliche Kunst in Rom und Konstantinopel. Schätze aus dem Museum für Spätantike und byzantinische Kunst Berlin*, exhibition catalogue, Diözesanmuseum Paderborn, Paderborn.

Cat. Paris 2000
L'art copte en Égypte. 2000 ans de christianisme, Institut du monde arabe, 15 mai–3 Septembre 2000, Paris.

Cat. Paris 2001
L'Orient de Saladin. L'art des Ayyoubides, Institut du monde arabe, 23 octobre 2001– 10 mars 2002, Paris.

Cat. Rouen 2003
Durand, M. and Saragoza, F. (eds.), *Égypte, la trame de l'histoire: Textiles pharaoniques, coptes et islamiques*, Musée départemental des Antiquités, Rouen, 19 Octobre 2002–20 Janvier 2002, and Institut du monde arabe, Paris, mi-Juin–mi-Septembre 2004.

Cat. Schallaburg 2012
Daim, F. (ed.), *Das goldene Byzanz und der Orient*, Ausstellung Schallaburg, Mainz.

Cat. Stuttgart 1984
Brunner-Traut, E., Brunner, H. and Zick-Nissen, J. (eds.), *Osiris, Kreuz und Halbmond. Die drei Religionen Ägyptens*, exhibition catalogue, Kunstgebäude am Schlossplatz, Stuttgart, Mainz.

Cat. Stuttgart 2007
Ägyptische Mumien. Unsterblichkeit im Land der Pharaonen, exhibition catalogue, Landesmuseum Württemberg, Stuttgart, Mainz.

Cat. Tongres 2000
Willems, H. (ed.) and Clarysse. W. (ed.), *Les Empereurs du Nil*, exhibition catalogue, Musée Gallo-romain, Tongres and Herent.

Cat. Vienna 1998
Kesser, A., 'Coptic Textiles from Burial Grounds in Egypt', in *Graphis Annual* 90, 1960/61, Zurich.

Ceresa-Castaldo 1991
Ceresa-Castaldo, A., *Il bilinguismo degli antichi. XVIII giornate filologiche genovesi*, Genoa.

Chilton 2008
Chilton, B., *Abraham's Curse. Child Sacrifice in the Legacies of the West. The Roots of Violence in Judaism, Christianity, and Islam*, New York.

Choat 2009
Choat, M., 'Language and Culture in Late Antique Egypt', in Rousseau, P. (ed.), *A Companion to Late Antiquity*, Chichester and Oxford, pp. 342–56.

Clackson 2000
Clackson, J., 'A Greek Papyrus in Armenian Script', *Zeitschrift für Papyrologie und Epigraphik* 129, pp. 223–58.

Clackson 2001
Clackson, J., 'A Greek Educational Papyrus in Armenian Script', in Andorlini, I. et al. (ed.), *Atti del XXII Congresso Internazionale di Papirologia, Firenze, 23–29 agosto 1998* I, Florence, pp. 207–18.

Clarysse 1995
Clarysse, W., 'The Coptic Martyr Cult', in Lamberigts, M. and van Deun, P. (ed.), *Martyrium in Multidisciplinary Perspective: Memorial Louis Reekmans*, Leuven, pp. 377–95.

Clauss 2012
Clauss, M., *Mithras. Kult und Mysterium*, Darmstadt.

Clédat 1904–1906
Clédat, J., *Le monastère et la nécropole de Baouît*, Mémoires publiés par les membres de l'Institut Français d'Archéologie Orientale du Caire 12, Cairo.

Cohen 1996
Cohen, N., 'A Notice of Birth of a Girl', in Katzoff, R., Petroff, Y. and Schaps, D. (eds.), *Classical Studies in Honor of David Sohlberg*, Ramat Gan, pp. 385–98.

Cohen and Landau 2007
Cohen, H.J. and Landau, J.M., 'Egypt', in *Encyclopaedia Judaica* 6, 2nd ed., pp. 222–36.

Colpe 1969
Colpe, C., 'Christentum und Gnosis im Ägypterevangelium von Nag Hammadi', in Eltester, W. (ed.), *Christentum und Gnosis*, Berlin, pp. 129–32.

Colpe 1981
Colpe, C., 'Gnosis II (Gnostizismus)', in *Reallexikon für Antike und Christentum* 11, pp. 538–659.

Contadini 1998
Contadini, A., *Fatimid Art at the Victoria & Albert Museum*, London.

Coquin 1974
Coquin, C., *Les édifices chrétiens du Vieux-Caire I, Bibliographie et Topographie Historiques*, Cairo.

Cortes 2012
Cortes, E., 'Recovering contexts. The Roman Mummies Excavated by the Metropolitan Museum of Art at Dahshur, Egypt 2012', in Carrol, M. and Wild, J.P. (eds.), *Dressing the Dead in Classical Antiquity*, Gloucestershire, pp. 75–88.

Cortopassi 2010
Cortopassi, R., 'Broderies coptes du XIXe et du début du XXe siècle', in Boud'hors, A. and Louis, C. (eds.), *Cahiers de la Bibliothèque copte 17 – Études coptes XI*, Paris, pp. 95–106.

Courbage and Fargues 1992
Courbage, Y. and Fargues, P., *Chrétiens et Juifs dans l'Islam arabe et turc*, Paris.

Cramer 1941
Cramer, M., *Die Totenklage bei den Kopten*, Vienna and Leipzig.

Cramer 1955
Cramer, M., *Das altägyptische Lebenszeichen im christlichen (koptischen) Ägypten*, 3rd ed., Wiesbaden.

Creswell 1969
Creswell, K.A.C., *Early Muslim Architecture 1*, 2nd ed., Oxford.

Cribiore 1996
Cribiore, R., *Writing, Teachers and Students in Graeco-Roman Egypt*, Atlanta.

Cribiore 1999
Cribiore, R., 'Greek and Coptic Education in Late Antique Egypt', in Emmel, S., Krause, M. et al. (eds.), *Ägypten und Nubien in spätantiker und christlicher Zeit 2. Schrifttum, Sprache und Gedankenwelt. Akten des 6. Internationalen Koptologenkongresses. Münster 20–26 Juli 1996*, Sprachen und Kulturen des Christlichen Orients 6/2, Wiesbaden, pp. 279–86.

Cribiore 2001
Cribiore, R., *Gymnastics of the Mind. Greek Education in Hellenistic and Roman Egypt*, Princeton.

Cribiore 2009
Cribiore, R., 'Education in the Papyri', in Bagnall, R.S. (ed.), *The Oxford Handbook of Papyrology*, Oxford, pp. 320–37.

Cromwell 2010
Cromwell, J., 'Aristophanes, Son of Johannes. An 8th-century Bilingual Scribe?' in Papaconstantinou 2010, pp. 221–32.

Crum 1902
Crum, W.E., 'A Bilingual Charm', in *Proceedings of the Society of Biblical Archaology 24*, pp. 329–31.

Crum 1905
Crum, W.E., *Catalogue of the Coptic Manuscripts in the British Museum*, London.

Crum 1908
Crum, W.E., 'A Greek Diptych of the Seventh Century', *Proceedings of the Society of Biblical Archaeology 30*, pp. 255–65.

Cuffel 2013
Cuffel, A., 'Environmental Disasters and Political Dominance in Shared Festivals and Intercessions among Medieval Muslims', in Cormack, M. (ed.), *Muslims & Others in Sacred Space*, Oxford, pp. 108–46.

Czaja-Szewczak 2003
Czaja-Szewczak, B., 'Burial Tunics from Naqlun', in *Polish Archaeology in the Mediterranean 14*, pp. 177–84.

Czaja-Szewczak 2004
Czaja-Szewczak, B., 'Naqlun 2003: From Scraps to Tunic', in *Polish Archaeology in the Mediterranean 15*, pp. 159–64.

Czaja-Szewczak 2011
Czaja-Szewczak, B., 'Funerary textiles from the Medieval Cemetery of Naqlun', in *Polish Archaeology in the Mediterranean 20*, pp. 413–20.

Dagron 1969
Dagron, G., 'Aux origines de la civilisation byzantine. Langue de culture et langue d'État', *Revue historique 489*, pp. 23–56.

Dalton 1909
Dalton, O.M., *Catalogue of the Ivory Carvings of the Christian Era With Examples of Mohammedan Art and Carvings in Bone in the Department of British and Mediaeval Antiquities and Ethnography of the British Musuem*, London.

Dalton 1916
Dalton, O.M., 'A Coptic Wall Painting from Wadi Sarga', *Journal of Egyptian Archaeology 3*, pp. 35–37.

Dalton 1921
Dalton, O. M., *A Guide to the Early Christian and Byzantine Antiquities in the Department of British and Mediaeval Antiquities*, 2nd ed., Oxford.

Dassmann 1999
Dassmann, E., *Kirchengeschichte. II.2. Theologie und innerkirchliches Leben bis zum Ausgang der Spätantike*, Kohlhammer Studienbücher Theologie 11,2, Stuttgart.

Daxelmüller 1993
Daxelmüller, C., *Zauberpraktiken. Eine Ideengeschichte der Magie*, Zürich.

Davies 2009
Davies, O., *Grimoires. A History of Magic Books*, Oxford.

Davis 1998
Davis, S.J., 'Pilgrimage and the Cult of Saint Thecla in Late Antique Egypt', in Frankfurter 1998a, pp. 303–39.

Davis 2004
Davis, S.J., *The Early Coptic Papacy. The Egyptian Church and its Leadership in Late Antiquity*, Cairo.

Davis 2012
Davis, S.J., 'Life and Death in Lower and Upper Egypt: A Brief Survey of Recent Monastic Archaeology at Yale', *Journal for the Canadian Society for Coptic Studies 3–4*, pp. 9–26.

Deckers 1982
Deckers, J.G., 'Die Huldigung der Magier in der Kunst der Spätantike', in *Die Heiligen Drei Könige – Darstellung und Verehrung. Katalog der Ausstellung des Wallraf-Richartz-Museums in der Josef-Haubrich-Kunsthalle Köln, 1. Dezember 1982 bis 30. Januar 1983*, Cologne, pp. 20–32.

Deichmann 1975
Deichmann, F.W., *Die Spolien in Der Spätantiken Architektur*, Munich.

Deichmann, Feld and Grossmann 1988
Deichmann, F.W., Feld, O. and Grossmann, P., *Nubische Forschungen*, Archäologische Forschungen 17, Berlin.

Delattre 2006
Delattre, A., Un extrait du Psaume 90 en Copte, *Bulletin of the American Society of Papyrologists 43*, pp. 59–61.

Delia 1991
Delia, D., *Alexandrian Citizenship during the Roman Principate*, Atlanta.

De Moor et al. 2008
De Moor, A., Verhecken-Lammens, C. and Verhecken, A., *3500 jaar textielkunst. De collectie headquARTers*, Tielt.

De Moor and Fluck 2009
De Moor, A. and Fluck, C. (eds.), *Clothing the House. Furnishing Textiles of the 1st Millennium AD from Egypt and Neighbouring Countries. Proceedings of the 5th Conference of the Research Group 'Textiles from the Nile Valley', Antwerp, 6–7 October 2007*, Tielt.

De Moor and Fluck 2011
De Moor, A. and Fluck, C. (eds.), *Dress Accessories of the 1st millennium AD from Egypt. Proceedings of the 6th Conference of the Research Group 'Textiles from the Nile Valley', Antwerp, 2–3 October 2009*, Tielt.

De Moor, Fluck and Linscheid 2013
De Moor, A., Fluck, C. and Linscheid, P. (eds.), *Drawing the Threads Together. Textiles and Footwear of the 1st Millennium AD from Egypt. Proceedings of the 7th conference of the research group 'Textiles from the Nile Valley,' Antwerp, 7–9 October 2011*, Tielt.

De Moor et al. 2014
De Moor, A., Fluck, C., Van Strydonck, C. and Boudin, M., 'Radiocarbon Dating of Linen Hairnets in Sprang Technique', *British Museum Studies in Ancient Egypt and Sudan 21*, pp. 103–20.

Den Heijer 1996
Den Heijer, J., 'Coptic Historiography in the Fatimid, Ayyubid and Early Mamluk periods', *Medieval Encounters 2*, pp. 67–98.

Den Heijer 2008
Den Heijer, J., 'Religion, Ethnicity and Gender under Fatimid Rule. Three Recent Publications and Their Wider Research Context', in *Bibliotheca Orientalis 65*, pp. 38–72.

Denoix 1992
Denoix, S., *Décrire le Caire. Fustat Misr d'après Ibn Duqmaq et Maqrizi. L'histoire d'une partie de la ville du Caire d'après deux historiens Égyptiens des XIV–XVe siècles*, Études urbaines III, Cairo.

Derda 2008
Derda, T., *Deir el-Naqlun. The Greek Papyri* II, Journal of Juristic Papyrology Supplement IX, Warsaw.

Derda, Majcherek and Wipszycka 2007
Derda, T., Majcherek, T. and Wipszycka, E. (eds.), *Alexandria. Auditoria of Kom el-Dikka and Late Antique Education*, Warsaw.

Dessus-Lamare 1938
Dessus-Lamare, A., 'Le musaf de la mosquée de Cordue et son mobilier mécanique', *Journal Asiatique CCXXX*, pp. 566–68.

Destro and Pesce 2011
Destro, A. and Pesce, M., 'The Heavenly Journey in Paul: Tradition of a Jewish Apocalyptic Literary Genre or Cultural Practice in a Hellenistic-Roman Context?' in Casey, T.G. and Taylor, J. (eds.), *Paul's Jewish Matrix*, Rome, pp. 167–200.

De Vries Mzn 1981
De Vries Mzn, S.P., *Jüdische Riten und Symbole*, 1981.

Dickie 1976
Dickie, J., 'The Islamic Garden in Spain', in MacDougall, E.B. and Ettinghausen, R. (eds.), *The Islamic Garden*, Dumbarton Oaks, Washington D.C., pp. 87–105.

Dieleman 2005
Dieleman, J., *Priests, Tongues, and Rites. The London–Leiden Magical Manuscripts and Translation in Egyptian ritual (100–300 CE)*, Religions in the Graeco-Roman World 153, Leiden and Boston.

Dijkstra 2008
Dijkstra, J.H.F., *Philae and the End of Ancient Egyptian Religion. A Regional Study of Religious Transformation (298–642 CE)*, Leuven.

Dijkstra 2011a
Dijkstra, J.H.F., 'The Fate of the Temples in Late Antique Egypt', in Lavan, L. and Mulryan, M. (eds.), *The Archaeology of Late Antique 'Paganism'*, Late Antique Archaeology 7, Leiden, pp. 389–436.

Dijkstra 2011b
Dijkstra, J.H.F., 'Das Schicksal der Tempel in der Spätantike', in M. Stadler and D. von Recklinghausen (eds.), *KultOrte. Mythen, Wissenschaft und Alltag in den Tempeln Ägyptens*, Berlin, pp. 201–17.

Dijkstra 2015
Dijkstra, J.H.F., 'Philae', in Klauser, T. et al. (eds.), *Reallexikon für Antike und Christentum 27* (forthcoming).

DiTommaso 2010
DiTommaso, L., 'Daniel, Book of', in Collins, J.J. and Harlow, D.C. (eds.), *Eerdmans Dictionary of Early Judaism*, Grand Rapids and Cambridge, pp. 513–16.

Doxiadis 1995
Doxiadis, E., *The Mysterious Fayyum Portraits. Faces from Ancient Egypt*, New York.

Du Bourguet 1964
Du Bourguet, P., *Catalogue des étoffes coptes* I, Musée National du Louvre, Paris.

Du Bourguet 1975
Du Bourguet, P., 'Ensemble magique de la période romaine en Égypte', *La Revue du Louvre et des musées de France 4*, pp. 255–57.

Du Bourguet 1980
Du Bourguet, P., 'Un ancêtre des figurines d'envoûtement percées d'aiguilles, avec ses compléments magiques, au Louvre', in *Livre du centenaire: 1880–1980*, Mémoires de l'Institut Français d'Archéologie Orientale,104, Cairo, pp. 225–38, plates XXXIV – XXXVIII.

Dünzl 2006
Dünzl, F., *Kleine Geschichte des trinitarischen Dogmas in der Alten Kirche*, Freiburg i. Br.

Dunand 2007
Dunand, F., 'Between Tradition and Innovation. Egyptian Funerary Practices in Late Antiquity', in Bagnall, R.S. (ed.), *Egypt in the Byzantine world, 300–700*, Cambridge, pp. 163–84.

Dunand and Lichtenberg 2006
Dunand, F. and Lichtenberg, R., 'The Last Mummies', in Dunand, F. and Lichtenberg, R. (eds.), *Mummies and Death in Egypt*, Cornell, pp. 123–30.

Dyer, O'Connell and Simpson 2014
Dyer, J., O'Connell, E.R. and Simpson, A., 'Polychromy in Roman Egypt: A Study of a Limestone Sculpture of the Egyptian God Horus', *British Museum Technical Research Bulletin 8*, pp. 93–103.

Ebstein 2014
Ebstein, M., 'Du l-Nun al-Misri and Early Muslim Mysticism', in *Arabica 61*, pp. 559–612.

Effenberger (forthcoming)
Effenberger, A., 'Maria als Vermittlerin und Fürbitterin – Zum Marienbild in der spätantiken und frühbyzantinischen Kunst Ägyptens', in Allen, P., Külzer, A. and Peltomaa L.M. (eds.), *The Intercessory Role of Mary Across Times and Places in Byzantium (4th to 9th century)*, Vienna (forthcoming).

Effenberger and Rasemowitz 1975
Effenberger, A. and Rasemowitz, E., 'Der Pfau im Blütengezweig. Zu einem restaurierten spätantiken Stoff in der Frühchristlich-Byzantinischen Sammlung', *Forschungen und Berichte 16*, pp. 241–54.

Effland, von Falck and Graeff 2009
Effland, A., von Falck, M. and Graeff, J.-P., 'Inschriften des ptolemäerzeitlichen Tempels von Edfu', in Effland, A., Graeff, J.-P., von Falck, M. (eds.), 'Nunmehr ein offenes Buch...' – Das Edfu-Projekt, herausgegeben zum 160. Geburtstag des Marquis Maxence de Rochemonteix (1849–1891), Informationsbroschüre zum Edfu-Projekt, Heft 1 (IBE 1), Hamburg, pp. 7–33.

Eichhorn and Rasche 2013
Eichhorn-Johannsen, M. and Rasche, A. (eds.), 25.000 Jahre Schmuck aus den Sammlungen der Staatlichen Museen zu Berlin, Berlin.

Elm 1994
Elm, S., Virgins of God: The Making of Asceticism in Late Antiquity, Oxford.

Elm 1996
Elm, S., '"Pierced by bronze needles": Anti-Montanist Charges of Ritual Stigmatization in Their Fourth-century Context', Journal of Early Christian Studies 4, pp. 409–39.

Elsässer 2014
Elsässer, S., The Coptic Question in the Mubarak Era, New York.

El Shamsy 2013
El Shamsy, A., The Canonization of Islamic Law. A Social and Intellectual History, Cambridge.

Emmel 2008
Emmel, S., 'Shenoute of Atripe and the Christian Destruction of Temples in Egypt. Rhetoric and Reality', in Hahn, J., Emmel, S. and Gotter, U. (eds.), From Temple to Church. Destruction and Renewal of Local Cultic Topography in Late Antiquity, Religions in the Graeco-Roman World 163, Leiden, pp. 161–201.

Emmel 2008a
Emmel, S., 'Shenoute's Place in the History of Monasticism', in Gabra, G. and Takla, H. (eds.), Christianity and Monasticism in Upper Egypt 1, Akhmim and Sohag, Cairo, pp. 31–46.

Empereur 1998
Empereur, J.-Y., Alexandria Rediscovered, London.

Erman 1899
Ermann, A., Ausführliches Verzeichnis der Aegyptischen Altertümer und Gipsabgüsse, 2nd ed., Berlin.

Erman and Krebs 1899
Erman, A. and Krebs F., Aus den Papyrus der königlichen Museen, Berlin.

Entwistle and Corby Finney 2013
Entwistle, C. and Corby Finney, P., 'Late Antique Glass Pendants in the British Museum', in Entwistle, C. and James, L. (eds.), New Light on Old Glass: Recent Research on Byzantine Mosaics and Glass, British Museum Research Publication 179, London, pp. 131–77.

Ettinghausen 1933
Ettinghausen, R., 'Ägyptische Holzschnitzereien aus islamischer Zeit', in Berliner Museen. Berichte aus den preußischen Kunstsammlungen 44, Berlin, pp. 17–20.

Evelyn-White 1932
Evelyn-White, H.G., The Monasteries of the Wâdi 'n Natrûn II: The History of the Monasteries of Nitria and of Scetis, New York.

Evetts and Butler 1895
Evetts, B.T.A. and Butler, A.J. (eds.), The Churches and Monasteries of Egypt and Some Neighbouring Countries Attributed to Abu Salih, the Armenian, Oxford (reprint 2001).

Evetts 1910
Evetts, B.T.A., History of the Patriarchs of the Coptic Church of Alexandria III, Patrologia Orientalis V, Paris.

Fähndrich 2005
Fähndrick, H. (ed.), Der Islam in Originalzeugnissen 2. Religion und Gesellschaft, Lenningen.

Fahd 1966
Fahd, T., 'Le monde du sorcier en Islam', in Le monde du sorcier, Sources orientales 7, Paris, pp. 155–204.

Fahd 1997
Fahd, T., 'sihr.', in Encyclopaedia of Islam 9, new ed., Leiden, pp. 567–71.

Fahmy 1950
Fahmy, A.M., Muslim Sea Power in the Eastern Mediterranean from the Seventh to the Tenth Century A.D., Cairo.

Fansa and Aydin 2010
Fansa, M. and Aydin, K. (eds.), Wasserwelten: Badekultur und Technik. Begleitschrift zur Ausstellung Wasserwelten im Landesmuseum Natur und Mensch Oldenburg, 15. August – 17. Oktober 2010, Mainz.

Feder and Lohwasser 2013
Feder, F. and Lohwasser, A. (eds.), Ägypten und sein Umfeld in der Spätantike. Vom Regierungsantritt Diokletians 284/285 bis zur arabischen Eroberung des Vorderen Orients um 635–646, Philippika 61, Wiesbaden.

Fehérvári 1993
Fehérvári, G., 'Mihrab', in Encyclopaedia of Islam 7, new ed., Leiden and New York, pp. 7–15.

Feissel 2008
Feissel, D. 2008, 'Deux modèles de cursive latine dans l'ordre alphabétique grec', in Hoogendijk,F.A.J. and Muhs, B.P. (eds.), Sixty-five Papyrological Texts Presented to Klaas A. Worp on the Occasion of his 65th Birthday, Papyrologica Lugduno-Batava 33, Leiden, pp. 53–64.

Feissel 2008a
Feissel, D., 'Écrire grec en alphabet latin: le cas des documents protobyzantins', in Biville, F., Decourt, J.-C. and Rougemont, G. (eds.), Bilinguisme gréco-latin et épigraphie, Collection de la Maison de l'Orient 37, Série épigraphique et historique 6, Lyon, pp. 213–30.

Feldman 1996
Feldman, L.H., 'Diaspora Synagogues. New Light from Inscriptions and Papyri', in Cat. New York 1996, pp. 48–66.

Felten 1972
Felten, R., 'Die Stellung Rabs in der haggadischen Überlieferung' (dissertation), Cologne.

Fewster 2002
Fewster, P., 'Bilingualism in Roman Egypt', in Adams, J.N., Janse, M. and Swain, S. (eds.), Bilingualism in Ancient Society. Language Contact and the Written Text, Oxford, pp. 233–35.

Fikhman 1974
Fikhman, I.F., 'Slaves in Byzantine Oxyrhynchus,' in Kiessling, E. and Rupprecht, H.-A. (eds.), Akten des XIII. Internationalen Papyrologenkongresses Marburg/Lahn 1971, Munich, pp. 117–24.

Fine 1996
Fine, S., 'From Meeting House to Sacred Realm. Holiness and the Ancient Synagogue', in Cat. New York 1996, pp. 21–47.

Fine 2010
Fine, S., Art and Judaism in the Graeco-Roman World: Toward a New Jewish Archaeology, New York.

Firestone 1990
Firestone, R., Journeys in Holy Lands. The Evolution of the Abraham–Ishmael Legends in Islamic Exegesis, New York.

Fischel 1937 and 1969
Fischel W.J., Jews in the Economic and Political Life of Mediaeval Islam, London and New York.

Fischer 1994
Fischer, J., Griechisch–Römische Terrakotten aus Ägypten. Die Sammlung Sieglin und Schreiber, Dresden, Leipzig, Stuttgart, Tübingen, Tübinger Studien zur Archäologie und Kunstgeschichte 14, Berlin.

Fischer and Kittel 1943
Fischer, E. and Kittel, G., Das antike Weltjudentum. Tatsachen, Texte, Bilder, Schriften des Reichsinstituts für Geschichte des Neuen Deutschlands, Forschungen zur Judenfrage 7, Hamburg.

Fischhaber 1997
Fischhaber, G., Mumifizierung im koptischen Ägypten. Eine Untersuchung zur Körperlichkeit im 1. Jahrtausend n. Chr., Wiesbaden.

Fitzenreiter 2003
Fitzenreiter M. (ed.), Tierkulte im pharaonischen Ägypten und im Kulturvergleich, Internet-Beiträge zur Ägyptologie und Sudanarchäologie (IBAES) IV, http://www2.rz.hu-berlin.de/nilus/net-publications,ibaes4. (Last accessed 6 September 2015.)

Fluck 2004
Fluck, C., 'Textilien spätantiker, christlicher und islamischer Zeit aus Ägypten', in von Falck, M. and Fluck, C., Die Ägyptische Sammlung des Gustav-Lübcke-Museums Hamm, Bönen, pp. 208–61.

Fluck 2004a
Fluck, C., 'Ägyptische Puppen aus römischer bis früharabischer Zeit. Ein Streifzug durch die Sammlungen des Ägyptischen Museums in Berlin, des Museums für angewandte Kunst in Wien und des Benaki-Museums in Athen', in Harrauer, H. and Pintaudi, R. (eds.), Gedenkschrift Ulrike Horak (P. Horak), Florence, pp. 383–400.

Fluck 2008
Fluck, C., Ein buntes Kleid für Josef. Biblische Geschichten auf ägyptischen Wirkereien aus dem Museum für Byzantinische Kunst, Berlin, Berlin.

Fluck 2010
Fluck, C., 'The Portrait of Abraham of Hermonthis', in Gabra, G. and Takla, H.N. (eds.), Christianity and Monasticism in Upper Egypt 2: Nag Hammadi–Esna, Cairo, pp. 211–23.

Fluck and Finneiser 2009
Fluck, C. and Finneiser, K., Kindheit am Nil. Spielzeug – Kleidung – Kinderbilder aus Ägypten in den Staatlichen Museen zu Berlin, Berlin.

Fluck and Helmecke 2014
Fluck, C. and Helmecke G., 'Egypt's Post-Pharaonic textiles', in Gabra, G. (ed.), Coptic Civilization. Two Thousand Years of Christianity in Egypt, Cairo and New York, pp. 231–55.

Fluck, Linscheid and Merz 2000
Fluck, C., Linscheid, P. and Merz, S., Textilien aus Ägypten. Staatliche Museen zu Berlin – Preußischer Kulturbesitz, Skulpturensammlung und Museum für Byzantinische Kunst Bestandskataloge 1, Wiesbaden.

Fodor 2004
Fodor, A., 'The Rod of Moses in Arabic Magic', in Savage-Smith 2004, pp. 1–21.

Förster 2007
Förster, H., Die Anfänge von Weihnachten und Epiphanias – Eine Anfrage an die Entstehungshypothesen, Studien und Texte zu Antike und Christentum, Tübingen.

Foss 2007
Foss, C., 'Egypt under Mu'awiya, Part I. Flavius Papas and Upper Egypt', Bulletin of the School of Oriental and African Studies 72.1, pp. 1–24.

Foss 2010
Foss, C., 'Mu'awiya's state', in Haldon, J.H. (ed.), Money, Power and Politics in Early Islamic Syria. A Review of Current Debates, Farnham.

Fournet 1999
Fournet, J.-L., Hellénisme dans l'Égypte du VIe siècle. La bibliothèque et l'œuvre de Dioscore d'Aphrodité, Mémoires publiés par les membres de l'Institut Français d'Archéologie Orientale du Caire 115, Cairo.

Fournet 2003
Fournet, J.-L., 'Between Literary Tradition and Cultural Change. The Poetic and Documentary Production of Dioscorus of Aphrodite', in MacDonald, A.A, Twomey, M.W. and Reinink, G. (eds.), Learned Antiquity. Scholarship and Society in the Near East, the Graeco-Roman World and the Early Medieval West, Groningen Studies in Cultural Change 5, Leuven, Paris and Dudley, MA, pp. 101–14.

Fournet 2003a
Fournet, J.L., 'Langue et culture dans les praesidia', in Cuvigny, H. (ed.), La route de Myos Hormos. L'armée romaine dans le désert oriental. Praesidia du désert de Bérénice I, 2, Fouilles de l'Institut Français d'Archéologie Orientale 48, Cairo, pp. 427–500.

Fournet 2009
Fournet, J.-L., 'The Multilingual Environment of Late Antique Egypt. Greek, Latin, Coptic, and Persian documentation', in Bagnall, R.S. (ed.), The Oxford Handbook of Papyrology, Oxford, pp. 418–51.

Frank 2000
Frank, G., The Memory of the Eyes. Pilgrims to Living Saints in Christian Late Antiquity, Berkeley.

Frankfurter 1993
Frankfurter, D., Elijah in Upper Egypt. The Coptic Apocalypse of Elijah and Early Egyptian Christianity, Minneapolis.

Frankfurter 1994
Frankfurter, D., 'The Cult of the Martyrs in Egypt before Constantine. The Evidence of the Coptic Apocalypse of Elijah', in Vigiliae Christianae 48, pp. 25–47.

Frankfurter 1994a
Frankfurter, D., 'The Magic of Writing and the Writing of Magic. The Power of the Word in Egyptian and Greek traditions', *Helios* 21, pp. 189–221.

Frankfurter 1995
Frankfurter, D., 'Narrating Power. The Theory and Practice of the Magical Historiola in Ritual Spells', in Meyer and Mirecki, pp. 457–76.

Frankfurter 1998
Frankfurter, D., *Religion in Roman Egypt. Assimilation and Resistance*, Princeton.

Frankfurter 1998a
Frankfurter, D. (ed.), *Pilgrimage and Holy Space in Late Antique Egypt*, Leiden.

Frankfurter 1998b
Frankfurter, D., 'Introduction: Approaches to Coptic Pilgrimage', in Frankfurter 1998a, pp. 3–48.

Frankfurter 2003
Frankfurter, D., 'Syncretism and the Holy Man in Late Antique Egypt', *Journal of Early Christian Studies* 11, pp. 339–85.

Frankfurter 2005
Frankfurter, D., 'Voices, Books, and Dreams. The Diversification of Divination Media in Late Antique Egypt', in Johnston, S.I. and Struck, P.T. (eds.), *Mantike. Studies in Ancient Divination*, Leiden, pp. 233–54.

Frankfurter 2009
Frankfurter, D., 'The Laments of Horus in Coptic. Myth, Folklore, and Syncretism in Late Antique Egypt', in Dill, U. and Walde, C. (eds.), *Antike Mythen. Medien, Transformationen und Konstruktionen*, Berlin and New York, pp. 229–47.

Frankfurter 2010
Frankfurter, D., 'Where the Spirits Dwell. Possession, Christianization, and Saint-Shrines in Late Antiquity', in *Harvard Theological Review* 103, pp. 27–46.

Frantz-Murphy 2001
Frantz-Murphy, G., *Arabic Agricultural Leases and Tax Receipts from Egypt 148–427 A. H. / 765–1035 A.D.*, Corpus Papyrorum Raineri, Vienna.

Fraser 1972
Fraser, P.M., *Ptolemaic Alexandria*, 3 vols, Oxford.

Frederiksen and Irshai 2006
Frederiksen, P. and Irshai, O., 'Christian Anti-Judaism: Polemics and Policies', in Katz, T. (ed.), *The Cambridge History of Judaism 4: The Late Roman–Rabbinic Period*, Cambridge, pp. 977–1034.

Frenschkowski 2009
Frenschkowski, M., 'Magie', in *Reallexikon für Antike und Christentum* 23, pp. 857–957.

Frey 2012
Frey, J., 'Die Fragmente judenchristlicher Evangelien', in Markschies, C. and Schröter, J. (eds.), *Antike christliche Apokryphen in deutscher Übersetzung. I, 1. Evangelien und Verwandtes*, Tübingen, pp. 560–92.

Froschauer, Gastgeber and Harrauer 2003
Froschauer, H., Gastgeber, C. and Harrauer, H. (eds.), *Tod am Nil. Tod und Totenkult im antiken Ägypten*, Vienna.

Gaborit-Chopin 2003
Gaborit-Chopin, D., *Ivoires médiévaux, Ve–XVe siècles*, Musée du Louvre, Département des objets d'art, Paris.

Gabra 2004
Gabra, G., 'Notes on Coptic and Muslim Mulids in Egypt', *Hallesche Beiträge zur Orientwissenschaft* 38, pp. 145–50.

Gabra and van Loon 2007
Gabra, G. and van Loon, G.J.M., *The Churches of Egypt. From the Journey of the Holy Family to the Present Day*, Cairo.

Gaddis 2005
Gaddis, M. *There is No Crime for Those who Have Christ. Religious Violence in the Christian Roman Empire*, Berkeley.

Gager 1972
Gager, J., *Moses in Greco-Roman Paganism*, Society of Biblical Literature, Monograph Series 16, Nashville and New York.

Gager 1994
Gager, J., 'Moses the Magician. Hero of an Ancient Counter-Culture?', *Helios* 21, pp. 179–88.

Garcin 1976
Garcin, J.-C., 'Un centre musulman de la Haute-Égypte médiévale: Qus', *Texte Arabes et Études Islamiques* 6, Cairo.

Gardet 1965
Gardet, L., 'Djanna', in *Encyclopaedia of Islam* 2, Leiden and London, pp. 447–52.

Gascou 2006
Gascou, J., *Sophrone de Jérusalem. Miracles des Saints Cyr et Jean*, Paris.

Gaubert and Mouton 2004
Gaubert, C. and Mouton, J.-M., 'Présentation des archives d'une famille copte du Fayoum à l'époque fatimide', in Immerzeel, M. and van der Vliet, J. (eds.), *Coptic Studies on the Threshold of a New Millennium,* Orientalia Lovaniensia Analecta 133, Leuven, pp. 505–17.

Gayraud 1998
Gayraud, R.-P., 'Fostat. Évolution d'une capitale arabe du VIIe au XIIe siècle d'après les fouilles d'Istabl 'Antar', in Gayraud, R.-P. (ed.), *Colloque international d'Archéologie islamique*, Cairo, pp. 435–60.

Gayraud 1999
Gayraud, R.-P, 'Le Qarafa al-Kubra, dernière demeure des Fatimides', in Barrucand, M. (ed.), *L'Égypte fatimide – son art et son histoire. Actes du colloque organisé à Paris les 28, 29 et 30 mai 1998*, Paris, pp. 443–64.

Gayraud, Björnesjö, Muller-Woulkoff et al. 1991
Gayraud, R.-P., Björnesjö, S., Muller-Woulkoff, J.-M. et al., 'Istabl 'Antar (Fostat). Rapport de fouilles', *Annales Islamologiques* 25.1, pp. 57–87.

Gerhards and Brakmann 1994
Gerhards, A. and Brakmann, H. (eds.), *Die koptische Kirche. Einführung in das ägyptische Christentum*, Stuttgart.

Germer 1988
Germer, R., *Katalog der Altägyptischen Pflanzenreste der Berliner Museen*, Wiesbaden.

Germer 2011
Germer, R., 'Die Pflanzen der altägyptischen Gärten', in Tietze, C. (ed.), *Ägyptische Gärten*, Cologne, pp. 118–52.

Germer, Kischkewitz and Lüning 2009
Germer, R., Kischkewitz, H. and Lüning, M., *Berliner Mumiengeschichten. Ergebnisse eines multidisziplinären Forschungsprojektes*, Regensburg.

Gessler-Löhr, Grabbe, Raab and Schultz 2007
Gessler-Löhr, B., Grabbe, E., Raab, B.-W., and Schultz, M., 'Ausklang. Eine koptische Mumie aus christlicher Zeit', in Cat. Stuttgart 2007, pp. 254–77.

Gibb and Kramer 1974
Gibb, H. and Kramers, J.H. (eds.), *Shorter Encyclopedia of Islam*, Leiden.

Gibb, Defremery and Sanguinetti 1994
Gibb, H.A.R., Defrémery, C. and Saguinetti, B.R., *The Travels of Ibn Battuta A.D. 1325–1354*, translated with revisions and notes from the Arabian text, 3 vols, New Delhi.

Gibbs 2012
Gibbs, M., 'Manufacture, Trade and the Economy', in Riggs, C. (ed.), *The Oxford Handbook of Roman Egypt*, Oxford, pp. 38–55.

Ginsberg, Rothkoff, and Dan 2007
Ginsberg, H.L., Rothkoff, A. and Dan, J., 'Michael and Gabriel', *Encyclopaedia Judaica* 14, 2nd ed., pp. 167–69.

Ginzberg 1909–1938
Ginzberg, L., *Legends of the Jews*, 7 vols, Philadelphia.

von Gladiss 1998
von Gladiss, A., *Schmuck im Museum für Islamische Kunst*, Veröffentlichungen des Museums für Islamische Kunst 2, Berlin.

Goddio, Bernard, Bernard et al. 1998
Goddio, F., Bernard, A., Bernand, E., et al., *Alexandria. The Submerged Royal Quarters*, London.

Godlewski 1986
Godlewski, W., *Deir el-Bahari* V: *Le Monastére de St Phoibammon*, Warsaw.

Godlewski 2000
Godlewski, W., 'Les peintures de l'église de l'archange Gabriel à Naqlun', *Bulletin de la Société d'Archéologie Copte* 39, pp. 89–101.

Godlewski 2003
Godlewski, W., 'Naqlun. Excavation, 2002', *Polish Archaeology in the Mediterranean* 14, pp. 163–71.

Godlewski 2011
Godlewski, W. 2011, 'Naqlun. The Earliest Hermitages', in Bagnall, R.S., Davoli, P. and Hope, C. H. (eds.), *Proceedings of the Six International Conference of the Dakhleh Oasis Project*, The Oasis Papers 6, Oxford, pp. 475–89.

Godlewski 2011a
Godlewski, W., 'In the Shade of the Nekloni Monastery (Deir el Malak Gubrail, Fayyum)', in *Polish Archaeology in the Mediterranean* 20, pp. 467–82.

Godlewski 2012
Godlewski, W., 'Naqlun (nekloni). Excavations in 2008–2009', *Polish Archaeology in the Mediterranean* 21, pp. 193–211.

Godlewski and Czaja-Szewczak 2009
Godlewski, W. and Czaja-Szewczak, B., 'Naqlun Cemetery C.1 and its Cartonages', *Polish Archaeology in the Mediterranean* 18, pp. 247–60.

Godlewski and Łajtar 2006
Godlewski, W. and Łajtar, A., 'Grave Stelae from Deir el Naqlun', *Journal of Juristic Papyrology* 36, pp. 43–62.

Goehring 1999
Goehring, J.E., *Ascetics, Society, and the Desert: Studies in Early Egyptian Monasticism*, Harrisburg, PA.

Goehring 2007
Goehring, J.E., 'Monasticism in Byzantine Egypt', in Bagnall, R.S., *Egypt in the Byzantine World, 300–700*, Cambridge, pp. 390–407.

Goette 1989
Goette, H.R., 'Kaiserzeitliche Bildnisse von Sarapispriestern', *Mitteilungen des deutschen Archäologischen Instituts Kairo*, 45, pp. 173–86.

Goitein 1964
Goitein, S.D., 'The Synagogue Building and its Furnishing According to the Records of the Cairo Geniza', *Eretz-Israel* 7, pp. 81–97.

Goitein 1967–88
Goitein, S.D., *A Mediterranean Society. The Jewish Communities of the Arab World as Portrayed in the Documents of the Cairo Geniza*, 6 vols, Berkeley.

Goldberg 2012
Goldberg, J., *Trade and Institutions in the Mediterranean*, Cambridge.

Goldziher 1890
Goldziher, I., 'Die Heiligenverehrung im Islam' in Goldziher, I., *Muhammedanische Studien* 2, Halle, pp. 275–378.

Goldziher 1894
Goldziher, I., 'Hebräische Elemente in muhammedanischen Zaubersprüchen', *Zeitschrift der Deutschen Morgenländischen Gesellschaft* 48, pp. 358–60.

Goldziher 1971
Goldziher, I., 'Veneration of Saints in Islam' in Goldziher, I., *Muslim Studies* 2, London (reprint of 1890 edition), pp. 255–341.

Gardner 2007
Gardner, I., *Kellis Literary Texts* 2, Oxford.

Górecki 2008
Górecki, T., 'Archaeological Research in the Hermitage in Tomb 1152 in Sheikh Abd el-Gurna (West Thebes)', in *Polish Archaeology in the Mediterranean* 20, pp. 225–36.

Goodenough 1953
Goodenough, E.R., *Jewish Symbols in the Graeco-Roman Period* 2 and 3, Kingsport.

Graf 1996
Graf, F., *Schadenszauber und Gottesnähe. Die Magie in der griechisch–römischen Antike*, Munich.

Greifenhagen 1975
Greifenhagen, A., *Schmuckarbeiten in Edelmetall* 2, *Einzelstücke*, Berlin.

Greiner, Janowski and Lichtenberger 2007
Greiner, B., Janowski, B. and Lichtenberger, H. (eds.), *Opfere deinen Sohn! 'Das Isaak-Opfer' in Judentum, Christentum und Islam*, Tübingen.

Grenier 1977
Grenier, J.-C., 'Anubis Alexandrin et Romain', *Études préliminaires aux religions orientales dans l'empire romain* 57, Leiden.

Grenier 1983
Grenier, J.-C., 'La stèle funéraire du dernier taureau Bouchis (Caire JE 31901 – Stèle Bucheum 20)', *Bulletin de l'Institut Français d'Archéologie Orientale* 83, pp. 197–208.

Griffith 1890
Griffith, F.Ll., 'The Antiquities of Tell el Yahûdîyeh', in Naville, E., *Mound of the Jew and the City of Onias*, The Egypt Exploration Fund, London, pp. 33–74.

Griggs 1993
Griggs, C.W., *Early Egyptian Christianity. From its Origin to 451 C.E.*, Leiden.

Grimm 1974
Grimm, G., *Die römischen Mumienmasken aus Ägypten*, Wiesbaden.

Grohmann 1934
Grohmann, A., 'Islamische Zaubertexte', in *Griechische, koptische und arabische Texte zur Religion und religiösen Literatur in Ägyptens Spätzeit*, Veröffentlichungen aus den badischen Papyrus-Sammlungen 5, Heidelberg, pp. 415–51.

Grohmann 1952
Grohmann, A., *From the World of Arabic Papyri*, Cairo.

Grohmann 1957
Grohmann, A., 'The Origin and Development of Floriated Kufic', *Ars Orientalis* 2, pp. 184–213.

Grohmann 2, 1971
Grohmann, A., *Arabische Paläographie 2: Das Schriftwesen. Die Lapidarschrift*, Österreichische Akademie der Wissenschaften. Philosophisch-historische Klasse, Denkschriften 94/2: Forschungen zur islamischen Philologie und Kulturgeschichte 2, Vienna.

Gros 1996
Gros, P., *L'architecture romaine du début du IIIe siècle av. J.-C. à la fin du Haut-Empire* I, Paris.

Grossmann 1971–1980
Grossmann, P. 'Reinigungsarbeiten im Jeremiaskloster von Saqqara I–III', *Mitteilungen des Deutschen Archäologischen Instituts Kairo* 27, 1971, pp. 173–80; 28, 1972, pp. 145–52; 36, 1980, pp. 193–202.

Grossmann 1980
Grossmann, P., *Elephantine* II. *Kirche und spätantike Hausanlagen im Chnumtempelhof*, Archäologische Veröffentlichungen 25, Mainz.

Grossmann 1989
Grossmann, P., *Abu Mina* I. *Die Gruftkirche und die Gruft*, Archäologische Veröffentlichungen 44, Mainz.

Grossmann 1990
Grossmann, P., 'Typologische Probleme der nubischen Vierstützenbauten', in Godlewski, W. (ed.), *Coptic Studies, Acts of the Third International Congress of Coptic Studies*, Warsaw, pp. 151–59.

Grossmann 1998
Grossmann, P., 'The Pilgrimage Center of Abu Mina', in Frankfurter 1998a, pp. 281–302.

Grossmann 2002
Grossmann, P., *Christliche Architektur in Ägypten*, Handbuch der Orientalistik 62, Leiden, Boston and Cologne.

Grossmann 2005
Grossmann, P., 'Frühe fünfschiffige Kirchen und die Anfänge des Kirchenbaus in Ägypten', in Jánosi, P. (ed.), *Structure and Significance*, Festschrift für Dieter Arnold, Denkschrift der österreichischen Akademie der Wissenschaften 33, Vienna, pp. 283–303.

Grossmann 2013
Grossmann, P., 'Überlegungen zum ursprünglichen Grundriß der Kirche von Orléansville und ein Beitrag zur Entstehung der christlichen Basilika', *Antiquité Tardive* 21, pp. 313–20.

Grossmann and al-Taher 1997
Grossmann, P. and al-Taher, R., 'Excavation of the Circular Church at Farama-West', in *Mitteilungen des deutschen archäologischen Instituts Kairo* 53, pp. 255–62.

Gruen 2002
Gruen, E.S., *Diaspora. Jews amidst Greeks and Romans*, Cambridge, MA and London.

Guillaumont 1991
Guillaumont, A. et al., 'Kellia' in *Coptic Encyclopedia* 5, pp. 1396–410.

Guirguis and van Doorn-Harder 2011
Guirguis, M. and van Doorn-Harder, N., *The Emergence of the Modern Coptic Papacy. The Egyptian Church and its Leadership from the Ottoman Period to the Present*, Cairo.

Gulácsi 2001
Gulácsi, Z., *Manichaean Art in Berlin collections. A Comprehensive Catalogue*, Corpus Fontium Manichaeorum, Series Archaeologica et Iconographica 1, Turnhout.

Guyot and Klein 1993
Guyot, P. and Klein, R., *Das frühe Christentum bis zum Ende der Verfolgungen. Eine Dokumentation. I. Die Christen im heidnischen Staat*, Texte zur Forschung 60, Darmstadt.

Haas 1997
Haas, C., *Alexandria in Late Antiquity. Topography and Social Conflict*, Baltimore and London.

Hachlili 1988
Hachlili, R., *Ancient Jewish Art and Archaeology in the Land of Israel*, Leiden.

Hachlili 1998
Hachlili, R., *Ancient Jewish Art and Archaeology in the Diaspora*, Handbook of Oriental Studies 35, Leiden, Boston and Cologne.

Hachlili 2005
Hachlili, R., *Jewish Funerary Customs, Practices and Rites in the Second Temple Period*, Leiden and Boston.

Hachlili 2010
Hachlili, R., 'Art', in Collins, J.J. and Harlow, D.C. (eds.), *Eerdmans Dictionary of Early Judaism*, Grand Rapids and Cambridge, pp. 381–86.

Hadas-Lebel 2012
Hadas-Lebel, M., *Studies in Philo of Alexandria. A Thinker in the Jewish Diaspora*, Leiden.

Hahn 2004
Hahn, J., *Gewalt und religiöser Konflikt. Studien zu den Auseinandersetzungen zwischen Christen, Heiden und Juden im Osten des Römischen Reiches*, Berlin.

Hahn 2008
Hahn, J., 'Die Zerstörung der Kulte von Philae', in Hahn, Emmel and Gotter 2008, pp. 203–42.

Hahn, Emmel and Gotter 2008
Hahn, J., Emmel, S. and Gotter, U. (eds.), *From Temple to Church. Destruction and Renewal of Local Cultic Topography in Late Antiquity*, Leiden.

Hahn 2013
Hahn, J., 'Schenute von Atripe, die kaiserliche Religionspolitik und der Kampf gegen das Heidentum in Oberägypten', in Feder and Lohwasser 2013, pp. 81–108.

Hall 1905
Hall, H.R. 1905, *Coptic and Greek Texts of the Christian Period from Ostraka, Stelae, etc. in the British Museum*, London.

Halm 2003
Halm, H., *Die Kalifen von Kairo. Die Fatimiden in Ägypten 973–1074*, Munich.

Hamdy 2003
Hamdy, R., *Floral Bouquets and Garlands in Egypt*, Cairo.

Hanafi 2010
Hanafi, A., 'An Arabic Will Written on a Ship', in Gagos, T. (ed.), *Proceedings of the Twenty-fifth International Congress of Papyrology, Ann Arbor 2007*, Ann Arbor, pp. 299–306.

Harker 2008
Harker, A., *Loyalty and Dissidence in Roman Egypt*, Cambridge.

Harnack 1924
Harnack, A. von, *Die Mission und Ausbreitung des Christentums in den ersten drei Jahrhunderten*, 4th ed., Leipzig.

Harrauer 2003
Harrauer, H., 'Tod in den Papyri', in Froschauer, Gastgeber and Harrauer 2003, pp. 21–32.

Harrauer 2006
Harrauer, H., 'Die drei Landessprachen im ersten Jahrtausend n. Chr.', in Fluck, C. and Helmecke, G. (eds.), *Textile Messages. Inscribed Fabrics from Roman to Abbasid Egypt*, Studies in Textile and Costume History 4, Leiden and Boston, pp. 3–14.

Hauben 2012
Hauben, H., *Studies on the Melitian Schism in Egypt (AD 306–335)*, Aldershot.

Hawary and Rashed 1932 and 1939
Hawary, M.H. and Rashed, H., *Catalogue Général du Musée Arabe du Caire, Stèles funéraires* I and II, Cairo.

Heemstra 2010
Heemstra, M., *The Fiscus Judaicus and the Parting of the Ways*, Tübingen 2010.

Hees 2002
Hees, S. von, *Enzyklopädie als Spiegel des Weltbildes. Qazwīnīs Wunder der Schöpfung – eine Naturkunde des 13. Jahrhunderts*, Diskurse der Arabistik 4, Wiesbaden.

Heiden 2002
Heiden, D., 'Pharaonische Baumaterialien in der mittelalterlichen Stadtbefestigung von Kairo', in *Mitteilungen des Deutschen Archäologischen Instituts Kairo* 58, pp. 257–75.

Heiden 2010
Heiden, D., 'Auf der Suche nach dem verlorenen Minbar. Verstreute Kunstobjekte in der internationalen Kunstlandschaft', in Frenger, M. and Müller-Wiener, M. (eds.), *Von Gibraltar bis zum Ganges: Studien zur Islamischen Kunstgeschichte in memoriam Christian Ewert*, Bonner Asienstudien 7, Berlin, pp. 75–95.

Helmbold-Doyé 2015
Helmbold-Doyé, J., *Die Grabung der Deutschen Orient-Gesellschaft (DOG) unter der Leitung von Walter Honroth (12.01.–22.01.1913)*.

Heilmeyer and Lack 1997
Heilmeyer, M. and Lack, H.W., 'Le ghirlande del Fayyum nella collezione Georg Schweinfurth', in Walker, S. and Bierbrier, M. (eds.), *Fayyum – Misteriosi volti dell'Egitto*, Rome, pp. 256–65.

Heilmeyer and Schirarend 1996
Heilmeyer M. and Schirarend C., *Die Goldenen Äpfel*, Berlin.

Heinemann 1931
Heinemann, I., *Philons griechische und jüdische Bildung. Kulturvergleichende Untersuchungen zu Philons Darstellung der jüdischen Gesetze,* Breslau (reprint Darmstadt 1962)

Helck 1986
Helck, W., 'Westen', in *Lexikon der Ägyptologie* 6, p. 1235.

Helmecke 1999
Helmecke, G., 'Priestergewänder oder Votivgaben?', in Emmel, S., Krause, M. et al. (eds.), *Ägypten und Nubien in spätantiker und christlicher Zeit*, 2. *Schrifttum, Sprache und Gedankenwelt. Akten des 6. Internationalen Koptologenkongresses. Münster 20–26 Juli 1996*, Sprachen und Kulturen des Christlichen Orients 6/2, Wiesbaden, pp. 163–74.

Helmecke 2005
Helmecke, G., 'Textiles with Arab inscriptions excavated in Naqlun 1999–2003', in *Polish Archaeology in the Mediterranean* 16, pp. 195–202.

Helmecke 2006
Helmecke, G., 'Tiraz-Inschriften im Berliner Museum für Islamische Kunst, Berlin', in Fluck, C. and Helmecke, G. (eds.), *Textile Messages. Inscribed Fabrics from Roman to Abbasid Egypt*, Studies in Textile and Costume History 4, Leiden and Boston, pp. 173–91.

Helmecke 2013
Helmecke, G., 'Mat fragments in the Museum of Islamic Art in Berlin', in De Moor, Fluck and Linscheid, pp. 100–7.

Henein and Bianquis 2009
Henein, N.H. and Bianquis, T. 2009, 'La magie par les psaumes', *Bibliothèque d'études coptes* 12, 2nd ed., Cairo.

Hengel 1976
Hengel, M., 'Die Ursprünge der Gnosis und das Urchristentum', in Adna, J., Hafeman S.J. and Hofius, O. (eds.), *Rechtfertigung. Festschrift für Ernst Käsemann zum 70. Geburtstag*, Tübingen and Göttingen, pp. 125–84.

Hinterhuber 2009
Hinterhuber, E.M., *Abrahamischer Trialog und Zivilgesellschaft. Eine Untersuchung zum sozialintegrativen Potenzial des Dialogs zwischen Juden, Christen und Muslimen*, Stuttgart.

Hodak 2013
Hodak, S., 'Die Thebais im Morgen- und Abendland', in Feder and Lohwasser 2013, pp. 157–91.

Hoffman and Cole 2011
Hoffman, A. and Cole, P., *Sacred Trash. The Lost and Found World of the Cairo Geniza*, New York.

Holmes Katz 2007
Holmes Katz, M., *The Birth of the Prophet Muhammad: Devotional Piety in Sunni Islam*, London.

Honroth 1913
Honroth, W., 'Tell-el-Amarna 1912–13. Informationsgrabung auf dem Westufer bei Dirweh. Oberleitung Honroth (12.–22. Januar 1913)', unpublished manuscript.

Horak 1995
Horak, U., 'Koptische Mumien. Der koptische Tote in Grabungsberichten, Funden und literarischen

Nachrichten', *Biblos* 44, pp. 39–71.

Horbury and Noy 1992
Horbury, W. and Noy, D., *Jewish Inscriptions of Graeco-Roman Egypt*, Cambridge.

Horn 2013
Horn, J., 'Die Ausstrahlung des ägyptischen Mönchtums auf den Westen. Zur Vermittlerrolle der Kirchenväter Hieronymus und Johannes Cassianus', in Feder and Lohwasser 2013, pp. 139–56.

Hornung 1986
Hornung, E., 'Amentet', in *Lexikon der Ägyptologie* 1, p. 223.

Huber 2013
Hubert, B., 'Eine Tunika fürs Jenseits', in De Moor, Fluck and Linscheid 2013, pp. 12–21.

Humphrey 1986
Humphrey, J. H., *Roman Circuses: Arenas for Chariot Racing*, Berkeley.

Hunt 1989
Hunt, L.A., 'The al-Mu'allaqa Doors Reconstructed: An Early 14th-century Sanctuary Screen from Old Cairo,' *Gesta* 28.1, pp. 61–77.

Hussein 1981
Hussein, M.I., *Die Vergnügungen des Hofes und Alltagsleben. Eine ikonographische Untersuchung der Darstellungen in der Malerei der Fatimidenzeit und deren Wirkung auf die nachfolgenden Epochen in Ägypten*, Berlin.

Hüttenmeister and Reeg 1977
Hüttenmeister, F. and Reeg, G., *Die antiken Synagogen in Israel*, Wiesbaden.

Ibn al-Wašša' 1984
Ibn al-Wašša', *Abu t-Tayyib Muhammad Ibn Ishaq Ibn Yahya, Das Buch des buntbestickten Kleides*, 3 vols, Leipzig and Weimar.

Ibn Arabi 1990
Ibn Arabi, *La vie merveilleuse de Dhu-l-Nun l'Égyptien*, Paris.

Ibn Battuta 2010
Ibn Battuta, *Die Wunder des Morgenlandes. Reisen durch Afrika und Asien, nach der arabischen Ausgabe von Muhammad al-Bailuni ins Deutsche übertragen, kommentiert und mit einem Nachwort versehen von R. Elger*, Munich.

Ibn Dschubair 1988
Ibn Dschubair, *Tagebuch eines Mekkapilgers, aus dem Arabischen übertragen und bearbeitet von Regina Günther*, Stuttgart.

Imbach 2012
Imbach, J., *Mit Abraham unterwegs. Vom Abenteuer des Glaubens*, Würzburg.

Innemée 2000
Innemée, K.C., 'Deir al-Baramus, Excavations at the So-called Site of Moses the Black', *Bulletin de la Société d'Archéologie Copte* 39, pp. 123–35.

Isele 2010
Isele, B., *Kampf um Kirchen. Religiöse Gewalt, heiliger Raum und christliche Topographie in Alexandria und Konstantinopel (4. Jh.)*, Münster.

Iskander 2012
Iskander, E., *Sectarian Conflict in Egypt*, London.

Islamische Kunst 1984
Islamische Kunst, *Loseblattkatalog unpublizierter Werke aus deutschen Museen.*

1: *Glas; bearbeitet von Jens Kröger*, Mainz.

Islamische Kunst 1985
Islamische Kunst, *Loseblattkatalog unpublizierter Werke aus deutschen Museen. 2: Metall, Stein, Stuck, Holz, Elfenbein, Stoffe; bearbeitet von Almut Hauptmann von Gladiss und Jens Kröger*, Mainz.

Islamische Kunst 1986
Islamische Kunst, *Verborgene Schätze. Ausstellung des Museums für Islamische Kunst, Berlin. Selm, Schloß Cappenberg 10.9.–23.11.1986; Berlin-Dahlem 18.12.1986–15.2.1987*, Berlin.

Johnston 2002
Johnston, S.I., 'The Testament of Solomon from Late Antiquity to the Renaissance', in Bremmer, J.N. and Veenstra, J.R. (eds.), *The Metamorphosis of Magic from Late Antiquity to the Early Modern Period*, Leuven, pp. 35–49.

Jones 1987
Jones, C., 'Stigma: Tattooing and Branding in Graeco-Roman Antiquity', *Journal of Roman Studies* 77, pp. 139–55.

Jördens 2009
Jördens, A., *Statthalterliche Verwaltung in der römischen Kaiserzeit. Studien zum praefectus Aegypti*, Stuttgart.

Judge 1977
Judge, E.A., 'The Earliest Use of Monachos for "Monk" (P.Coll.Youtie. 77) and the Origins of Monasticism', *Jahrbuch für Antike und Christentum* 20, pp. 72–89.

Judge 1987
Judge, E., 'The Magical Use of Scripture in the Papyri', in Conrad, E.W. and Newing, E.G. (eds.), *Perspectives on Language and Text*, Winona Lake, pp. 339–49.

Juergensmeyer et al. 2013
Juergensmeyer, M. et al. (ed.), *The Oxford Handbook of Religion and Violence*, Oxford.

Kaiser 1967
Kaiser, W., *Ägyptisches Museum Berlin, Östlicher Stülerbau am Schloss Charlottenburg*, Berlin.

Kaiser Friedrich II 2008
Fansa, M. and Ermete, K. (eds.), *Kaiser Friedrich II (1194–1250). Welt und Kultur des Mittelmeerraums. Begleitband zur Sonderausstellung, 'Kaiser Friedrich II (1194–1250), Welt und Kultur des Mittelmeerraums'*, in Landesmuseum für Natur und Mensch, Oldenburg, Mainz.

Kambatisis 1976
Kambatisis, S., 'Une nouvelle tablette magique d'Égypte. Musée du Louvre, Inv. E 27145-IIIe-IVe siècle', *Bulletin de l'Institut Français d'Archéologie Orientale* 76, pp. 213–23.

Kaper 2003
Kaper, O.E., *The Egyptian God Tutu. A Study of the Sphinx-god and Master of Demons with a Corpus of Monuments*, Orienatlia Lovaniensia Analecta 119, Leuven, Paris and Dudley.

Kaplan 1999
Kaplan, I., *Grabmalerei und Grabreliefs der Römerzeit. Wechselwirkungen zwischen den ägyptischen und griechisch-alexandrinischen Kunst*, Beiträge zur Ägyptologie 16; Veröffentlichungen der Institute für Afrikanistik und Ägyptologie der Universität Wien, Vienna.

Kaptein 1993
Kaptein, N.J., *Muhammad's Birthday Festival*,

Leiden.

Kayser 1967
Kayser, H., *Führer durch die Sammlungen des Roemer-Pelizaeus-Museums*, Hildesheim.

Kayser 1994
Kayser, F., *Recueil des inscriptions grecques et latines (non funéraires) d'Alexandrie impériale (Ier-IIIe s. apr. J.-C.)*, Cairo.

Kendrick 1921 and 1922
Kendrick, A.F., *Catalogue of Textiles from Burying-grounds in Egypt*, Victoria and Albert Museum, Department of Textiles, London.

Kennedy 1998
Kennedy, H., 'Egypt as a Province in the Islamic Caliphate', in Petry, C.F. (ed.), *The Cambridge History of Egypt* 1, 640–1517, Cambridge, pp. 62–85.

Kennedy 2012
Kennedy, H., 'Journey to Mecca: A History', in Porter, V. (ed.), *Hajj Journey to the Heart of Islam*, London, pp. 68–136.

Kerkeslager 1998
Kerkeslager, A. 1998, 'Jewish Pilgrimage and Jewish Identity in Hellenistic and Early Roman Egypt', in Frankfurter 1998a, pp. 99–225.

Kerkeslager 2006
Kerkeslager, A., 'The Jews in Egypt and Cyrenaica, 66–c.235 CE', in Kratz, S.T. (ed.), *The Cambridge History of Judaism* 4, *The Late Roman–Rabbinic Period*, Cambridge, pp. 53–68.

Kessler 1989
Kessler, D., *Die heiligen Tiere und der König. Teil I. Beiträge zu Organisation, Kult und Theologie der spätzeitlichen Tierfriedhöfe*, Ägypten und Altes Testament 16, Wiesbaden.

Kessler 2000
Kessler, D., 'Das Hellenistische Serapeum in Alexandria und Ägypten in ägyptologischer Sicht', in Görg, M. and Hölbl, G. (eds.), *Ägypten und der östliche Mittelmeerraum im 1. Jahrtausend v. Chr. Akten des Interdisziplinären Symposions am Institut für Ägyptologie der Universität München 25.–27.10.1996*, Ägypten und Altes Testament 44, Wiesbaden, pp. 163–230.

Kessler and Brose 2008
Kessler, D. and Brose, P. (eds.), *Ägyptens letzte Pyramide. Das Grab des Seuta(s) in Tuna el-Gebel*, Munich.

Khan 1994
Khan, G., 'The Pre-Islamic Background of Muslim Legal Formularies', *Aram Periodical* 6, pp. 193–224.

Khan 2007
Khan, G., 'Newly Discovered Arabic Documents from Early Abbasid Khurasan', in Sijpesteijn, P. M., Sundelin, L., Torallas Tovar, S. and Zomeño, A., *From al-Andalus to Khurasan. Documents from the Medieval Muslim World*, Leiden, pp. 201–18.

Khater 1967
Khater, A., 'L'emploi des Psaumes en thérapie avec formules en caractères cryptographiques', *Bulletin de la Société d'Archéologie Copte* 19, pp. 123–76.

Khosroyev 1995
Khosroyev, A., *Die Bibliothek von Nag Hammadi. Einige Probleme des Christentums in Ägypten während der ersten Jahrhunderte*, Arbeiten zum spätantiken und koptischen Ägypten 7, Altenberge, pp. 158–66.

Khoury 1979
Khoury, R., 'Note sur les foires et pèlerinages juifs d'Égypte, Hommages à la mémoire de Serge Sauneron, 1927–1976', in Vercoutter, J. (ed.), *Égypte post-pharaonique*, pp. 459–69.

Kiltz and Kouriyhe
Kiltz, S.D. and Kouriyhe, Y., TUK 0603 'Hymnen auf das Paradies 7:18' in *Texte aus der Umwelt des Korans* (Datenbank des Corpus Coranicum).

Kinberg 2004
Kinberg, L., 'Paradise' in *Encyclopaedia of the Qur'an* 4, Washington D.C., pp. 12–20.

King 2004
King, D., 'Roman and Byzantine Dress in Egypt', in Muthesius, A. and King, M., *Collected Textile Studies*, London, pp. 246–67.

Kippenberg 2011
Kippenberg, H., *Violence as Worship. Religious Wars in the Age of Globalization*, Stanford.

Kiss 2007
Kiss, Z., 'Alexandria in the Fourth to Seventh Centuries', in Bagnall, R.S. (ed.), *Egypt in the Byzantine World, 300–700*, Cambridge, pp. 187–206.

Kister 1989
Kister, M.J., 'Do not assimilate yourselves …. la tashabbahu', *Jerusalem Studies in Arabic and Islam* 12, pp. 321–71.

Kitzinger 1938
Kitzinger, E., 'The Story of Joseph on a Coptic Tapestry', *Journal of the Warburg Institute* 1, pp. 266–68.

Klesse 1967
Klesse, B., *Seidenstoffe in der italienischen Malerei des 14. Jahrhunderts*, Bern.

Klotz 2010
Klotz, D., 'Triphis in the White Monastery. Reused Temple Blocks from Sohag', *Ancient Society* 40, pp. 197–213.

Koch 1993
Koch, K., *Geschichte der ägyptischen Religion von den Pyramiden bis zu den Mysterien der Isis*, Stuttgart and Berlin.

Koenen and Römer 1988
Koenen, L. and Römer, C., *Der Kölner Mani-Kodex. Über das Werden seines Leibes, Kritische Edition*, Opladen.

Kolpaktchy 1970
Kolpaktchy, G., *Das Ägyptische Totenbuch, übersetzt und kommentiert von G. Kolpaktchy*, 2nd ed., Weilheim.

Kominiko 2013
Kominko, Maja. *The World of Kosmas: Illustrated Byzantine Codices of the Christian Topography*, Cambridge.

Kraemer 1958
Kraemer, C. J., *Excavations at Nessana 3. Non-Literary Papyri*, Princeton.

Krämer 1982
Krämer, G., *Minderheit, Millet, Nation? Die Juden in Ägypten 1914–1952*, Wiesbaden.

Kraemer 1999
Kraemer, J., 'A Jewish Cult of the Saints in Fatimid Egypt', in Barrucand, M. (ed), *L'Égypte fatimide – son art et son histoire. Actes du colloque organisé à Paris les 28, 29 et 30 mai 1998*, Paris, pp. 579–601.

Kramer, Shelton and Browne 1987
Kramer, B., Shelton, J.C. and Browne, G.M., *Das Archiv des Nepheros und verwandte Texte*, Mainz.

Kratz and Nagel 2003
Kratz, R.G. and Nagel, T. (eds.), '*Abraham, unser Vater*'. *Die gemeinsamen Wurzeln von Judentum, Christentum und Islam,* Göttingen.

Krause 1971
Krause, M., 'Zur Lokalisierung and Datierung koptischer Denkmäler. Das Tafelbild des Bischofs Abraham', *Zeitschrift für Ägyptische Sprache und Altertumskunde* 97, pp. 106–11.

Krause 1985
Krause, M., 'Zum Fortwirken altägyptischer Elemente im koptischen Ägypten', *Ägypten. Dauer und Wandel,* Sonderschrift, Deutsches Archäologisches Institut Kairo 18, Mainz, pp. 115–22.

Krause 1991
Krause, M., 'Bishops, correspondence of', in *Coptic Encyclopedia* 2, New York, pp. 400a–2b.

Krause 1994
Krause, M., 'Zum Silberschatz von Luxor', *Boreas* 17, pp. 149–57.

Krause 1998
Krause, M., 'Das Mönchtum in Ägypten', in Krause, M. (ed.), *Ägypten in spätantik- christlicher Zeit. Einführung in die koptische Kultur,* Sprachen und Kulturen des christlichen Orients 4, Wiesbaden, pp. 149– 74.

Krause 2003
Krause, M., 'Das Totenwesen der Kopten', in Froschauer, Gastgeber and Harrauer 2003, pp. 33–44.

Krauss 1985
Krauss, R., *Sothis- und Monddaten: Studien zur astronomischen und technischen Chronologie Altägyptens,* Hildesheim.

Kriss and Kriss-Heinrich 1962
Kriss, R. and Kriss-Heinrich, H., *Volksglaube im Bereich des Islam* 2, *Amulette, Zauberformeln und Beschwörungen,* Wiesbaden.

Kristensen 2012
Kristensen, T.M., 'Miraculous Bodies. Christian Viewers and the Transformation of "Pagan" Sculpture in Late Antiquity', in Birk, S. and Poulsen, B., *Patrons and Viewers in Late Antiquity,* Aarhus, pp. 31–66.

Kröger 1984
Kröger, J., *Glas, Loseblattkatalog unpublizierter Werke aus Deutschen Museen* 1, Berlin, Staatliche Museen zu Berlin Preußischer Kulturbesitz, Museum für Islamische Kunst, Mainz.

Kropp 1930/1931
Kropp, A.M., *Ausgewählte koptische Zaubertexte* 1: *Textpublikation* 2: *Übersetzungen und Anmerkungen* 3: *Einleitung in die koptischen Zaubertexte,* Brussels.

Kubiak 1976
Kubiak, W., 'The Burning of Misr al-Fustat in 1168. A Reconsideration of Historical Evidence', *Africana Bulletin* 25, pp. 51–64.

Kubiak 1987
Kubiak, W.B., *Al-Fustat. Its Foundation and Early Urban Development,* Cairo.

Kühnel 1927
Kühnel, E., *Islamische Stoffe aus ägyptischen Gräbern in der Islamischen Kunstabteilung und in der Stoffsammlung des Schlossmuseums,* Berlin.

Kühnel 1939
Kühnel, E., 'Islamische Brotstempel aus Ägypten', *Berliner Museen* 60/3, pp. 50–56.

Kühnel 1942
Kühnel, E., 'Islamische Schriftkunst', *Monographien künstlerischer Schrift* 9, 2nd ed., Graz.

Kühnel and Bellinger 1952
Kühnel, E. and Bellinger, L., *Catalogue of Dated Tiraz Fabrics. Umayyad, Abbasid, Fatimid. Technical Analysis by Louisa Bellinger,* Washington D.C.

Kugel 1990
Kugel, J., *In Potiphar's House: The Interpretive Life of a Biblical Text,* San Francisco.

Kulicka 2011
Kulicka, E., 'Remarks on the Typology of Islamic Graves from the Cemeteries on Kom el-Dikka in Alexandria', *Polish Archaeology in the Mediterranean* 20, pp. 483–98.

Kurth 1990
Kurth, D., *Der Sarg der Teüris. Eine Studie zum Totenglauben im römischen Ägypten,* Aegyptiaca Treverensia 6, Mainz.

Kurth, Behrmann, Budde et al. 2004
Kurth, D., Behrmann, A., Budde, D. et al., *Edfou VII: Die Inschriften des Tempels von Edfu, Abteilung I Übersetzung, Band 2,* Wiesbaden.

Kuschel 1994
Kuschel, K.-J., *Streit um Abraham. Was Juden, Christen und Muslime trennt – und was sie eint,* Munich.

Kuschel 2007
Kuschel, K.-J., *Juden – Christen – Muslime. Herkunft und Zukunft,* Düsseldorf.

Lambert 1994
Lambert, P. (ed.), *Fortifications and the Synagogue. The Fortress of Babylon and the Ben Ezra Synagogue, Cairo,* London.

Lambert 2001
Lambert, P. (ed.), *Fortifications and the Synagogue. The Fortress of Babylon and the Ben Ezra Synagogue, Cairo,* 2nd ed., Montreal.

Lambert 2001a
Lambert, P., 'Towards an Interfaith Centre. Archaeology, Preservation and History', in Lambert 2001, pp. 19–37.

Lamm 1928
Lamm, C.J., *Das Glas von Samarra,* Forschungen zur islamischen Kunst 2; Die Ausgrabungen von Samarra 4, Berlin.

Lamm 1929/1930
Lamm, C.J., *Mittelalterliche Gläser und Steinschnittarbeiten aus dem Nahen Osten,* 2 vols, Forschungen zur islamischen Kunst 5, Berlin.

Langener 1996
Langener, L., *Isis lactans – Maria lactans. Untersuchungen zur koptischen Ikonographie,* Arbeiten zum spätantiken und koptischen Ägypten 9, Munich.

Langner 1983
Langner, B., *Untersuchungen zur historischen Volkskunde Ägyptens nach mamlukischen Quellen,* Islamkundliche Untersuchungen 74, Berlin

Lasser 2010
Lasser, J.M. 2010, 'Coptic Orthodoxy', in J.A. McGuckin (ed.), *Encyclopedia of Eastern Orthodox Christianity,* Oxford, pp. 146–59.

Lauer and Picard 1955
Lauer, J.P. and Picard, C., *Les Statues ptolémaïques du Sarapieion de Memphis,* Publications de l'Institut d'art et d'archéologie de l'Université de Paris 3, Paris.

Lavan and Mulryan 2011
Lavan, L. and Mulryan, M. (eds.), *The Archaeology of Late Antique 'Paganism',* Late Antique Archaeology 7, Leiden and Boston.

Le Coz 2006
Le Coz, R., *Les chrétiens dans la médecine arabe,* Paris.

Lefort 1954
Lefort, L.-T., 'La chasse aux reliques des martyrs en Égypte au IVè siècle', *La nouvelle Clio* 6, pp. 225–30.

Lefort 1958
Lefort, L.-T., 'L'homélie de S. Athanase des papyrus de Turin', *Le muséon* 71, pp. 5–50, 209–39.

Leibovitch 1942
Leibovitch, J., 'Stèles funéraires de Tell el- Yahoudieh', *Annales du Service des Antiquités de l'Égypte* 41, pp. 41–47.

Leipoldt 1964
Leipoldt, J., 'Ein Kloster lindert Kriegsnot. Schenutes Bericht über die Tätigkeit des Weißen Klosters bei Sohag während eines Einfalls der Kuschiten', in *. . . und fragten nach Jesus. Beiträge aus Theologie, Kirche und Geschichte. Festschrift für Ernst Barnikol zum 70. Geburtstag,* Berlin, pp. 52–56.

Lehrmann 1980
Lehrman, J., *Earthly Paradise: Garden and Courtyard in Islam,* London.

Lembke 2004
Lembke, K., 'Gräber und Mumien. Römer im Leben, Ägypter im Tod', in Lembke, K., Fluck, C. and Vittmann, G., *Ägyptens späte Blüte. Die Römer am Nil,* Mainz, pp. 51–65.

Leonhardt 2001
Leonhardt, J., *Jewish Worship in Philo of Alexandria,* Text and Studies in Ancient Judaism 84, Tübingen.

Lepper 2012
Lepper, V.M., 'Die ägyptisch-orientalische "Rubensohn-Bibliothek" von Elephantine', in Lepper, V.M. (eds.), *Forschung in der Papyrussammlung. Eine Festgabe für das Neue Museum,* Ägyptische und Orientalische Papyri und Handschriften des Ägyptischen Museums und Papyrussammlung Berlin 1, Berlin, pp. 497–507.

Lepper (forthcoming)
Lepper, V.M., 'Die aramäo-jüdische Gemeinde von Elephantine. Ein ägyptologischer Ansatz', in *Festschrift Ursula Rößler-Köhler,* Göttinger Orientforschungen, Göttingen.

Le Quesne 2001
Le Quesne, C., 'The Synagogue', in Lambert 2011a, pp. 79–97.

Le Quesne 2013
Le Quesne, C., 'Hajj Ports of the Red Sea: A Historical and Archaeological Overview', in V. Porter and L. Saif (eds.), *The Hajj: Collected Essays,* The British Museum Research Publication 193, London, pp. 74–83.

Lehrmann 1980
Lehrmann, J., *Earthly Paradise: Garden and Courtyard in Islam,* London.

Lev 1981
Lev, Y., 'The Fatimid vizier Ya'qub ibn Killis and the Beginning of the Fatimid Administration in Egypt', *Der Islam* 58, pp. 287–349.

Levine 2005
Levine, L.I., *The Ancient Synagogue. The First Thousand Years,* 2nd ed., New Haven and London.

Lieu 1992
Lieu, S.N.C., *Manichaeism in the Later Roman Empire and Medieval China,* Tübingen.

Lieu et al. 2012
Lieu, S.N.C., Eccles, L., Franzmann, M., Gardner I. and Parry, K., 'Medieval Christian and Manichaean Remains from Quanzhou (Zayton)', *CFM, Series Archaeologica et Iconographica,* 2, Turnhout. See also: http://mq.edu.au/research/centres_and_ groups/ancient_cultures_research_centre/ research/cultural_ex_silkroad/zayton/

Lieu, Eccles, Franzmann et al. 2012
Lieu, S.N.C., Eccles, L., Franzmann, M., Gardner, I. and Parry, K., *Medieval Christian and Manichaean Remains from Quanzhou (Zayton),* Corpus fontium Manichaeorum, Series archaeologica et iconographica 2, Turnhout.

Lintz and Coudert 2013
Lintz, Y. and Coudert, M. (eds.), *Antinoé. Momies, textiles, céramiques et autres antiques,* Paris.

Loebenstein 1982
Loebenstein, H., *Koranfragmente auf Pergament aus der Papyrussammlung der Österreichischen Nationalbibliothek.* Mitteilungen aus der Papyrussammlung der Österreichischen Nationalbibliothek (Papyrus Erzherzog Rainer), Neue Serie, XIV, Folge, Vienna.

Löfgren 1972
Löfgren, O., 'Der Spiegel Salomons. Ein äthiopischer Zaubertext', in Bergman, J. (ed.), *Ex orbe religionum. Studia Geo Widengren XXIV mense apr. MCMLXXII quo die lustra tredecim feliciter explevit oblata ab collegis, discipulis, amicis, collegae magistro amico congratulantibus,* Studies in the History of Religions 21–22, vol. 1, pp. 208–23.

Löhr 1996
Löhr, W.A., *Basilides und seine Schule. Eine Studie zur Theologie- und Kirchengeschichte des zweiten Jahrhunderts,* Wissenschaftliche Untersuchungen zum Neuen Testament 83, Tübingen.

Löw 1934
Löw, I., *Flora der Juden,* Vienna.

López 2013
López, A.G., *Shenoute of Atripe and the Uses of Poverty. Rural Patronage, Religious Conflict, and Monasticism in Late Antique Egypt,* Berkeley.

Lother 1929
Lother, H., *Der Pfau in der altchristlichen Kunst. Eine Studie über das Verhältnis von Ornament und Symbol,* Leipzig.

Lubomierski 2008
Lubomierski, N., 'The Coptic Life of Shenoute', in Gabra, G. and Takla, H.N. (eds.), *Christianity and Monasticism in Upper Egypt* 1, Cairo, pp. 91–8.

Lucchesi Palli 1978
Lucchesi Palli, E., 'Observations sur l'iconographie de l'aigle funéraire copte et nubien', in *Actes du Colloque d'Études Nubiennes, Chantilly, 2–6 juillet 1975,* Publications de l'Institut Français d'Archéologie Orientale 526, Cairo, pp. 175–91.

Lucchesi Palli 1995
Lucchesi Palli, E., 'Der Adlerfries der ersten Kathedrale von Faras: Liegen ihm koptische Quellen zugrunde?', *Biblos* 44, Vienna, pp. 33–38.

Lüddeckens, Thissen and Brunsch 1979–2000
Lüddeckens, E., Thissen, H.-J., Brunsch, W., *Demotisches Namenbuch*, Wiesbaden.

Lüdemann 1987
Lüdemann, G., *Das frühe Christentum nach den Traditionen der Apostelgeschichte*, Göttingen.

Luft and Poethke 1991
Luft, U. and Poethke, G., *Leben im ägyptischen Altertum. Literatur, Urkunden, Briefe aus vier Jahrtausenden*, Berlin.

Lührmann 2000
Lührmann, D. (ed.) *Fragmente apokryph gewordener Evangelien in griechischer und lateinischer Sprache*, Marburger Theologische Studien 59, Marburg.

Luijendijk 2008
Luijendijk, A.M. *Greetings in the Lord: Early Christians and the Oxyrhynchus Papyri*. Cambridge, MA.

Luijendijk 2014
Luijendijk, A.M., *Forbidden Oracles? The Gospel of the Lots of Mary*, Tübingen.

Lutfi 1998
Lutfi, H., 'Coptic Festivals of the Nile. Aberrations of the Past?', in Philipp, T. and Haarmann, U. (eds.), *The Mamluks in Egyptian Politics and Society*, Cambridge, pp. 254–82.

Luttikhuizen 2010
Luttikhuizen, G.P., 'Gnostische Erklärungen der Genesiserzählung', in Tubach, J., Drost-Abgarjan, A. and Vashalomidze, S. (eds.), *Sehnsucht nach dem Paradies*, Wiesbaden, pp. 71–81.

Luxenberg 2000
Luxenberg, C., *Die Syro-aramäische Lesart des Korans*, 2000.

Luz 2002
Luz, U., *Das Evangelium nach Matthäus. I. Mt 1–7*, Evangelisch-Katholischer Kommentar zum Neuen Testament, 1.1, 5th ed., Düsseldorf and Zürich.

Lyzwa-Piber 2011
Lyzwa-Piber, A., 'Mats and Baskets from Cemetery A at Naqlun in Fayyum Oasis', *Polish Archaeology in the Mediterranean* 20, pp. 509–23.

Majcherek 2007
Majcherek, G., 'The Late Roman Auditoria of Alexandria. An Archaeological Overview', in Derda, Majcherek and Wipszycka 2007, pp. 11–50.

Mango 1963
Mango, C., 'Antique Statuary and the Byzantine Beholder', *Dumbarton Oaks Papers* 17, pp. 53–75.

Ma'oz 1995
Ma'oz, Z.U., 'The Judean Synagogues as a Reflection of Alexandrine Architecture', in *Alessandria e il mondo ellenistico-romano, Atti del II Congresso Internazionale Italo-Egiziano*, Rome, pp. 192–201.

Markschies 1991
Markschies, C., 'Gnosis/Gnostizismus', in Görg, M. and Lang, B. (eds.), *Neues Bibel-Lexikon*, Düsseldorf and Zürich, pp. 868–71.

Markschies 1992
Markschies, C., *Valentinus Gnosticus? Untersuchungen zur valentinianischen Gnosis mit einem Kommentar zu den Fragmenten Valentins*, Wissenschaftliche Untersuchungen zum Neuen Testament 65, Tübingen.

Markschies 2012
Markschies, C., 'Das Evangelium nach den Ägyptern', in Markschies, Schröter and Heiser 2012, pp. 661–82.

Markschies, Schröter and Heiser 2012
Markschies, C., Schröter, J. and Heiser, A. (eds.), *Antike christliche Apokryphen in deutscher Übersetzung*, 7th edition der von E. Hennecke begründeten und von W. Schneemelcher fortgeführten Sammlung der neutestamentlichen Apokryphen 1 Evangelien und Verwandtes, Teilband 1 und 2, Tübingen.

Marzinzik 2013
Marzinzik, S., *Masterpieces: Early Medieval Art*, London.

Massignon 1958
Massignon, L., *La cité des morts au Caire (Qarâfa – Darb al-Ahmar)*, Cairo.

Mathews 2005
Mathews, T.F., 'Isis and Mary in Early Icons', in Vassilaki, M. (ed.) *Images of the Mother of God. Perceptions of the Theotokos in Byzantium*, Aldershot, pp. 3–11.

Mathews 2006
Mathews, T.F., 'Early Icons of the Holy Monastery of Saint Catherine at Sinai', in Nelson, R. and Collins, K.M. (eds.), *Holy Image – Hallowed Ground. Icons from Sinai. The Paul Getty Museum, Los Angeles, November 14, 2006 – March 4, 2007*, Los Angeles, pp. 39–55.

Mayer 2013
Mayer, W., 'Religious Conflict. Definitions, Problems and Theoretical Approaches', in W. Mayer and B. Neil (eds.), *Religious Conflict from Early Christianity to the Rise of Islam*, Berlin, pp. 1–20.

MacCoull 1988
MacCoull, L.S.B., *Dioscorus of Aphrodito: His Work and his World*, Berkeley.

Macdonald and Madelung 1991
Macdonald, D.B. and Madelung, W., 'Mala'ika.', in *The Encyclopaedia of Islam* 6, new ed., Leiden, pp. 216–19.

McGing 1990
McGing, B.C.M., 'Melitian Monks at Labla', *Tyche* 5, pp. 67–94.

McGuckin 1994
McGuckin, J.A., *St. Cyril of Alexandria. The Christological Controversy. Its History, Theology, and Texts*, Leiden, New York and Cologne.

McKendrick, Parker and O'Hogen 2015
McKendrick, S., Parker, S.D., and O'Hogen, C., eds, *Codex Sinaiticus: New Perspectives on the Ancient Biblical Manuscript*, London.

McKenzie 2007
McKenzie, J., *The Architecture of Alexandria and Egypt c.300 BC to AD 700*, New Haven.

McKenzie, Gibson and Reyes 2004
McKenzie, J., Gibson, S. and Reyes, A.T., 'Reconstructing the Serapeum in Alexandria from the Archaeological Evidence', *Journal of Roman Studies* 94, pp. 73–121.

McMullen 1966

McMullen, R., 'Provincial Languages in the Roman Empire', *The American Journal of Philology* 87, pp. 1–17.

Meischner 2001
Meischner, J., *Bildnisse der Spätantike 193–500. Problemfelder: die Privatpoträts*, Berlin.

Merkelbach 1995
Merkelbach, R., *Isis regina – Zeus Serapis. Die griechisch-ägyptische Religion nach den Quellen dargestellt*, Stuttgart and Leipzig.

Merkelbach 2001
Merkelbach, R., *Isis Regina – Zeus Serapis. Die griechisch-ägyptische Religion nach den Quellen dargestellt*, 2nd ed., Munich and Leipzig.

Meyer 2007
Meyer, M. (ed.) *The Nag Hammadi Scriptures*, New York.

Meyers 1996
Meyers, E., 'Ancient Synagogues. An Archaeological Introduction', in Cat. New York 1996, pp. 3–20.

Meyer and Smith 1994
Meyer, M. and Smith, R., *Ancient Christian Magic. Coptic Texts of Ritual Power*, San Francisco.

Meyer and Mirecki 1995
Meyer, M. and Mirecki, P., *Ancient Magic and Ritual Power*, Leiden.

Michl 1962
Michl, J., 'Engel VI (Gabriel)', *Reallexikon für Antike und Christentum* 5, pp. 239–43.

Miles 1957
Miles, G., 'Early Islamic Tombstones from Egypt in the Museum of Fine Arts, Boston', *Ars Orientalis* 11, pp. 151–57.

Moaz and Ory 1977
Moaz, K. and Ory, S., *Inscriptions arabes de Damas: Les stèles funéraires I. Cimetière d'al-Bab al-Sagir*, Damascus.

Modrzejewski 1995
Modrzejewski, J.M., *The Jews of Egypt. From Rameses II to Emperor Hadrian*, Edinburgh.

Mokbel 1966
Mokbel, A., 'La Règle de Saint Antoine le Grand', *Malto* 2, pp. 207–27.

Moldenke 1952
Moldenke, H., *Plants of the Bible*, New York.

Möller 1913
Möller, G., *Demotische Texte aus den königlichen Museen zu Berlin, 1: Mumienschilder*, Leipzig.

Möller 1919
Möller, G., 'Das Mumienporträt', *Wasmuths Kunsthefte* 1, Berlin.

Mond and Myers 1934
Mond, R. and Myers, O.H., *The Bucheum*, Egypt Explorararion Society Memoirs 41, 3 vols, London.

Monneret de Villard 1924
Monneret de Villard, U., 'Ricerche sulla Topografia di Qasr esh-Sham', *Bulletin de la Société de Géographie d'Égypte* 12, pp. 205–32 and 13, pp. 73–94.

Montserrat 1998
Montserrat, D., 'Pilgrimage to the Shrine of SS Cyrus and John at Menouthis in Late Antiquity', in Frankfurter 1998a, pp. 257–79.

Morelli 1998
Morelli, F., 'Legname, palazzo e moschee. P. Vindob. G 31 e il contributo dell'Egitto alla prima architettura islamica', *Tyche* 13,

pp. 165–90.

Morelli 2001
Morelli, F., *Documenti greci per la fiscalità e la amministrazione dell'Egitto arabo*, Corpus Papyrorum Raineri. Griechische Texte XV, Vienna.

Morenz 1951
Morenz, S., *Die Geschichte von Joseph dem Zimmermann*, Berlin.

Morenz 1975
Morenz, S., 'Altägyptischer und hellenistisch-paulinischer Jenseitsglaube bei Schenute' in Morenz, S., *Religion und Geschichte des Alten Ägypten. Gesammelte Aufsätze*, Weimar, pp. 590–95.

Mortley and Colpe 1981
Mortley, R. and Colpe, C., 'Gnosis I (Erkenntnislehre)', *Reallexikon für Antike und Christentum* 11, pp. 446–537.

Mühling 2011
Mühling, A., *'Blickt auf Abraham, euren Vater': Abraham als Identifikationsfigur des Judentums in der Zeit des Exils und des Zweiten Tempels*, Göttingen.

Müller 1954
Müller, C.D.G., 'Die alte koptische Predigt. Versuch eines Überblicks' (dissertation), Darmstadt.

Müller 1959
Müller, C.D.G., *Die Engellehre der koptischen Kirche. Untersuchungen zur Geschichte der christlichen Frömmigkeit in Ägypten*, Wiesbaden.

Müller 1962
Müller, C.D.G., *Die Bücher der Einsetzung der Erzengel Michael und Gabriel*, CSCO 225–26, Scriptores coptici 31–32, Leuven.

Müller 1969
Müller, C.D.G., *Grundzüge des christlich-islamischen Ägypten*, Grundzüge 11, Darmstadt.

Müller 1998
Müller, H.P., 'Eine Parallele zur Weingartenmetapher des Hohenliedes aus der frühgriechischen Lyrik', in Dietrich, M. und Kottsieper, I. (ed.), *'Und Mose schrieb dieses Lied auf'. Studien zum Alten Testament und zum Alten Orient. Festschrift Oswald Loretz zur Vollendung seines 70. Lebensjahres*, Münster, pp. 569–84.

Murray 1926
Murray, G.W., 'Aidhab', *The Geographical Journal* 68, pp. 235–40.

Museum für Islamische Kunst 1971 and 1979
Museum für Islamische Kunst Berlin, catalogue, expanded edition 1979, Berlin-Dahlem.

Nagel 1966
Nagel, P., *Die Motivierung der Askese in der Alten Kirche und der Ursprung des Mönchtums*, Texte and Untersuchen 95, Berlin.

Naser-e-Khosrou 1993
Safarname. Ein Reisebericht aus dem Orient des 11. Jahrhunderts. Herausgegeben, bearbeitet und aus dem Persischen übersetzt von S. Najmabadi und S. Weber, Munich.

Nauerth 1978
Nauerth, C., 'Die Josefsgeschichte auf koptischen Stoffen', *Enchoria* 8, p. 107.

Nautin 1967
Nautin, P., 'La conversion du temple de Philae en église chrétienne', *Cahiers archéologiques* 17, pp. 1–43.

Naville 1890
Naville, E., *Mound of the Jew and the City of Onias*, London.

Neumann and Untermann 1980
Neumann, G. and Untermann, J., *Die Sprachen im römischen Reich der Kaiserzeit*, Cologne.

Niehaus and Peters 2009
Niehaus, M. and Peters, W. (eds.), *Mythos Abraham. Texte von der Genesis bis Franz Kafka*, Stuttgart.

Nielsen 2014
Nielsen, I., *Housing the Chosen. The Architectural Context of Mystery Groups and Religious Associations in the Ancient World*, Turnhout.

Niewöhner-Eberhard 2006
Niewöhner-Eberhard, E., 'Die Tiraz-Inschrift aus dem Lüneburger Schatz der Goldenen Tafel', in Fluck, C. and Helmecke, G. (eds.), *Textile Messages. Inscribed Fabrics from Roman to Abbasid Egypt*, Studies in Textile and Costume History 4, Leiden and Boston, pp. 193–219.

Nirenberg 2013
Nirenberg, D., *Anti-Judaism. The Western Tradition*, New York.

O'Connell 2007
O'Connell, E.R., 'Transforming Monumental Landscapes in Late Antique Egypt', *Journal of Early Christian Studies* 15, pp. 239–74.

O'Connell 2010
O'Connell, E.R., 'Excavating Late Antique Western Thebes. A History', in Gabra, G. and Takla, H. N. (eds.), *Christianity and Monasticism in Upper Egypt 2: Nag Hammadi-Esna*, Cairo, pp. 253–70.

O'Connell 2014
O'Connell, E.R., 'Settlements and Cemeteries in Late Antique Egypt. An Introduction', in O'Connell 2014b, pp. 1–19.

O'Connell 2014a
O'Connell, E.R., 'R. Campbell Thompson's 1913/14 Excavation of Wadi Sarga and Other Sites', *British Museum Studies in Ancient Egypt and Sudan* 21, pp. 121–92.

O'Connell 2014b
O'Connell, E.R. (ed.), *Egypt in the First Millennium AD: Perspectives from New Fieldwork*, British Museum Publications on Egypt and Sudan 2, Leuven.

O'Connell 2014c
O'Connell, E.R. (ed), 'Catalogue of British Museum Objects from The Egypt Exploration Fund's 1913/14 Excavation at Antinoupolis (Antinoë) with Contributions by A.J. Dowler, F. Pritchard, St J. Simpson, R.I. Thomas and A.J. Veldmeijer', in Pintaudi, R. (eds.), *Antinoupolis II: Scavi e materiali* III, Florence, pp. 467–504.

O'Kane 2006
O'Kane, Bernard, *The Treasures of Islamic Art in the Museums of Cairo*, Cairo and New York, pp. 138–41, no. 125.

Opper 2014
Opper, T., *The Meroë Head of Augustus*, London.

Orlandi 1981
Orlandi, T., 'Omelie copte. Scelte e tradotte, con una introduzione sulla letteratura copta', *Corona Patrum* 7, Turin.

Orlandi 2008
Orlandi, T., *Coptic Texts Relating to the Virgin Mary. An Overview*, Rome.

Osterhammel and Petersson 2003
Osterhammel, J. and Petersson, N.P., *Geschichte der Globalisierung. Dimensionen Prozesse Epochen*, Munich.

Palanque 1906
Palanque, C., 'Rapport sur les recherches effectuées à Baouit en 1903', *Bulletin de l'Institut Français d'Archéologie Orientale* 5, pp. 1–21.

Palme 2007
Palme, B., 'The Imperial Presence. Government and Army', in Bagnall, R.S., *Egypt in the Byzantine World, 300–700*, Cambridge, pp. 244–71.

Panaino 1983
Panaino, A., 'Uranographia Iranica I. The Three Havens in the Zoroastrian Tradition and the Mesopotamian Background' in Gyselen, R. (ed.), *Au carrefour des religions. Mélanges offerts à Philippe Gignoux*, Bures-sur-Yvette, pp. 5–21.

Papaconstantinou 2001
Papaconstantinou, A., *Le culte des saints en Égypte des Byzantins aux Abbassides. L'apport des inscriptions et des papyrus grecs et coptes*, Paris.

Papaconstantinou 2007
Papaconstantinou, A., '"They Shall Speak the Arabic Language and Take Pride In It". Reconsidering the Fate of Coptic after the Arab Conquest', *Le Muséon* 120, pp. 273–99.

Papaconstantinou 2008
Papaconstantinou, A., 'Dioscore et le bilinguisme dans l'Égypte du VIe siècle', in J.-L. Fournet (ed.), *Les archives de Dioscore d'Aphroditè cent ans après leur découverte. Histoire et culture dans l'Égypte byzantine*, Paris, pp. 77–88.

Papaconstantinou 2009
Papaconstantinou, A., '"What Remains Behind". Hellenism and *Romanitas* in Christian Egypt after the Arab Conquest", in Cotton, H., Hoyland, R., Price, J. et al. (eds.), *From Hellenism to Islam: Cultural and Linguistic Change in the Roman Near East*, Cambridge, pp. 455–57.

Papaconstantinou 2010
Papaconstantinou, A. (ed.), *The Multilingual Experience. Egypt from the Ptolemies to the 'Abbasids*, Farnham.

Papaconstantinou 2013
Papaconstantinou, A., 'L'enseignement en Égypte à la fin de l'Antiquité', in Vallet, É., Aube, S. and Kouamé, T. (eds.), *Lumières de la sagesse. Écoles médiévales d'Orient et d'Occident*, exhibition catalogue, Paris, pp. 30–31.

Paret 1971
Paret, R., 'Ibrahim', in *Encylopaedia of Islam* 3, new ed., Leiden and London.

Parker 1950
Parker, R.A., *The Calendars of Ancient Egypt*, Chicago.

Parlasca 1966
Parlasca, K., *Mumienporträts und verwandte Denkmäler*, Mainz.

Parlasca 1969
Parlasca, K., *Repertorio d'Arte dell'Egitto Greco-Romano*, Serie B, Volume I, Tavole 1-60-Numeri 1-246, Palermo.

Parsons 2007
Parsons, P.J., *City of the Sharp-nosed Fish: Greek Lives in Roman Egypt*, London.

Peacock 2008
Peacock, D., 'The Enigma of 'Aydhab. A Medieval Islamic Port on the Red Sea Coast', *International Journal of Nautical Archaeology* 37.1, pp. 32–48.

Pearson 2006
Pearson, B., 'Egypt', in Mitchell, M.M. and Young, F.M. (eds.), *The Cambridge History of Christianity* I. *Origins to Constantine*, Cambridge, pp. 331–50.

Pedersen 1965
Pedersen, J., 'Djabra'il', in *Encyclopaedia of Islam* 2, new ed., Leiden and London, pp. 362–64.

Pedersen 1993
Pedersen, J., 'Minbar 1', in *Encyclopaedia of Islam* 7, Leiden and New York.

Pedersen and Golmohammad 1993
Pedersen, J. and Golmohammad, J., 'Minbar 1 and 2', in *Encyclopaedia of Islam* 7, Leiden and New York.

Peltomaa 2004
Peltomaa, L.M., 'Die berühmteste Marien-Predigt der Spätantike. Zur chronologischen und mariologischen Einordnung der Predigt des Proklos. Mit einem Anhang von J. Koder. Übersetzung der Predigt', in *Jahrbuch der Österreichischen Byzantinistik* 54, pp. 77–96.

Perles 1905
Perles, F., 'Synagogue', in *Jewish Encyclopedia* 11, New York and London, pp. 619–28.

Pernigotti 1995
Pernigotti, S., 'La magia copta. I testi', in *Aufstieg und Niedergang der Römischen Welt*, II.18.5, Berlin and New York, pp. 3685–730.

Pernigotti 2000
Pernigotti, S., *Testi della magia copta*, Imola (Bo).

Peters 1994
Peters, F.E., *The Hajj. The Muslim Pilgrimage to Mecca and the Holy Places*, Princeton.

Petrie 1889
Petrie, W.M.F., *Hawara, Biahmu and Arsinoe*, London.

Petrie 1906
Petrie, W.M.F., *Hyksos and Israelite Cities*, London.

Petrie 1911
Petrie, W.M.F., *Roman Portraits and Memphis (IV)*, British School of Archaeology in Egypt and Egyptian Research Account 20, London.

Philipp 1972
Philipp, H., *Terrakotten aus Ägypten*, Bilderheft der Staatlichen Museen Preußischer Kulturbesitz – Berlin 18/19, Berlin.

Philipp 1985
Philipp, T., *The Syrians in Egypt, 1725–1975*, Stuttgart.

Philipp 1986
Philipp, H., *Mira et Magica. Gemmen im Ägyptischen Museum der Staatlichen Museen Preußischer Kulturbesitz Berlin-Charlottenburg*, Mainz am Rhein.

Piccirillo 2010
Piccirillo, M., 'Mosaics', in Collins, J.J. and Harlow, D.C. (eds.), *The Eerdmans Dictionary of Early Judaism*, Grand Rapids and Cambridge, pp. 965–67.

Pink 2007
Pink, J., 'Der Mufti, der Scheich und der Religionsminister. Ägyptische Religionspolitik zwischen Verstaatlichung, Toleranzrhetorik und Repression', in Faath, S. (ed.), *Staatliche Religionspolitik in Nordafrika/Nahost. Ein Instrument für modernisierende Reformen?*, Hamburg, pp. 27–56.

Popović and Zangenberg 2013
Popović, M. and Zangenberg, J.K., 'Dagelijks leven in Judea en de materiële cultuur van Qumran in regionale context', in Popovic, M., *De Dode Zee rollen. Nieuw licht op de schatten van Qumran*, Amsterdam, pp. 72–93.

Popper 1951
Popper, W., *The Cairo Nilometer. Studies in Ibn Taghri Biri's Chronicles of Egypt*, University of California Publications in Semitic Philology 12, Berkeley and Los Angeles.

Pormann and Savage-Smith 2007
Pormann, P.E. and Savage-Smith, E., *Medieval Islamic Medicine*, Cairo.

Porten 1969
Porten, B., *Archives from Elephantine. The Life of an Ancient Jewish Military Community*, Berkeley.

Porten and Yardeni 1999
Porten, B. and Yardeni, A., *Textbook of Aramaic Documents from Ancient Egypt*, 4th ed., Jerusalem.

Porter 2012
Porter, V., 'Textiles of Mecca and Medina', in Porter, V. (ed.), *Hajj: Journey to the Heart of Islam*, London, pp. 256–65.

Power and Sheehan
Power, T.C. and Sheehan, P.D., 'Babylon–Fustat': http://www.encyclopediaanciethistory.com. (Last accessed 6 September 2015.)

Price 2008
Price, R.M., 'The Theotokos and the Council of Ephesus', in Maunder, C. (ed.), *Origins of the Cult of the Virgin*, London, pp. 89–103.

Priese 1991
Priese, K.-H. (ed.), *Ägyptisches Museum Berlin, Museumsinsel Berlin*, Berlin.

Pritchard 2006
Pritchard, F., *Clothing Culture. Dress in Egypt in the First Millenium AD. Clothing from Egypt in the Collection of the Whitworth Art Gallery*, Manchester.

Pritchard 2013
Pritchard, F., 'A Survey of Textiles in the UK from the 1913–14 Egypt Exploration Fund Season at Antinoupolis', in De Moor, Fluck and Linscheid 2013, pp. 34–55.

Pucci Ben Zeev 2005
Pucci Ben Zeev, M., *Diaspora Judaism in Turmoil, 116/117 CE: Ancient Sources and Modern Insights*, Leuven and Dudley.

Quibell 1909
Quibell, J.E., *Excavations of Saqqara (1907–1908)*, Cairo.

Quibell 1912
Quibell, J.E., *Excavations at Saqqara (1908–9, 1909–10): The Monastery of Apa Jeremias*, Cairo.

Radtke 2002
Radtke, B., 'Wali', in *Encyclopaedia of Islam* 11, new ed., Leiden, pp. 109–12.

Ragheb 2013
Ragheb, Y., 'Les premiers documents arabes de l'ère musulmane', in Zuckerman, C., *Constructing the Seventh Century*, Paris, pp. 679–726.

Ragib 1976
Ragib, Y., 'Al-Sayyida Nafisa, sa légende, son culte et son cimetière', *Studia Islamica* 44, pp. 61–86.
Ragib 1977
Ragib, Y., 'Al-Sayyida Nafisa, sa légende, son culte et son cimetière (Suite et fin)', *Studia Islamica* 45, pp. 27–55.
Raphael 2009
Raphael, R.P., *Jewish Views of the Afterlife*, 2nd ed., Lanham.
Rapoport and Savage-Smith 2014
Rapoport, Y. and E. Savage-Smith, *An Eleventh-century Egyptian Guide to the Universe. The Book of Curiosities*, Leiden.
Raspe 1996
Raspe, M., 'Josef. In der Kunst', in *Lexikon für Theologie und Kirche* 5, 3rd ed., Freiburg et al, col. 998–99.
Rathbone 1991
Rathbone, D., *Economic Rationalism and Rural Society in Third-Century A.D. Egypt. The Heroninos Archive and the Appianus Estate*, 1991.
RCEA 2 1932 and RCEA 8 1937
Combe, É., Sauvaget, J. and Wiet, G. (eds.), *Répertoire chronologique d'épigraphie arabe*, Cairo.
Rebiger 2003
Rebiger, B., 'Die magische Verwendung von Psalmen im Judentum', in Zenger, E. (ed.), *Ritual und Poesie. Formen und Orte religiöser Dichtung im Alten Orient, im Judentum und im Christentum*, Herders Biblische Studien 36, Freiburg i. Br., pp. 265–81.
Rebiger 2007
Rebiger, B., 'Angels in Rabbinic Literature', in F.V. Reiterer, T. Nicklas and K. Schöpflin (eds.), *Angels. The Concept of Celestial Beings, Origins, Development and Reception*. Deuterocanonical and Cognate Literature Yearbook 2007, Berlin, pp. 629–44.
Rebiger 2010
Rebiger, B., *Sefer Shimmush Tehillim. Buch vom magischen Gebrauch der Psalmen, Edition, Übersetzung und Kommentar*, Texte und Studien zum antiken Judentum 137, Tübingen.
Rebiger, Schäfer et al. 2009
Rebiger, B., Schäfer, P., et al., *Sefer ha-Razim I und II. Das Buch der Geheimnisse I und II* 1 and 2, Texte und Studien zum antiken Judentum 125 and 132, Tübingen.
Reif 2000
Reif, S.C., *A Jewish Archive from Old Cairo*, Richmond.
Reif 2013
Reif, S., 'The Jewish Heritage of Old Cairo', in Ludwig, C. and Jackson, M. (eds.), *The History and Religious Heritage of Old Cairo. Its Fortress, Churches, Synagogue, and Mosque*, Cairo and New York, pp. 36–71.
Reimbold 1983
Reimbold, E.T., *Der Pfau. Mythologie und Symbolik*, Munich.
Richter, S.G. 1997
Richter, S.G., *Die Aufstiegspsalmen des Herakleides. Untersuchungen zum Seelenaufstieg und zur Seelenmesse bei den Manichäern*, Sprachen und Kulturen des christlichen Orients 1, Wiesbaden.

Richter, S.G. 1998
Richter, S.G., *Die Herakleides-Psalmen*, Corpus fontium Manichaeorum. Series Coptica 1. Liber Psalmorum 2 fasc. 2, Turnhout.
Richter, S.G. 2004
Richter, S.G., 'Vom mönchischen Leben. Entwicklungslinien des Mönchtums in Ägypten', in Boochs, W. (ed.) *Geschichte und Geist der koptischen Kirche,* Langwaden, pp. 131–49.
Richter, S.G. 2008
Richter, S.G., 'Manichaeism and gnosticism in the Panopolitan region between Lykopolis and Nag Hammadi', in Gabra, G. and Takla, H.N. (eds.), *Christianity and Monasticism in Upper Egypt* 1. *Akhmim and Sohag*, Cairo, pp. 121–30.
Richter, S.G. 2010
Richter, S.G., 'The Desert Fathers', in P. Whitfield, N. Tomoum and S. Marei (eds.), *Coptic Art Revealed*, Cairo, pp. 90–105.
Richter, S.G. 2012
Richter, S.G., 'Gnosis und Manichäismus in Ägypten – eine kleine Einführung': http://faszinierendes-aegypten.de/gnoundman_01.php
Richter, T.S. 2002
Richter, T.S., 'Miscellanea Magica, I. Das Rebus//š/ im altkoptischen Papyrus Schmidt II. Was warf Horus auf dem Berg aus? Zum koptischen Homonym oyelle "Lied"/"Fangseil"' in Papyrus Berlin P 8313, *Journal of Egyptian Archaeology* 88, pp. 247–52.
Richter, T.S. 2005
Richter, T.S., 'Quellen aus römischer, byzantinischer und arabischer Zeit' in Fischer-Elfert, H.-W. (ed.), *Altägyptische Magie*, Stuttgart, pp. 115–29, 166–76.
Richter, T.S. 2009
Richter, T.S., 'Greek, Coptic, and the "Language of the *Hijra*". The Rise and Decline of the Coptic Language in Late Antique and Medieval Egypt', in Cotton, H., Hoyland, R., Price, J. et al. (eds.), *From Hellenism to Islam. Cultural and Linguistic Change in the Roman Near East*, Cambridge, pp. 403–14.
Richter, T.S. 2010
Richter, T.S., 'Language Choice in the Qurra Papyri', in Papaconstantinou, A. (ed.), *The Multilingual Experience. Egypt from the Ptolemies to the 'Abbâsids*, Paris and Oxford, pp. 189–219.
Riederer 1978
Riederer, J., 'Die naturwissenschaftliche Untersuchung der Bronzen des Ägyptischen Museums Stiftung Preussischer Kulturbesitz Berlin', in *Berliner Beiträge zur Archäometrie*, 3, pp. 5–42.
Rigsby 1996
Rigsby, K.J., *Asylia. Territorial Inviolability in the Hellenistic World*, Hellenistic Culture and Society 22, Berkeley.
Rigsby 2003
Rigsby, K.J., 'A Jewish Asylum in Greco-Roman Egypt', in Dreher, M. (ed.) *Das antike Asyl. Kultische Grundlagen, rechtliche Ausgestaltung und politische Funktion*, Cologne, Weimar and Vienna, pp. 127–42.
Ritner 1993
Ritner, R.K., *The Mechanics of Ancient Egyptian Magical Practice*, Studies in Ancient Oriental Civilization 54, Chicago.

Ritner 1995
Ritner, R.K., 'Egyptian Magical Practice under the Roman Empire. The Demotic Spells and Their Religious Context', in *Aufstieg und Niedergang der Römischen Welt* II.18.5, Berlin and New York, pp. 3333–79.
Roberts 1979
Roberts, C.H., *Manuscript, Society and Belief in Early Christian Egypt*, London and New York.
Robinson 2005
Robinson, C.F., *'Abd al-Malik*, Oxford.
Rochette 1994
Rochette, B., 'Traducteurs et traductions dans l'Égypte gréco-romaine', *Chronique d'Égypte*, 69, pp. 313–22.
Rodziewicz 1984
Rodziewicz, M., *Alexandrie III: Les habitations romaines tardives d'Alexandrie*, Warsaw.
Roeder 1956
Roeder, G., *Ägyptische Bronzefiguren*, Mitteilungen aus der Ägyptischen Sammlung 6, Berlin.
Rössler-Köhler 1980
Rössler-Köhler, U., 'Jenseitsvorstellungen', in *Lexikon der Ägyptologie* 3, pp. 252–67.
Rondot 2013
Rondot, V., *Derniers visages des dieux d'Égypte: Iconographies, panthéons et cultes dans le Fayoum hellénisé des IIe-IIIe siècles de notre ère*, Paris.
Rosenthal-Heginbottom 2009
Rosenthal-Heginbottom, R., 'The Curtain (*Parochet*) in Jewish and Samaritan Synagogues', in De Moor, A. and Fluck, C. (eds.), *Clothing the House. Furnishing Textiles of the 1st millennium AD from Egypt and Neighbouring Countries*, Tielt, pp. 155–69.
Rousseau 1999
Rousseau, P., *Pachomius, the Making of a Community in Fourth-century Egypt*, Berkeley, Los Angeles and London.
Rubenson 1990
Rubenson, S., *The Letters of St. Antony. Origenist Theology, Monastic Tradition and the Making of a Saint*, Lund.
Rudolph 1990
Rudolph, K., *Die Gnosis. Wesen und Geschichte einer spätantiken Religion*, 3rd ed., Göttingen.
Ruffing 2008
Ruffing, K., *Die berufliche Spezialisierung in Handel und Handwerk. Untersuchungen zu ihrer Entwicklung und zu ihren Bedingungen in der römischen Kaiserzeit im östlichen Mittelmeerraum auf der Grundlage griechischer Inschriften und Papyri*, Rahden.
Russell 1981
Russell, N., *The Lives of the Desert Fathers*, Cistercian Publications 34, Kalamazoo.
Rutschowscaya 2012a
Rutschowscaya, M.-H., 'Les tissus d'ameublement', in *L'Orient romain et byzantin au Louvre*, Paris, pp. 112–217.
Rutschowscaya 2012b
Rutschowscaya, M.-H., 'Les vêtements', in *L'Orient romain et byzantin au Louvre*, Paris, pp. 118–25.
Sachau and Schwally 1905–1940
Sachau, E. and Schwally, F. (eds.), *Ibn Saad*, 9 vols in 14 books, Leiden.
Sanders 1994
Sanders, P., *Ritual, Politics and the City in Fatimid Cairo*, Albany.

Saradi-Mendelovici 1990
Saradi-Mendelovici, H., 'Christian Attitudes Towards Pagan Monuments in Late Antiquity and Their Legacy in Later Byzantine Centuries', *Dumbarton Oaks Papers* 44, Washington, pp. 4–61.
Sauer 2003
Sauer, E., *The Archaeology of Religious Hatred in the Roman and Early Medieval World*, Stroud.
Savage-Smith 2004
Savage-Smith, E. (ed.), *Magic and Divination in Early Islam*, The Formation of the Classical Islamic World 42, Aldershot.
el-Sayed 2010
el-Sayed, R., 'Schenute und die Tempel von Atripe. Zur Umnutzung des Triphisbezirks in der Spätantike', in Knuf, H., Leitz, C. and von Recklinghausen, D. (eds.), *Honi soit qui mal y pense. Studien zum pharaonischen, griechisch-römischen und spätantiken Ägypten zu Ehren von Heinz-Josef Thissen*, Leuven, pp. 519–38.
Scanlon 1972
Scanlon, G.T., 'Fustat. Archaeological Reconsiderations', in *Proceedings of the International Colloquium on the History of Fustat, Kairo* 7, pp. 415–28.
Scanlon 1986
Scanlon, G.T., 'Catalogue of Filters', *Fustat Expedition Final Reports* 1, Cairo.
Schäfer 1910
Schäfer, H., *Ägyptische Goldschmiedearbeiten*, Königliche Museen zu Berlin, Mitteilungen aus der Ägyptischen Sammlung 1, Berlin.
Scharff 1923
Scharff, A., *Götter Ägyptens*, Berlin.
Schenke et al. 2001–2003
Schenke, H.M. et al. (eds.), *Nag Hammadi Deutsch 1: NHC I,1–V,1; 2: NHC V,2–XIII,1, BG 1 und 4*, Berlin and New York.
Schiller 1932
Schiller, A.A., *Ten Coptic Legal Texts*, New York.
Schimmel 1995
Schimmel, A., *Mystische Dimensionen des Islam. Die Geschichte des Sufismus*, 3rd ed., Munich.
Schmelz 2004
Schmelz, G., 'Das Christentum im Fayyum bis zum 5. Jahrhundert', in Gemeinhardt, P. (ed.), *Patristica et oecumenica. Festschrift für Wolfgang A. Bienert zum 65. Geburtstag*. Marburger theologische Studien 85, Marburg, pp. 147–56.
Schneemelcher 2009
Schneemelcher, W. (ed.), *Neutestamentliche Apokryphen II: Apostolisches, Apokalypsen und Verwandtes*, 6th ed., Tübingen.
Schneider 1983
Schneider, M., *Stèles funéraires musulmanes des îles Dahlak (Mer rouge)*, 2 vols, Cairo.
Schröter and Bethge 2012
Schröter, J. and Bethge, H.-G., 'Das Evangelium nach Thomas (Thomasevangelium [NHC II,2 p. 32,10–51,28])'. Oxyrhynchos-Papyri I 1, IV 654 und IV 655 (P. Oxy. I 1, IV 654 und IV 655)', in Markschies, Schröter and Heiser, pp. 483–526.
Schulman 1972/1973
Schulman, A.R., 'A Rare Representation of Tutu from Tel el-Fada (Sinai)', *Museum Haaretz Yearbook* 15/16, pp. 69–76.
Schulz-Flügel 1990
Schulz-Flügel, E. (ed.), *Rufinus, Historia Monachorum sive de Vita Sanctorum Patrum*, Berlin and New York.

Schulz and Ziemer 2010
Schulz, G. and Ziemer, J., *Mit Wüstenvätern und Wüstenmüttern im Gespräch,* Göttingen.

Schwarz 1966
Schwarz, J., 'La fin du serapeum d'Alexandrine', in Samuel A.E. (ed.), *Essays in Honor of C. Bradford Welles,* American Studies in Papyrology 1, New Haven, pp. 97–111.

Schwartze 2011
Schwartze, D.R., 'Macabees, books of' in J.R. Baskin (ed.), *The Cambridge Dictionary of Judaism and Jewish Culture,* New York, p. 408.

Schweizer 2014
Schweizer, H., 'Josefsgeschichte in Islam und Judentum': http://www-ct.informatik.uni-tuebingen.de/daten/jguebers.pdf. (Last accessed 6 September 2015.)

Seeber 1980
Seeber, Ch., 'Jenseitsgericht', in *Lexikon der Ägyptologie* 3, pp. 249–52.

Seidelmayer 2001
Seidlmayer, S., *Historische und moderne Nilstände. Untersuchungen zu den Pegelablesungen des Nils von der Frühzeit bis zur Gegenwart,* Berlin.

Seipel 1998
W. Seipel (ed.), *Schätze der Kalifen. Islamische Kunst zur Fatimidenzeit,* exhibition in the Kunsthistorisches Museum Vienna, Vienna.

Sells 2001
Sells, M., 'Ascension', *Encyclopaedia of the Qur'an* 1, pp. 176–81.

Serjeant 1942
Serjeant, R.B., 'Material for a History of Islamic Textiles up to the Mongol Conquest', *Ars Islamica* 9, pp. 54–92.

Severin 1982
Severin, H.-G., 'Zur spätantiken Bauskulptur im Jeremiaskloster', *Mitteilungen des Deutschen Archäologischen Instituts Kairo* 38, pp. 170–93.

Severin 1991
Severin, H.-G., 'Bawit, Archaeology, Architecture, and Sculpture', in *Coptic Encyclopedia* 2, New York and Toronto, p. 365.

Schätze der Kalifen 1998
Seipel, W. (ed.), *Schätze der Kalifen. Islamische Kunst zur Fatimidenzeit,* exhibition catalogue, Künstlerhaus, Vienna.

Shaw 2011
Shaw, B., *Sacred Violence. African Christians and Sectarian Hatred in the Age of Augustine,* Cambridge.

Sheehan 2010
Sheehan, P., *Babylon of Egypt. The Archaeology of Old Cairo and the Origins of the City,* American Research Center in Egypt. Conservation Series 4, Cairo.

Sheehan 2012
Sheehan, P., 'The Port of Babylon in Egypt', in Agius, D.A., Cooper, J.P., Trakadas, A. and Zazzaro, C. (eds.), *Navigated Spaces, Connected Places. Proceedings of Red Sea Project V Held at the University of Exeter, 16–19 September 2010,* Oxford, pp. 103–15.

Shoshan 1993
Shoshan, B., *Popular Culture in Medieval Cairo,* Cambridge.

Shoshan 2006
Shoshan, B., 'Nile', in Meri, J.W. (ed.) *Medieval Islamic Civilization: An Encyclopedia* 2, New York, pp. 561–62.

Shoshan 2006a
Shoshan B., 'Nawruz', in Meri, J.W. (ed.), *Medieval Islamic Civilization: An Encyclopedia* 2, New York, pp. 559–60.

Sidarus 2007
Sidarus, A., 'Multilingualism and Lexicography in Egyptian Late Antiquity', *Hallesche Beiträge zur Orientwissenschaft* 44, pp. 173–95.

Sidarus 2013
Sidarus, A., 'From Coptic to Arabic in the Christian Literature of Egypt', *Coptica* 12, pp. 35–56.

Sidebotham
Sidebotham, S.E., *Berenike and the Ancient Maritime Spice Route,* Berkeley.

Sijpesteijn 2007
Sijpesteijn, P.M., 'The Arab Conquest of Egypt and the Beginning of Muslim Rule', in Bagnall, R.S., *Egypt in the Byzantine World 300–700,* Cambridge, pp. 437–59.

Sijpesteijn 2009
Sijpesteijn, P.M., 'Landholding Patterns in Early Islamic Egypt', in *Journal of Agrarian Change* 9.1, pp. 120–33.

Sijpesteijn 2011
Sijpesteijn, P.M., 'Building an Egyptian Identity', in A. Ahmed, M. Bonner and B. Sadeghi (eds.), *Scholars and Scholarship of the Islamic World: Studies in Islamic History, Law and Thought in Honor of Professor Michael Allan Cook on his Seventieth Birthday,* Leiden, pp. 97–123.

Sijpesteijn 2013
Sijpesteijn, P.M., *Shaping a Muslim State. The World of a Mid-eighth-century Egyptian Official,* Oxford.

Sijpesteijn 2014
Sijpesteijn, P.M., 'An Early Umayyad Papyrus-invitation for the Hajj', *Journal of Near Eastern Studies* 73.2, pp. 179–90.

Sizgorich 2009
Sizgorich, T., *Violence and Belief in Late Antiquity. Militant Devotion in Christianity and Islam,* Philadelphia.

SKD 1996
Von Sure Yusuf bis Sure An-Nur, Sure 12–24, Die Bedeutung des Korans 3, Munich.

Smith 1928/2010
Smith, M., *Rabi'a the Mystic and her Fellow Saints in Islam. Beeing the Life and Teachings of Rabi'a al-'Adawiyya al-Qaysiyya of Basra Together with Some Account of the Place of the Women Saints in Islam,* Cambridge (reprint 2010).

Speiser 2013
Speiser, P., 'Umayyad, Tulunid and Fatimid Tombs at Aswan', in Raue, D., Seidlmyer, S.J., Speiser, P. et al. (eds.), *The First Cataract of the Nile. One Region – Diverse Perspectives,* Sonderschrift. Deutsches Archäologisches Institut, Abteilung Kairo 36, Berlin and Boston, pp. 211–22.

Speyer 1981
Speyer, W., *Büchervernichtung und Zensur des Geistes bei Heiden, Juden und Christen,* Stuttgart.

Staffa 1977
Staffa, S.J., *Conquest and Fusion. The Social Evolution of Cairo A.D. 642–1850,* Leiden.

Starowieyski 1989
Starowieyski, M., 'Le titre θεοτόκος avant le concile d'Ephèse', in Livingstone, E. (ed.), *Papers Presented at the Tenth International Conference on Patristic Studies Held in Oxford 1983. Historica, Theologica, Gnostica, Biblica et Apocrypha,* Studia Patristica 19, Leuven, pp. 236–42.

Das Staunen der Welt 1995
Das Staunen der Welt 1995. Das Morgenland und Friedrich II. (1194–1250). Bilderheft der Staatlichen Museen zu Berlin, Preußischer Kulturbesitz 77/78. Exhibition catalogue, Museum für Islamische Kunst, Berlin.

Stewart 1991
Stewart, C., *Demons and the Devil. Moral Imagination in Modern Greek Culture,* Princeton.

Stillman 1988
Stillman, Y.K., *Female Attire of Medieval Egypt. According to the Trousseau Lists and Cognate Material from the Cairo Geniza,* Ann Arbor.

Stillman and Sanders 2000
Stillman, Y.K. and Sanders, P., 'Tiraz', in *Encyclopaedia of Islam* 10, new ed., Leiden, pp. 534–39.

Strzygowski 1904
Strzygowski, J., 'Mschatta. II: Kunstwissenschaftliche Untersuchung', in *Jahrbuch der königlich preuszischen Kunstsammlungen* 25, pp. 225–72.

Strzygowski 1904b
Strzygowski, J., *Koptische Kunst, Catalogue général des antiquités égyptiennes du Musée du Caire,* Vienna (reprint Osnabrück 1973).

Sullivan and Abed-Kotob 1999
Sullivan, D.J. and Abed-Kotob, S., *Islam in Contemporary Egypt. Civil Society vs. the State,* Boulder.

Swanson 2010
Swanson, M.N., *The Coptic Papacy in Islamic Egypt 641–1517,* Cairo.

Tadros 2013
Tadros, M., *Copts at the Crossroads. The Challenges of Building Inclusive Democracy in Egypt,* Cairo.

Tagher 1998
Tagher, J., *Christians in Muslim Egypt. An Historical Study of the Relations Between Copts and Muslims from 640 to 1922,* Altenberge.

ten Hacken 2004
ten Hacken, C., 'The Legend of Aur. Arabic Texts Concerning the Foundation of the Monastery of Naqlun', in Immerzeel, M. and van der Vliet, J. (eds.), *Coptic Studies on the Threshold of a New Millennium* 1, Leuven, Paris and Dudley, pp. 337–48.

ten Hacken 2006
ten Hacken, C., 'The Description of Antioch in Abu al-Makarim's' "History of the Churches and Monasteries of Egypt and some neighbouring Countries"', in Ciggaar, K. and Metcalf, M. (eds.), *East and West in the Medieval Eastern Mediterranean* 1, Orientalia Lovaniensia Analecta 147, Leuven, Paris and Dudley, pp. 185–216.

Thackeray 1921
Thackeray, H. St. J., *The Septuagint and the Jewish Worship,* London.

Thackston 1978
Thackston, W.M. (ed.), *The Tales of the Prophets of al-Kisa'i. Translated from the Arabic, With Notes,* Library of Classical Arabic Literature 2, Boston.

Thackston 1986
Thackston, W.M (ed.), *Naser-e Khosraw's Book of Travels (Safarnama). Translated from Persian, with Introduction and Annotations by W.M. Thackston,* Bibliotheca Persica 36, New York.

Thalmayer 2001
Thalmayer, L., *Abraham und das Vermächtnis seiner Frauen. Eine Vision für Frieden zwischen Juden und Arabern im Sinne der Abrahamischen Ökumene,* Oberursel.

Thenayian 1999
Rashed al-Thenayian, Mohammed A., *An Archaeological Study of the Yemeni Highland Pilgrim Route between San'a and Mecca,* Riyadh.

Thomas 2000
Thomas, T.K., *Late Antique Egyptian Funerary Sculpture. Images for This World and the Next,* Princeton.

Thompson 1994
Thompson, D.J., 'Literacy and Power in Ptolemaic Egypt', in Bowman, A.K. and Wolff, G. (eds.), *Literacy and Power in the Ancient World,* Cambridge, pp. 67–83.

Till 1935
Till, W.C., *Koptische Heiligen- und Martyrerlegenden* I.II, Rome (reprint 1962).

Tillier 2011
Tillier, M. (ed.), *Abû Hilâl Al-'Askarî, Livre des califes qui s'en remirent au jugement d'un cadi,* Cahier des Annales islamologiques 30 2011.

Timbie 1998
Timbie, J., 'A Liturgical Procession in the Desert of Apa Shenoute', in Frankfurter 1998a, pp. 415–41.

Timm 1985
Timm, S., *Das christlich-koptische Ägypten in arabischer Zeit,* Tübinger Atlas des Vorderen Orients, Beihefte B 41.3, Wiesbaden.

Tkaczow 1993
Tkaczow, B., *The Topography of Ancient Alexandria. An Archaeological Map,* Warsaw.

Toelken 1835
Toelken, E.H., *Erklärendes Verzeichnis der antiken vertieft geschnittenen Steine der Königlich Preußischen Gemmensammlung,* Berlin.

Tomber 2008
Tomber, R., *Indo-Roman Trade. From Pots to Pepper,* London.

Torallas Tovar 2004
Torallas Tovar, S., 'Egyptian Lexical Interference in the Greek of Byzantine and Early Islamic Egypt', in Sijpesteijn, P. and Sundelin, L. (eds.), *Papyrology and the History of Early Islamic Egypt,* Islamic History and Civilization 55, Leiden, pp. 163–77.

Torallas Tovar 2013
Torallas Tovar, S., 'Egyptian Burial Practices in Late Antiquity. The Case of Christian Mummy Labels', in Torallas Tovar, S. and Monferrer, P. (eds.), *Cultures in Contact. Transfer of Knowledge in the Mediterranean Context. Selected papers,* Cordoba, pp. 15–26.

Török 2005
Török, L., *Transfigurations of Hellenism: Aspects of Late Antique Art in Egypt, AD 250–700,* Probleme der Ägyptologie 23, Leiden and Boston, MA.

Torp 2006
Torp, H., 'The *Laura* of Apa Apollo at Bawit, Considerations on the Founder's Monastic Ideals and the South Church', *Arte Medievale, Neue Serie,* V, 2, pp. 9–46.

Tran Tam Tinh 1973
Tran Tam Tinh, V., *Isis Lactans. Corpus des monuments gréco-romains d'Isis allaitant Harpocrate*, Études préliminaires aux religions orientales dans l'empire romain 37, Leiden.
Treasures 2006
O'Kane, B. (ed.), *The Treasures of Islamic Art in the Museums of Cairo*, Cairo and New York.
Tricoche 2012
Tricoche, A., 'Graffiti figurés d'Égypte sous la domination romaine', in Ballet, P. (ed.), *Grecs et Romains en Égypte. Territoires, espaces de la vie et de la mort, objets de prestige et du quotidien*, Bibliothèque d'Étude 157, Cairo, pp. 93–100.
Tritton 2008
Tritton, A.S., *Caliphs and Their Non-Muslim Subjects. A Critical Study of the Covenant of 'Umar*, London and New York.
Trombley 2009
Trombley, F.R., ''Amr b. Al-'As Refurbishment of Trajan's Canal', in Blue, L., Cooper, J., Thomas, R. et al. (eds.), *Connected Hinterlands: Proceedings of Red Sea Project IV Held at the University of Southampton, September 2008*, Society for Arabian Studies Monographs 8, Oxford, pp. 99–110.
Tubach 1998
Tubach, J., 'Die Prolepsis des Eschatons in der Onnophrios-Vita', *Hallesche Beiträge zur Orientwissenschaft* 26, pp. 89–95.
Türkis and Azur 1999
Busz, R. and Gercke, P. (eds.), *Türkis und Azur. Quarzkeramik im Orient und im Okzident*, exhibition catalogue, Kassel, Wilhelmshöhe 18.7.–3.10.1999.
Ullmann 1972
Ullmann, M., *Die Natur- und Geheimwissenschaften im Islam*, Handbuch der Orientalistik I/VI, 2, Leiden and Cologne.
Untermann 2011
Untermann, M. (ed.), *Ägyptische Magie im Wandel der Zeiten. Eine Ausstellung des Instituts für Papyrologie in Zusammenarbeit mit dem Institut für Ägyptologie der Universität Heidelberg*, Universitätsmuseum Heidelberg, Kataloge 5, Heidelberg.
Vajda 1948
Vajda, G.' 'Sur quelques éléments juifs et pseudo-juifs dans l'encyclopédie magique de Bûni', in *Ignace Goldziher Memorial Volume, ed. by Samuel Löwinger* 1, Budapest, pp. 387–92.
van der Vliet 2000
van der Vliet, J., 'Les anges du Soleil. À propos d'un texte magique copte récemment découvert à Deir el-Naqloun (N. 45/95)', in Bosson, N. (ed.), *Cahiers de la Bibliothèque copte XII – Études coptes VII*, Paris et al., pp. 319–37.
van der Vliet 2014
van der Vliet, J., 'Warding off Evil, Attracting Charm. Magic in Late Antique and Early Medieval Egypt,' in Gabra, G: (ed.), *Coptic Civilization. Two Thousand Years of Christianity in Egypt*, Cairo, pp. 123–31.
Vansleb 1678
Vansleb, J.M., *The Present State of Egypt, or a New Relation of a Late Voyage into That Kingdom Performed in the Years 1672 and 1673*, London.
Viereck 1928
Viereck, P., *Philadelphia. Die Gründung einer hellenistischen Militärkolonie in Ägypten*, Morgenland: Darstellungen aus Geschichte und Kultur des Ostens 16, Leipzig.

Vikan 1979
Vikan, G., 'Joseph Iconography on Coptic Textiles', *Gesta. International Center of Medieval Art* 18, Chicago and New York, pp. 99–108.
Vikan 1991/1992
Vikan, G., 'Two Byzantine Amuletic Armbands and the Group to Which They Belong', *Journal of the Walters Art Gallery* 49/50, pp. 33–51.
Vikan 2010
Vikan, G., *Early Byzantine Pilgrimage Art*, Washington D.C.
Vivian 1993
Vivian, T., *Histories of the Monks of Upper Egypt and the Life of Onnophrius*, Cistercian Studies Series 140, Kalamazoo.
Vleeming 2011
Vleeming, S.P., *Short Texts II 278–1200: Demotic and Greek-Demotic Mummy Labels and Other Short Texts Gathered from Many Publications*, Studia Demotica 9, Leuven, Paris and Walpole.
Vorsicht Glas 2010
Kühn, M. (ed.), *Vorsicht Glas! Zerbrechliche Kunst 700–2010*, Sammlungen des Museums für Islamische Kunst; exhibition catalogue, Museum für Islamische Kunst 10.9.2010 – 9.1.2011, Berlin.
Walker 2009
Walker, P.E., *Caliph of Cairo. Al-Hakim bi-Amr Allah, 996–1021*, Cairo and New York.
Ward-Perkins 1994
Ward-Perkins, J.B., 'Constantine and the Origin of the Christian Basilica', *Studies in Roman and Early Christian Architecture*, London 1994, pp. 447–68 (first published as *Papers of the British School at Rome*, 22), pp. 447–68.
Ward-Perkins 2003
Ward-Perkins, B., 'Reconfiguring Sacred Space. From Pagan Shrines to Christian Churches', in Brands, G. and Severin, H.G. (eds.), *Die spätantike Stadt und ihre Christianisierung*, Wiesbaden, pp. 285–90.
Webb 2001
Webb, G., 'Angel', *Encyclopaedia of the Qur'an* 1, pp. 84–92.
Webb 2002
Webb, G., 'Gabriel', *Encyclopaedia of the Qur'an* 2, pp. 278–80.
Weber 1914
Weber, W., *Die ägyptisch-griechischen Terrakotten*, Mitteilungen aus der Ägyptischen Sammlung 2, Berlin.
Weimar 1996
Weimar, P., 'Josef. Josef der Patriarch, Josefsgeschichte', *Lexikon für Theologie und Kirche* 5, 3rd ed., Freiburg et al., pp. 997–98.
Weiss 2005
Weiss, Z., *The Sepphoris Synagogue. Deciphering an Ancient Message Through its Archaeological and Socio-Historical Contexts*, Jerusalem.
Weitzmann and Kessler 1986
Weitzmann, K. and Kessler, H.L., *The Cotton Genesis*, British Library Codex Cotton Otho B. VI, Princeton.
Wessel 1957
Wessel, K., *Rom – Byzanz – Russland. Ein Führer durch die Frühchristlich-byzantinische Sammlung*, Berlin.
Wessel 1963
Wessel, K., *Koptische Kunst. Die Spätantike in Ägypten*, Recklinghausen.

Wiet 1939–1942
Wiett, G., *Catalogue général du Musée Arabe du Caire, stèles funéraires*, II. (1936), IV (1936), V (1937), VI (1939), VII (1940), VIII (1941), IX (1941), X (1942), Cairo.
Wiet 1971
Wiet, G., *Inscriptions historiques sur pierre*, Catalogue général du Musée d'art islamique du Caire, Cairo.
Willburger 2007
Willburger, N., 'Zeugnisse römischer Mumiendekoration aus Ägypten', in Cat. Stuttgart, pp. 228–53.
Wills 2002
Wills, L.N., *Ancient Jewish Novels: An Anthology*, Oxford.
Wimmer and Leimgruber 2007
Wimmer, S.J. and Leimgruber, S., *Von Adam bis Muhammad. Bibel und Koran im Vergleich*, Stuttgart.
Winkler 1930
Winkler, H.A., *Siegel und Charaktere in der mohammedanischen Zauberei*, Studien zur Geschichte und Kultur des islamischen Orients 7, Berlin and Leipzig.
Winlock and Crum 1926
Winlock, H.E and Crum, W.E., *The Monastery of Epiphanius at Thebes*, New York.
Wipszycka 2009
Wipszycka, E., *Moines et communautés monastiques en Égypte (IVe–VIIIe siècles)*, Journal of Juristic Papyrology, Supplement XI, Warsaw.
Worman 1905
Worman, E.J., 'Notes on the Jews in Fustat from Cambridge Genizah documents', *Jewish Quarterly Review* 18.1, Philadelphia, pp. 1–39.
Worrell 1923
Worrell, W.H., *The Coptic Manuscripts in the Freer Collection*, University of Michigan Studies, Humanistic Series 10, New York and London (reprint New York and London 1972).
Wright 1887
Wright, W., 'Kufic tombstones in the British Museum', *Proceedings of the Society of Biblical Archaeology*, 17th Session, pp. 329–49.
Wright 2010
Wright, A.T., 'Angels', in Collins, J.J. and Harlow, D.C. (eds.), *Eerdmans Dictionary of Early Judaism*, Grand Rapids and Cambridge, pp. 328–31.
Wulff 1909
Wulff, O., *Altchristliche und mittelalterliche byzantinische und italienische Bildwerke*, Teil 1: Altchristliche Bildwerke, Königliche Museen zu Berlin. Beschreibung der Bildwerke der Christlichen Epochen 3, Berlin.
Wulff and Volbach 1926
Wulff, O. and Volbach W.F., *Spätantike und koptische Stoffe aus ägyptischen Grabfunden in den Staatlichen Museen Kaiser-Friedrich-Museum, Ägyptisches Museum, Schliemann-Sammlung*, Berlin.
Xanthopoulou 2010
Xanthopoulou, M., *Les lampes en bronze à l'époque paléochrétienne*, Bibliothèque de l'Antiquité tardive 16, Turnhout.
Yusuf 1999
Yusuf, Abd el-Ra'uf Ali, 'A Rock-crystal Specimen in the Museum of Islamic Art, Cairo, and the Seven Fatimid Domes in the Qarafa al-Kubra, Cairo', in Barrucand, M. (ed.), *L'Égypte*

fatimide – son art et son histoire. Actes du colloque organisé à Paris les 28, 29 et 30 mai 1998, Paris, pp. 312–17.
Zaborowski 2008
Zaborowski, J., 'From Coptic to Arabic in Medieval Egypt', *Medieval Encounters. Jewish, Christian, and Muslim Culture in Confluence and Dialogue*, 14, Leiden et al., pp. 15–40.
Zanetti 1994
Zanetti, U., 'Fêtes des anges dans les calendriers et synaxaires orientaux', in Carletti, C. and Otranto, G. (eds.), *Culto e insediamenti Micaelici nell'Italia meridionale fra tarda antichità e medioevo (Atti del Convegno Internazionale Monte Sant'Angelo 18–21 novembre 1992)*, Bari, pp. 323–49.
Zanetti 1995
Zanetti, U., 'Abu 'l-Makarim et Abu Salih', *Bulletin de la Société d'Archéologie Copte* 34, Cairo, pp. 85–138.
Zenger 2007
Zenger, E. (ed.), *Herders theologischer Kommentar zum Alten Testament. Genesis 37–50, übersetzt und ausgelegt von J. Ebach*, Freiburg i. Br. et al.
Zibawi 2003
Zibawi, M., *Images de l'Égypte chrétienne. Iconologie copte*, Paris.
Ziebarth 1913
Ziebarth E., *Aus der antiken Schule*, 2nd ed., Bonn.
Zotenberg 1958
Zotenberg, M.H., *Chronique de Abou-Djafar-Mohammed-Ben-Djarîr-Ben-Yezid Tabari, traduite sur la version persane d'Abou-'Ali Mohammed Bel'ami, d'après les manuscrits de Paris, de Gotha, de Londres et de Canterbury*, 4 vols, Paris.
Zuri 1918
Zuri, J. Sch., *Rab. Sein Leben und seine Anschauungen*, Zürich.
Zych 2005
Zych, I., 'Wooden Coffins from Cemetery A in Naqlun', *Polish Archaeology in the Mediterranean* 16, pp. 211–21.
Zych 2008
Zych, I., 'Cemetery C in Naqlun: Preliminary Report on the Excavation in 2006', *Polish Archaeology in the Mediterranean* 18, pp. 230–46.

WEB RESOURCES

(last accessed 6 September 2015)
Papyri cited according to Oates et al, *Checklist of Editions of Greek, Latin, Demotic and Coptic Papyri, Ostraca and Tablets*:
http://library.duke.edu/rubenstein/scriptorium/papyrus/texts/clist_papyri.html
Arachne: Objektdatenbank des Deutschen Archäologischen Instituts:
http://arachne.uni-koeln.de
Arbeitsstelle für Manichäismusforschung, Universität Münster:
http://www.uni-muenster.de/IAEK/forschen/kop/mani/index.html
Berliner Papyrusdatenbank:
http://smb.museum/berlpap/index.php
British Museum, database:
https://www.britishmuseum.org/research/collection_online/search.aspx
Staatliche Museen zu Berlin, database:
http://www.smb-digital.de/eMuseumPlus
Victoria and Albert Museum, database:
http://collections.vam.ac.uk
Yeshiva University Museum, New York:
www.yumuseum.tumblr.com/ArkDoor

Illustration Acknowledgements

Index

Figures in *italics* refer to illustrations; (c) refers to captions to illustrations.